NEW DIRECTIONS IN DIGITAL
TEXTUAL STUDIES

Bloomsbury Studies in Digital Cultures

Series Editors
Anthony Mandal and Jenny Kidd

This series responds to a rapidly changing digital world, one which permeates both our everyday lives and the broader philosophical challenges that accrue in its wake. It is inter- and trans-disciplinary, situated at the meeting points of the digital humanities, digital media and cultural studies, and research into digital ethics.

While the series will tackle the 'digital humanities' in its broadest sense, its ambition is to broaden focus beyond areas typically associated with the digital humanities to encompass a range of approaches to the digital, whether these be digital humanities, digital media studies or digital arts practice.

Titles in the series
Ambient Stories in Practice and Research, edited by Amy Spencer
Digital Humanities and the Cyberspace Decade, 1990-2001, Claire Warwick
Drone Cultures, John Muthyala
Hacking in the Humanities, Aaron Mauro
Listening In, Toby Heys, David Jackson and Marsha Courneya
Metamodernism and the Postdigital in the Contemporary Novel, Spencer Jordan
Representing the New AI in Film and Television, Graham Allen
Resisting Big Tech, Niels Niessen
The Trouble With Big Data, Jennifer Edmond, Nicola Horsley, Jörg Lehmann and Mike Priddy

Forthcoming titles
The Generic Person, Sophie Day, Celia Lury, Helen Ward
Cultural Institutions and Digital Inequality, Indigo Holcombe-James
Provoking Online Drama, Crystal Abidin and Jin Lee

NEW DIRECTIONS IN DIGITAL TEXTUAL STUDIES

BOOK HISTORY, SCHOLARLY EDITING AND CURATION IN CONVERSATION

Christopher Ohge and Kristen Schuster

BLOOMSBURY ACADEMIC
LONDON • NEW YORK • OXFORD • NEW DELHI • SYDNEY

BLOOMSBURY ACADEMIC

Bloomsbury Publishing Plc, 50 Bedford Square, London, WC1B 3DP, UK
Bloomsbury Publishing Inc, 1359 Broadway, New York, NY 10018, USA
Bloomsbury Publishing Ireland, 29 Earlsfort Terrace, Dublin 2, D02 AY28, Ireland

BLOOMSBURY, BLOOMSBURY ACADEMIC and the Diana logo are trademarks of Bloomsbury Publishing Plc

First published in Great Britain 2026

Copyright © Christopher Ohge & Kristen Schuster, 2026

Christopher Ohge & Kristen Schuster have asserted their right under the Copyright, Designs and Patents Act, 1988, to be identified as Authors of this work.

Cover design by Megan Wilson
Cover image: Eugene Deacons via Adobe Stock and illustrated by Megan Wilson

All rights reserved. No part of this publication may be: i) reproduced or transmitted in any form, electronic or mechanical, including photocopying, recording or by means of any information storage or retrieval system without prior permission in writing from the publishers; or ii) used or reproduced in any way for the training, development or operation of artificial intelligence (AI) technologies, including generative AI technologies. The rights holders expressly reserve this publication from the text and data mining exception as per Article 4(3) of the Digital Single Market Directive (EU) 2019/790.

Bloomsbury Publishing Plc does not have any control over, or responsibility for, any third-party websites referred to or in this book. All internet addresses given in this book were correct at the time of going to press. The author and publisher regret any inconvenience caused if addresses have changed or sites have ceased to exist, but can accept no responsibility for any such changes.

A catalogue record for this book is available from the British Library.

A catalog record for this book is available from the Library of Congress.

ISBN: HB: 978-1-350-40677-3
PB: 978-1-350-40676-6
ePDF: 978-1-350-40678-0
eBook: 978-1-350-40679-7

Series: Bloomsbury Studies in Digital Cultures

Typeset by Deanta Global Publishing Services, Chennai, India
Printed and bound in Great Britain

For product safety related questions contact productsafety@bloomsbury.com.

To find out more about our authors and books visit www.bloomsbury.com and sign up for our newsletters.

CONTENTS

Figures	vii
Notes on contributors	x
Introduction: This is Not a Book *Christopher Ohge and Kristen Schuster*	1
Part I: Methods and case studies	13
1 Cataloguing the Enlightenment: Legacy Practices of Organized Knowledge *Zoe Screti*	15
2 Editing Authenticity in the Manuscript Text: Prefaces, Diplomatic Transcriptions and Photographs *Geoffrey Turnovsky*	37
3 The Printing Surface in the Age of Digital Reproduction *Giles Bergel*	55
4 From Bookshelves to Bytes: Navigating the Digital Transformation of Writers' Libraries *Anke Jaspers and Martina Schönbächler*	79
5 A Graph Database Approach to Editing and Publishing Infinitely Recombinant Digital Texts with OCHRE *Miller C. Prosser*	99
6 Pragmatic Digital Editing, Data Analysis and Creative-Critical Practices: The Case of the Anti-Slavery Anthology *The Bow in the Cloud* (1834) *Christopher Ohge*	117
7 Extracting for Experience: Material Annotation and its Affordances in Textual Studies *Mary Erica Zimmer*	133
8 Reading the Edited Collection, Distantly: Some Trends in British Theological Publishing in the Twentieth Century *Peter Webster*	157
Part II: Interdisciplinary reflections	173
9 Unlocking Literary Heritage: From Cabinets of Curiosities to Digital Storytelling *Wim Van Mierlo*	175

Contents

10 Folklore Archives in the Digital Age *Karoline Strittmater* 191

11 Teaching Truman with Hypertext Methods: Project Whistlestop over Two Decades *Ashney V. Randle, Logan F. Thompson, Renee M. Jones and Sarah A. Buchanan* 205

12 Digital Publishing Practices in Museums: Old Habits, New Platforms *Ellen Charlesworth and Claire Warwick* 227

13 Describing New Media: Strategies and Recommendations for Teaching Structured Data in Multidisciplinary Humanities Contexts *Kristen Schuster* 247

14 Honey, AI shrunk the Archive: Artificial Intelligence as Compression Algorithm *Jon Ippolito* 263

15 Book History for the Future: Connecting Communications Media *Leah Henrickson* 281

Afterword: On Textual Editing and Digital Scholarly Curation *Dirk Van Hulle* 297

Index 305

FIGURES

1.1	'Systême figuré des connoissances humaines' in Diderot and d'Alembert's *Encyclopédie*. Image from Wikipedia Commons.	21
2.1	Mme du Châtelet's letter to Maupertuis, 10 January 1734. BnF, Ms Fr. 12268 (https://archivesetmanuscrits.bnf.fr/ark:/12148/cc43457c). The digitized image can be found here: https://gallica.bnf.fr/ark:/12148/btv1b6000754n/f17.item#.	44
2.2	Du Châtelet's letter juxtaposed with Besterman's transcription, as rendered in the *Electronic Enlightenment*.	45
3.1	William Hone, *Ancient Mysteries Described, Especially the English Miracle Plays, Founded on Apocryphal New Testament Story, Extant Among the Unpublished Manuscripts in the British Museum: Including Notices of Ecclesiastical Shows, the Festivals of Fools and Asses, the English Boy Bishop, the Descent Into Hell, the Lord Mayor's Show, the Guildhall Giants, Christmas Carols, &c* (printed for William Hone, 1823), 100–1.	56
3.2	Hone and Cruikshank depicted in their 1823 joint publication *Facetiae and Miscellanies With one hundred and twenty engravings, drawn by George Cruikshank*, London: Hunt & Clarke, printed by: J. M'Creery et al. 1827.	58
3.3	'Gravure en Bois, Principes,' *Encyclopédie ou Dictionnaire raisonné des sciences, des arts et des métiers*, vol. 5 (plates). Paris, 1765, http://hdl.handle.net/2027/spo.did2222.0001.502.	59
3.4	A ballad and chapbook block (McGill University Library Woodblocks Collection Box 13 Item 672) with an antiquarian offprint (*Specimens of early wood-engraving, being impressions of woodcuts in the possession of the publisher*, Newcastle-upon-Tyne: William Dodd, 1862).	61
3.5	Object detection of illustrations in chapbooks printed in Scotland (Dutta, Bergel and Zisserman 2021).	64
3.6	Block impressions of chapbooks, matched using VGG Visual Search Engine (VISE) software (Dutta, Arandjelović and Zisserman 2021).	64
3.7	A timeline of broadside ballad block impressions, as seen by computer vision, accessible at https://www.robots.ox.ac.uk/~vgg/demo/ballads/ (Chung et al, 2014).	65
3.8	Impression 16, highlighted on 40 Rawlinson 566, fol. 12r.	67
3.9	Impression 628, as shown in 3.7, highlighted on Bodleian Douce Ballads 1, fol. 22r.	67
3.10	An overlay visualization of details of Figures 3.8 and 3.9 in the VGG Image Compare software collator.	68

Figures

3.11	Details of Figures 3.8 and 3.9. Note in particular the progressive damage to the bottom frame of the 3.8 woodcut.	69
3.12	RTI capture of a Newcastle ballad-printer's woodblock, now in the British Museum.	71
5.1	Simplified relational database schema tables recording U.S. Presidents and political party names in normalized tables. The use of primary and foreign keys to join data from the tables prevents duplication of string data in the database.	106
5.2	Schematic representation of a semi-structured graph database approach to texts. Each word and each letter are individual database items linked to other items. The database extracts the required items to produce a reading text.	106
5.3	Facsimile text edition of an alphabetic cuneiform text from Ras Shamra (RS 15.032, Miller Prosser editor; photos by John Ellison; copyright PhoTEO).	111
5.4	A comparison of multiple Hebrew manuscripts of the Book of Genesis, chapter 1.	112
6.1	Digitized facsimile of Ann Gilbert's illustration to accompany her poem 'The Mother', in *The Bow in the Cloud* (John Rylands Library, Manchester).	120
6.2	Religious affiliations for contributors published in *The Bow in the Cloud*.	126
6.3	Sentiment values in *The Bow in the Cloud* (published text, 1834), with Rolling Means.	126
6.4	Data story: Thomas Buxton's 'Compensation'.	129
7.1	Text of *Moby-Dick*, represented through word cloud software.	135
7.2	'Or, the Whale,' by Jos Sances (2020–1).	136
7.3a	'Or, the Whale,' with section headings (credit: Jos Sances, 2020–1).	137
7.3b	Detail from 'Or, the Eye' StoryMap (credit: Erica Zimmer and Jeff Peterson, 2021).	137
7.4	3D-printed quadrant (credit: Mirkoengineer, on Thingiverse).	140
7.5a	'Artefact Analysis' slides. (Credit: Wilson Taylor.)	143
7.5b	'Artefact Analysis' slides. (Credit: Wilson Taylor.)	143
7.6a	Concordance view of 'quadrant' in *Moby-Dick* (AntConc).	145
7.6b	Concordance plot of 'quadrant' in *Moby-Dick* (AntConc).	146
7.7a	Zipf's Law, visualized.	147
7.7b	Distribution plot for corpus following Zipf's Law.	148
7.8	Whale images carved by participants Elizabeth Sobikw-Williams and Alicia DeMaio.	151
8.1	Authorship and gender in theological edited collections.	164
8.2	Chronological proportions. Authorship by professional status in theological edited collections.	167
8.3	Geographic proportions in theological edited collections.	168
11.1	Screenshot of the Project Whistlestop homepage on 5 December 1998. https://web.archive.org/web/19991012034516/http://whistlestop.org/.	210

11.2	Screenshot of the Truman Presidential Library & Museum website on 16 May 2020. https://www.trumanlibrary.gov/.	219
12.1	A table of interview participants including details of their museum's collection, size and area.	231
13.1	Getty Art and Architecture thesaurus results for 'Blue'.	251
13.2	FRBRoo Group 1 entities.	256
13.3	FFRBR Group 1 entities as *Alice in Wonderland*.	258

NOTES ON CONTRIBUTORS

Giles Bergel is Senior Researcher in Digital Humanities in the Department of Engineering Science at the University of Oxford. He contributes to various digital resources for the study of the printed book, including an archive of the ballad *The Wandering Jews's Chronicle*; Bodleian Ballads Online; and Stationers' Register Online. He collaborates extensively with the Visual Geometry Group on computer vision software aimed at book historians and other researchers in the humanities and information sciences.

Sarah A. Buchanan is Associate Professor of Archival Studies at the University of Missouri. She investigates provenance research methods, data storytelling with archives and preservation of audiovisual collections. She is active in the Society of American Archivists as a student chapter faculty advisor and serves as the reviews editor for *Digital Humanities Quarterly*.

Ellen Charlesworth is an AHRC-funded PhD candidate at Durham University. Having studied art history at the Courtauld Institute of Art and then data science at Birkbeck, her current research spans digital humanities, museum studies and digital art history. Funded by the Alan Turing Institute, her most recent project investigates the way algorithms mediate our experience of the online cultural landscape.

Leah Henrickson is Senior Lecturer in Digital Media and Cultures at the University of Queensland. She is the author of *Reading Computer-Generated Texts* (2021) and numerous articles on text generation systems and output, artificial intelligence and digital media environments. She also studies digital storytelling for critical self-reflection, community building and commercial benefit, and is the author of *Digital Storytelling: An Introduction* (2025).

Jon Ippolito is an artist, writer and curator who teaches new media and digital curation at the University of Maine. Ippolito is the co-founder of the Variable Media Network for preserving new media art, UMaine's Digital Curation and Just-in-Time Learning programmes, and Learning with AI. His AI focus is creators – writers, programmers and media makers – and how the technical, aesthetic and legal ramifications of generative AI empower and frustrate them.

Anke Jaspers is Senior Lecturer in German at the University of Graz. She is the author of *Suhrkamp und DDR. Literaturhistorische, praxeologische und werktheoretische Perspektiven auf ein Verlagsarchiv* (2022), as well as several writings on writers' libraries in edited collections. Her current book project *Intertextualität im Regal: Die Autor:innenbibliothek* *in der literarischen Produktion* seeks to advance the theory of the writers' library and to integrate the category 'library' into central concepts of literary studies.

Renee M. Jones is a librarian in the Rare Books and Manuscripts Department at St. Louis Public Library, where she also serves as administrator for digital collections and supervises the history and fine arts departments. Her work with the library's obituary database earned her the Missouri Library Association's 2019 Excellence in Genealogy and Local History Award.

Christopher Ohge is Senior Lecturer in Digital Approaches to Literature at the School of Advanced Study, University of London, where he teaches in the MA programme in the History of the Book. He is the author of the book *Publishing Scholarly Editions: Archives, Computing, and Experience* (2021) and other writings on Herman Melville, textual editing and digital humanities. In 2023, he was awarded a fellowship from the National Endowment for the Humanities and the Mellon Foundation to complete a digital edition of the 1834 British anti-slavery anthology *The Bow in the Cloud*.

Miller C. Prosser is the Director of Online Publications in the Forum for Digital Culture at the University of Chicago, where he teaches courses on data management and data publication for the humanities. His research focuses on the socioeconomic organization of the Late Bronze Age kingdom of Ugarit and surrounding regions. He is the co-director of the Ras Shamra Tablet Inventory, a digital publication of inscribed objects from Ras Shamra-Ugarit.

Ashney V. Randle is an archivist at the National Archives at College Park, MD, United States. Ashney is a member of Beta Phi Mu since graduating with her MLIS from the University of Missouri, and she received her bachelor's in history from Missouri State University. While Ashney is an employee of the National Archives, the views, thoughts and opinions expressed in her co-authored chapter do not reflect any official policy or position of the National Archives and Records Administration or any other government agency.

Martina Schönbächler specializes in digital projects and editions at ETH Zurich's Literary Archives. She is the author of *Splitterpoetologie. Thomas Manns Gerda-Komplex zwischen Bibliothek, Frühwerk und 'Joseph in Ägypten'* (2024) and various publications on writers' libraries, digital editions and writing processes. Her research interests include the poetics of literary prose, gender studies and new materialism. She is currently working on writing processes in trans- and posthuman contexts.

Kristen Schuster (they/them) is Lecturer in Digital Humanities at the University of Southampton. Their research blends gender theories with critical studies of men and masculinities to conceptualize new methods for engaging with histories of information systems and computing.

Notes on Contributors

Zoe Screti is Leverhulme Early Career Fellow at the Voltaire Foundation, University of Oxford, a Research Fellow of Harris Manchester College and an associated member of the Institut des textes et manuscrits modernes (ITEM)'s *Équipe Écritures des Lumières*. She was the Astra Foundation Research Fellow in Manuscript Studies at the Voltaire Foundation from 2022 to 2024. Zoe holds a PhD in history from the University of Birmingham (2022), where her thesis explored the relationship between alchemy and religious reform in England between 1450 and 1650.

Karoline Strittmater is a graduate of the University of Missouri with a master's in both museum studies and library and information science. She has been a member of Beta Phi Mu since 2022.

Logan F. Thompson is the Metadata Strategist (Senior Archivist) at the University of Oklahoma Libraries. He holds a Digital Humanities Graduate Certificate and MLIS from the University of Missouri and is currently pursuing a MSc in history from the University of Edinburgh. His interactive research project Visualize KC at https://visualizekc.org/ features geolocated maps and postcards documenting the Kansas City area's built environment in the first half of the twentieth century.

Geoffrey Turnovsky is Professor of French and co-director of the Textual Studies Program at the University of Washington. He specializes in the cultural history of early modern France and Europe, emphasizing the history of print, books, authorship and reading. He published *The Literary Market. Authorship and Modernity in the Old Regime* (2011) and *Reading Typographically. Immersed in Print in Early Modern France* (2024). As co-director of UW Textual Studies, Turnovsky spearheaded the creation of and oversees the graduate certificate in Textual and Digital Studies and the minor in Textual Studies and Digital Humanities.

Dirk Van Hulle is Professor of Bibliography and Modern Book History at the University of Oxford, director of the Oxford Centre for Textual Editing and Theory (OCTET), and of the Centre for Manuscript Genetics at the University of Antwerp. With Mark Nixon, he is director of the MLA award-winning *Beckett Digital Manuscript Project* (www.beckettarchive.org). His publications include *Textual Awareness* (2004), *Modern Manuscripts* (2014), *Samuel Beckett's Library* (2013, with Mark Nixon), *The New Cambridge Companion to Samuel Beckett* (2015), *James Joyce's Work in Progress* (2016), *Genetic Criticism: Tracing Creativity in Literature* (2022) and *Write Cut Rewrite* (2024, with Mark Nixon).

Wim Van Mierlo is Senior Lecturer in English at Loughborough University, where he convenes LETS: the Loughborough Editing and Textual Scholarship research group. He is the author of *James Joyce and Cultural Genetics: The Joycean Genome* (2023) and *Scholarly Editing in Perspective* (2025). He is also the editor of *Where There is Nothing and The Unicorn from the Stars: Manuscript Materials*, the penultimate volume in the

Cornell Yeats series (2012). His current project is called 'The Archaeology of the Poem', an archival study of creative practice and manuscript culture between c. 1750 and 1990.

Claire Warwick is Professor of Digital Humanities in the Department of English at Durham University. Her research is concerned with the way that digital resources, including artificial intelligence techniques, are used in the humanities and cultural heritage and in reading behaviour in physical and digital spaces. She has recently completed a monograph: *Digital Humanities and the Cyberspace Decade: A World Elsewhere*. She has served on various advisory boards in digital humanities, for example, the British Library's BL Labs and was a member of the Conseil Scientifique du Campus Condorcet in Paris.

Peter Webster is a scholar of twentieth-century British Christianity and has published widely on the history of the Church of England as well as religion, law and art. He is the author of the book *The Edited Collection: Pasts, Present and Futures* (2020). In 2014, he founded Webster Research and Consulting to help archives and academic libraries understand their users and make better digital resources for research. He is now Head of Digital Scholarship and Innovation in the Hartley Library, University of Southampton.

Mary Erica Zimmer is Principal Lecturer within the Concourse Program at the Massachusetts Institute of Technology (MIT), where her teaching and research focuses on book history, material culture, poetry and poetics. She also serves as Associate Director for Bookshops with *The Map of Early Modern London*, is Co-Director of the MIT Beaver Press, and has recently joined the *Bibliography of Editions of Early English Drama* (BEEED). In 2021 and 2024, she served as Digital Pedagogy Lead for the NEH Summer Institute: *Teaching Melville:* Moby-Dick *and the World of Whaling in the Digital Age*.

INTRODUCTION

THIS IS NOT A BOOK

Christopher Ohge and Kristen Schuster

The title of this introduction may pique the reader's curiosity, while potentially perplexing those with experience in many fields: book history, new media studies and digital curation, to name a few. *This is Not a Book – It's Data . . . This is Not a Book – It's a Digital Archive . . . This is Not a Book – It's Information.* We intend our title to suggest that the simple and enduring codex (individually, or as collected in an archive) is not quite what we think it is because of the ways we can interact with texts. Given the rise of material studies of the book and the wide availability of digital facsimiles, we now have literary scholars who regularly 'read' aspects of a text's physical form as fully as its content (Holahan, Malcolm and Trettien 2024). Embracing the polysemous nature of text technologies offers opportunities to invoke and explore further disciplinary perspectives.

This volume presents interdisciplinary arguments on text-based scholarship from editing, bibliography, publishing, digitizing, archiving and curating, while reconsidering these activities in light of new media. It also manifests the conviction that combining perspectives from related disciplines (ones with which we may not interact) brings forward the many thought-provoking concerns we share. By offering these perspectives and putting them into conversation, we aim to advance our scholarship: the book historian may become more attentive to digital curation and social media as publishing practices; the textual editor may rethink editorial theories based on information theory and generative AI tools, or may develop inclusive approaches to negotiate the impact of digital facsimiles and archival methods or perhaps consider material such as folklore, anthologies or woodblocks as objects of scholarly attention; the cultural heritage professional may register the changing scholarly dynamics occasioned by the rise of new media and literary methodologies such as techniques of macroanalysis (Bode 2012; Da 2019) or, as Jon Ippolito suggests in his essay in this volume, by strategies focused on *discovering* knowledge rather than *generating* facts in digital archives. All these conversations destabilize assumptions about what constitutes the text and book by reflecting on how we conceptualize data within interdisciplinary contexts of emerging technologies.

By bringing in experts from book history, publishing history, scholarly editing, museum and archival curation, information science, and new media studies, we offer redescriptions of our understanding of material texts – documents, books, images and data – and promote interdisciplinary perspectives on how the digital humanities

(DH) can bring together research about (new) media. These approaches underpin our interest in using new media to destabilize and transform the conceptualization of texts within these disciplines. We argue that creative-critical uses of information science and curation can bridge different practices and research involving digital approaches to textual studies. Considering a plurality of technologies as tools that enable our access to text as media enhances our appreciation of materiality itself – not only in terms of objects' physical properties, but also in light of their underlying constitutive processes of communication, representation and composition (Treharne and Willan 2019).

New Directions in Textual Studies attends to the conditions of writing and composition in their many forms of mediation: as documents, books, printed materials, visual art and data sets, as well as in the forms that collections of writing and composed materials might take, including libraries and digital archives. We need to reconsider such entities as forms of information that are now primarily mediated as data through digital technologies such as publishing platforms, text technologies, databases and artificial intelligence. Yet we are also thinking of these forms of writing as modes of narration, as well as ways to grapple with a data-rich world. To begin to address these issues, the volume puts three related themes into conversation:

- **Digital approaches to book history and textual scholarship:** explorations of technology and media that focus on editorial practices and how texts and books have been made, published, distributed and archived.
- **Theories of new media as a lens for evaluating digital methods and publication:** theories of new media that offer insights into how DH projects use text, as well as how these uses then affect more discipline-specific approaches to book history and textual editing.
- **Information science and digital curation:** strategies of selecting, preserving, representing and structuring data, as well as communicating about archives and (new) media, are ingrained within information science and digital curation.

To address these themes, we have invited scholars and practitioners from a variety of career stages and national contexts: postgraduate students, information science professionals and non-tenured researchers are published alongside established academics hailing from North America, Europe and Australia. The idea for this volume arose from ongoing conversations between its two editors. One is an literary scholar and book historian; the other is a library and information science scholar who works in digital curation. We met in the middle through DH. In the course of these conversations, we realized that while digital textual studies and book history had much in common with digital curation, these fields could do more to exchange ideas and use the tools of new media studies to reconsider the material focus of book history.

Following in the tradition of Lev Manovich, Matthew Kirschenbaum and N. Katherine Hayles, we are attempting to reframe 'text' as one of many possible codifications of information, rather than as immutable words transmitted through documents and books. In doing so, we think it is possible to imagine texts and books beyond printed forms and technology beyond binary codes that produce algorithms. Martin Paul Eve's *Theses on the Metaphors of Digital-Textual History* (2024) shows how to study the various metaphors that print has offered readers and how those metaphors eventually rupture in digital forms. Yet important metaphors such as hypertext are assumed to be the product of digital media but may function as a method to capture associative processes of thought in the literary mind using digital approaches (Atzenbeck and Nürnberg 2019; Antonini et al. 2025; Blackburn-Daniels and Bradley 2024). In particular, Kirschenbaum's recent book *Bitstreams* (2021) offers an important template for exploring how digital media affect the creation, preservation and interpretation of literary material. Preserving digital artefacts, such as authors' digital drafts and email archives, creates both opportunities and challenges of digital archiving for memory institutions. Building on these ideas, we consider how editing and curation could facilitate innovative experiences of these new forms of heritage. Traditional editorial, bibliographical and archival methods were developed for analog materials and are often inadequate to the task of capturing the complexities of new media. Thus, it becomes possible to also ask: how could textual studies benefit from a creative, curatorial approach to thinking about text as media?

A recent presentation by Gill Partington and Adam Smyth at the 'Out of Practice' seminar at the Institute of English Studies, University of London, focused on the physical processes involved in Partington's reading Vladimir Nabokov's *Pale Fire*: including, for instance, those of photographing her hand holding the book, making notes, checking her phone, spilling her drink and so on. The photographs were printed and bound. As Partington spoke, Smyth projected his hands, flipping the pages of Partington's book on a large screen. Their approach made not only clear, but visible and tangible, the layers of mediation involved in any textual experience while highlighting how the digital can help us appreciate materiality and tactility on a deeper level, reflecting recent experiments in 'post-publishing' (Adema 2021).

Texts are now complex forms of media – and the product of many layers of abstraction that are computable – which enable new ways of reading and analysis. As Laura Dietz has shown, digital proxies of texts and books also have significant value as 'real' readerly objects of 'bookness' (2025, 4). The production, publication and archiving of texts have been changing with new scholarship on digitized archives, text collections and artificial intelligence. The authors in this collection are invested in using technology to do research and research-led teaching about the challenges, promises and biases of textual studies in media-rich contexts.

* * *

Despite its long-standing history in academic practice, textual studies can be difficult to situate. Is it about the making of books, creativity and authorship or a cultural analysis of printing, publishing and reading? How is it different from its predecessor philology, or from other forms of bibliography? Textual studies can be all of those things; that said, the question of how digital technologies have changed our approaches to what text is, while complicating the cultural status that texts themselves may have, still lingers.

Digital approaches to textual scholarship already have a rich history going back to the 1990s. Although DH continues to grow and gain recognition, it is sometimes accused of being uncritical or under-theorized (Warwick 2015). Notwithstanding these issues, the successes of digital textual scholarship have been impressive, including the new scholarly editions that have been developed using the standards of the Text Encoding Initiative (TEI): the Jane Austen Fiction Manuscripts Project, the Samuel Beckett Digital Manuscript Project, the William Blake Archive, the Julian Bond Papers, the Theodor Fontane Archive, the digital historical-critical edition of Goethe's *Faust*, the Herman Melville Electronic Library (MEL), the Rossetti Archive, the Mark Twain Project Online, the Walt Whitman Archive and the digital edition of Vetusta Monumenta – to name a few. As these projects' names suggest, some conceptual blurring exists between the 'archive' and the 'edition' (Price 2009). Yet it is clear that new media makes it possible to build editions *out of* (not *separate from*) archives. Doubtless many more digital editions will continue to appear because the scholarly work involved in their creation is itself enhanced by access to searchable digital editions, manuscript facsimiles and further linked items (Driscoll and Pierazzo 2016).

In digital bibliography, impressive initiatives such as Cristina Dondi's international database *Material Evidence in Incunabula* (MEI, launched in 2009) have published data from over 80,000 books (Dondi 2020). Other important databases – including Early English Books Online (EEBO), Eighteenth Century Collections Online (ECCO) and the Universal Short Title Catalogue (USTC) – have expanded access to textual scholars and book historians (Gregg 2020). Projects such as Print & Probability show the affordances of combining book history, computer vision and machine learning to re-discover letterpress printers whose identities have eluded scholars for hundreds of years (Lemley et al. 2024).[1]

Alongside database projects, digital archives of writers' libraries have also innovated since the early days of DH. Melville's Marginalia Online (MMO), which was launched in 2006 by Steven Olsen-Smith, began as an online catalog of books owned, borrowed and consulted by Herman Melville, based on the pioneering work of Merton Sealts, Jr., yet has more recently been releasing digital facsimiles of Melville's annotated books as well as innovative data analysis tools to understand the fragmentary evidence of marginalia. The Beckett, Fontane and Whitman projects have also added marginalia sections to their editions, and some others (for example, of John Stuart Mill and Thomas Mann) focus on libraries and marginalia. Other projects, such as the Archaeology of Reading (which focuses on Gabriel Harvey and John Dee's libraries), have made use of the improved digital image delivery application programming interface (API) offered by the International Image Interoperability Framework (IIIF). In this volume, Anke Jaspers and

---

[1] See also the Print & Probability project website at https://printprobability.org/.

Martina Schönbächler show that many other fascinating authorial library projects are in development. In addition to these kinds of enterprises, as argued by scholars such as Lorna Hughes, Melissa Terras and Jane Winters, DH has been changing our conceptions of media, theories and methodologies, and approaches for preserving, cataloguing and curating heritage.

In his 2014 Lyell Lectures in Bibliography, H. R. Woudhuysen said that digitized books are undeniably useful to book history research. However, he also emphasized that one must also be aware of the 'fallibility of people making digital images' – they make mistakes, omit some information and are often reproducing just one copy of a book without being clear about the history of that copy. They also choose specific file formats (which is not without risk of obsolescence or quirks in compression). The bibliographical makeup of these copies is often hidden or difficult to dissemble without advanced technical skills, unlike those who have handled a hand press, which shows how easy it is to make printing mistakes (Lawrence and Franklin 2023; Grafton 2022; Trettien 2021). Digitized books are editions in their own right: they come with decisions – a kind of computational editorial hand – and a new set of type (in the sense of data structuring and other supports like transcription). In his chapter, Geoffrey Turnovsky likewise argues that a digital facsimile illustrates a 'transformed text'. Terms such as 'edition' are evolving in the digital age.

Simultaneously balancing critical awareness with the pursuit of novelty and innovation poses challenges to newer iterations of book history; this offers scope for integrating theories of new media into book history methods and practices. The objects are undeniably useful, but the user also needs to be aware of what they are seeing.[2] As the late Will Noel put it in his 2019 Sandars Lectures, 'The Medieval Manuscript and its Digital Image,' digitized books should no longer be called 'surrogates'.[3] What then should we call them? Treating books as media and text as data opens a realm of possibilities. As editorial constructs, digital facsimiles are worthy of textual scholarship and critical awareness. Therefore, they should be taken seriously, but not so seriously that they overlook the possibilities for new areas of discussion, perspectives on access, and the evolution of ownership and creativity. Studying the materiality of books can only be enhanced by an understanding of their underlying information through digital tools. In this volume, contributors consider how to evolve traditional humanities debates about meaning and form and look to more varied approaches to imagining and interrogating textual artefacts and data.

Digitized books are only one part of digital book history, and the novelty of digitized texts has abated, and access to digital copies has become a near requirement for research and teaching. Using digital methods in book history is now a necessity. Yet resistance – and misunderstandings – still arise. These issues suggest that we are still emerging out of a 'digital incunable' phase (Turnovsky 2024, 295; Whearty 2022, 121–67). With

---

[2] https://podcasts.ox.ac.uk/almost-identical-copying-books-england-1600-1900.
[3] https://www.youtube.com/watch?v=7S45VsnUxG0&t=2s.

technologies such as generative AI and Handwritten Text Recognition, we are in the midst of leaving the digital incunable phase, which will produce a new wave of tools and methods for processing, retrieving and presenting digital texts. Some textual editors are now using Transkribus to transcribe manuscripts and generative AI to encode and annotate those transcriptions in TEI-XML. Other recent initiatives, such as Sophie Whittle's prototype digital teaching edition of Chaucer's 'Pardoner's Tale' using machine-assisted AI methods, show that scholars will need to be equipped to ask critical questions about the consequences of new digital tools. As Mark Vareschi and Heather Wacha show in their collection *Intermediate Horizons* (2022), book history and digital practices are integrated through approach, access and assessment. The interconnected 'horizons' at the intersections of texts, technology and culture could return us to a more human-centred study of the humanities in the digital age. Doing so has the potential, to quote Whitney Trettien, to give textual scholars 'a renewed commitment to how we compose and share our work ... [and] how we use technologies to make public the stories we spin about texts and their lives' (Trettien 2021, 6). This volume of essays seeks to add more examples and provocations to expand this conversation.

* * *

This collection follows several lines of recent thought in textual scholarship. Adam Smyth has argued in his introduction to *The Oxford Handbook of the History of the Book in Early Modern England* (2023) that bibliography and book history have, in the past, engaged in narrow and excluding narratives of their remit and practices. Justin Tonra (2021), reflecting on D. F. McKenzie's groundbreaking work, makes a similar point that expanding that remit also enhances what we now know about the book: 'As book historians subject e-books and born-digital texts to the bibliographical scrutiny once reserved for rare books, digital humanists are concerned with the epistemological consequences of the shift from print to digital as a means of humanistic inquiry and production.' In another recent collection, *DH+BH*, the editors Spencer Keralis and Cait Coker argue that DH and book history are 'potentially expansive tools for advocacy, activism, and recovery work in our current moment', inviting readers to reflect on power, privilege and potential in the wider fields of DH and history of the book. Examples published in *American Contact* (2024) and innovative DH projects such as the Colored Conventions Project, the Early Caribbean Digital Archive, and the Black Bibliography Project explore these dynamics through the medium of material texts to redefine the boundaries of the book.[4] It is also important to recognize the professional practices of librarians and archivists as active research partners and reckon with the fact that the twenty-first-century archive is a fluid and polyvocal domain influenced by a range of subject matter expertise (Russell

---

[4] https://coloredconventions.org/. https://ecda.northeastern.edu/. https://blackbibliog.org/. See also the Colored Conventions Project's extensive list of Black Digital Humanities Projects and Resources at bit.ly/Black-DH-List.

and Layne-Worthey 2024; Prescott and Wiggins 2023). DH may be a capacious concept, but it is intertwined with library, archival and information sciences.

Contributions in this collection come from an international community of scholars exploring the limitations of digital collections, the potential of digital methodologies to enrich bibliographical research, and the pleasures and challenges of interdisciplinary approaches to textual studies. Combined with this idea are the creative-critical practices that have started to be incorporated into textual studies (Nabugodi and Ohge 2022). As Dirk Van Hulle puts it, one of the most promising aspects of this work 'is a sustained attempt to think in terms of *creative ecologies* instead of dichotomies' (Van Hulle 2024). This collection takes a similar spirit and focuses on the intersections between textual scholarship, museum and archival studies and new media studies to address important questions of materiality, remediation, creativity, curation, textual authority and storytelling.

The rationale of this volume is to stimulate new research and digital approaches through an interdisciplinary exchange of case studies, methodologies and interdisciplinary reflections, which should be applicable not only to academics but also to curators in libraries, archives and museums. This will push readers of this volume not to accept technologies in their work but to *ask questions about those technologies* – to think about how technologies are used, to improve them and to ensure better access and experiences of textual and archival materials.

We have divided this volume into two sections. Chapters in the first section offer methodological reflections on the related disciplines of scholarly editing and book history. Authors take a broad view of textual data and present alternative practices to the value of digital facsimiles, the technical needs for databases and digital libraries, and the functional requirements for creating new kinds of digital editions. Case studies and methods shared by authors transcend what could have been accomplished in the print publishing era and articulate the complex entanglements between technologies, data, text and media. In taking a broad view of data, authors are able to grapple with the fact that many digital concepts are metaphors of material texts and that aspects of materiality persist in the digital age, but that new forms of data structuring are also necessary (sometimes for good and sometimes not, as Miller C. Prosser shows in Chapter 5).

The collection begins with Zoe Screti's 'Cataloguing the Enlightenment: Legacy Practices of Organized Knowledge', which engages with the histories of cataloguing and classification as a method for understanding the materiality of knowledge. Her propositions shed light on how collections of books influence our thinking about the historical value of information. Continuing in this theme, Geoffrey Turnovsky's chapter, 'Editing Authenticity in the Manuscript Text: Prefaces, Diplomatic Transcriptions and Photographs', uses prefaces to eighteenth-century manuscript letter editions to analyse the dynamics of editing a handwritten text for readability, or faithfully representing these texts in editions, and how digital facsimiles of such manuscripts should change our conception of authenticity. Giles Bergel's chapter, 'The Printing Surface in the Age of Digital Reproduction', traces the interconnections of print technology and image reproduction to destabilize notions of media being 'new' and the hegemony of text in book history projects. Anke Jaspers and Martina Schönbächler's chapter, 'From Bookshelves to Bytes: Navigating the Digital Transformation of Writers' Libraries', offers a multifaceted conceptualization of the writer's library and the development of a shared theory and methodology for producing digital archives and editions of these collections. Their chapter shows how digital methods can shed more light on how authors used their books in distinct moments of thinking and composition, envisaging a hypertext mode of reading. Weaving all of these themes together, Miller C. Prosser's chapter, 'A Graph Database Approach to Editing and Publishing Infinitely Recombinant Digital Texts with OCHRE', combines Ted Nelson's hypertextual idea of 'intertwingularity' and textual scholar Jerome McGann's ideas on digital editing to argue for the utility of graph databases in textual scholarship. By doing so, he is able to consider the complex connections between atomized bits of textual information. Christopher Ohge's chapter, 'Pragmatic Digital Editing, Data Analysis and Creative-Critical Practices', focuses on his recent digital edition of the British anti-slavery anthology *The Bow in the Cloud* (1834), compiled by Mary Anne Rawson, which exemplifies pragmatic approaches to curating open data with multiple analysis and publishing tools, as well as creative-critical approaches. It also pushes new thinking about editorial theory and modes of digital publishing. Echoing these critical points, Mary Erica Zimmer's chapter, 'Extracting for Experience: Material Annotation and its Affordances in Textual Studies', proposes creative strategies and pedagogies for engaging with Herman Melville's novel *Moby-Dick*. Through community engagement, object-oriented learning and creative praxis, Zimmer's chapter presents opportunities to imagine the editorially adjacent idea of 'material annotation' with haptic modes of experience, from creating artworks to 3D printing. Her case study shines a light on the value of textual studies, book history and curatorial collaborations to enable user-oriented interpretations of complex canonical texts. Peter Webster's chapter, 'Reading the Edited Collection, Distantly', offers a discipline-specific methodology for using digital methods to study publication histories. This configuration of practices is important because Webster is a historian who uses texts to uncover people who contributed to theological scholarship. His aim then is not to study texts as objects but texts as the manifestation of ideas and ideas as the product of communities of practice. Taken together, chapters in this section provide an excellent example of the possibilities for using digital approaches to materials like edited collections to contribute to discussions of evolving disciplinary histories.

The second section of this volume shows the possibilities of digital curation when it is informed by textual scholarship, literary techniques of storytelling and new media studies. Wim Van Mierlo's chapter, 'Unlocking Literary Heritage: From Cabinets of Curiosities to Digital Storytelling', further offers reflective and critical interrogations of the curatorial practices that ought to inform digital approaches to literary collections. Curation can push the boundaries of knowledge representation and community engagement. In the context of information and archival science, digital curation consists of interconnected practices that support the selection, appraisal and preservation of media. These practices provide an opportunity to reflect on editing in relation to theories of new media. In 'Folklore Archives in the Digital Age', Karoline Strittmater reviews the cultural and disciplinary history of folklore archives and presents a comprehensive review of opportunities and challenges involved in the curation and preservation of folklore collections – issues which also overlap with many concerns of book historians and textual scholars. Ashney Randle, Logan Thompson, Renee Jones and Sarah Buchanan's chapter, 'Teaching Truman with Hypertext Methods: Project Whistlestop over Two Decades', provides a detailed history of the digital archive of Harry Truman's presidential library. Their case study further reflects on the challenges of curating historical documents with innovative digital technologies and hypertext methodology. Ellen Charlesworth and Claire Warwick's chapter, 'Digital Publishing Practices in Museums: Old Habits, New Platforms', analyses museums' social media strategies, offering insights into the challenges and requirements of new media publishing practices in the GLAM sector. Charlesworth and Warwick show how social media content may not reach its intended audiences and suggest that the act of creating new media is a valuable first step to re-imagining museum outreach; it is only a first step towards transforming how museums communicate the significance and accessibility of their collections. Through their data-driven analyses of social media use, they identify opportunities for creative engagement with audiences, while attending to the complexities of formulating creative approaches to establishing who comprises their targeted audiences. Kristen Schuster's chapter, 'Describing New Media: Strategies and Recommendations for Teaching Structured Data in Multidisciplinary Humanities Contexts', situates language as a fundamental part of cataloguing practices and highlights the need for collaboration to generate creative and innovative data structuring methods.

Jon Ippolito's chapter, 'Honey, AI Shrunk the Archive: Artificial Intelligence as Compression Algorithm', offers an important critique of applying an animate metaphor to artificial intelligence, which has the danger of homogenizing the digital archive. Ippolito encourages us to understand large language models as statistical engines rather than brains (or stochastic parrots). We conclude the collection of essays in a provocative vein with Leah Henrickson's 'Book History for the Future: Connecting Communications Media', which proposes approaches for studying computer-generated and mediated text to situate book history within wider conversations about data and human-computer interactions.

The chapters in each section investigate how interdisciplinary engagements with textual artefacts open up analytical and creative possibilities. We have used our three themes to engage in editorial conversations with contributors and to present new thinking in book history, textual scholarship, new media and digital curation. Instead of rejecting the value of disciplinary expertise, these chapters showcase the possibilities for expertise to foster creative praxes and new conceptualizations of the materials, ideas and histories central to humanities scholarship. In thinking about technology in relation to these themes, we have challenged disciplinary approaches to digital methods to theorize new ways of working with texts. Through interdisciplinary uses of digital editing, trans-disciplinary critiques of cataloguing and inquiries into the possibilities of AI, it is possible to conceptualize text as media and media as text in new ways. The reason for this approach is that so many texts on book history or textual editing or new media studies are directed to their own disciplinary communities, whereas this volume aims to open up these disciplines by focusing on their overlapping and complementary practices.

* * *

No edited collection should presume to cover everything and will not account for some creative, critical and innovative scholarship. This is not meant as an excuse but as a statement to acknowledge the limitations of our editorial work and to encourage future work that provokes, highlights and expands upon digital approaches to textual studies. We aim to present a sample of innovative, cross-disciplinary work that is meant to spark conversations, instead of defining the field or discipline. This is not done for the sake of ignoring disciplinary debates and politics within the field of humanities research, but to foster inclusive and reflexive methods to conceptualize data, databases and computational practices in more approachable and collaborative ways.

Through this work, we have found areas of overlap that in turn highlight the boundaries within our disciplines and open up opportunities for discussion, debate and research. While we both work in academic contexts, collaborative and iterative discussions have reinforced the value of practice-based work that makes histories of books, ideas and technologies more accessible. The importance of access to textual materials, books and archives appears in many of the chapters in this volume – access through critiques of tradition, innovation in the management of information and creative interventions that break down barriers. Many of the questions we have posed are not new, but they propose new directions in studying text technologies that look to the future while attending to the past. We hope that readers can make note of areas for future research and see themselves within inquiries that strive to imagine more diverse modes of collaborative inquiry.

Bibliography

Adema, Janneke. *Living Books: Experiments in the Posthumanities*. Cambridge, MA: MIT Press, 2021.

Antonini, Alessio, Francesca Benatti, Sam Brooker, and Christopher Ohge. 'Hypertext as Method in Book History and Beyond'. In *DH + BH: An Interdisciplinary Collection on Digital Humanities and Book History*. Edited by Spencer D. C. Keralis and Cait Coker. Urbana-Champaign, IL: Windsor & Downs Press, 2025.

Atzenbeck, Claus and Peter Nürnberg. 'Hypertext as Method'. *HT '19: Proceedings of the 30th ACM Conference on Hypertext and Social Media* (2019): 29–38. https://doi.org/10.1145/3342220.3343669.

Barnes, Rhae Lynn and Glenda Goodman, eds. *American Contact: Objects of Intercultural Encounters and the Boundaries of Book History*. Philadelphia: University of Pennsylvania Press, 2024.

Blackburn-Daniels, Sally and Matthew Bradley. 'The Handling of Vernon Lee's Words: Developing Scholarly Editions in the Age of Hypertext'. In *35th ACM Conference on Hypertext and Social Media (HT '24)*, 10–13 September 2024, Poznan, Poland. ACM. https://doi.org/10.1145/3648188.3678212.

Bode, Katherine. *Reading by Numbers: Recalibrating the Literary Field*. London: Anthem Press, 2012.

Da, Nan Z. 'The Computational Case against Computational Literary Studies'. *Critical Inquiry* 45, no. 3 (2019): 601–39.

Dietz, Laura. *E-books and 'Real Books': Digital Reading and the Experience of Bookness*. Cambridge: Cambridge University Press, 2025.

Dondi, Cristina, ed. *Printing R-Evolution and Society 1450–1500*. Venice: Edizioni Ca' Foscari, 2020.

Driscoll, Matthew James and Elena Pierazzo. *Digital Scholarly Editing: Theories and Practices*. Cambridge: OpenBook Publishers, 2016.

Eve, Martin Paul. *Theses on the Metaphors of Digital-Textual History*. Redwood City, CA: Stanford University Press, 2024.

Grafton, Anthony. *Inky Fingers: The Making of Books in Early Modern Europe*. Cambridge, MA: Harvard University Press, 2022.

Gregg, Stephen H. *Old Books and Digital Publishing: Eighteenth-Century Collections Online*. Cambridge: Cambridge University Press, 2020.

Holahan, Cassidy, Aylin Malcolm and Whitney Trettien. 'Not Reading the Edition'. In *Futures of Digital Scholarly Editing*. Edited by Matt Cohen, Kenneth M. Price, and Caterina Bernardini. Minneapolis: University of Minnesota Press, 2024.

Hughes, Lorna, ed. *Evaluating and Measuring the Value, Use and Impact of Digital Collections*. London: Facet, 2011.

Keralis, Spencer D. C. and Cait Coker, eds. *DH + BH: An Interdisciplinary Collection on Digital Humanities and Book History*. Urbana-Champaign, IL: Windsor & Downs Press, 2025.

Kirschenbaum, Matthew G. *Bitstreams: The Future of Digital Literary Heritage*. Philadelphia: University of Pennsylvania Press, 2021.

Lawrence, Richard and Alexandra Franklin. 'Printing and Book History: Insights from Practice'. In *The Oxford Handbook to the History of the Book in Early Modern England*, 123–39. Edited by Adam Smyth. Oxford: Oxford University Press, 2023.

Lemley, Samuel V., Nikolai Vogler, Christopher N. Warren, D. J. Schuldt, Laura S. DeLuca, Kari Thomas, Taylor Berg-Kirkpatrick, Elizabeth Dieterich, Kartik Goyal, and Max G'Sell. 2024. 'Everything There is to be Learned about Seventeenth-Century Types: Computational Bibliography & The Printers of Shakespeare's Fourth Folio'. In *The Four Shakespeare Folios, 1623–2023*. Edited by Samuel V. Lemley. University Park, PA: Penn State University Press.

McKenzie, D. F. *Bibliography and the Sociology of Texts*. London: The British Library, 1986.

Nabugodi, Mathelinda and Christopher Ohge, eds. Special Issue: 'Creative-Critical Provocations'. *Textual Cultures* 15, no. 1 (2022). https://www.jstor.org/stable/e48511031.

Prescott, Andrew and Alison Wiggins, eds. *Archives: Power, Truth, and Fiction*. Oxford: Oxford University Press, 2023.

Price, Kenneth M. 'Edition, Project, Database, Archive, Thematic Research Collection: What's in a Name?' *Digital Humanities Quarterly* 3, no. 3 (2009). https://www.digitalhumanities.org/dhq/vol/3/3/000053/000053.html.

Russell, Isabel Galina and Glen Layne-Worthey, eds. *The Routledge Companion to Libraries, Archives, and the Digital Humanities*. London: Routledge, 2024.

Smyth, Adam, ed. *The Oxford Handbook of the History of the Book in Early Modern England*. Oxford: Oxford University Press, 2023.

Terras, Melissa. 'Digital Humanities and Digitised Cultural Heritage'. In *The Bloomsbury Handbook to the Digital Humanities*, 255–66. Edited by James O'Sullivan. London: Bloomsbury Academic, 2022.

Tonra, Justin, ed. 'Book History and Digital Humanities in the Long Eighteenth Century'. Special issue of *Eighteenth Century Studies* 54 no. 4 (2021): 765–83.

Treharne, Elaine and Claude Willan. *Text Technologies: A History*. Redwood City, CA: Stanford University Press, 2019.

Trettien, Whitney. *Cut/Copy/Paste: Fragments from the History of Bookwork*. Minneapolis: University of Minnesota Press, 2021.

Turnovsky, Geoffrey. *Reading Typographically: Immersed in Print in Early Modern France*. Redwood City, CA: Stanford University Press, 2024.

Van Hulle, Dirk. 'Creative Ecologies: The Complete-Works Edition in a Digital Paradigm'. In *Futures of Digital Scholarly Editing*. Edited by Matt Cohen, Kenneth M. Price and Caterina Bernardini. Minneapolis: University of Minnesota Press, 2024.

Vareschi, Mark and Heather Wacha, eds. *Intermediate Horizons: Book History and Digital Humanities*. Madison: University of Wisconsin Press, 2022.

Warwick, Claire. 'Building Theories or Theories of Building? A Tension at the Heart of Digital Humanities'. In *A New Companion to Digital Humanities*. Edited by Susan Schreibman, Ray Siemens, John Unsworth. Oxford: Wiley-Blackwell, 2015.

Whearty, Bridget. *Digital Codicology: Medieval Books and Modern Labor*. Redwood City, CA: Stanford University Press, 2022.

Winters, Jane. 'Digital Humanities and the Academic Books of the Future'. In *The Bloomsbury Handbook to the Digital Humanities*, 245–54. Edited by James O'Sullivan. London: Bloomsbury Academic, 2022.

PART I
METHODS AND CASE STUDIES

CHAPTER 1
CATALOGUING THE ENLIGHTENMENT
LEGACY PRACTICES OF ORGANIZED KNOWLEDGE
Zoe Screti

Catalogues are essential tools for scholarly research, allowing users to locate curated lists of sources they want to consult and documenting the depth and breadth of a given collection – whether they are books, manuscripts, objects or remedies. For that reason, they have been used for many centuries by a host of scholars and library users ranging from medieval monks to twenty-first-century academics. But for all of the wonderful opportunities that catalogues offer, they are often inherently flawed, shaping and directing our research in implicit and sometimes problematic ways.

Although catalogues had a long history, many of these problems were introduced and formalized during the Enlightenment, a period of categorization in which the sum of human knowledge was rationally organized into a series of classifications and subclassifications that were linked in relational and hierarchical ways (Hodacs, Nyberg and Van Damme 2018). Medieval catalogues had also employed classifications but adopted a two-pronged approach, as identified by Philip Gaskell, that lacked the relational nature of later catalogues (Gaskell 1980, 108, 112). The first of these was an ecclesiastical system that privileged theology and was then followed by the liberal arts. The second was an academic system that reflected the division of knowledge into the *trivium* and *quadrivium* within the university system. It was during the long eighteenth century that these classifications would be divided further, expanded, and turned into the relational hierarchies that privileged some categories over others in problematic ways. While some of these categories have since been revised, the persistence of such approaches to classification continues to shape the ways in which we discuss and value the world today. This is especially true of library classifications, the conceptual containers into which books and manuscripts are sorted according to their subject matter.

By exploring how these subject classifications came into being and reflecting on their consequences for library users and cataloguers today, this reflection is a timely one as the digital age attempts to reshape traditional cataloguing and classification methods and overcome problems introduced during the Enlightenment.

Cataloguing practices before the eighteenth century

Although it is typical to think of the Enlightenment as a period of expanding knowledge, it was also a period in which the diversity of the world was forced into neat classifications.

Despite this desire to rationalize the world into a series of systems, relationships, and hierarchies that made the sum of human knowledge seem comprehensible, these same categories and classifications simultaneously made multidimensional objects, ideas, and concepts distinctly one-dimensional. Nowhere is this dynamic more apparent than within library catalogues, which today seek to provide a complete, ordered, and logical account of a collection of books and/or manuscripts that not only differ from one another in unique ways but also have their own complex constitutions.

Before discussing the problems introduced during the Enlightenment, it is first pertinent to define what a catalogue is and how definitions have changed over time, as only then can the implications of Enlightenment influences on cataloguing methods be fully appreciated. The likes of G. Thomas Tanselle have notably argued that catalogue is a flexible term whose meaning is defined at an individual level, making it all the more important to explore the multifaceted nature of the term and its genesis (Tanselle 1977, 1–56). Catalogues for many centuries had typically been simple lists or registers, often used as a calendar of saints, to map the genealogy of royalty, to organize a library collection or to provide an overview of medicinal treatments. Indeed, the term catalogue in Old French refers to a list or index, while the Greek katalogos from which the term derived refers to a list or register (kata meaning completely, and legein meaning to say or count). In a manuscript translation of Guy de Chauliac's *Grande Chirurgie* (c.1425), one of the earliest recorded descriptions of the term 'catalogo' or 'catalogue' in English, de Chauliac remarks:

> þe degreez of medicinez may more liztly be founden, be þai ordeyned vnder þe cathologo i. ordre or noumbre of þe a.b.c. of latine menne.[1]

Thus, a catalogue was a list of information that had been structured in some way, such as alphabetically, in the case of de Chauliac, or thematically, as was the case with monastic catalogues in the medieval period. While many varieties of manuscript and printed catalogues continued to be produced into the seventeenth century, most of these works are divisible into three key categories: science and medicine, bibliographies, and sales.

Like de Chauliac, seventeenth-century authors often used catalogues of remedies for distinctly medical or scientific purposes, using the form to list and record experiments, observations, ingredients, and remedial concoctions. On 6 September 1665, for instance, Robert Boyle described in a letter to Henry Oldenburg a 'Catalogue of all the Simples & other easily parable Medicines that have been found successful against the Plague' that he found in an old book (Hunter et al., *Robert Boyle* vol. 2, 537–8, and vol. 2, 516–17). Similarly, Robert Hooke wrote on 6 October 1665 that 'I have in my catalogue already

---

[1]'The degrees of medicines may more easily be found, if they are ordained under the catalogue in order or number of the a.b.c. of the Latin type.' New York Academy of Medicine, New York, 'New York Academy of Medicine 12', f.140.

thought on divers experiments of heat and cold, of gravity and levity, of condensation and rarefaction of pressure, of pendulous motions and motions of descent...', while John Read wrote in 1666 of a 'Catalogue of about 200 select Chymicall Medicines' (Hunter et al., *Robert Boyle* vol. 2, 537–8, and vol. 3, 2–5). Seventeenth-century catalogues were thus used in scientific and medical contexts. In this way, they were uniquely indebted more to natural history than they were to library science as we now conceive of it, as a sense of activity, investigation, experimentation, and observation underpinned their construction.

Additionally, the term 'catalogue' was used in this period in bibliographical ways, often to refer to the totality of a given author's works or to organize the contents of a library. Amongst these authorial catalogues were the sermons of prominent clergymen such as John Bramhall, successively Bishop of Derry and Archbishop of Armagh, and John Tillotson, Archbishop of Canterbury (Bramhall 1676; Tillotson 1696). Catalogues of the works of key literary figures likewise rolled off the presses in vast quantities; a catalogue of John Milton's works appeared at the end of *The Life of John Milton*, published in 1699, for instance, while Henry Oldenburg wrote to Robert Boyle in December 1664 of a work that consisted of:

> the name and position of all who excel in all arts and sciences, the books which they have published, and those they plan; the death of men of letters of any repute, including the principle [sic] events of their lives with a catalogue of all they have published in order to aid in writing an éloge. (Hunter et al., *Robert Boyle* vol. 2, 531–4)

Finally, catalogues were used in entrepreneurial ways in the seventeenth century to advertise and sell wares, usually books, by both booksellers and printers, as H. R. Woudhuysen has demonstrated (Woudhuysen 2023). In another letter to Robert Boyle, for instance, Oldenburg notes that he saw in the catalogue of Bishops Head Bookshop in Pauls Churchyard that 'the same Kircher has publisht [sic] a Scrutinium Physicomedicum Pestis, which I never saw before' (Hunter et al., *Robert Boyle*, vol. 2, 531–4). Meanwhile, in the correspondence between John Locke and Philippus van Limborch, there are multiple references to the 'Frankfurt catalogue which contains the books to be offered to the public at the next fair'.[2] These lists were variably arranged chronologically, alphabetically, or without any logical ordering at all, as in the case of *A Catalogue of Bookes Printed For, and to be Sold by Richard Davis at his shop neer Oriell Colledge in Oxford*, printed in 1660 (Davis 1660).

Despite their variable subject matter, there are two qualities that united seventeenth-century catalogues in their various forms: first, a sense of dynamism, and second the form of the list. While these were records of doing – of testing, observing, printing, selling,

---

[2]See, for example, de Beer 1978.

collecting, and writing – they also conformed to the textual format of the standardized list. Although there are some similarities between these lists and today's catalogues, these seventeenth-century examples lack a crucial element popularized in the eighteenth century that has since become the fundamental principle of cataloguing in the modern world: subject classification. This is an important methodological distinction to make; as catalogues are often used by historians of the book, an awareness of the genesis of subject classifications and the altered approaches taken to cataloguing over the long eighteenth century, is pivotal in understanding the literary cultures underpinning their construction.

Cataloguing in the Enlightenment

During the eighteenth century, new approaches to cataloguing generated a shift in the meaning of the term. Fundamentally, it was still used to refer to a list. However, the focus of catalogues came increasingly to fall on library collections, manipulating the textual form to record and document the bibliophilic collecting achievements of a given institution or individual. Even sales catalogues came to focus on the vast libraries of individuals, often at the time of their death. In England and France, for instance, at least 2,390 library catalogues and 2,080 book catalogues were printed between 1700 and 1800, compared to just 33 library catalogues and 188 book catalogues for the previous century.[3] Even taking into account survival rates and the expansion of print in the eighteenth century, this constitutes a significant rise in the number of catalogues pertaining specifically to books. The growth in popularity of the library catalogue (rather than the catalogue of scientific discoveries or authors' works aforementioned) mirrored wider Enlightenment trends to develop one's intellectual identity through one's library, with numerous manuals on the 'proper' construction of library collections circulating. While the library catalogue had been used prior to the Enlightenment, it was during this period that they were popularized and incorporated into countless domestic (as well as institutional) spaces as a means of curating learned personas (Montoya 2021).

There was a secondary simultaneous shift: whereas catalogues had previously been records of achievements such as scientific experiments or literary prowess, they became active participants in scholarly endeavours. Individuals would, for instance, ask for specific catalogues to be sent to them so that they could consult given entries or advise one another on which catalogues and/or catalogue entries to read. In 1760, for instance, Thomas Gray advised Horace Walpole to 'Look in Casley's Catalogue of the King's Library at 17. D. 4to. VI. 1. & you will find the Mss of Occleve & Painting of Chaucer' (Toynbee and Whibley 1935, 696–703, Letter 320). Meanwhile, in 1762, Thomas Percy, who was researching copies of works by Copland, wrote to Thomas Warton of the

---

[3] These figures are based on a search of GoogleBooks for the term 'catalogue', with results filtered by two time ranges: 1600–99 and 1700–99. These figures are based on a search conducted in February 2024.

Bodleian Library catalogue produced by Thomas Hyde, noting that 'fol. 1674, led me into the Error about the Edit. 1528. See that Catalog. Art. BEVIS' (Dennis 1931, 1178–180, Letter 13). Thus, catalogues become part of the enquiry process rather than just recording active processes, with scholars interrogating them as they would other source materials. This also served to associate particular items with a given collection and/or institution, providing a legal record of the collections and providing scholars with a means of not only locating the sources they required but also localizing their research within specific collections.

Individuals also directly compared catalogue entries in their scholarly enquiries. In 1778, George Mason wrote in a letter to Thomas Warton that he had noticed some discrepancies between different versions of the *Temple of Glass*, presumed to have been written by John Lydgate. He notes:

> There are some slight differences which may occasion a doubt, viz: Ames says 27 leaves, this Copy has 28; Ames calls it Octavo, West's Catalogue call'd it Quarto; (which I believe it is, but more resembling Octavo in shape) Ames spells the word in the Title bygenneth but in the book it is begynneth. Yet without some evidence of the existence of a book nearer to Ames's description, I cannot help regarding these small variations as instances of Ames's inaccuracy. (Fairer 1995, 405–8, Letter 366)

By the eighteenth century, catalogues referred in many instances to library collections and were regarded critically by their users. While they were still lists, the definition of a catalogue now had a narrower focus and had captured the imagination in a bibliocentric way.

By far the most significant change of the eighteenth century, however, was the introduction of subject classification as a means of ordering catalogues. Wider changes in attitudes towards knowledge – and knowledge organization – played a crucial role in determining the textual format of these catalogues, enhancing the simple list by introducing a hierarchical structure grouped thematically by subject. This change in attitudes towards the division of knowledge was pivotal in transforming cataloguing methods and introduced problematic practices that have endured to the present day.

During the Medieval period, it was generally held that all that it was possible to know had been known at one time or another. As such, acquiring knowledge was a process of uncovering and relearning from books of ancient and contemporary wisdom, rather than making discoveries or pioneering theories. The Renaissance began to challenge this belief. Between the voyages of discovery, the emergence of printing technologies and the increasing institutionalization of the sciences, scholars began to question the completeness of the knowledge of the ancients and instead began to think about and quantify knowledge in new ways. In the seventeenth century, John Locke, for instance, argued that knowledge is an understanding of the relations of things, and so it is a process of decomposition and recomposition, of breaking down the totalities of things into smaller units in order to perceive the relations between them, while others argued that human reasoning could generate new knowledge to the benefit of mankind (Gibson 2010). In particular, an emphasis on empirical knowledge emerged: knowledge that could be quantified, interrogated, and tested in a rigorous and systematic manner (Crignon, Zelle and Nunzio 2014).

The growing belief in knowledge as relational, useful, systematic, and limitless in potential had significant consequences for cataloguing methodologies; it encouraged cataloguers to present their lists in hierarchical and relational ways that would allow for the easy introduction of new concepts into those lists. This approach was influenced in no small part by the emergence of the encyclopaedia as both a genre and a methodology for the organization of knowledge via relational and hierarchical means, as opposed to the trivium/quadrivium division of knowledge used in preceding centuries. In Denis Diderot and Jean le Rond d'Alembert's *Encyclopédie*, for instance, published in Paris between 1751 and 1772, d'Alembert expressly noted that the purpose of the encyclopaedia was 'to set forth the order and connection of the parts of human knowledge' (Alambert, vol. 1). The *Encyclopédie* was therefore intended to show the relationality of information to enable users to draw connections, directly contrasting the trivium/quadrivium division of knowledge that had influenced earlier catalogues, as noted above. To allow for the efficient identification of relationships, the information it provided needed to be encoded. In this way, the *Encylopédie* functioned almost as a pre-digital relational database or TEI-encoded text, using common descriptors to link multiple entities across a vast field of metadata, though with many idiosyncrasies. Diderot and d'Alembert ascribed a so-called 'class of knowledge' to each entry to draw connections between them, totalling 55,248 classes (Horton et al. 2009). In 2009, Russell Horton, et al. identified the most common of these, revealing the ways in which such relational, or hierarchical, classifications functioned (Horton et al. 2009). Three of the most popular classes, for instance, mention geography: 'Géographie', 'Géographie moderne' and 'Géographie ancienne'. A further five mention history: 'Histoire naturelle botanique,' 'Histoire moderne,' 'Histoire naturelle,' 'Histoire ancienne' and 'Histoire ecclésiastique'.

That this relationality was intentional is evidenced in the authors' diagram to explain how their classification system functioned, dubbed the 'Système figuré des connoissances humaines' (Figure 1.1). Here, *entendement* (understanding) is broken down into three categories: *mémoire* (memory), *raison* (reason) and *imagination* (imagination), with each of these being divided and subdivided into increasingly granular classes. Under *mémoire*, for instance, is history, itself divided into sacred history; ecclesiastical history; civil, ancient and modern history; and natural history. The third of these four sub-categories is further divided into civil history and literary history, with these again being divided into the classes of memoirs, antiquities and universal histories. The system devised for the *Encyclopédie*, then, was at once relational and hierarchical, allowing the authors to demonstrate the ties between classes such as 'botanique' and 'histoire naturelle botanique', while also revealing their place within a hierarchical, ordered system of knowledge.

This division and subdivision of knowledge was judged by some to be a crucial opportunity to make new discoveries and glean enhanced understandings. In 1768 Joseph Priestley argued:

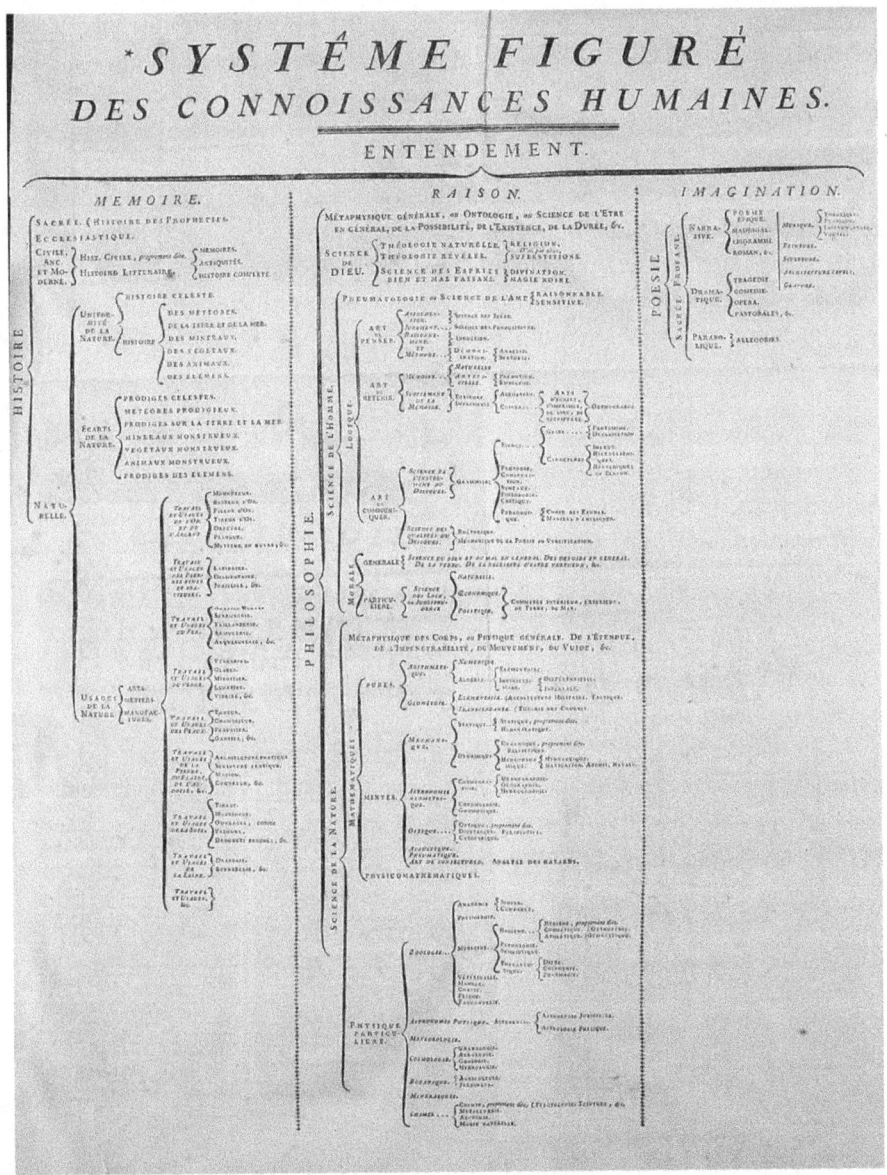

Figure 1.1 'Système figuré des connoissances humaines' in Diderot and d'Alembert's *Encyclopédie*. Image from Wikipedia Commons.

If, by this means, one art or science should grow too large for an easy comprehension in a modest space of time, a commodious subdivision will be made. Thus all knowledge will be subdivided and extended, and knowledge [. . .] being power, the human powers will be increased. (Priestley 1771, 4)

For Priestley, this carving up of knowledge represented more than just the identification of relationships and hierarchies within knowledge; it was about breaking the sum of knowledge down into more easily digestible chunks in order to facilitate new thoughts, ideas, and discoveries. Just as the library catalogue had become an active participant in scholarship, so too had subject classifications.

Altered attitudes towards, and presentation of, knowledge played a critical role in shaping cataloguing practices during the Enlightenment. In an early iteration of the Enlightenment's drive to systematize and organize knowledge, Gabriel Naudé published a guide for library owners, advising them on how to arrange their books in a logical and orderly manner. Translated by John Evelyn into English in 1661, this guide instructed readers:

> I conceive that to be always the best which is most facil, the least intricate, most natural, practified, and which follows the Faculties of theology, physick, jurisprudence, mathematics, humanity, and others, which should be subdivided each of them into particulars, according to their several members. (Naudé 1661, 77)

A library was, Naudé argued, to be arranged according to the contents of the books it contained. Furthermore, this arrangement was to have a sense of hierarchy, with each category being subdivided into smaller subject areas, foreshadowing the system employed a century later by Diderot and d'Alembert.

Others followed Naudé, Diderot, and d'Alembert's methods in their library catalogues, arranging books according to a hierarchical and relational methodology. In a letter to Richard Steele in 1721 James Anderson remarked:

> I made a catalogue of the books as they were ranged in shelves, which I am now altering and making up, according to the several subjects of the enclosed general account of them. (Blanchard 1941, 160–1, Letter 171)

Rather than creating a list of the books in his library as they appeared on his shelves, Anderson instead speaks of his deliberate decision to arrange them by their subject classifications within his catalogue.

Similar subject-based classifications were also incorporated into sales catalogues. In 1764, for instance, the *Catalogue of the Large and Curious English Library of Mr. John Hutton* was divided into several subject-based clusters, each of which listed individual subject headings.[4] Not only does this catalogue employ granular subject headings but also conveys relationality in a similar vein to the *Encyclopédie*. History, for example, is represented as history and chronology, history of arts and sciences, natural history,

---

[4] For further information on these headings, see Peterson and Bristow (1764).

marvellous history, church history, English history and antiquities, Oriental history and voyages, Turkish history, history of the Reformation and of the British churches, history of the different kingdoms and states of Europe, and natural and civil history of several of the counties of England. Like Diderot and d'Alembert's *Encyclopédie*, this catalogue followed hierarchical and relational methodologies to divide, subdivide and link their entries.

During the eighteenth century, then, library catalogues were arranged in ways that reflected new approaches to knowledge encoded within the Enlightenment ideals of classification and categorization. In the nineteenth century, these methodologies were codified for universal application, ensuring Enlightenment ideals prevailed in cataloguing methodologies for perpetuity.

Enumerative cataloguing

Early ideas about how this codification could be undertaken were first expressed by the marquis de Condorcet, a mathematician and philosopher who studied under d'Alembert. In a posthumously printed work of 1805, the marquis set out his plan to apply classifications and categorizations to the process of cataloguing, arguing that cataloguers should employ what he dubbed 'technical methods':

> I mean by technical methods the art of arranging a large number of subjects in a system so that we may straightaway grasp their relations, quickly perceive their combinations, and readily form new combinations out of them. (Baker 1962, 100)

Condorcet's system of technical methods was a decimal one. The cataloguer selects a number of primary qualities according to which an object (such as a book) can be classified, and each of these will have up to ten modifications or subdivisions that are expressed numerically. The first quality is 1–9, the second is 01–09, the third is 001–009 and so on. This system could be applied to a variety of subjects and could thus be used to denote relationships and hierarchies while classifying and categorizing.

Condorcet's enumerative system was expanded upon further in the nineteenth century by two systems that sought to universalize library cataloguing practices, perpetuating Enlightenment ideals and understandings of knowledge. These systems, both of which were published in 1876, are now the two most widely used systems in global libraries: the Dewey Decimal System and the Cutter Expansive Classification system, which formed the basis of the Library of Congress Classification System (LCC).

Drawing on the 'technical methods' called for by Condorcet, Melvil Dewey, chief librarian at Columbia University, published a wide-scale classification and categorization system in 1876 that represents a book's subject(s) with numerical values. The main classifications of texts (General Works, Philosophy and Psychology, Religion, Social Science, Language, Natural Science and Mathematics, Technology, The Arts, Literature,

Geography and History) are given a three-digit number, while the sub-classifications are represented as fractional decimals. For instance, a book about butterflies would have the reference 595.789. This reference is devised in the following way:

- 500 denotes the class 'Natural Science'.
- 590 denotes the class 'Zoological Sciences'.
- 595 denotes the class 'Other Invertebrates'.
- 595.7 denotes the subclass 'Insects'.
- 595.78 denotes the subclass 'Lepidoptera'.
- 595.789 denotes the subclass 'Butterflies'.

The Dewey Decimal System (DDC) achieved widespread popularity and is now used in 200,000 libraries in at least 135 countries (Hayes 2013).

Charles Ammi Cutter, head librarian at the Boston Athenaeum and later director of Forbes, adopted a similar approach in his Expansive Classification System that was published in his *Rules for a Printed Dictionary and Catalogue*, also in 1876. Inspired by Dewey, Cutter proposed a decimal classification system in which different subjects were expressed numerically. However, many smaller libraries complained that this system was too detailed and complex. Cutter therefore devised seven schedules of complexity, allowing smaller libraries to use less detailed versions of his system (eight classifications in total) and the largest libraries the most complex (twenty-six classifications). Cutter's system now forms the basis of the LCC, used by most large academic and research libraries.

These two popular enumerative, relational and hierarchical classification systems are indebted to Enlightenment efforts to understand and order knowledge in new ways. With their origins in the likes of Condorcet's 'technical methods' and Diderot and d'Alembert's *Encyclopédie*, they have come to dominate cataloguing practices over the past 200 years, providing as close to a universal system as has thus far been possible. They also pre-empted the Digital Age, adopting proto-computational methods of data structuring that have ensured their continued relevance into the present day despite technological advancements transforming the ways in which data is accessed and interpreted.

Legacy practices and inherent biases

While these universal systems were a positive development, offering scholars the chance to navigate larger sets of materials in a systematic way, they also contain implicit biases.

In the first instance, ordered classifications of knowledge create artificial divisions between disciplines, occluding the inter- and trans-disciplinarity of innumerable works. This division runs contrary to the Enlightenment ideal of gaining universal knowledge that encouraged figures such as Carl Linnaeus, Francis Bacon and Denis Diderot to attempt to classify, for instance, all things in the natural world. Yet, the cataloguing methods creating these divisions were founded in the very same period. That this was problematic was remarked upon at the time. Gottfried Wilhelm Leibniz, for instance, in his *New Essays Concerning Human Understanding*, wrote:

> It is usually found that one and the same truth may be put in different places, according to the terms it contains, and also according to the mediate terms or causes upon which it depends, and according to the inferences and results it may have [...] one and the same truth may have many places according to the different relations it can have. Those who arrange a library very often do not know where to place certain books, being in suspense between two or three places equally suitable. (Leibniz 1896, 623)

Condorcet similarly noted in reference to classification tables that:

> the observers themselves would have taken different results from the tables, according to the ideas they had in mind, the goal which they had set themselves. (Baker 1962, 104)

Both authors acknowledged that cataloguing, classifying, and categorizing are all subjective processes in which the opinions of one individual may differ radically from another's, making it difficult to classify a book or manuscript according to its subject and causing uncertainty over where to place the work on a library shelf.

The physicality of book placement on shelves and the limitations of the printed library catalogue make it necessary for a decision to be made if materials are organized according to subject, but this necessity does not render this selection process unproblematic. Take, for instance, the *Mabinogion*, one of the Matter of Britain, which is foundational in the mythology of Wales. In both the DDC and LCC, this work is listed under Welsh literature (891.6631 and PB2363.M2, respectively). While this is a logical category for the work, the *Mabinogion* is also a series of tales steeped in folklore and Celtic mythology that draws upon the romance trope familiarized by Arthurian legends and has central themes of rulership, magic, and love. The singular classification of Welsh literature, then, does a disservice to the contents and style of the work and prevents researchers interested in these aspects who are not solely seeking Welsh examples from finding the book.

The example of the *Mabinogion* reveals how this decision-making process prioritizes some subjects over others. However, this system of prioritization is often a problematic one, especially as catalogues rely on hierarchical structures and thus a system of superiors and inferiors. In LCC, for instance, the *Mabinogion* falls under the subclass PB: modern languages and Celtic languages. This group is divided into several sub-classifications, including 'Goidelic and Gaelic', 'Pict', 'Brittanic group' and 'Gaulish', each of which is subdivided further. As a result, the work is not counted in the 'Literature (general)' class of PN that primarily concerns English-language works, separating English works from those originating in the rest of the British Isles and creating a sense of hierarchy in which English is the assumed norm (and thus superior) and Celtic the 'other' (and thus inferior).

While this division speaks of historic tensions between England and their neighbouring countries, the LCC's 'Class P' features other examples of structural hierarchies that carry damaging associations (Fleming and O'Day 2018; Jones and Vale 1989; Smout 2005).[5]

Subclass PM, for instance, is a conglomerate of 'Hyperborean, Indian and artificial languages', combining the languages of a variety of peoples who have all been historically subjugated by the West: those of the Arctic regions, such as the Inuit; those of Mexico, Central America, South America and the West Indies; and those who use Creole languages, such as those in the Caribbean, Western Africa and the Philippines. The conjunction of these languages with so-called 'artificial' languages such as Esperanto, picture languages and secret languages appears to belittle these languages, and by extension those who use them, compared to their English-speaking counterparts. This subclass uses language that further reinforces this denigration. The use of the term 'hyperborean' to describe individuals living in the extreme North, for instance, perpetuates a Greco-Roman notion that Scandinavians identified themselves as Hyperboreans when confronted with the Roman Empire, though such individuals today claim no descent from the ancient Hyperboreans. Employed as a catch-all to group a diverse and often unrelated group of Northern languages this term both occludes the complex individuality of the languages, and relates the peoples it describes to an ancient group who lay beyond the 'civilized' worlds of Ancient Greece and Rome.

Enumerative systems based on subject classifications have thus introduced biases into knowledge organization. While some of these biases derive more from the need to place a physical book in a logical place – the *Mabinogion* is, after all, an epic of Welsh literature – other decisions are founded in the cataloguer's own biases or biases enforced upon cataloguers and users by standardized frameworks that employ unsuitable classifications and language.

Digital solutions

Since the 1990s, calls to radically rethink standardized cataloguing have gained momentum and visibility. Many of the early proponents of this call cited the subjectivity of cataloguers whose profession centred on decision-making. Sheila Intner, for instance, argued that it was important for cataloguers to recognize 'the rationale for observing standards as well as the trade-offs to be made in departing from them', as doing so would allow them to think critically of the standards themselves but also make more informed decisions about how to implement them to best suit their users' needs, their collections, and their local environment (Intner 1989, 237). Beatrice Kovacs likewise noted that it was important for cataloguers to recognize that theirs was a profession of decision-making, emphasizing the need for cataloguers to be taught that they always

---

[5] For criticisms of the Library of Congress cataloguing system, see Slatcher (2023, 43–7).

have multiple options in the classifications that they use and that there could be multiple ways in which an item might be described, with none of these necessarily being 'right' or 'wrong' (Kovacs 1989, 377).

Though Inter and Kovacs raised valuable concerns about cataloguing approaches, these evolved with the rise of digital cataloguing. In 1971, Ohio University's Alden Library launched an electronic cataloguing system in which libraries could share records across a network, rather than relying on physical card catalogues, forming the basis of what is now OCLC World Cat. The subsequent rise of Linked Open Data, MARC 21 Authority Records and TEI-XML tagging, amongst other developments, has placed pressure on cataloguers to adopt standardized, universal vocabularies to aid inter- and intra-operability and thereby enhance the user experience. While the cataloguer makes a choice, they cannot make exceptions to the authority lists they draw upon, as Kovacs had argued was once a common practice (Kovacs 1989).

This notion of authority has since been questioned, with Hope A. Olsen noting:

> Underlying this model of authority control is the assumption that a universal language is necessary. This assumption results in the exclusion of marginalized topics and groups in that all systems have limits which define them and, therefore, a system cannot be all-inclusive [. . .]. Authority control is the means by which we enforce conformity to the 'universal language' so it is the means by which we include, marginalize or exclude. (Olson 1997)

If digital catalogues call for uniformity and standardization, however, how can this conformity to marginalization and exclusion be overcome?

Digital methods present cataloguers with three (non-mutually exclusive) possible solutions. The first is to use topic modelling to determine subjects based on the content of individual texts, thereby reducing reliance on individual cataloguers and their implicit, or indeed explicit, biases. The second is to adopt approaches that enable a single work to be classified in multiple different ways. The third is to engage with critical cataloguing guidelines and adopt universal changes to problematic terminologies.

Topic modelling

Topic modelling offers cataloguers a chance to use digital approaches to limit biases in the cataloguing process, with decisions as to the subject matter of a text being made based upon its quantified content alone. Many topic models are founded in Bayesian statistics, which suggests that parameters within a statistical model, both observed and unobserved, have two probability distributions that are linked: prior distributions and data distributions (van de Schoot et al. 2021). This Bayesian approach combines knowledge of parameters with observed data and can thus be used in conjunction with text mining to establish observable patterns within the text that fit into given knowledge of the parameters of a subject classification, or topic. Of the various topic models to have emerged in recent years, by far the most popular has been Latent Dirichlet Allocation (LDA) – first applied to machine learning in 2003 by David Blei, Andrew Ng and Michael Jordan – that attributes words within a given corpus to the topics present within the said corpus (Blei, Ng and Jordan 2003). While this model works well for corpora with previously established topics, such as a set of scientific texts dealing with molecular chemistry, the success of the model for interpreting topics that are not previously known is far more limited, with the model typically identifying too few or too many topics to be useful (Weizhong et al. 2015). As such, its application to extensive and diverse library collections has thus far seen limited success.

The most successful application of these methods in library cataloguing at present is Annif, a digital tool for automated indexing and classifying, which has since been developed further into Finto AI. Developed by the National Library of Finland (NLF) and launched in 2017, Annif is an open-source digital tool that automates the subject indexing process. It adopts a twofold approach, one lexical and one associative, for algorithm implementation (Suominen, Inkinen and Lehtinen 2022). The lexical approach matches words within a given document with a list of terms associated with a predetermined subject vocabulary, allowing the model to suggest a number of potential subjects based on the frequency of these matches. For instance, if the phrase 'Ancient Rome' appears frequently within the text, this will be identified as one possible subject classification. The associative approach, on the other hand, trains the model with a dataset taken from manually indexed materials in order to establish correlations between words and subjects. For instance, the subject of 'Ancient Rome' may show a high level of correlation with words like 'centurion', 'patrician,' 'caesar,' 'colosseum' and 'gladiator' if these terms appear frequently in the corpus identified as having the subject classification of 'Ancient Rome'. If a document analysed through Annif mentions these terms, the associative approach enables the model to suggest a subject classification of 'Ancient Rome' even where the classification has not been expressed lexically. This combined approach is similar to that of Edoardo Airoldi and Jonathan Bischof, who in 2012 argued that subject determinism based on the frequency of relationships between words was insufficient as these could vary depending on the subject matter (Airoldi and Bischof 2016). Using Hierarchical Poisson Convolution and a 'bag of words' textual data representation to model on multiple corpora, Airoldi and Bischof demonstrated that when word use in varying contexts is quantified, modelling can attain the same levels of accuracy in subject classification as human cataloguers.

While the quality of results was marginally higher for human cataloguers over the machine, Annif, like Airoldi and Bischof's study, demonstrated that the application of these tools could be used successfully and continues to be implemented by NLF and expanded to include diverse and complex classifications. Other libraries too have adopted the tool, including the German National Library, the National Library of Sweden and the Leibniz Information Centre for Economics (Golub et al. 2024). A similar prototype tool, Kratt, has also been developed for the National Library of Estonia (Asula et al. 2021). Drawing upon a dataset of keywords drawn from the Estonian Subject Thesaurus, *Eesti Märksõnastik*, and the Universal Decimal Classification Summary, Kratt currently uses

22 per cent of the possible subject headings available, limiting its current effectiveness. It takes extracted texts, lemmatizes the data, and then tags the lemmas using Hybrid Tagger, a tool developed as part of the TEXTA Toolkit. The most frequent tags are then translated into subject classifications. In contrast to Annif, Kratt only adopts a lexical approach, and this, combined with its use of a fraction of the possible subject header terms, renders it, at present, less effective. Topic modelling thus offers a potentially exciting digital solution. However, widely accessible software based on developed models is not yet available, and the development and/or training of such models are costly in terms of both time and money. Added to this, the models rely on digital versions of texts, meaning they can only be applied to a fraction of library collections unless institutions invest in the digitization of their full holdings. As such, though presenting a possible future innovation and seeing some success in the Finnish context, they are not yet a widely used solution.

Multiple subject classifications

One of the fundamental principles of topic modelling is that individual works may have multiple subjects. In the pre-Digital Age, the need to place a book in one location on a physical shelf made it impractical for books to be catalogued with multiple subject headings. However, the use of digital management software, and indeed the existence of e-books, reduces the need for singular classification, enabling cataloguers to select a range of labels that, combined, represent the totality of the work described.

Many university and research libraries, especially those using Primo software developed by Ex Libris to catalogue their collections, follow this methodology. Sharing entries for the same work across the Primo network, numerous institutions offer multiple subjects for a single work. The Bodleian Library's *SOLO* system, for instance, frequently provides multiple subjects for a single work. Sioned Davies's translation of *The Mabinogion* (2018), for instance, features four subjects: 'Tales, Medieval'; 'Tales – Wales'; 'Mythology, Welsh'; and 'Mythology, Celtic – Wales'.[6] These multiple categories go further than previously noted, identifying the work as not only Welsh literature but also as mythology and medieval literature. However, the subjects identified still derive from classification systems such as DDC and LCC and thus remain limited by the outmoded and often problematic biases and hierarchies these systems perpetuate. Thus, while an improvement that partially increases the findability of the work, the reliance on previous practices undermines this progress.

Others have begun to crowdsource this metadata, complementing traditionally classified items with user-generated tags. User-generated tags offer significant benefits, often being more reflective of contemporary trends and standards and thus overcoming the terminology and implications inherited from older systems such as DDC and LCC.

---

[6]https://solo.bodleian.ox.ac.uk/permalink/44OXF_INST/q6b76e/alma990211884690107026.

Melissa Adler, for instance, has revealed the positive impact that user-based tags in LibraryThing have had in the cataloguing of books with transgender themes, arguing that folksonomies are responsive and expansive (Adler 2009). However, this user-based approach also raises concerns. Primarily, user tags are often unregulated, with no standardized means of checking that the tags added accurately reflect the content of the work being described. Furthermore, as Adler has argued, the introduction of unstandardized folksonomies may inhibit findability, again revealing the complexity of developing classification systems that are inclusive and adaptable but nevertheless standardized (Adler 2009).

Some librarians have raised concerns that increased granularity in classifications is causing the process of subject indexing and classification to become irrelevant, a matter compounded by the increasing quantity and quality of metadata that provides alternative entry points into library collections. Isidoro Gil Leiva et al., for instance, surveyed 123 university libraries in South America and discovered that of those surveyed, 59 per cent of librarians claimed not to assign classification codes because they considered them to be unnecessary, and 23 per cent of respondents remarked that the high-volume purchase of e-books rendered the assigning of subject classifications impractical (Leiva et al. 2024). Birger Hjørland once asked, 'Is classification necessary after Google?', arguing that improvements in search capabilities can transcend the need to classify texts at all as they offer new pathways into library collections (Hjørland 2012). Hjørland suggests that classification systems should pivot away from ideas of standardization and instead be based on the localized needs of a given collection. Thus, while increased granularity is more representative of collections and their users, some concern has been raised over the viability of subject classification in the face of increased quantities of metadata and the ever more complex capabilities of search functions.

Critical cataloguing

Although the development of automatic subject classification tools and the ability to list multiple subjects in a digital platform offer significant benefits to cataloguers in the digital age, many of the implementations of these two approaches are still marred by their reliance on outdated terms and hierarchies. In order to supersede the problems introduced to cataloguing in the eighteenth century, later codified by the likes of DDC and LCC, it is vital to challenge the terminologies and hierarchies that these classification systems perpetuate. Calls for such action have been repeated since 1993, with the likes of Heather Moorcroft, Emily Drabinski, Hope Olson, Sandy Littletree and Cheryl Metoyer all arguing for the dismantling of problematic terms and hierarchies within classification systems (Dabrinski 2013; Littletree and Metoyer 2015; Moorcroft 1993; Olsen 2001). Likewise, Kate Ozment has challenged the ways in which bibliographical practices (such as cataloguing) can be revised to better represent women's texts and labour (2020). Critical Cataloguing, a movement focused on 'radical empathy' that prompts online discussion about the inequalities and insensitivities of existing catalogues using #critcat, has also emerged (Ozment 2016). Numerous cataloguers have begun implementing changes based on this movement, reviewing problematic subject classifications and implementing alternatives.

As much as library catalogues have traditionally 'constructed silences', to borrow from Moorcroft, digital catalogues offer a vital chance to equitably represent the diversities of human society, culture, and history. Steven W. Holloway et al. have shown how James Madison University has subverted Library of Congress controlled vocabularies that take whiteness as typical by crowdsourcing tags and using Wikidata URIs so as to make visible the Black characters and the contribution of Black creators in their comic book collections (Holloway, Kaiser and Flota 2022). The Trans Metadata Collective (TMDC) issued a report in 2022 that offered recommendations for uses of LCC subject headings that better reflected trans experiences (Watson et al. 2023). They argued that the terms 'Coming out – Sexual orientation' and 'Outing – Sexual orientation', erased their experience, as there is a distinction between 'coming out' and telling others of your trans status (disclosing). TMDC also recommended that cataloguers eschew LCC terminology in favour of vocabularies developed by the likes of Homosaurus that are intended to nuance and enrich LCC terminologies in beneficial ways, making the trans experience visible, just as James Madison University made Black experiences visible within the context of comic books.

The ability to make real-time changes to library metadata in digital catalogues enables cataloguers to quickly, efficiently, and consistently implement updates to problematic words and hierarchies, whether this be in the alteration of terminology or the introduction of new classifications. In doing so, it is easier than ever before to enact radical change within catalogues to ensure their equitability and inclusivity, helping to overcome the inherent biases that shape DDC and LCC. Critical cataloguing is an ongoing, ever-changing movement, and the dynamism of digital catalogues supports this, with cataloguers needing to continually review and update their metadata as sociocultural standards change.

As with the other digital solutions outlined above, there are some impediments to the success of critical cataloguing, namely that there is not a universal consensus regarding which problematic terms require change. In 2016 the Library of Congress issued its plans to remove the subject headings of 'Illegal Aliens' and 'Illegal Immigration', replacing the headings instead with 'Noncitizens' and 'Unauthorized Immigration', respectively. The then Republican-led House of Representatives moved to stop this change, instructing the Library of Congress not to make the change, an instruction they followed (Library of Congress 2016). Though this change was later introduced in 2021, the interplay between politics and cataloguing was nevertheless made apparent. Despite significant calls for change, such alterations can only be enacted in concordance with wider sociopolitical and cultural change. Further problematic is the fact that the LCC system is used internationally. As such, decisions such as those outlined above made in the United States have a ripple effect throughout the rest of the world, imposing one hegemonic viewpoint on numerous diverse individuals and collections.

Conclusion

Library catalogues perform a key mediating function between collections of books and manuscripts and their users, determining the sorts of questions that can be asked of a given collection, directing users to specific resources, and thereby shaping the subsequent views and scholarship of the user. Where implicit biases exist, this mediation process becomes dysfunctional, contributing to the wider dispersal of prejudices and injustices, many of which originated in Enlightenment ideas regarding cataloguing practices and later nineteenth-century notions of evolution, gender, class and race. The digital age poses its own problems: while digital tools can enhance the activities of critical cataloguers and provide new, less biased approaches, the pressing need for Linked Open Data using standardized vocabularies forces many cataloguers to resort to problematic universal languages for which there is not a universal solution. As cataloguers continue to digitize their catalogues, the majority of which will conform to standards set out by the likes of the Library of Congress, it will be important for them to do so critically, working together with diverse individuals to tackle problematic terminology, reshape hierarchies into webs, and inform readers openly of the processes that have shaped the resources they use. Such digital tools have transformative capabilities, shaping not only the ways in which scholars use catalogues but also making digital library spaces more representative.

Bibliography

Archival source

New York Academy of Medicine, New York, 'New York Academy of Medicine 12', f.140.

Printed sources

Adler, Melissa. 'Transcending Library Catalogs: A Comparative Study of Controlled Terms in Library of Congress Subject Headings and User-Generated Tags in LibraryThing for Transgender Books'. *Journal of Web Librarianship* 3, no. 4 (2009): 309–31.

Airoldi, Edoardo M. and Jonathan M. Bischof. 'Improving and Evaluating Topic Models and Other Models of Text', *Journal of the American Statistical Association* 111, no. 516 (2016): 1381–403.

Asula, Marit, Jane Makke, Linda Freienthal, Hele-Andra Kuulmets and Raul Sirel. 'Kratt: Developing an Automatic Subject Indexing Tool for the National Library of Estonia'. *Cataloging and Classification Quarterly* 59, no. 8 (2021): 775–93.

Baker, K. M. 'An Unpublished Essay of Condorcet on Technical Methods of Classification'. *Annals of Science* 18, no. 2 (1962): 99–123.

Blanchard, Rae, ed. 'Letter 171'. In *The Correspondence of Richard Steele*, 160–1. Oxford: Oxford University Press, 1941.

Blei, David M., Andrew Y. Ng and Michael I. Jordan. 'Latent Dirichlet Allocation'. *Journal of Machine Learning Research* 3, no. 4–5 (2003): 993–1022.
Bodleian Library, 'The Mabinogion. Davies, Sioned, Translator': https://solo.bodleian.ox.ac.uk/permalink/44OXF_INST/q6b76e/alma990211884690107026
Bramhall, John. *The Works of the Most Revered Father, in God, John Bramhall D.D.* Dublin, 1676.
Caswell, Michelle and Marika Cifor. 'From Human Rights to Feminist Ethics: Radical Empathy in the Archives'. *Archivaria* 81 (2016): 24–43.
Crignon, Claire, Carsten Zelle and Nunzio Allocca, eds. *Medical Empiricism and Philosophy of Human Nature in the 17th and 18th Century*. Leiden: Brill, 2014.
d'Alembert, Jean le Rond and Denis Diderot, eds. *Encyclopédie ou dictionnaire reaisonné des sciences, des arts et des métiers*, vol. 1. Paris, 1751.
Dabrinski, Emily. 'Queering the Catalogue: Queer Theory and the Politics of Correction'. *The Library Quarterly* 83, no. 2 (2013): 94–111.
Davis, Richard. *A Catalogue of Bookes Printed for, and to be Sold by Richard Davis at His Shop neer Oriell Colledge in Oxford*. Oxford, 1660.
de Beer, E. S., ed. *The Correspondence of John Locke: Letters nos. 849–1241*, vol. 3. Oxford: Oxford University Press, 1978.
Dennis, Leah. 'The Text of the Percy-Warton Letters'. *PMLA* 46, no. 4 (1931): 1178–80.
Fairer, David, ed. *The Correspondence of Thomas Warton*. Athens, GA: University of Georgia Press, 1995.
Fleming, N. C. and Alan O'Day, eds. *Ireland and Anglo-Irish Relations since 1800: Critical Essays*. Abingdon: Routledge, 2018.
Gaskell, Philip. *Trinity College Library: The First 150 Years*. Cambridge: Cambridge University Press, 1980.
Gibson, James. *Locke's Theory Knowledge and Its Historical Relations*. Cambridge: Cambridge University Press, 2010.
Golub, Koralijka, Osma Suominen, Ahmed Taiye Mohammed, Harriest Aagaard and Olof Osterman. 'Automated Dewey Decimal Classification of Swedish Library Metadata using Annif Software'. *Journal of Documentation* 80, no. 5 (2024). https://doi.org/10.1108/JD-01-2022-0026.
Hayes, Patrick. 'Dewey Decimal System in The 21st Century Library', *StateTech*, 14 March 2013. https://shorturl.at/GZWuM.
Hjørland, Birger. 'Is Classification Necessary after Google?'. *Journal of Documentation* 68, no. 3 (2012): 299–317.
Hodacs, Hanna, Kenneth Nyberg and Stéphane Van Damme, eds. *Linnaeus, Natural History and the Circulation of Knowledge*. Liverpool: Liverpool University Press, Oxford Studies in the Enlightenment, 2018.
Holloway, Steven W., Justina Kaiser and Brian Flota. 'Re-imagining (black) Comic Cataloguing: Increasing Accessibility Through Metadata at One University Library', *Journal of Graphic Novels and Comics* 13, no. 6 (2022): 884–914.
Horning, Audrey. *A Cultural History of Objects in the Age of Enlightenment*. London: Bloomsbury, 2022.
Horton, Russell, Robert Morrissey, Mark Olsen, Glenn Roe and Robert Voyer. 'Mining Eighteenth Century Ontologies: Machine Learning and Knowledge Classification in the Encyclopédie'. *Digital Humanities Quarterly* 3, no. 2 (2009). http://digitalhumanities.org/dhq/vol/3/2/000044/000044.html.
Hunter, Michael, Antonio Clericuzio and Lawrence Principe eds. *The Correspondence of Robert Boyle: 1662–1665*, vol. 2. London: Pickering & Chatto, 2001.

Intner, Sheila. 'Responding to Change: New Goals and Strategies for Core Cataloging Courses'. In *Recruiting, Educating, and Training Cataloging Librarians: Solving the Problems*, 227–43. Edited by Sheila Intner and Janet Swan Hill. Westport, CN: Greenwood Press, 1989.

Jones, Michael and Malcolm Vale, eds. *England and Her Neighbours, 1066-1453: Essays in Honour of Pierre Chaplais*. London: Hambledon Press, 1989.

Kovacs, Beatrice. 'An Educational Challenge: Teaching Cataloging and Classification'. *Library Resources & Technical Services* 3, no. 4 (1989): 375–81.

Lefèvre, Wolfgang. 'Natural or Artificial Systems? The Eighteenth-Century Controversy on Classification of Animals and Plants and Its Philosophical Contexts'. In *Between Leibniz, Newton, and Kant: Philosophy and Science in the Eighteenth Century*, 191–209. Edited by Wolfgang Lefèvre. New York: Springer, 2023.

Leibniz, Gottfried Wilhelm, *New Essays Concerning Human Understanding*. Translated by Alfred Gideon Langley. London: Macmillan, 1896.

Leiva, Isidoro Gil, Maria Carolina Andrade e Cruz, Franciele Marques Redigolo and Mariângela Spotti Lopes Fujita. 'Assignment of Subject Headings and Classification Codes to e-books in South American University Libraries'. *Revista Española de Documentación Científica* 47, no. 2 (2024). https://doi.org/10.3989/redc.2024.1513.

Library of Congress. 'Library of Congress to Cancel the Subject Heading "Illegal Aliens"'. Executive Summary. Washington, DC: Library of Congress, 2016. https://www.loc.gov/catdir/cpso/illegal-aliens-decision.pdf.

Littletree, Sandy and Cheryl Metoyer. 'Knowledge Organization from an Indigenous Perspective: The Mashantucket Pequot Thesaurus of American Indian Terminology Project'. *Cataloging & Classification Quarterly* 53, no. 5–6 (2015): 640-657.

Makris, Nikolaos and Nikolaos Mitrou. 'Multisubject Analysis and Classification of Books and Book Collections, Based on a Subject Term Vocabulary and the Latent Dirichlet Allocation'. *IEEE Access* 11 (2023): 120881–98.

Moorcroft, Heather. 'The Construction of Silence'. *The Astralian Library Journal* 42, no. 1 (1993): 27–32.

Montoya, Alicia C. 'Building the *Bibliothèque Choisie*, from Jean Le Clerc to Samuel Formey: Library Manuals, Review Journals, and Auction Catalogues in the Long Eighteenth Century'. In *Book Trade Catalogues in Early Modern Europe*, 426–62. Edited by Arthur der Weduwen, Andrew Pettegree, and Graeme Kemp. Leiden: Brill, 2021.

Naudé, Gabriel. *Instructions Concerning Erecting of a Library*. Translated by John Evelyn. London, 1661.

Olson, Hope A. 'The Power to Name: Representation in Library Catalogs'. *Signs: Journal of Women in Culture and Society* 26, no. 3 (2001): 639–68.

Olson, Hope A. 'Thinking Professionals: Teaching Critical Cataloguing'. *Technical Services Quarterly* 15, nos. 1–2 (1997): 51–66.

Ozment, Kate. 'A Rationale for Feminist Bibliography'. *Textual Cultures* 13, no. 1 (2020): 149–78.

Peterson, Samuel and W. Bristow. *A Catalogue of the Large and Curious English Library of Mr. John Hutton*. London, 1764.

Priestley, Joseph. *An Essay on the First Principles of Government, and on the Nature of Political, Civil, and Religious Liberty*. London: J. Johnson, 1771.

Slatcher, Rebecca. 'Indigenous Languages in the British Library Catalogue: A Critique of 'Indians of North America-Languages''. *Art Libraries Journal* 48, no. 2 (2023): 43–7.

Smout, T. C., ed. *Anglo-Scottish Relations from 1603 to 1900*. Oxford: Oxford University Press, 2005.

Suominen, Osma, Juho Inkinen and Mona Lehtinen. 'Annif and Finto AI: Developing and Implementing Automated Subject Indexing'. *JLIS.it* 13, no. 1 (2022). https://doi.org/10.4403/jlis.it-12740.

Tanselle, G. Thomas. 'Bibliography and Library Cataloguing'. *Studies in Bibliography* 30 (1977): 1–56.

Tillotson, John. *The Works of the Most Reverand Dr. John Tillotson, late Lord Archbishop of Canterbury*. London, 1696.

Toynbee, Paget and Leonard Whibley, eds. *Correspondence of Thomas Gray*, vol. 2. Oxford: Oxford University Press, 1935.

van de Schoot, Rens, Sara Depaoli, Ruth King, Bianca Kramer, Kaspar Märtens, Mahlet G. Tadesse, Marina Vannucci, Andrew Gelman, Duco Veen, Joukje Willemsen and Christopher Yau. 'Bayesian Statistics and Modelling'. *Nature Reviews: Methods Primer* 1, no. 1 (2021). https://doi.org/10.1038/s43586-020-00001-2.

Watson, B. M., Devon Murphy, Beck Schaefer and Jackson Huang. '"Our Metadata, Ourselves": The Trans Metadata Collective'. *Proceedings of the Association for Information Science and Technology* 60, no. 1 (2023): 433–41.

Weizhong, Zhao, James J. Chen, Roger Perkins, Zhichao Liu, Weigong Ge, Yijun Ding and Wen Zou. 'A Heuristic Approach to Determine an Appropriate Number of Topics in Topic Modeling'. *BMC Bioinformatics* 16, no. S8 (2015). http://www.biomedcentral.com/1471-2105/16/S13/S8.

Woudhuysen, H. R. 'From Duck Lane to Lazarus Seaman: Buying and Selling Old Books in England during the Sixteenth and Seventeenth Centuries'. In *The Oxford Handbook of the History of the Book in Early Modern England*. Edited by Adam Smyth. Oxford: Oxford University Press, 2023.

CHAPTER 2
EDITING AUTHENTICITY IN THE MANUSCRIPT TEXT
PREFACES, DIPLOMATIC TRANSCRIPTIONS AND PHOTOGRAPHS
Geoffrey Turnovsky

Montesquieu's introduction to *The Persian Letters* offers a classic framing for an epistolary narrative of the era. Insisting on the letters' authenticity, it presents Montesquieu as 'only' the translator of letters exchanged by the Persians who as guests in his home had let him copy their correspondence. 'I am, then, only a translator,' he writes, 'and all my efforts have been to adapt the work to our tastes' (Montesquieu 1999, 7).[1] Today, the statement conjures the art and artifice of the eighteenth-century novel along with the distinct horizons of expectations that defined fiction in this period, shaped partly by the ostensible naïveté of readers who may or may not have believed these conceits and by conventions governing the writing of 'pseudofactual' fiction before the advent of literary realism in the nineteenth century and its 'willing suspension of disbelief' (Darnton 1984, 215–56; Foley 1986; Paige 2011).

The introduction also intersects with a related yet distinct history, which is that of the editing of correspondence, both fictional and real. Editions of letters may have been less direct in confirming their authenticity than as we observe in volumes of fictional letters, where the prefatory claim was at the core of a narrative strategy. But editorial and paratextual framing of letters in editions of correspondence fulfills the same basic function of establishing the letters' defining qualities as *real* letters: the fact, first, that the letters were private and written with no eye towards circulation beyond their addressees, let alone to publication in a printed edition, and second, that the printed text presented to the reader was derived from handwritten documents that comprised the correspondence. In this sense, the prefatory text stands in tension with the texts of the letters themselves. Unlike the prefaces, the edited and published letters were themselves not vehicles for communicating the qualities of privacy and handwritten-ness or the authenticity they affirmed. On the contrary, the texts of the letters were normally transformed unabashedly for publication in print, as Montesquieu makes clear. Not only did the edited texts no longer manifest the traits of a private, handwritten letter, but these qualities were what

---

[1] The first edition appeared with a false imprint as *Lettres persanes* (Cologne: Chez Pierre Marteau, 1721) but was published in Amsterdam.

the editors' interventions targeted: private and intimate details and language, inside exchanges opaque to a non-addressed reader, disorder and disorganization, and non-standard, inconsistent and variegated forms (spellings, formulations, punctuation), all presumed to detract from the experience of 'general' readers to whom the print edition, in contrast with the letter, was pitched. The preface staged and projected the editorial work. And it was the testimony of this work, rather than the letters themselves, that bore witness to the letters' authenticity.

We can cite many examples from seventeenth- and eighteenth-century editions of letters in which, textually, in their style, spelling and punctuation, the letters observe a respect for the rules and decorum of printed texts that fully obfuscates the texts' origins as handwritten letters. The defining epistolary qualities of the letters are instead established in prefaces attesting to the disordered, unsystematic, and intimate nature of the unpublished writings as the editor had discovered them – in handwritten originals and contemporary copies (without necessarily privileging the autograph over the copy) – and then to all the editorial labour that was necessary to render those handwritten texts readable by a large public not addressed by them. This work involved not just imposing standardized grammar, spelling and punctuation on texts that were, in their original states, inconsistent in these areas, but more substantial manipulations as well: removing passages, clarifying and polishing language, filling in gaps, and reorganizing the sequence of letters, or imposing an organization that does not exist in often dispersed or indiscriminately stored, undated originals. In the preface to his 1650 edition of the court poet Vincent Voiture's works, Voiture's nephew, Martin Pinchesne, describes the 'extreme disorder' of the poet's papers as he found them. The paratextual address to the reader foregrounds the prodigious efforts then required to impose regularity on the chaos and make the texts readable, partly by placing the letters in an approximate chronological order as best as Pinchesne could guess (since Voiture did not date his letters) and partly through a triage such that 'not all [of the letters] would be reproduced indifferently'. Collaborating with mutual friends Jean Chapelain and Valentin Conrart, Pinchesne selected those letters that were 'the most suited to be seen'. Despite all the work, Pinchesne remained apologetic for the raw state of the text, noting that the print run was kept small in order to see if Voiture's writings 'will please the public', and if they do, Pinchesne promised a 'second edition in better order and more exactly corrected' (Voiture 1650, ĩ iii v–ĩ iv r).

Perhaps the best-known, albeit decidedly equivocal, examples of editorial polishing for publication of letters in early French-language editions are the two editions of Marie de Rabutin-Chantal, Marquise de Sévigné's correspondence, first edited and published by Denis-Marius Perrin in 1734–7 and republished, in a 'new expanded edition', in 1754. These editions were the first of Sévigné's letters undertaken with 'official authorization', specifically, that of Sévigné's grand-daughter, Pauline de Simiane (who inherited the letters from her mother, Sévigné's daughter, Mme de Grignan). Consisting mostly of letters to her daughter, the editions were instrumental in establishing the canonical status of Sévigné's letters in the French literary tradition as the model for a new kind of 'personal' writing defined by the intimacy of a private correspondence between mother and child. Perrin was cognizant of this shift towards more intimate and affective content, noting at the start of his preface to the 1734-7 edition that 'the letters of a mother to her daughter, as perfect as they may be, would seem destined to be forgotten'. He further underscores, as key to the letters' appeal, 'the feelings of maternal love that so frequently appear' and 'the noble, delicate and varied turns of phrase which she uses to express this tenderness' (Sévigné 1734, 1: iii, xiii). Perrin's framing of the correspondence as a glimpse into something private and, by nature, unpublished is bolstered by repeated references to the autograph manuscripts and the special access he had had to them as Simiane's chosen editor, in contrast with the editors of previous (unauthorized) editions, especially from the mid-1720s, who had access only to 'inaccurate' copies that had been widely circulating without sanction. These copies were inaccurate precisely because they had been 'polished' for circulation. Entrusting Perrin to supersede these editions with corrected – that is, more controlled – versions of the letters, Simiane passed along to him the originals that she had inherited, and Perrin makes his privileged access clear to readers through long, detailed comparisons of passages from the existing faulty editions with Sévigné's autograph texts, noting 'an infinity of incoherencies and horrible mistakes', which his edition now, of course, corrects in a return to the 'originals' (Sévigné 1734, 1: v–vi).

But in fact, Perrin also made extensive changes to the text of Sévigné's letters in order to render them 'worthy of print', as he stated himself (Sévigné 1754, 1: ix). He acknowledged in the 1734 preface 'suppressing a number of purely domestic details of no interest to the public' (Sévigné 1734, one: xii). An apparent contradiction presents itself in editions that celebrate Sévigné's 'noble, delicate and varied' ([1734], xiii) style – 'négligé' is the key term in French (a term that itself has an important history)[2] – insofar as the letters were written with no thought to publication ([1754], iv–v), while significantly reworking this style specifically *for* publication in line with the prevailing sensibilities and expectations of contemporary readers. The contradiction, however, is at the heart of an editorial philosophy for letters: a text's 'singularity' – a term Perrin uses – as an idiosyncratic scribal expression is established as much, or even more, in the paratextual affirmation of all the editorial labours needed to make the expression publishable as on anything the reader will find in the published text itself, which is, in turn, presumed to offer only a mediated hint of this singularity. Polishing for publication does not, in this sense, undermine the paratextual affirmation of the text's epistolarity.

This established editorial paradigm rested on a specific view of the printed text and the manuscript and of the defining incommensurability of their relationship. Print and manuscript are distinct writing systems, which are impossible to fully reconcile. Print can no better convey the written text of a manuscript than we could imagine a photocopy conveying a painting. Print can convey only a mediated 'translation' of the manuscript text into the language of print, which was necessarily ordered and obeyed a

---

[2] Roger Duchêne, who will be discussed further down, published an article on 'Mme de Sévigné et le style négligé', *Œuvres & Critiques* I, 2 (1976).

standardized set of rules and conventions shaped by the orientation of printed writing towards a readership implied by printing's scaled-up reproductive capacities (a broad public of non-initiates and non-addressees), and by typesetting technology. Manuscript text by contrast was written for a single in-the-know reader, replete with private detail, insider references, deeply personalized formulations and scribal shorthands, which, in their raw state on the handwritten pages of the letter, would be bewildering, chaotic, and inaccessible to anyone not addressed. It was the editor's job to transform this generally illegible text into something readable for a public not imputed by the letters, a task Perrin conceives as anticipating the revisions the letter writer would herself have undoubtedly made if, with an eye to print publication, she 'had had the time to revise [d'y mettre la dernière main]' (Sévigné 1754, 1: iii–iv).[3] But the manuscript text disappeared in the process. Print was opaque with respect to it. The printed edition could not deliver a glimpse of the manuscript text beyond the editor's descriptive memorialization of it.

Three hundred years later, the world of epistolary editing could hardly be more different. Sévigné's preeminent modern editor, Roger Duchêne, frames his Gallimard Pléiade edition as a pointed rebuke of Perrin's cavalier willingness to alter Sévigné's text and of the editorial philosophy that underlay it. The editor's role for Duchêne is not to *translate* the manuscript text for a print public while bearing witness to all the labours of this transformation and acknowledging, through the changes made, the ultimate impossibility of it. It is to make the manuscript text accessible to the print reader *as the manuscript text it is*. It is to deliver the original document, through print, in a form that is nonetheless as close as possible to the form in which the letters were first composed and delivered to their intended recipients. Discussing an early eighteenth-century manuscript collection of Sévigné's letters ostensibly copied from her autographs, Duchêne emphasized a suggestive distinction between the 'text' and an 'edition of the text', with the latter referring to the text as polished for a readership. Charles Capmas rediscovered this lost manuscript in the 1870s as he was preparing his own edition of the letters, and the collection seemed to offer a new, more immediate access to Sévigné's originals.[4] But in Duchêne's assessment, while the manuscript was unprecedentedly close to originals, it had nonetheless been finessed and corrected for the benefit of other readers. '[T]he Capmas was meant to be read,' Duchêne asserts (775), and as such, it was not the text but an edition of it. Ironically, the epistolary editor's task was not to establish an edition but to recover and convey the text with as little intervention as possible.

---

[3] He adds that the editor 'never has the right to add anything of his or her own into the Work of another; but by the same measure', he asks, 'would we contest him or her the freedom the suppress what appears to him or her as not proper to be published?'

[4] Capmas's edition was published in 1876. The copy was seen as having been directly copied from autographs to which Nicolas Amé Bussy de Rabutin, son of Roger, Bussy de Rabutin, who was a cousin and frequent correspondent of Sévigné's, had access. Nicolas had himself been preparing an 'authorized' edition of Sévigné's letters but died before he was able to complete the work. See Duchêne's 'Note sur le texte' in his edition of Marie de Rabutin-Chantal Sévigné, *Correspondance* (Paris: Gallimard, 1972), 1: 755–832. Duchêne talks about the Capmas manuscript on 769–78.

Duchêne's views reflect for us what might seem a more professionalized and modern editorial philosophy. But more than a process of modernization, this shift in perspectives on print, the manuscript, and on the relationship between the two underlies a distinct editorial paradigm. The original manuscripts are now deemed readable. They are no longer evoked as hopelessly difficult, disordered documents legible only to those addressed by them and to hard-working editors specially positioned – often by their personal connections with the letter writers as well as by their training and dedication – to decipher them, as was the case in early modern editions. The original documents are now the privileged sites of the authentic text, a trend we saw emerge with Perrin – an equivocal figure, as noted earlier – who discredited faulty existing editions through comparison with the 'correct' text of what he called the 'original', itself a weighty term in a framework in which so many editions of correspondence were established on copies made of the letters – by the writer, the recipient or a secretary – rather than on anything clearly identifiable as original. Yet like editors before him, Perrin assumed the reader of his edition would not be able to read the original, at least not in its pure form. The transitional moment he represents elevates the original, to be sure, but as that which cannot be read. By contrast, Duchêne's preface emphasizes not his work imposing order on chaotic originals but his efforts to recover original texts that had been disfigured by two centuries of bad editing, including above all Perrin's own efforts to counter bad editing. His project was in the vein of 'unediting', though with the important caveat that for Duchêne, what was most salient was the absence of the great majority of the autograph letters (e.g. McLeod 1981 and Marcus 1996). This likely made it easier for Duchêne to envision the readability of the manuscripts (which are, in truth, not easy to read), a point to which we will return.

It also made it easier for him to imagine, *contra* Perrin, that the printed book *could be* a medium for delivering the manuscript. Manuscript and print are no longer incommensurable because, in parallel with the editor's defining efforts of self-obfuscation, the printed medium is re-envisioned as *transparent*; not a text in and of itself, with its own distinct grammar and norms, but a window onto a text presumed to exist separately from the printed medium, which in this case is the letter exactly as Sévigné had written it, with all the inside references, shorthands, and eccentric formulations. The development of conventions for diplomatic transcription reflects this new perspective on print and print's capacity to present the manuscript text in its original form, *as a manuscript text*. Diplomatic transcription refers to the relatively modern practice of replicating, in print, a text exactly as it appears in the source document, including idiosyncratic spelling and punctuation that would generally be normalized in a critical editing paradigm that distinguishes in the text the substantives – the words chosen by the author – from the accidentals (spellings and punctuation) (Greg 1950/1951, 19–36). The distinction and the hierarchy implicit in the terminology are rooted in the historic practice by which print-shop professionals, in the course of preparing a printed edition, were expected to 'translate' the text into print, imposing a standardized spelling and punctuation on an author's text, whose manuscript was assumed to be inconsistent and unsystematic in this respect. 'It happens very often that an Author, who is more concerned about the order of his Work than the care required to punctuate correctly the items in his clauses, sometimes, out of a lack of attention, adds punctuation that is directly in opposition to what should be there,' writes Martin Dominique Fertel in his 1723 *Science pratique de l'imprimerie*. Compositors should thus not replicate what is in the copies they are transcribing from, but should make adjustments in accordance with the uses and norms consistent with print publication, which Fertel goes on to delineate in sections covering different punctuation marks (Fertel 1723; Chartier 2004, 66). In the Anglo-American tradition of literary editing, the distinction between substantives and accidentals helped to separate authorial intent from the other agencies that shaped the text as it circulated, especially those from within the print shop. The model works fine when one additionally presumes an intent (on the author's part) to publish and disseminate copies, in and through which the author's 'work' would acquire an abstract identity apart from its instantiation in copies, including in manuscript drafts, and thus from the contingencies and variations embodied in those copies. When the goal, however, is to publish a hitherto unpublished and (therefore) unique document such as a manuscript letter, the hierarchy has to be inverted since now the idiosyncratic orthography and punctuation are among those qualities of the text that most define it in its documentary singularity. The letter writer's quirky spelling and punctuation are no longer incidental, external to the author's conceptualization of the work, but are constitutive of the text's nature as a personal letter.

This view has prevailed among modern editors of the correspondence of eighteenth-century French writers, who variously argue that the spelling and punctuation of the manuscript are, in their quirks, integral rather than accidental to the author's letters. Jean Sgard, Jeroom Vercruysse, Henri Coulet, and Jacques Proust each have their own takes on the matter (Sgard 1981, Vercruysee 1988, Coulet 1988, Proust 1978). Vercruysse describes a 'typographic translation', by which a 'print-shop orthography [orthographe d'atelier]' is imposed on a handwritten text that typically did not follow any systematic or consistent method (Vercruysse, 99). Sgard defines 'epistolary punctuation' as an expression of the writer's familiarity with the addressee. The purpose of punctuation in a personal letter is not to enforce grammatical regularity and order on a text such that it can be better understood by a general readership. It is to accentuate the emotivity and affect of a concrete interpersonal interaction between two people. Sgard counts punctuation marks per one hundred words to quantify the difference, calculating thirteen as the threshold between 'epistolary' punctuation (which tends to fewer marks) and typographic punctuation (which tends to more). All the editors emphasize that typographic punctuation was not only more grammatical and logical but also more frequent and denser. A letter written by hand could, for one thing, rely on the layout of the page to indicate semantic units or events such as the ending of a sentence, as evidenced in a letter dated 10 January 1734 by the Marquise du Châtelet to Pierre Louis Moreau de Maupertuis discussed by Sgard that includes just five punctuation marks – four commas and a period – over 10 lines and 133 words. Most importantly, all the editors agree that there is something meaningful and evocative of the author's voice in the idiosyncrasies of the writing as it appears in the manuscript, which needs to be maintained in any edition as an integral part of the letters' text. The punctuation, spelling or non-systematic syntax

Editing Authenticity in the Manuscript Text

in the manuscript text conveyed the 'spontaneous', 'personal', 'natural' or 'expressive' qualities – terms employed by these editors – that have come to define the letter as a letter.[5] 'The time has come,' writes Proust, 'to respect original punctuation religiously. It was more expressive, livelier, than that of the pedants, which we have become; and it was, paradoxically, much more modern' (Proust 1978). (See Figure 2.1)

But Sgard also sees the problem. The Marquise du Châtelet's manuscript letter does not simply illustrate 'epistolary punctuation'. In Sgard's more equivocal discussion, it exemplifies in addition a 'non-transcribable' text (34).[6] The letter renders manifest the fact that, on closer inspection, diplomatic transcription is never what it is cracked up to be, particularly when it comes to punctuation. The limitations are easy to enumerate when we juxtapose du Châtelet's manuscript, digitized by the Bibliothèque nationale de France and available in its digital library, Gallica, with the diplomatic transcription provided in the *Electronic Enlightenment* database of early modern letters, the text of which is based on the transcription in Theodore Besterman's *Oeuvres complètes de Voltaire* (OCV), where the letter was included. (See Figure 2.2)

Looking at just the first few lines, we see in Besterman's print edition that grave accents were added to the preposition 'à' whereas they are absent in the manuscript. Apostrophes separate 'J'ay' and 'm'aves' in the OCV but do not appear in the original. A period ends the first sentence after the word 'lu'. Yet it is clear in the manuscript that du Châtelet added a comma here, followed by the uncapitalized 'iay', which is in turn transcribed in print with a capitalized 'I'ay'. The edition adds another period after 'deux manuscrits', but with those two words in the manuscript coming at the end of line 3, du Châtelet added no punctuation at all, likely assuming the line break forced by the end of the paper sufficed to indicate to Maupertuis that a new thought (beginning with another uncapitalized 'i'ay', but with an apostrophe this time) began.

My purpose is not to criticize Besterman's transcription. I am far too uncertain about many aspects of the original text mentioned here to be in a position to do that: is that a dot over a lowercase 'i' in 'iay été' or an apostrophe following an un-dotted capital I in 'I'ay été' (as transcribed by Besterman)? It looks like the former to me – the i's are almost all dotted throughout the letter – but I cannot say for sure. Is there even a basis in this context for distinguishing between a majuscule and a minuscule letter? I cannot honestly say that I see a single letter in the text that I recognize as unambiguously majuscule, including the 'v' of 'versailles' in the sign-off, though every letter at the beginning of a sentence is capitalized by Besterman, despite the diplomatic spellings of 'Je' as 'Ie'. Of the seven sentences transcribed in the print edition, six begin with 'Ie' or 'I'' as a spelling for

---

[5] See especially Coulet, who uses 'ponctuation spontanée' and 'punctuation expressive' synonymously with epistolary punctuation. 'Ponctuation spontanée' is also used in Proust, who additionally notes that eighteenth-century writers have accustomed us to an 'infinitely more personal punctuation than that of Maupassant or Zola'.
[6] Sgard is the least programmatic of the three and, while advocating for the attempt to get as close as possible to the original text of the eighteenth-century letter – 'dans la mesure du possible' – he raises the most questions about the ability to produce a perfectly diplomatic transcription of it. See for example, footnote 3, p. 32.

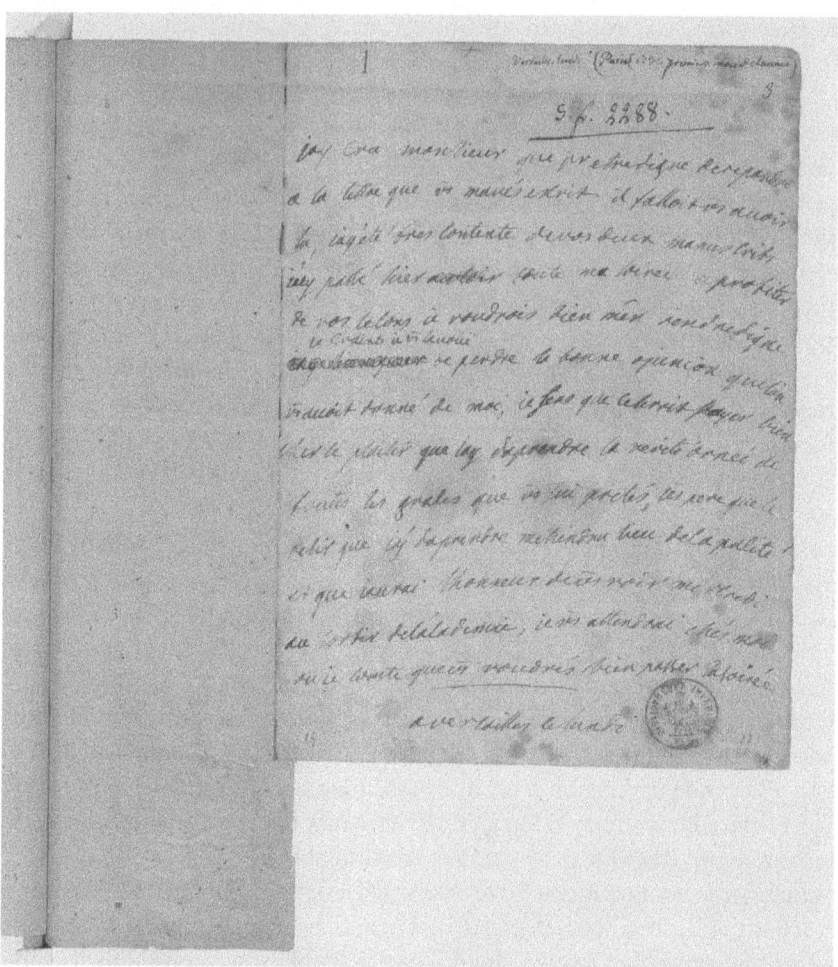

Figure 2.1 Mme du Châtelet's letter to Maupertuis, 10 January 1734. BnF, Ms Fr. 12268 (https://archivesetmanuscrits.bnf.fr/ark:/12148/cc43457c). The digitized image can be found here: https://gallica.bnf.fr/ark:/12148/btv1b6000754n/f17.item#.

'Je' or 'J'. The first begins 'J'ay', but is that a 'j' or an 'i'? I can see why Besterman transcribed the glyph as 'j' since there does seem to be the beginnings of a descender relative to other i's, but was that a calculated choice of du Châtelet's to use 'j' in this instance, whereas throughout her text, she exclusively used 'i' to spell 'je'? Or is the hint of a descender no more than a slip of the pen? And did she choose to only use minuscule, as was once fashionable in email? Or was capitalizing the first letter of a sentence – when she even thought that that's what she was doing: beginning a new sentence – simply not the rigid grammatical and orthographic rule in her mind that we take it to be today, including when we write by hand? The eighteenth-century French grammarian Nicolas Beauzée points out, much like Fertel and many others had, how inattentive authors tended to

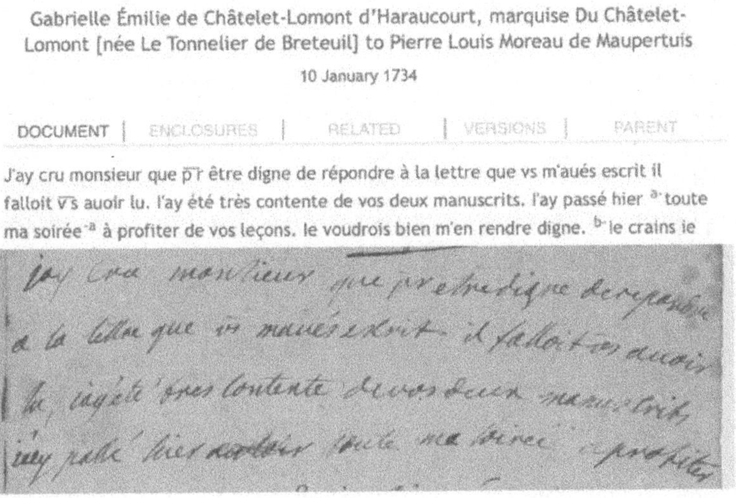

Editing Authenticity in the Manuscript Text

Gabrielle Émilie de Châtelet-Lomont d'Haraucourt, marquise Du Châtelet-Lomont [née Le Tonnelier de Breteuil] to Pierre Louis Moreau de Maupertuis

10 January 1734

DOCUMENT | ENCLOSURES | RELATED | VERSIONS | PARENT

J'ay cru monsieur que p̄r̄ être digne de répondre à la lettre que vs m'aués escrit il falloit v̄s auoir lu. l'ay été très contente de vos deux manuscrits. l'ay passé hier ᵃ˙toute ma soirée ˙ᵃ à profiter de vos leçons. le voudrois bien m'en rendre digne. ᵇ˙le crains le

Figure 2.2 Du Châtelet's letter juxtaposed with Besterman's transcription, as rendered in the *Electronic Enlightenment*.

be with respect to punctuation: 'how is it possible that, so long after the invention of distinctive signs for punctuation, we still have copyists and perhaps authors who write with so little care?' (Beauzée 1767, 570)

In transcribing for a print edition, Besterman has to make choices that work. As did eighteenth-century printers, bound not just to abstract spelling and punctuation standards but to the more concrete constraints of movable type (which those abstract rules reflected). The ambiguities could exist in handwriting – though they would ultimately be squelched as handwriting was increasingly subjected to the rationality of typographic writing – but they could not exist in print since in print, there was a stark, moulded-in-lead difference between an uppercase and a lowercase letterform, one famously manifest in the arrangement of the typecases themselves. There is similarly an inexorable distinction between apostrophes and dots over i's, which are represented by two separate type sorts. The ambiguities we see in the letters of du Châtelet cannot be reproduced using typographic characters unless new sorts are forged specifically to imitate the ambiguous usages seen on the manuscript page. In fact, early printers and typefounders had assiduously endeavoured to imitate all the variety of forms of handwritten text, and in the effort, they produced expansive founts of type that included the variant letterforms, combinations (ligatures), shorthands and abbreviations that typified the handwriting of the period. But while the multiplication of letterforms, glyphs, and diacritical marks sped up (and reflected the speeding up) of handwriting, it dramatically slowed down the printing process. Movable type printing, for which each character had to be carved and forged into distinct pieces of type that were, in turn, stored in separate compartments in typecases for compositors to pull from, benefited far more than handwriting did from a restricted character set. Unsurprisingly, by the eighteenth century, founts had been substantially streamlined to reflect not scribal richness and diversity but a much more rarefied set of letterforms and punctuation marks (Turnovsky 2024).

As such, when eighteenth-century printers sought to imitate handwriting, they had recourse to other technologies, such as copper-plate engraving and lithography. Yet we consider the texts produced by these alternative printing methods to be facsimiles, not diplomatic transcriptions. As far as I know, the latter refers specifically to the attempt to reproduce textual idiosyncrasy with movable type characters, an endeavour that is often – maybe always? – doomed to failure, as we have seen, at least when remediating handwriting (Salzman 2023).[7] Could we even have a concept of 'diplomatic transcription' in the absence of doomed-to-fail efforts to replicate idiosyncrasy, that is, in a case where a 'diplomatic' transcription would look exactly the same as a normalized transcription? This raises the question of whether an exact reproduction of the text in its original form is even the goal. Is the point of diplomatic transcription the often impossible goal of rendering the text exactly as it appears on the pages of the original, or is it instead to offer readers a compelling impression of the original now via the transcription of the text, a rhetorical gesture that is, in a sense, analogous to that of evoking in a preface the disorder of the originals and the labours of the editor in making them readable? Both are efforts to 'produce belief' in the reader, to use the language of Pierre Bourdieu (Bourdieu 1992, 237–45). The difference is that diplomatic transcription builds on a distinct set of beliefs about print, on one hand, assumed now to operate as a medium of transparency capable of conveying the manuscript text, and about the manuscript, on the other, conceived no longer as an unreadable mess needing to be 'translated' in order to be legible, but as a privileged source for the author's voice (Duranti 1989, 12).[8]

There is an irony in the fact that the editorial conceit of an 'exact transcription' of an original would be undermined by the presence of the original itself, or in the event, by a photographic representation of it, now easily available from the digital library of the Bibliothèque nationale de France. Peter Robinson compares texts to quantum particles whose nature is affected by the position of the observer: '[the] text [...] changes depending on how we look at it' (Robinson 1996, 106–7). The circumstances of our observation of texts define and redefine them. On their own, printed diplomatic transcriptions project meticulous, objective, quasi-scientific accuracy. Each oddly spelled word and unconventional punctuation mark screams that this is reliably the real thing. But juxtaposed against images of the originals they represent, they suddenly appear hardly

---

[7] In his study, Salzman (2023) focuses on type facsimiles, which in some ways blur the line between diplomatic edition and facsimile since the issues attendant to 'translating' from one medium to another are not as patent. But even within the framework of movable type print, differences invariably emerge. In 'Electronic Textual Editing: Levels of Transcription', tei-c.org, M. J. Driscoll defines as 'strictly diplomatic' transcriptions 'in which every feature which may reasonably be reproduced in print is retained', https://tei-c.org/Vault/ETE/Preview/driscoll.html.

[8] Luciana Duranti argues that a document's 'authenticity' is not an intrinsic quality but a historical one. The ancients did not have a concept of a document's inherent authenticity. Authenticity was established situationally (Duranti 1989, 12).

less approximate and arbitrary in the editorial choices they reflect than did Perrin's editions, advancing claims to accuracy that are not borne out by the comparison. In this last part, we turn to implications of the rise of photographic images in the framework of digital editions, of their increased availability and their technical improvement, and of the development of increasingly seamless pipelines for integrating them (such as the International Image Interoperability Framework [IIIF]) for transcription and editing. Above all, the editorial paradigm of which current transcription practices are the product is predicated on a belief in medium and inter-medium transparency and in the priority and reliability of the original source. To what extent do photographic transcriptions trouble this now established paradigm and call for a new one? Or to what extent, conversely, might we deem the incorporation of digital images of originals into editions to be simply this modern paradigm's next logical step? Are image-enhanced digital editions today equivalent in some ways to Perrin's hybrid editions of the early eighteenth century, introducing new ethics and protocols around transcription (for Perrin, a heretofore unprecedented fidelity to the original) but lacking a clear model for what the new edition should then be?

What jumps out is a sense of progress towards exactitude. The photographic image may delegitimize the diplomatic transcription by revealing its limitations. It does so, however, not by interrogating the premises of the diplomatic transcription's claim to exactness but, on the contrary, insofar as it takes on for itself the diplomatic transcription's goal to offer an even more 'exact' representation of a source and more effectively bring the reader closer and closer to the original, as scanning technologies improve and resolutions and network bandwidth increase. In this sense, the digital image would seem to be a product of the same editorial model, integrating a new technology into it but conceiving of the edition similarly.

The same critique of diplomatic transcriptions can be leveled against photographic transcriptions that now appear to deliver not only the exact text as attested by the original source but the text as the object itself, now including, as integral to the experience of the text, material elements like blank pages and covers. The myth of presence that the image upholds is predicated on a continuing belief in the invisibility of the medium, even though the medium is most assuredly there, and on the medium's effectiveness at sustaining this belief. Photos build from print in this regard, offering even more powerful experiences of unmediated contact with an authentic source. But no less than with print, these experiences are cultivated. Photos transform the text just as any other medium invariably does, despite the fact that the transformations seem less noticeable, partly because they are often subtle but partly because we do not process the transformations as substantive emendations to the original, and in this sense, we fail to 'notice' them. Photos, for instance, inevitably distort the size of what they are representing. The dimensions of images on the screen (whatever the device being used) seldom have any relation to the size of the object they depict. And the vast majority of interfaces regularize dimensions, presenting differently sized items as images and in image templates of a standardized size. We know this to be true, of course, but we do not consider this standardization to impact the accuracy of the text we are looking at.

This is true as well for the order and organization of documents. Practices in this domain have evolved substantially from the early days of photography for microfilm when the norm was to skip pages considered not to be part of the text, such as blank flyleaves. More recent photography for digitization tends to include blank pages and similar paratextual matter that might be considered extraneous to the text, such as half-title pages, pages with publisher, binder, provenance or library and cataloguing information, as well as front and back covers, and sometimes the spine and side views of the text block. The photos begin to function not so much as a transcription tool but as a precise documentary record of the text as object integrating, in this sense, an updated conceptualization of the text in Jerome McGann's framework as the product of linguistic *and* bibliographic codes, and not just the former (McGann 1991, 77). Yet photos only do so by disaggregating the object and representing it in a way – as a sequence of disconnected pages or openings – that is pointedly different from how one experiences the object itself in one's hands, defined above all by its boundedness, if bound, or by whatever device or platform is used to gather the pages and leaves, whether a folder, carton, or something else. Again, the important thing is not so much the difference itself, which like standardized image dimensions is intuitive and obvious. It is our ability to downplay the difference as we encounter the text on the screen as inessential to its nature.

Image resolution is another domain where significant changes have occurred in the direction of improved accuracy. Early, low-resolution, black-and-white photography would alter the text as perceived in the image in obvious ways, leading to misconstruals or to the inability to read parts of the text in the photo, not to mention uncertainty and lack of confidence about how the text should be read (Gadd 2009, 680–92; Mak 2015, 1515–26; Gavin 2017, 70–105).[9] Big improvements in resolution (and in the network infrastructure necessary for the dissemination of larger image files) ostensibly offer more 'accurate' representations of texts, in which the reader can have more confidence. They do not, however, offer the 'true text'. They offer a transformed text that, among other things, allows for an ability to zoom and perceive microscopic detail – in the paper, in the ink – of a kind that would be far less perceptible when reading the physical object

---

[9]Many examples can be found in the digital collection Early English Books Online (EEBO). EEBO digitizations were generated from low-resolution, black and white microfilm photographs dating to as far back as the 1930s. The TEI markup for one work selected somewhat at random, *Ane acte anent the registring of saisings, reversiones, and some vther writtes, etc.* (1599) includes eighteen instances of the tag <gap reason='illegible'> – indicating that the transcriber could not determine the text – in a 1-page broadsheet, with the majority of these tags reflecting issues in the reproduction of the document rather than the printing itself. The TEI transcriptions were hand-copied from the existing photos rather than from the originals. For a sense of how broad this phenomenon is in EEBO, the search query 'org:textcreationpartnership reason="illegible" path:*.xml', which looks for the string 'reason="illegible"' in all XML documents in the TCP Github repository, yields 13,200 documents. The repository contains over 61,300 XML transcriptions of texts in the EEBO database, according to the list of TCP texts compiled in the spreadsheets here: https://github.com/textcreationpartnership/Texts. The search results include many instances of illegibility encountered by transcribers due to printing or the condition of the physical book or document. But many of the legibility issues have to do with the quality of the photographic reproduction (https://github.com/textcreationpartnership/A11642/blob/b93516bce509f31a915e88c275a3a6ec640e0400/A11642.xml#L123).

under normal circumstances, without the necessary magnification tools. To return to Robinson's insight, the higher resolution alters our vantage point – it not only brings us closer to the text in the sense posited by the idea of accuracy, but it also provides a proximity that is beyond what the object and our physical capacities, *in real life*, provide. This technologically enhanced proximity, in turn, alters the text.

The key in these observations lies not in the alterations in and of themselves, but in the fact that, from the standardization of size to the disaggregation of the bound text to the possibilities of seeing the text in quasi-microscopic detail, we consider none of these reconfigurations of the text to undermine our sense of access, through the photographic image, to the text as it exists in its original form. In this respect, photographic transcription partakes of the order of medium transparency in its powerful claims to accuracy and in its capacity to obfuscate its mediated nature, to the point where we habitually and without much thought downplay, ignore or forget obvious transformations of the text of the kind just described.

Photographic transcriptions are, though, different from printed diplomatic transcriptions in at least one significant way. In an editorial framework, the photographic image does not exist in isolation. A diplomatic transcription can operate on its own, as seen in Besterman's edition of Du Châtelet's letter to Maupertuis, where the transcription of the letter is not accompanied by, say, a regularized text. By contrast, on its own, a photographic remediation of a text produces a facsimile, and, as Hans Walter Gabler has argued, 'facsimile editions tend only marginally to be considered *editions*'; and insofar as they might be editions, it is 'only to the extent that they are bolstered by paratexts – and among such above all by transcriptions'. The accompanying transcriptions, Gabler goes on to assert, 'allow us *to read* what in the facsimile can only be *seen*' (Gabler 2007, 198). The difference between *reading* and *seeing* the text leaves much to ponder. Gabler's point is that the text is *readable* insofar as it can be 'lifted off' (in his terms) from its documentary conveyance and reinscribed into a new platform. Transmissibility is integral to readability, which is itself understood as a function or outcome of editing. Editing is what transforms a document into a text or constructs a text out of a document, and in Gabler's view, in contrast with Duchêne, only an edited text can be read. The unedited document is 'merely' seen.

McGann clarifies the issue in his reflection on the relationship between text and image of the text in the framework of editing for digital publication. 'The emergence of electronic texts [. . .] has completely changed the traditional situation,' he writes. We can foresee 'a marriage of facsimile and critical editing' in the development of encoding techniques that computationally link a text with images of that text and thus with the idiosyncratic documentary and material features that the image is especially amenable to representing. McGann's 1997 article detailed efforts with the Rossetti Archive to move past the early 'linguistic' biases of the guidelines of the Text Encoding Initiative, which favoured the abstract text – with XML elements prioritizing textual structures and genre – while downplaying the 'bibliographic codes' inhering in the text's physical and visual instantiations. The TEI Guidelines have since that time evolved substantially in the direction of offering alternative models for representing a text, notably with the

<facsimile> element introduced in TEI P5 in 2007. <facsimile> operates at the same level as the <text> element, at the top of the XML hierarchy, a child of the <TEI> document itself, extending the possibility of representing a 'written source' not as 'transcribed or encoded text' but as a 'set of images' and visual surfaces onto which the text is inscribed.[10]

But efforts to theorize greater integration between text and image of the text hit up against nuts-and-bolts realities in which image- and text-processing technologies are 'all but irreconcilable', as Matthew Kirschenbaum put it (Kirschenbaum 2003, 138). Despite the <facsimile> element and related tools for representing the text 'by prioritizing the encoding of their spatial features over their logical textual structure', as we read in chapter 12 of the TEI Guidelines,[11] the base technical reality represented by TEI is the need ultimately to translate the image of a text into the plain text of XML in order for the text to be 'read', in this instance by a computer. The same can be said of increasingly powerful and accurate Optical Character Recognition (OCR) tools, which ostensibly afford us the ability to 'read' images, but only via the mediation of an algorithm programmed to detect the contours of writing symbols in the image and, now aided by machine learning, to render those symbols as tractable text, editable in the sense Gabler conceives it, which can then be copied, pasted, and emended. Ryan Cordell argues that OCR output, for all of its well-known accuracy problems, should be seen as a new edition of the text it is representing, even with all the distortions (Cordell 2017, 188–225). Cordell's case is persuasive to me; the text has been reset and rekeyed. But it is notable that only the OCR output is to be considered an edition, not the scanned image from which it is derived. The hierarchy between text and image is reasserted, with the image, in itself, opaque to editing.

Assumptions about agency are, of course, critical. In the digital realm, an edition is only an edition insofar as it can be read not just by humans, but also by computers. I would say that this is a reasonable assumption to make. No digital edition can present itself today without at least basic text search capabilities – would we deem it a 'digital edition' otherwise? – and most readers are surely looking for more in terms of text-processing functionality (Ohge 2021). The chain of transmissibility needs, in this sense, to integrate machines. And machines copy texts in very specific ways, that is, by recognizing at a granular level *characters*, which have been encoded according to particular schemas. The past fifty years of scholarship in the humanities, from Post-Structuralism to New Historicism to Social Bibliography, have greatly expanded traditional conceptions of the text in order to identify semiotic systems, open to interpretation and 'reading', in phenomena where they were not historically sought or found: in images, for one thing, as well as in all sorts of verbal and non-verbal 'discourses', including, as D. F. McKenzie affirmed, in landscape (McKenzie 1999, 29–41). In the world of computing, by contrast,

---

[10] See the entry for <facsimile> in the TEI P5 Guidelines: https://www.tei-c.org/release/doc/tei-p5-doc/en/html/ref-facsimile.html.
[11] TEI Guidelines, chapter 12, 'Representation of Primary Sources', (https://tei-c.org/release/doc/tei-p5-doc/en/html/PH.html).

the definition of text has remained decidedly narrow and categorical: text is a datatype comprised of strings of characters – alphanumeric and special symbols (letters, numbers and punctuation marks, along with spaces and line-breaks) – with each one defined abstractly and in isolation (the letter 'a' is always the letter 'a' no matter what other characters surround a singular instance of it and no matter how each instance might be formatted), and each encoded with a distinct binary value according to a standardized, recognized schema.

To be sure, the set of symbols that can be included as readable text data has massively expanded with the evolution of encoding schemas from the 7-bit ASCII of the 1980s (able to encode 128 characters) to the exponentially larger 8-, 16- and 32-bit Unicode standards prevalent in our time. UTF-8, the most commonly used system today, offers codepoints for 1.1 million characters, including a vast array of non-Latin glyphs and diacritical marks excluded in ASCII. This has, of course, been critical for integrating non-Anglophone, non-European, and non-alphabetic text into the transmission chain of machine-readable text, but on a critical condition, which is that the language and writing systems out of which these texts come are able to adapt to two ineluctable rules for character encoding: the separation (and separability) of distinct characters (with each assigned a unique binary code) and their abstract standardization, with each character assuming a stable identity apart from any concrete use and formatting.

Unicode is a standard for digitized writing, but it is worthy of note that these two rules are the products of typography, not computation or digitization *per se*, which did no more than adopt for its uses the preexisting typographic writing system based on the use of metal type – reproducible sorts, cast in moulds that function as a kind of encoding system. The 1960s fantasized highly pixelated letterforms on low-resolution green screens as the future of writing. But in reality, the vast majority of digital writing today looks far more like the typographic writing of early print from 500 years ago than the printed texts of the late sixteenth century looked like the manuscripts of merely a hundred years prior. The decision to distil European writing into a streamlined collection of discrete, abstracted, and easily replicable and referenced characters, characters that would in turn demonstrate unprecedented durability over the ensuing five centuries, was made by printers and typesetters of the first decades of the 1500s, rapidly consolidating around roman typeface as an all-purpose, degree-zero letterform. The text-processing functionalities we expect and take for granted in a digital platform, including keyword searching, would not exist in the forms they do without these decisions of early sixteenth-century printers.

In this sense, Gabler's conception of the transmissibility of texts is not only about the ability to reproduce a text, which is easily done with any image file. It entails the ability to reproduce a text as a succession of typographic characters: tractable in their autonomy and abstraction. The transcriptions necessary to turn documents into edited texts translate a source, in whatever form it might take, into a sequence of separated and standardized glyphs, which then defines the text's transmissibility, and thus, for Gabler, its readability. When the document being converted is a printed document – which we should understand broadly here to refer to a document intended for circulation in print (even if the specific source is a manuscript) – this translation is, as one might expect, relatively seamless. Characters can either be converted typographically as they exist in the source. Or in the case of a regularized transcription, changes can be rationalized in the goal of legibility. The problem comes with non-print documents, specifically when the document's non-printedness – its qualities as a handwritten letter – is a key feature of the text one seeks to edit and transmit. The qualities that characterize the manuscript as *manuscript* – irregular punctuation, spelling and grammar, and ambiguous glyphs that anchor the writing in a concrete affective context, giving the letter meaning as a letter reflective of the emotion and interpersonal intensity with which it was written – are precisely what the standardizing tendencies of character encoding systems, from typecasting to UTF, exclude. In this context, both diplomatic transcription and transcription for machine reading will always fail. Inevitably, their 'accuracy' with respect to the original documentary qualities of the text will be impressions of accuracy, contingent on the vantage point of the reader and the frameworks that sustain the reader's belief in the transcription's reliability as a point of access to the original.

The effects of manuscript spontaneity and individuality are, in truth, not intrinsic to handwriting. Far from it; handwriting can certainly be and for centuries was as regular and formulaic as print would become (though the formulas of the scribal world pushed in directions very different than that of streamlined character sets). The association of handwriting with individuality and affect took root in the shadow of print, in opposition to print's standardizing tendencies. The idea of the handwritten document as an inherently idiosyncratic and therefore personal form of writing only makes sense in the age of print (Stallybrass 2001; Turnovsky 2024). The editors of French eighteenth-century correspondence cited above, in promoting adherence to 'epistolary punctuation' and related scribal quirks in their editions, conceived of the meanings of these quirks in pointed contrast with print: 'epistolary punctuation [. . .] does not have the same function as typographic punctuation', writes Sgard in 'La punctuation épistolaire' (32). This media cross-pollination raises all the key questions we face today. How, in turn, will digitization change not only our access to the texts generated by earlier transcription technologies but our conceptions of those technologies and of the texts they produce, as print changed our perceptions of manuscript text? And how will these conceptions transform our techniques for editing, remediating, and representing the texts? What equivalent of 'diplomatic transcription' might emerge? Digitization pulls in two distinct, even conflictual directions: towards character-based, large-scale databases which advance an unprecedented level of abstraction with respect to the original sources; and towards a heightened sense of the original's materiality, through higher- and higher-resolution images. It is hard to say what new configurations will emerge from this juxtaposition, and how techniques of editing will evolve. But what is clear is the necessity for new kinds of collaboration entailed by new media forms interacting with old forms and old texts, between book historians, editors and literary scholars and librarians, information and computer scientists.

Bibliography

Beauzée, Nicolas. *Grammaire générale, ou exposition raisonnée des éléments nécessaires du langage, pour servir de fondement à l'étude de toutes les langues*. Paris. Imprimerie de J. Barbou, 1767.

Bourdieu, Pierre. *Les règles de l'art. Genèse et structure du champ littéraire*. Paris. Éditions du Seuil, 1992.

Chartier, Roger. 'The Text Between the Voice and the Book'. In *Voice, Text, Hypertext: Emerging Practices in Textual Studies*, 54–71. Edited by R. Modiano, L. F. Searle and P. Shillingsburg. Seattle: University of Washington Press, 2004.

Cordell, Ryan. '"Q i-jtb the Raven": Taking Dirty OCR Seriously'. *Book History* 20, no. 1 (2017): 188–225.

Coulet, Henri, "Ponctuation originale et ponctuation éditée." In *Les éditions critiques. Problèmes techniques et éditoriaux. Actes de la Table ronde internationale de 1984*. Special issue of *Annales littéraires de l'Université de Besançon* 370 (1988): 57–64.

Darnton, Robert. 'Readers Respond to Rousseau: The Fabrication of Romantic Sensitivity'. In *The Great Cat Massacre and Other Episodes in French Cultural History*, 215–56. New York: Vintage Press, 1984.

Driscoll, M. J. 'Electronic Textual Editing: Levels of Transcription'. *tei-c.org*, 2007. https://tei-c.org/Vault/ETE/Preview/driscoll.html.

Duchêne, Roger. 'Mme de Sévigné et le style négligé'. *Œuvres & Critiques*, no. 1–2 (1976), 113–27.

Duchêne, Roger, 'Note sur le texte'. In Marie de Rabutin-Chantal, marquise de Sévigné, *Correspondance*, vol. 1, 755–832. Paris: Gallimard, 1972.

Duranti, Luciana. 'Diplomatics: New Uses for an Old Science, Part I'. *Archivaria* 28 (1989): 7–27.

Fertel, Martin Dominique. *La science pratique de l'imprimerie*. Saint Omer: Fertel, 1723.

Foley, Barbara C. *Telling the Truth: The Theory and Practice of Documentary Fiction*. Ithaca, NY: Cornell University Press, 1986.

Gabler, Hans Walter. 'The Primacy of the Document in Editing'. *Ecdotica* 4, no. 1 (2007): 197–207.

Gadd, Ian. 'The Use and Misuse of Early English Books Online'. *Literature Compass* 6/3 (2009): 680–92.

Gavin, Michael. 'How to Think about EEBO'. *Textual Cultures* 11, no. 1/2 (2017): 70–105.

Greg, Walter Wilson. 'The rationale of copy-text'. *Studies in Bibliography* 3 (1950): 19–36.

Kirschenbaum, Matthew. 'The Word as Image in an Age of Digital Reproduction'. In *Eloquent Images: Word and Image in the Age of New Media*, 137–56. Edited by Mary E. Hocks and Michelle R. Kendrick. Cambridge, MA: MIT Press, 2003.

Lettres de la marquise du Châtelet à M. de Maupertuis (1734–1741), BnF, Ms Fr. 12268. https://archivesetmanuscrits.bnf.fr/ark:/12148/cc43457c.

Mak, Bonnie. 'Archaeology of a Digitization'. *Journal of the Association for Information Science and Technology* 65, no. 8 (2015): 1515–26.

Marcus, Leah. *Unediting the Renaissance: Shakespeare, Marlowe and Milton*. New York and London: Routledge, 1996.

McLeod, Randall. 'Un' Editing' Shak-speare'. *SubStance* 10 (1981): 26–55.

McGann, Jerome J. *The Textual Condition*. Princeton, NJ: Princeton University Press, 1991.

McKenzie, Donald F. *Bibliography and the Sociology of Texts*. Cambridge: Cambridge University Press, 1999.

Montesquieu, Charles-Louis de Secondat, baron de La Brède et de. *The Persian Letters*. Translated by George Healy. Indianapolis: Hackett Publishing, 1999.

Ohge, Christopher. *Publishing Scholarly Editions: Archives, Computing, and Experience.* Cambridge: Cambridge University Press, 2021.

Paige, Nicholas D. *Before Fiction: The Ancien Régime of the Novel.* Philadelphia: University of Pennsylvania Press, 2011.

Perrousseaux, Yves. *Histoire de l'écriture typographique,* vol. 1. Méolans-Revel: Atelier Perrousseaux, 2005.

Proust, Jacques. 'La ponctuation des textes de Diderot.' *Romanische Forschungen* 90, no. H. 4 (1978): 369–87.

Robinson, Peter. M. W. 'Is There a Text in These Variants?' In *The Literary Text in the Digital Age,* 99–115. Edited by Richard Finneran. Ann Arbor, MI: University of Michigan Press, 1996.

Salzman, Paul. *Facsimiles and the History of Shakespeare Editing.* Cambridge: Cambridge University Press, 2023.

Sévigné, Marie de Rabutin-Chantal, Marquise de. *Recueil des Lettres de Madame la Marquise de Sévigné, à Madame la Comtesse de Grignan, sa fille.* 6 vols. Paris: Simart, 1734-1737.

Sévigné, Marie de Rabutin-Chantal, Marquise de. *Recueil des lettres de Mme la Marquise de Sévigné à Mme la comtesse de Grignan, sa fille. Nouvelle édition augmentée.* 8 vols. Paris: Rollin, 1754.

Sgard, Jean. 'La ponctuation épistolaire'. In *Edition und Interpretation. Edition et Interprétation des Manuscrits Littéraires,* 32–43. Edited by Louis Hay and Winfried Woesler. Bern, Frankfurt, Las Vegas: Peter Lang, 1981.

Stallybrass, Peter. 'Books and Scrolls. Navigating the Bible'. In *Books and Readers in Early Modern England,* 42–79. Edited by Jennifer Anderson and Elizabeth Sauer. Philadelphia: University of Pennsylvania Press, 2001.

TEI P5 Guidelines. https://www.tei-c.org/release/doc/tei-p5-doc/en/html/index.html.

Turnovsky, Geoffrey. *Reading Typographically.* Redwood City, CA: Stanford University Press, 2024.

Vercruysse, Jeroom. "Les traductions typographiques de Voltaire." In *In Les éditions critiques. Problèmes techniques et éditoriaux. Actes de la Table ronde internationale de 1984.* Special issue of *Annales littéraires de l'Université de Besançon* 370 (1988): 98–106.

Voiture, Vincent. *Les Oevvres de Monsievr de Voitvre.* Paris: Courbé, 1650.

CHAPTER 3
THE PRINTING SURFACE IN THE AGE OF DIGITAL REPRODUCTION
Giles Bergel

Printing surfaces, one of the lowest-profile elements of the printing process, nonetheless fascinate. Embodying the basic mechanics of printing – perhaps more intelligibly than the press itself – they also epitomize its rarely realized ideal, namely the production of uniform copies from one composition. While printing surfaces are intrinsically generative (emphasized by the synonymous term 'printing matrix'), wood blocks and metal plates are products of art and industry in their own right. They are attracting increasing attention thanks to work such as a collection of essays edited by Elizabeth Savage and Femke Speelman (Savage and Speelman, forthcoming); a number of digitization and cataloguing projects such as the collections of the Plantin-Moretus Museum in Antwerp; and a mailing list dedicated to early printing surfaces ('Blocks, Plates and Stones') that, at the time of writing, has just under 200 subscribers.[1] Surviving surfaces are boundary objects straddling the worlds of museums and print collections: since there are few common cataloguing standards across galleries, libraries and museums, they are rarely surfaced or described in full.

For bibliographers, printing surfaces are temporal and geographical milestones: a unique block, once separated from its inked impression on paper, may indicate the origins of an anonymously or pseudonymously printed book or may trace relationships between printers across time and space. This article outlines some computational aids to this task, focusing on relief woodblocks for letterpress printing. It places both the mechanical reproduction *of* blocks – and mechanical reproduction *from* blocks – that is to say, printing – in relation to digital imaging and discusses the impact of the latter on bibliographical methods. Last, it attempts to draw some parallels between block printing and digital facsimiles and other data. It will begin by exploring the history of one set of blocks along with their owners, copies and impressions, as a case study.

In 1820, the antiquary and radical satirist William Hone visited the London premises of Thomas Batchelar, printer of songbooks, single-sheet broadside ballads, carols and occasional longer works. Hone recalled the visit in his 1823 history of English popular religious drama *Ancient Mysteries Described* as follows:

---

[1] The Plantin-Moretus Museum in Antwerp has imaged their collection of woodblocks – see https://museumplantinmoretus.be/en/page/impressive-woodblocks. The Blocks, Plates and Stones mailing list is available at https://www.jiscmail.ac.uk/cgi-bin/wa-jisc.exe?A0=BLOCKSPLATESSTONES

The attachment of Carol buyers extends even to the wood cuts by which they are surrounded. Some of these, on a sheet of Christmas Carols, in 1820, were so rude in execution, that I requested the publisher, Mr. T. Batchelar, of 115, Long Alley, Moorfields, to sell me the original blocks. I was a little surprised by his telling me that he was afraid it would be impossible to get any of the same kind cut again. When I proffered to get much better engraved, and give them to him in exchange for his old ones, he said, 'Yes, but better are not so good; I can get better myself: now these are old favourites, and better cuts will not please my customers so well.' However, by assuring him that artists could copy any thing, I obtained them. (Hone, *Ancient Mysteries Described* 1823, 99)

Surrounding Hone's text, his printer John McCreery has arranged four woodcut illustrations of episodes in the life of Christ (see Figure 3.1).

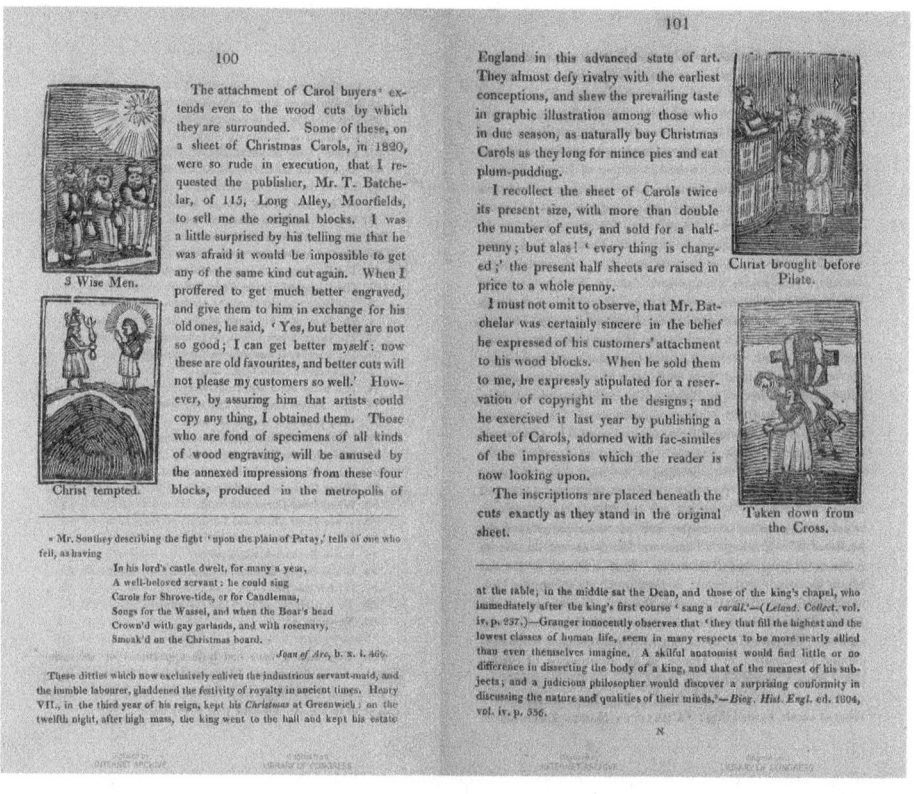

Figure 3.1 William Hone, *Ancient Mysteries Described, Especially the English Miracle Plays, Founded on Apocryphal New Testament Story, Extant Among the Unpublished Manuscripts in the British Museum: Including Notices of Ecclesiastical Shows, the Festivals of Fools and Asses, the English Boy Bishop, the Descent Into Hell, the Lord Mayor's Show, the Guildhall Giants, Christmas Carols, &c* (printed for William Hone, 1823), 100–1.

Hone's book is a detailed history of and commentary on the transmission of the apocryphal Christian gospels within broadside carols, mystery plays and other forms of folklore and popular culture. As J. W. Robinson puts it, Hone is seeking to uncover the 'unofficial piety and poetry of the people' (Robinson 1978, 36). His appraisal of Batchelar's carols places them within a history of the persistence of a canon of popular knowledge and taste over time:

> Those who are fond of specimens of all kinds of wood engraving, will be amused by the annexed impressions from these four blocks, produced in the metropolis of England in this advanced state of art. They almost defy rivalry with the earliest conceptions, and shew the prevailing taste in graphic illustration among those who in due season, as naturally buy Christmas Carols as they long for mince pies and eat plum-pudding. (Hone, *Ancient Mysteries*, 100)

Hone's attestation that Batchelar's reluctance to sell the blocks is solid evidence for the popularity of their designs has been accepted in most repetitions of the story, despite the fact that his book contains what may be the only surviving impressions from the blocks (Marsh 2016, 79; Shepard 1969, 63). Broadside songs of any kind rarely survive: carols, used to decorate walls at Christmas, were particularly ephemeral. Hone anticipates the suspicion that Batchelar's testimony was a negotiation tactic, assuring the reader of Batchelar's interest in printing from the copied blocks exchanged for his originals:

> I must not omit to observe, that Mr. Batchelar was certainly sincere in the belief he expressed in the belief he expressed of his customers' attachment to his wood blocks. When he sold them to me, he expressly stipulated for a reservation of copyright in the designs; and he exercised it last year by publishing a sheet of Carols, adorned with fac-similes of the impressions which the reader is now looking upon. (Hone, *Ancient Mysteries*, 101)

Hone is certainly at pains to document both the mutual benefits resulting from the transaction and his own familiarity with the mechanics of printing, which, as at various times a bookseller, librarian and publisher as well as an author, he understood very well. As the author of illustrated political satires and histories, he worked closely with engravers such as George Cruikshank, a collaboration illustrated in one of their joint productions (see Figure 3.2).

As Mercedes Cerón notes of Hone and his associates, 'Regency radicalism benefited from recent developments in printing techniques while adopting the visual language associated with popular ephemera' (Cerón 2015, 225). Images constitute both evidence and argument in many of Hone's publications, whether acting as visual quotations in his antiquarian treatises or polemical counterparts to the incisive prose of his satires and

Figure 3.2 Hone and Cruikshank depicted in their 1823 joint publication *Facetiae and Miscellanies With one hundred and twenty engravings, drawn by George Cruikshank,* London: Hunt & Clarke, printed by: J. M'Creery et al. 1827.

political writings.[2] Relief woodcuts, unlike engravings printed from metal plates, can be printed simultaneously on the same press as type, allowing Hone in the *Ancient Mysteries* both to show the blocks and to tell their story at the same time. He exploits the obvious fact that printing surfaces can be printed as well as documented, departing from the usual antiquarian practice of rendering historical specimens in three-dimensional relief, as seen, for example, in an article on woodcut in Diderot and d'Alembert's *Encyclopédie*. (See Figure 3.3)

Hone, then, does not so much put the blocks on show as show them in action. Their messages are reproduced, while the accompanying text places them within a

---

[2] See Jason McElligott, 'William Hone (1780–1842), Print-Culture, and the Nature of Radicalism,' in *Varieties of Seventeenth-and Early Eighteenth-Century English Radicalism in Context* (Abingdon: Routledge, 2016), 241–60; Rick Bowers, 'Parody, Performance and Self-Defence: William Hone's Ancient Mysteries Described (1823),' *English Studies* 94, no. 1 (2013): 42–56; Kyle Grimes, 'Before the Trials: William Hone and the Rise of the Watchdog Press,' *English Studies* 103, no. 8 (2022): 1178–90, and Grimes, *Hone Bio-Text: A Biography, Bibliography and e-text archive*. https://honearchive.org (accessed 21/2/2025).

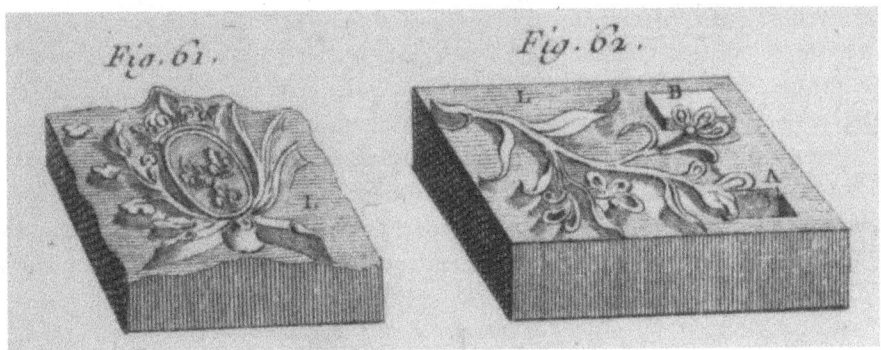

Figure 3.3 'Gravure en Bois, Principes,' *Encyclopédie ou Dictionnaire raisonné des sciences, des arts et des métiers*, vol. 5 (plates). Paris, 1765, http://hdl.handle.net/2027/spo.did2222.0001.502.

history of printing and of books from 'the earliest conceptions' up until the present. We are told that work in this style had become practically extinct: this perhaps undercuts their imputed popularity, but it is true that printing was becoming in some respects a more 'advanced art'. Hone may have had in mind technical developments such as the improved iron press, followed by the steam press, or the burgeoning of a substantial industry of typefounders, designers, etchers and engravers that, in contrast to a century earlier, were increasingly able to supply British printers with paper, type and other materials. Books themselves were still costly, but the cheap formats, such as broadside ballads that had entertained, informed and educated readers and audiences for centuries, were joined by songsters, prints, newspapers and other literatures able to reach increasingly large publics (Raven 2007 and 2009; Finkelstein and Nash 2024). From this perspective, the traditional illustrated broadside was both in a relative decline compared to newer formats such as songsters, and paradoxically of a forerunner of a new age of mass media and literacy that had long been anticipated, but had not quite come to pass.

This quantitative shift in media production was also qualitative: appreciators could perceive certain differences between the woodcuts on Batchelar's sheets and reused in Hone's volume and the emerging technique now usually called wood-engraving. While designs in woodcut are carved *along* the grain, often with a knife, wood-engraving is carved *across* the end-grain of a harder wood, often with tools resembling those of a copper engraver. As shown by Hone's own broad usage of the term 'wood-engraving', a categorical distinction had yet to emerge, but a contrast was often visually apparent, most famously in the work of Thomas Bewick's studio. Wood-engraving, as developed by Bewick, makes extensive use of white (uninked) lines carved into the sub-surface of the block: woodcut composition relies more on relief features that pick up ink and print in black. Combined with the new iron presses working on the improved papers of this period and the centralization and division of labour that the metropolis engendered, fine wood-engraved lines could be skilfully orchestrated to generate a richly textured image at relatively low cost, enabling the copious illustration of popular books and periodicals such as the *Penny Magazine* and Hone's own *Everyday Book* and other publications.[3]

While aficionados of what we now called wood-engraving will sometimes refer to the lower status of woodcuts by way of Horace Walpole's sneer against 'slovenly stamps',[4] blocks for broadside ballads and chapbooks were in fact designed with some precision and care. What Batchelar told Hone about readers' familiarity with their appearance seems to bear this out, while a letter from the Glasgow chapbook printer James Lumsden to Thomas Bewick himself points to a fundamental design requirement for such blocks:

> I received yesterday a Number of cuts and coincide in opinion with you that they are done in a very superior manner, but the style is very farr from what I expressed to you, and I am extremely sorry to say are useless for the purpose intended ... Twould be useless to Putt them to press in the Present state as the coarseness of the paper we use would quite destroy them. (quoted in Tattersfield 2011, 149)

The coarseness of Lumsden's paper is a feature, not a defect, which allows his chapbooks to reach the widest possible market, priced at a penny or less. Bewick's exquisite blocks will not serve that market, while blocks with a simpler and bolder design will print strong and clear. Suitable for chapbook printers' narrow profit margins (and the narrow margins of chapbooks themselves), such blocks were both economical and durable: an original Newcastle printing block reproduced below was cut with a sparse pattern of hatched white lines and gouged white space, employing a robust and ingenious composition of rigid supporting elements (such as curtains and furniture) around the central design (see Figure 3.4).

This block was made to last, exhibiting a robustness that defines the aesthetic of many cheap print woodcuts, while its use of white lines also points to the emerging visual vocabulary of wood-engraving and its relationship with cheap print.

As printing was undergoing various interdependent technical, industrial and aesthetic revolutions, its history became of increasing interest to scholars and collectors, as traced by the emerging hobby and science of bibliography (Klancher 2009). The 1812 Roxburghe sale, an iconic moment in the rise of 'bibliomania', is famous for the unprecedented prices achieved by large books such as a copy of the *Decameron* (Connell

---

[3] See William Andrew Chatto, *A Treatise on Wood Engraving, Historical and Practical* (London: Charles Knight, 1839). On Thomas Bewick see Jennifer S. Uglow, *Nature's Engraver: A Life of Thomas Bewick* (Chicago: University of Chicago Press, 2009), and Nigel Tattersfield, *The Complete Illustrative Work of Thomas Bewick* (London: The British Library and The Bibliographical Society; Delaware: Oak Knoll Press, 2011).

[4] Jenny Uglow notes that 'engravings were the plain man's art, dismissed by the critic Horace Walpole in a cursory footnote in 1782 as "slovenly stamps," but Bewick transformed them into images of haunting depth and subtlety'. Ian Bain remarks that Bewick 'brought respectability to the woodblock as a medium for purposes more elevated than crude ballad sheets and chapbooks', 'Thomas Bewick and His Contemporaries', in Ian Bain, 'Thomas Bewick and His Contemporaries', in *Maps and Prints: Aspects of the English Book Trade*, ed. Robin Myers and Michael Harris (Oxford: Publishing Pathways, 1984), 67–80.

Figure 3.4 A ballad and chapbook block (McGill University Library Woodblocks Collection Box 13 Item 672) with an antiquarian offprint (*Specimens of early wood-engraving, being impressions of woodcuts in the possession of the publisher*, Newcastle-upon-Tyne: William Dodd, 1862). For these blocks see 'Pieces of Art: a Collection of Engraved Woodblocks'. https://blogs.library.mcgill.ca/rbsc/pieces-of-art-a-collection-of-engraved-woodblocks, and Leo DeFreitas, 'Newcastle Chapbooks, Broadsides, and Garlands: A Study of the Collection of Woodblocks in McGill University Library, Rare Books and Special Collections,' in Printers, Pedlars, Sailors and Nuns: Aspects of Street Literature, ed. David Atkinson and Steve Roud (London: Ballad Partners, 2019), 88–102.

2000; Ferris 2015), but it also saw the sale of a set of vanishingly rare broadside ballads from the previous three centuries.[5] Hone's visit to Batchelar superficially resembles a familiar narrative, in which the learned explorer 'discovers' and preserves the last relics of a dying culture. One example, much discussed by historians of popular print culture is the story of the young James Boswell buying and extravagantly binding twenty-four chapbooks, the 'old darlings' of his childhood, printed and sold in Bow Churchyard by the market-leading firm of Dicey (Boswell, quoted in Pottle 1991, 299). Pat Rogers accused Boswell of 'literary slumming' while conceding that he held 'a genuine affection' for chapbooks (Rogers 1985, 165; see also Mullan and Reid 2000, 10). Thomas Percy, later Bishop of Dromore, visited the same office and bought dozens of broadside ballads from Cluer Dicey, who he describes in a letter, using a printing metaphor, as being 'of a much lower stamp' than some of his other suppliers, but we know from the work of Nick Groom that Percy made (but did not acknowledge) extensive use of these sheets in his best-selling and influential *Reliques of English Poetry* (Groom 1999; see also Stoker, 2014). Frederic Madden, whose collections of ballads are now in Cambridge University Library, visited the Dicey firm's later owner, James Marshall, who convinced him that he was the direct descendant of the Ballad Partners, who dominated the ballad trade in the seventeenth century (Thomson 1987). William Hone is distinctive within this tradition because, while sharing these other collectors' genuine passion for printed traces of antiquity, his ambitions within the unreformed political culture of his day were distinctively and disruptively egalitarian.

---

[5]The Roxburghe ballads are held by the British Library and can be seen online through the English Broadside Ballad Archive, http://www.ebba.english.ucsb.edu (accessed 2 March 2025).

Hone's political radicalism was never far beneath the surface of his antiquarian writings – indeed, it animated his whole life's work. His political satires attracted prosecutions on such consequential charges as sedition and blasphemy, from which he was able to acquit himself by erudite use of the literary evidence reprinted in the *Ancient Mysteries* (Robinson 1978). Hone himself had been fascinated by print since childhood: in his *Everyday Book* he recalls at the age of twelve being lent a bundle of fragments of early printing by a cobbler:

> he lent me a folio of fragments from Caxton's 'Polychronicon', and Pynson's 'Shepherd's Kalendar', which he kept in the drawer of his seat, with 'St. Hugh's Bones', and the instruments of his 'gentle craft'. This black-letter lore, with its wood-cuts, created in me a desire to be acquainted with our old authors, and a love for engravings, which I have indulged without satiety. (Hone 1825, vol. 1 col. 859)

Hone's appetite is not unlike Boswell's for chapbooks, but while it is undeniable that we now understand cheap print chiefly through the rarefied, iconic collections of ballads and chapbooks collected by Samuel Pepys, James Boswell, Frederic Madden, Thomas Percy and Hone's confidant and ally Francis Douce, among others, Hone's collections are now dispersed, their energies directed outward in Hone's lifetime into his writing and radical activities. Many of his books were auctioned in 1828 in an attempt to address his debts, but the 1843 catalogue of his posthumous sale reveals that he retained the bulk of his ballads and carol-sheets – and a quantity of unidentifiable woodblocks – until his dying day.[6]

While Hone seems to have struck an acceptable bargain with Batchelar, it's unlikely that the latter was unaware that blocks could be copied: printers of broadsides and chapbooks had been using blocks copied with varying degrees of precision for centuries. Loose copies can be seen throughout the ballad corpus, while very close copies could be made by cutting through a printed impression onto a block (Ivins 1943, 124–5). The block itself could be moulded in metal through the stereotype process, which was rapidly becoming an industrial norm: Thomas Hodgson wrote in 1820 that 'there are now in London twelve establishments for the casting of stereotype plates' (Hodgson 1820, 121). Cliché reproduction, in which a woodblock was impressed into molten type metal, may also have been known to printers as part of a repertory of skills typically unrecorded in the few manuals that we have and from which few printers would have

---

[6] I am grateful to the library of the Grolier Club of New York for providing a copy of the *Catalogue of the Valuable and Interesting Collection of Books, Tracts, Ballads, Prints etc of the Late Mr William Hone* (Henry Southgate and Co, 1843). The catalogue contains multiple entries ballads, carols and woodblocks, few of which are listed in more than scant detail. The auctioneer touts these items as 'once so popular as to be printed in every large town in the kingdom but [. . .] now altogether supplanted by other literature, and are no longer published. Opportunities of acquiring them but very rarely occur'.

learnt their trade.[7] Judging from their appearance in Hone's reprint, Hone's blocks do not seem particularly well-worn, certainly compared to the cracked and worm-eaten blocks tirelessly worked across multiple decades by the ballad printers of the seventeenth-century monopoly period. Whether due to their antiquity, commercial value or sacred subject, Batchelar seems to have looked after his blocks. If he received metal stereotypes in return for his wooden originals, he may well have been glad to have had facsimiles that were both more durable than the wooden exemplars he sold to Hone and practically indistinguishable from their sources (Bevan 2023, 73 and fn. 20).

How we think about print now is captured by William Ivins's claim that it offers to generate an 'exactly repeatable pictorial statement', a characterization that was influential on Elizabeth Eisenstein's focus on 'fixity' (Ivins 1953, 180; Eisenstein 1979). But repeatability has always been partial. Bibliography, a science of difference, asks what, exactly, is meant by 'exactly'. The goal is generally not so much to debunk the very idea of repeatability but to manage deviations from the norm within certain pragmatic horizons: as Tom Davis puts it, 'If you ask an engineer to machine a metal rod a meter long, he or she will probably ask, "For what purpose?" in order to find out what kind of tolerances in measurement would be required' (Davis 1995, 148). Eminently practical and usually a service discipline to others, bibliography distinguishes authorial from other influences; detects earlier from later states within editions; tells originals from copies; and, perhaps most charismatically, uncovers forgeries and other mysteries. In contrast to the ideal of the exact copy, bibliography assigns epicurean gradations of difference. Differences include swollen or faded lines in illustrations, substituted or fallen type, cancelled or inserted pages, amended plates, or new combinations of old materials. Variously laborious, fastidious and sensual, bibliography delights as much in the puzzles it addresses as their logical solution. The state of an impression might differ only minutely: a crack in a block may appear, widen, or be offset by one of a thousand myriad hacks, workarounds, error corrections and trade secrets scarcely visible from the normative distance of the present. While it depends upon close observation, bibliography is often conjectural, as the phenomenology of matter in action inevitably outweighs what is visible on the surface. We weren't there when the book was made: our attempts to reconstruct what really happened in the printing house are necessarily imaginative, if not sometimes positively imaginary.[8]

As bibliography relies on observation, measurement, pattern recognition and tabulation, the computer is an obvious partner, but Davis's caution against drawing general inferences from what fits the researcher's specific purpose should apply no less to bibliography in the digital age. For studies of woodblocks, a range of computational

---

[7]See Hodgson's *Essay*, 38–44 and James Mosley, 'Dabbing, Abklatschen, Clichage,' *Journal of the Printing Historical Society* 23, 2015. An earlier version of this article can be found at http://typefoundry.blogspot.com/2006/01/dabbing-abklatschen-clichage.html (accessed 3 March 2025).

[8]That bibliographers had made fixed assumptions about printers' working practices was the central argument of D. F. McKenzie, 'Printers of the Mind: Some Notes on Bibliographical Theories and Printing-House Practices,' *Studies in Bibliography* 22 (1969): 1–75.

aids are available. Through machine learning – a family of methods in which computers are taught to detect features within training data that they then may be able to detect in fresh data – illustrations can be extracted from their surroundings (see Figure 3.5).

Other methods can match printed impressions apparently printed from the same block, yielding a history of its working life (see Figure 3.6).

Figure 3.5 Object detection of illustrations in chapbooks printed in Scotland (Dutta, Bergel and Zisserman 2021).

Figure 3.6 Block impressions of chapbooks, matched using VGG Visual Search Engine (VISE) software (Dutta, Arandjelović and Zisserman 2021).

The Printing Surface in the Age of Digital Reproduction

Unlike the broader task of image classification with which most visual AI is concerned, the software tool (VGG VISE) that generated the above gallery of matches does not employ training data: instead, images are matched by counting the number of spatially consistent geometric features within an image, ideally one that contains a high degree of visual texture or contrast, as is typical of black-and-white woodcut illustrations on paper (see Figure 3.7).

While the block matches such as the above are statistically demarcated, their lower bounds are set by an arbitrary threshold of difference defined – as with Davis's analogy of a metal rod – by the researcher who must take into account the exigencies of blockmaking and presswork, the historical materialities of paper, ink and blocks, and the latter-day

Figure 3.7 A timeline of broadside ballad block impressions, as seen by computer vision, accessible at https://www.robots.ox.ac.uk/~vgg/demo/ballads/ (Chung et al, 2014). This sequence is also visualized as an animation, controllable by scrubbing across the stack of registered images with a mouse pointer, at https://www.robots.ox.ac.uk/~vgg/demo/ballads/history/comp7.html.

materialities of digital imaging. We seek to reverse the printing process in order to isolate the bare block from the mediating layers of ink and presswork: the block is the 'signal', to borrow the foundational distinction in information theory made by Claude Shannon, while the medium through which it is reproduced is considered as 'noise' (Shannon 1948). While this bifurcation admittedly erases the materiality of presswork and the phenomenal effect of the impression, it does allow an archaeological reconstruction of a particular stratum of printing history – the one that included the block on the press prior to and during its printing.

While we consider the block as uniform across impressions, this uniformity, as with all matter in motion, is only relative. Blocks may have been deliberately altered: wood is also prone to cracking, warping, incidental damage, or consumption by woodworms (Hedges 2013). Such signs of entropy (which are in fact signs of life) can be exploited to generate timelines, in which the loss of ink is used as a proxy for the loss of the block's printable surface area.

This woodblock was heavily used over three decades: its deterioration provides a skeletal publishing history of the typically undated broadside ballads on which it appears. Each ballad may contain a number of woodcuts: each possesses its own timelines, and all intersect at the point of impression, in variable conditions at that time. The sequence has been computationally inferred from the images, but the captions providing date ranges (if known) are taken from external evidence, namely the conjectured dates in business of the printers and publisher.

The external dating is both a challenge to and a constraint around the visual analysis. On the one hand, histories of block decay can be used to refine an externally sourced publication date, particularly when multiple blocks have been set within a single form. On the other hand, a purely visually conjectured timeline needs to be viewed with an awareness of a wider set of material considerations than may be immediately apparent. Publication dating by block damage rests on the assumption that the history of a block is always one of relentless decay. But blocks can be divided or combined, sections can be cut out and plugged, and broken lines (particularly those framing the block, which are particularly liable to wear) can be repaired or replaced. The clarity of the impression itself may vary due to uneven inking, the dampness of the paper, the quality of the presswork or any other natural variance.

The fact that the date ranges are not continuous with the order of the impressions tellingly reveals the complexity of this matrix of impressions. In the case of Impressions 16 and 628, we can see that each belongs to what appears to be the same ballad, as is consistent with their date ranges but not their position in the visual sequence.

The two sheets in Figures 3.8 and 3.9 appear to be identical, but some differences can be seen when the sheets are digitally superimposed. (See Figure 3.10)

This method of digital registration and overlay follows on from earlier, optical and mechanical 'collators' devised by twentieth-century bibliographers, which are still in use alongside software collators (Smith 2000). As can be seen in the ImageCompare application shown above, the third block from the left is not quite the same across both sheets: the position of the first two blocks and that of the printers' imprint have shifted

The Printing Surface in the Age of Digital Reproduction

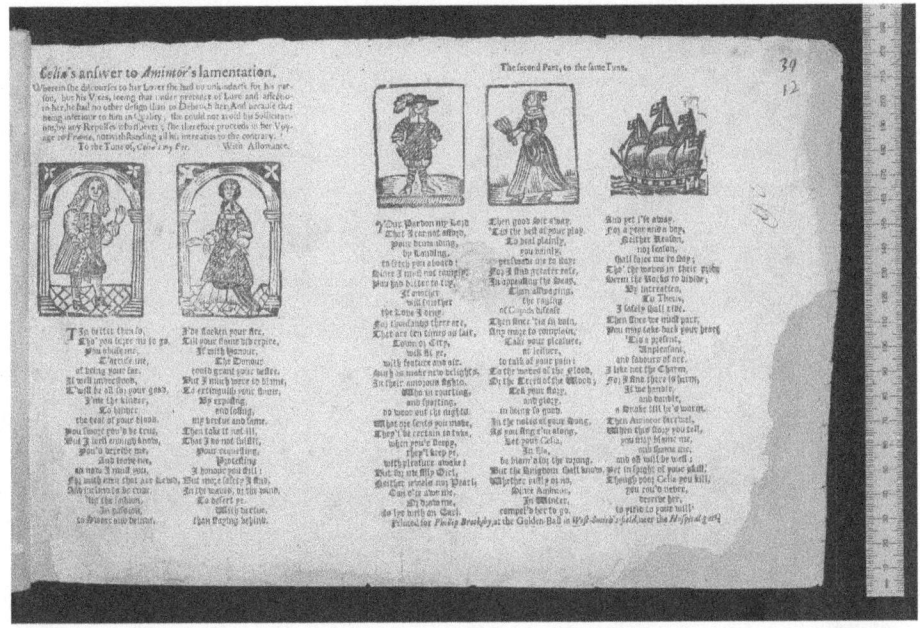

Figure 3.8 Impression 16, highlighted on 40 Rawlinson 566, fol. 12r.

Figure 3.9 Impression 628, as shown in Figure 3.7, highlighted on Bodleian Douce Ballads 1, fol. 22r.

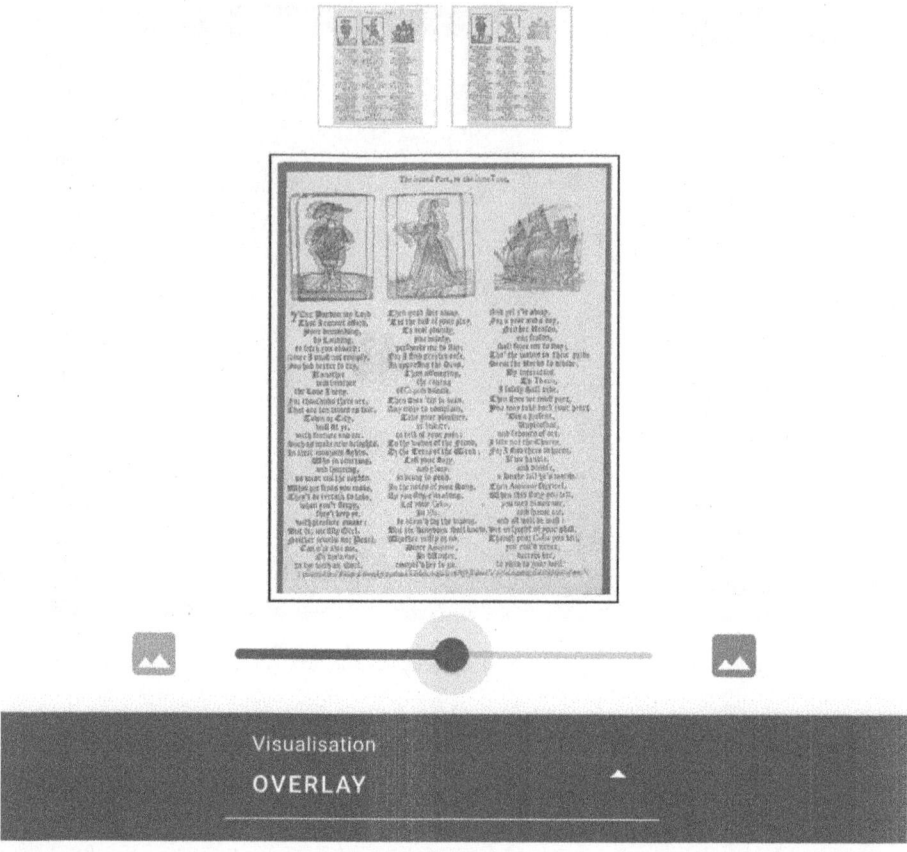

Figure 3.10 An overlay visualization of details of Figures 3.8 and 3.9 in the VGG Image Compare software collator. Prasanna Sridhar, Abhishek Dutta and Andrew Zisserman, VGG Image Compare. https://gitlab.com/vgg/image-compare.

somewhat in the form. Classical bibliography would tend to consider these sheets to be separate states within the same edition or, if the publication dates are known, to also be separate issues (Tanselle 1975). The latter of these two ballads was probably printed from type kept standing between print runs: prohibited by earlier printing ordinances in order to protect typesetters' labour, it was scarcely economical for books composed of many multiple forms, but it could evidently be justified for short ballads for which there was a reliable market; the use of standing type may therefore be an indication that this ballad was popular (Atkinson 2021). Damage to the block under examination might lead one to think that some time had passed between the two impressions, but damage such as warping and cracking can occur between as well as within print runs. At the least, the inferred condition of the blocks does positively indicate the order in which the two sheets were printed: this justifies the conjectured sequencing of the gallery of impressions as a whole. (See Figure 3.11)

Figure 3.11 Details of Figures 3.8 and 3.9. Note in particular the progressive damage to the bottom frame of the Figure 3.8 woodcut.

All of the methods that this article has described depend on digital imaging, perhaps the most revolutionary but underappreciated bibliographical advance of the last several decades. Preceded by the establishment of in-house imaging studios in libraries and by the funding of large-scale digitization projects, most special collections 'reading rooms' are now ad hoc picture studios (Dunning 2011; Wakelin 2021). The result is that more people can now see a broadside ballad than ever could in their heyday.

Digital photography has been joined by more advanced imaging modes such as hyperspectral and CT imaging, analytical methods based in image processing, and computer vision.[9] While it is not the case that computers can 'see' more deeply than humans, their bandwidth and memory can help us to see more broadly and consistently.

---

[9] On imaging, see, for example, Edward Potten, 'Dating the Rylands Apocalypse Wood-block: John Bagford and the Earliest Facsimiles of blockbooks,' *Journal of the Printing Historical Society* Third Series, 3 (2022), 14–46; Jana Dambrogio, Amanda Ghassaei, Daniel Starza Smith, Holly Jackson, Martin L. Demaine, Graham Davis, David Mills, Rebekah Ahrendt, Nadine Akkerman, David van der Linden and Erik D. Demaine, 'Unlocking History Through Automated Virtual Unfolding of Sealed Documents Imaged by X-ray Microtomography,' *Nature Communications* 12, no. 1184 (2021): 1–10; Federica Nicolardi, Stephen Parsons et al., 'Revealing Text from a Still-rolled Herculaneum Papyrus Scroll (PHerc. Paris. 4),' *Zeitschrift für Papyrologie und Epigraphik* 229 (2024): 1–13. Beyond block matching, the identification of recurring pieces of type demonstrates computer vision's aptitude for precise recall – see, for example, Christopher Warren, Avery Wiscomb, Pierce Williams, Samuel V. Lemley and Max G'Sell, 'Canst Thou Draw Out Leviathan with Computational Bibliography? New Angles on Printing Thomas Hobbes' Ornaments' Edition,' *Eighteenth-Century Studies* 54, no. 4 (2021): 827–59.

Many methods within the digital humanities are routinely criticized for merely automating rote tasks rather than providing qualitatively new insights, but analyses such as the above exercise in matching and sequencing impressions can *only* be done with computers, which, if nothing else, are good at storing and retrieving data.

The enhanced visibility of historical books has naturally turned our attention to their less visible aspects. These include the book's interface: its tactile dimensions and histories of ownership and use – an anthropological approach invoked in literary studies under the header of the 'material text'.[10] Textual materialism has been one of the main ways in which book history has been integrated into literary studies of, in particular, the early modern period, when printers' ledgers and publishers' archives are vanishingly scarce (at least in English), and book historians must largely rely on the book alone to account for itself. Early modern material-textualists have drawn attention to typography as, following Donald McKenzie, a means of 'making meaning', and to the interface and affect of the codex and other handheld formats – affordances that digitizations generally fail to communicate. The banner of the material text in this context is a kind of formal poetics: it somewhat resembles New Criticism but is informed by classical bibliography and graphic design, engendered in an age in which almost anyone can choose and manipulate type and page layout on-screen, even if the affordances of digital typography are no less materially bounded than the handpress printer's forme.

The framework of textual materialism can be usefully applied to the digitization of printing surfaces themselves. Digitization normally aims to capture the face of the block on which the design is cut, but this printable surface area can be difficult to capture, as both the relief and the supporting area are often darkened from ink and age. It helps to be able to print from the block, issues of conservation permitting, or else a three-dimensional depth map of the printing face of the block can capture the designed relief with some precision, from which a virtual offprint can be made (Bergel, Franklin and Harris, forthcoming). If standardized, this depth capture would permit the computational matching of undocumented blocks (of which there are many) with their printed impressions. A facsimile generated by a 3D printer could also be made (Hancher 2019), but the simpler and cheaper method of photo-etching (a successor to stereotype) may serve just as well, albeit it will not be as winningly punning as the act of 'printing' a printing surface. A digitization that is cognizant of textual materialism might, however, image not just the block's printing surface but also its back and sides – six faces in all. The reverse and sides of a block may include makers' or owners' marks, trial block designs, shims to raise up the block to type height and other artefacts of the block's material history. This panoptic materialism, analogous in some ways to the

---

[10] The term 'material text' seems to have been introduced, in distinction to a 'linguistic text', in Peter Shillingsburg, 'Text as Matter, Concept, and Action,' *Studies in Bibliography* 44 (1991): 31–82. Exemplary work includes the Material Texts series from Penn Press: see https://site.pennpress.org/material-texts-2021/material-texts/ (accessed 3 March 2025).

relief depictions of blocks in the *Encyclopédie*, may make a case for photogrammetric capture, which produces three-dimensional facsimiles showing all faces. While useful as documentation, such lustrous facsimiles are also reverential re-enchantments of the original: their weakness is that the state-of-the art of artificial shading and capture technologies is somewhat ephemeral. An arguably more informative imaging mode is Reflectance Transformation Imaging (RTI), which employs a lighting dome to capture a hemispheric, dynamically illuminated view of an object, which the following (non-interactive) image can only hint at. (See Figure 3.12)

RTI's specular enhancement mode, combined with the viewer software's interface in which the angle of light can be arbitrarily changed, provides a powerful simulation of turning a block in hand against the light: tool-marks are sharply revealed against the natural wood grain and tactility is almost made visible. We rarely know the names of makers of blocks, but these tool-marks are sometimes idiosyncratic, revealing the inferred dimensions of cutters' tools, methods or habits, such as their preference (or not) for clearing – Bewick for one is famously indifferent towards the the sub-surface under

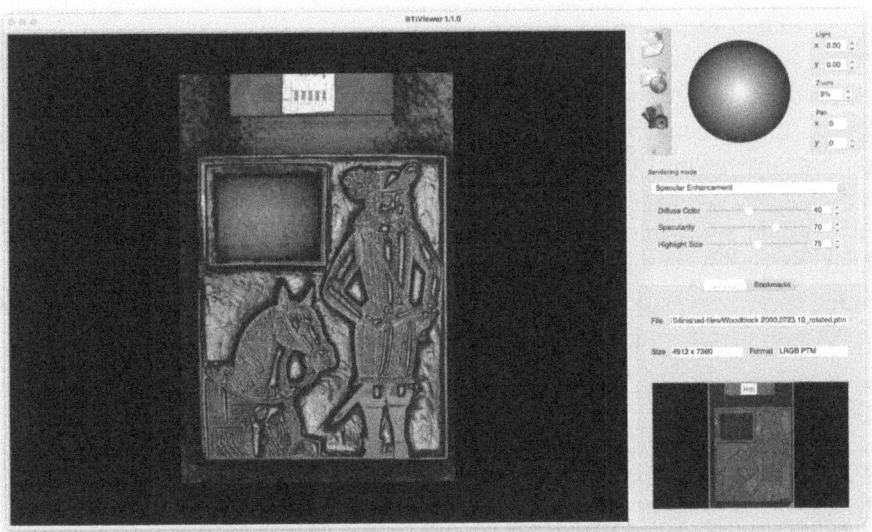

Figure 3.12 RTI capture of a Newcastle ballad-printer's woodblock, now in the British Museum. The block was owned and used by John White and his successors, now catalogued at https://www.britishmuseum.org/collection/object/P_2000-0723-10 (accessed 3 March 2025). It can be seen in use on several ballads, including *The Life and Death of the Duke of Berwick*, printed in Newcastle by John White, available at https://ebba.english.ucsb.edu/ballad/31056/album (accessed 3 March 2025). I am grateful to Sheila O'Connell, David Saunders and their colleagues at the British Museum for the RTI imaging work.

his design; other makers will almost devoutly clear and level the spaces that do not print and which, in most cases, only the printer will see.[11]

A strict textual materialist would object that digital mediations can never replace the original, and this is undeniably true: the proper function of a digital representation such as an image or a cloud of spatial coordinates is not so much to replace the object of interest but rather to provide a viewpoint on it. If done reflectively, appraising a digital facsimile can make us think about what it misses. Digital cataloguers can and do foreground many of the transformations of scale, lighting, tone and affect that photography introduces: digitization can and should therefore show its own workings, and by so doing can allow us to understand the affordances of digitization as well as its object.[12] The commonplace distinction between 'digital' and 'physical' copies of a book or other object is an important one but should turn our attention towards the materiality of the digital itself, including such entirely physical parameters of digital imaging as studio lighting, resolutions, file formats, and the professional and personal contexts of those taking the pictures. It is perhaps revealing of our moment that we lack a generally agreed term for the binary opposite of 'the digital', as is the habit of foregrounding the term 'digital' in any context where it's likely now the norm, such as photography. 'Digital' as a qualifier is unlikely to age particularly well.

Old media can teach us about new media, too. Book history's founding insistence on attending to the industrial economy of the book as closely as literary and textual scholars do for the 'message' and bibliographers for the 'medium' is a natural partner of the digital humanities and cognate fields such as media, communication and software studies. Sometimes narrowly conceived, the digital humanities are not just about humans making things with computers but also critically reflecting on how using computing remakes us (a dialectic that is also at the heart of book and media history); then it would seem important to look for the motives, mechanisms and histories behind the surface of technology. Just as books are made with blocks and type, on printing presses, by skilled operators, software too has a history and a socio-technical environment within which it is executed. Critics of AI as conceived of at the time of

---

[11]For reproductions of Bewick blocks and a discussion of the importance of press-work in determining results, see Graham Moss, *Thomas Bewick, Engraver and the Performance of Woodblocks* (Charing: Florin Press, 2021).
[12]Critical and historical work on both digital editions and mass digitization projects has foregrounded many of these materialities of the digital: see, for example, Alan Galey, 'The Enkindling Reciter: E-Books in the Bibliographical Imagination,' *Book History* 15 (2012): 210–47; Martin Paul Eve, 'You Have to Keep Track of Your Changes': The Version Variants and Publishing History of David Mitchell's Cloud Atlas's, *Open Library of Humanities* 2, no. 2 (2016): 1–34; Bonnie Mak, 'Archaeology of a Digitization,' *Journal of the Association for Information Science and Technology* 65, no. 8 (2014): 1515–26; Zachary Lesser and Whitney Trettien, 'Material / Digital,' in *Shakespeare / Text: Contemporary Readings in Textual Studies, Editing and Performance*, ed. Claire M. L. Bourne (London: The Arden Shakespeare, 2021), 402–23; and Whitney Trettien, 'The History of the Early Modern Book in the Digital Age,' in *The Oxford Handbook of the History of the Book in Early Modern England*, ed. Adam Smyth, Oxford Handbooks (2023; online edn, Oxford Academic, 18 September 2023). https://doi.org/10.1093/oxfordhb/9780198846239.013.25 (accessed 19 February 2025) and Ryan Cordell, '"Q i-tjb the Raven": Taking Dirty OCR Seriously,' *Book History* 20 (2017): 188–225.

writing have repeatedly shown how machine learning models are essentially compact indexes of training data, exhibiting all the biases intrinsic to the creation and selection of that data and requiring scrutiny towards how – and by who – that data was gathered (Devlin 2023; Gebru et al. 2021; Crawford and Paglen 2021). Artificial intelligence should properly be understood not in terms of models of thought but as a form of reproductive media, like printing.

Analogies between print and digital technology are commonplace, particularly as a prophecy of revolutionary change (Graham 2016): computers, or the Internet or AI are, we are told, the most disruptive developments since 'the invention' (tellingly and incorrectly singular) of 'the printing press' (also singular). Book history spends a lot of its time arguing otherwise – about the press and increasingly also the computer. As embodiments of labour, web pages or algorithms embedded in software are no less physical than printers' woodblocks, whose materiality unquestionably exists behind the scenes of the images they generate. Websites are built and break no less than blocks and printing presses, or as Friedrich Kittler and John Johnston argued, 'There is no software.'[13] A simple opposition between 'the digital' and the physical – or data and its support – similarly can't fail to define the digital as both secondary to and separate from the real world rather than as a concrete expression of human agency.

The gambit of textual materialism – that no two books are ever quite the same, either by design or from use, and that no facsimiles can quite capture the essence of their original source – in one sense reifies this distinction, but it is wholly congruent with a Kittlerian materialism, that the text cannot be distinguished from its support, perhaps even its environment. The text – or information, or data, or the message – is at best a social convention that allows us all to be literally on the same page as readers of what we agree to consider 'the same' book. Information overload, a supposed pathology of our age that book historians have taught us can be found in earlier ages (Blair 2010), also has information entropy as its materialist counterpart. Texts fall apart: reproductions merely take us farther away from an increasingly attenuated signal, and reading is not so much communication as it is conjectural restoration. While this pessimism makes both psychological and historical sense, it is somewhat one-dimensional as a theory of communications, focusing solely on what we can take from texts to the exclusion of what we can make from them.

We are, then, in a world of entanglement in which matter and meaning appear to intersect as much as do the things we make and that we are. Digital and other reproductions are not trade-offs between text and matter in which 'aura' is only ever diminished: reproduction is additive.[14] It is true that the bargain that Batchelar struck with Hone traded the irreducible original for a modern copy, but his stereotypes were at

---

[13] Kittler's point was that code is materially instantiated at all times – 'signifiers of voltage differences,' running on hardware: Friedrich A. Kittler and John Johnston. 'There Is No Software,' in *Literature, Media, Information Systems* (Abingdon: Routledge, 2013), 147–55.
[14] I take Benjamin's main meaning of 'aura' to be the artwork's traceable provenance.

least as good as Hone's woodblocks – or actually better, more durable and able in theory to illustrate new sheets, while Hone's antiquarian stewardship of the originals, along with his learned and loving commentary, sustains and magnifies their traditional value. This should inspire hope that other bargains might be struck between the book's matter and its message, as between agents of change like Hone and the vital forms of life that both he and Batchelar preserved and cherished.

Bibliography

Atkinson, David. 'Ballad and Street Literature Printing in Petticoat Lane, 1740s–1760s'. *Traditiones* 47, no. 2 (October 2018): 105–15.

Atkinson, David. 'Licenced and Entered According to Order: A Ballad and Chapbook Conundrum'. *Publishing History* 85 (2021).

Atkinson, David. 'Standing Type in Dicey/Marshall Issues of The Berkshire Tragedy'. *The Library* 21, no. 2 (2020): 216–25.

Atkinson, David. 'Was There Really a "Mass Extinction of Old Ballads" in the Romantic Period?' In *Street Ballads in Nineteenth-Century Britain, Ireland, and North America*, 19–36. Abingson: Routledge, 2016.

Bain, Ian. 'Thomas Bewick and His Contemporaries'. In *Maps and Prints: Aspects of the English Book Trade*. Edited by Robin Myers and Michael Harris. Oxford: Publishing Pathways, 1984.

Bergel, Giles, Alexandra Franklin and Stephen Harris. 'Rediscovering Copper Plates in the Bodleian Libraries'. In *Printing Things: Blocks, Plates and Other Printing Surfaces, 1400–1900*. Edited by Elizabeth Savage and Femke Speelberg. Oxford: Oxford University Press, 2024.

Bevan, Iain. 'Scottish Chapbooks, Their Woodcuts and Transient Print'. In *Transient Print: Essays on the History of Printed Ephemera*. Edited by Lisa Peters and Elaine Jackson. Lausanne: Peter Lang, 2023.

Blagden, Cyprian. 'Notes on the Ballad Market in the Second Half of the Seventeenth Century'. *Studies in Bibliography* 6 (1954): 161–180.

Blair, Anne M, *Too much to know: Managing scholarly information before the modern age*. New Haven: Yale University Press, 2010.

Boswell, James. *Boswell's London Journal 1762–1763*. Edited by Frederick A. Pottle. Edinburgh: Edinburgh University Press, 1991.

Bowers, Rick. 'Parody, Performance and Self-Defence: William Hone's Ancient Mysteries Described (1823)'. *English Studies* 94, no. 1 (2013): 42–56.

Cerón, Mercedes. 'Wood-Engravings from the Collection of Francis Douce at the Ashmolean Museum'. In *Burning Bright: Essays in Honour of David Bindman*, London: UCL Press, 224–233. 2015.

Chatto, William Andrew. *A Treatise on Wood Engraving, Historical and Practical*. London: Charles Knight, 1839.

Chung, Joon Son, Relja Arandjelović, Giles Bergel, Alexandra Franklin, and Andrew Zisserman. 'Re-presentations of art collections'. In *Computer Vision-ECCV 2014 Workshops: Zurich, Switzerland, September 6-7 and 12, 2014, Proceedings, Part I 13*, pp. 85-100. Springer International Publishing, 2015.

Connell, Philip. 'Bibliomania: Book Collecting, Cultural Politics, and the Rise of Literary Heritage in Romantic Britain'. *Representations* 71 (2000): 24–47.

Cordell, Ryan. '"Q i-tjb the Raven": Taking Dirty OCR Seriously'. *Book History* 20 (2017): 188–225.

Crawford, Kate and Trevor Paglen. 'Excavating AI: The Politics of Images in Machine Learning Training Sets'. *AI & Society* 36, no. 4 (2021): 1105–1116.

Dambrogio, Jana, Amanda Ghassaei, Daniel Starza Smith, Holly Jackson, Martin L. Demaine, Graham Davis, David Mills, et al., 'Unlocking History Through Automated Virtual Unfolding of Sealed Documents Imaged by X-ray Microtomography'. *Nature Communications* 12, no. 1184 (2021). https://doi.org/10.1038/s41467-021-21326-w.

Davis, Tom. 'The Epic of Bibliography: Alexander Pope and Textual Criticism'. *Text* 6 (1995).

DeFreitas, Leo John. *Newcastle Chapbooks, Broadsides, and Garlands: A Study of the Collection of Woodblocks in McGill University Library, Rare Books and Special Collections*, in *Printers, Pedlars, Sailors and Nuns: Aspects of Street Literature*, 88–102. Edited by David Atkinson and Steve Roud. London: The Ballad Partners, 2019.

Devlin, Kate. 'Power in AI: Inequality Within and Without the Algorithm'. In *The Handbook of Gender, Communication, and Women's Human Rights*, 123–139. Edited by Margaret Gallagher and Aimee Vega Montiel. Hoboken: John Wiley & Sons, 2023.

Dugaw, Dianne. 'The Popular Marketing of "Old Ballads": The Ballad Revival and Eighteenth-Century Antiquarianism Reconsidered'. *Eighteenth-Century Studies* 21, no. 1 (1987): 71–90.

Dunning, Alastair. 'List of Digitisation Projects Funded under the UK's AHRC Resource Enhancement Scheme', 2011. http://eprints.rclis.org/17517/.

Dutta, Abhishek, Giles Bergel and Andrew Zisserman. 'Visual Analysis of Chapbooks Printed in Scotland'. In *Proceedings of the 6th International Workshop on Historical Document Imaging and Processing*, Lausanne, Switzerland, 4–6 September 2021. New York: ACM, 2021. https://doi.org/10.1145/3476887.3476893.

Eisenstein, Elizabeth. *The Printing Press as an Agent of Change*. Cambridge: Cambridge University Press, 1979.

The Encyclopedia of Diderot & d'Alembert Collaborative Translation Project. Michigan Publishing, University of Michigan Library, 2010. http://hdl.handle.net/2027/spo.did2222.0001.502 (accessed 5 November 2024).

Eve, Martin Paul. '"You Have to Keep Track of Your Changes": The Version Variants and Publishing History of David Mitchell's *Cloud Atlas*'. *Open Library of Humanities* 2, no. 2 (2016): 1–34.

Feather, John. *Publishing, Piracy and Politics: An Historical Study of Copyright in Britain*. London: Mansell, 1994.

Ferris, Ina. *Book-Men, Book Clubs, and the Romantic Literary Sphere*. Basingstoke: Palgrave, 2015.

Finkelstein, David and Alistair Nash, eds. *The British Publishing Industry in the Nineteenth Century*, 3 vols. Abingdon: Routledge, 2024.

Galey, Alan. 'The Enkindling Reciter: E-Books in the Bibliographical Imagination'. *Book History* 15 (2012): 210–47.

Gebru, Timnit, Jamie Morgenstern, Briana Vecchione, Jennifer Wortman Vaughan, Hanna Wallach, Hal Daumé III and Kate Crawford. 'Datasheets for Datasets'. *Communications of the ACM* 64, no. 12 (2021): 86–92.

Graham, Elyse. 'The Printing Press as Metaphor'. *Digital Humanities Quarterly* 10, no. 3 (2016). https://www.digitalhumanities.org/dhq/vol/10/3/000264/000264.html (accessed 5 November 2024).

Grimes, K. 'Before the Trials: William Hone and the Rise of the Watchdog Press'. *English Studies* 103, no. 8 (2022): 1178–90.

Grimes, K. *Hone Bio-Text: A Biography, Bibliography and e-text archive*. https://honearchive.org (accessed 21 February 2025).

Groom, Nick. *The Making of Percy's 'Reliques'*. Oxfofd: Oxford University Press, 1999.

Hancher, Michael, Donald T. Luce, Colin McFadden and Samantha T. Porter. 'Two- and Three-Dimensional Representations of Thomas Bewick Woodblocks'. 2019, https://doi.org/10.13020/hw8q-c585.

Hedges, S. B. 'Wormholes Record Species History in Space and Time'. *Biology letters* 9, no. 1 (2013): 20120926.

Hodgson, Thomas. *An Essay on the Origin and Progress of Stereotype Printing; Including a Description of the Various Processes*. Newcastle: Printed by and for S. Hodgson, 1820.

Hone, William. *Ancient Mysteries Described, Especially the English Miracle Plays, Founded on Apocryphal New Testament Story*. London: Printed for William Hone, 1823. https://hdl.handle.net/2027/wu.89101414100?urlappend=%3Bseq=112%3Bownerid=13510798900588801-116.

Hone, William. *The Every-Day Book; or, the Guide to the Year*, vol. 1. London, 1825.

Hone, William. *Facetiae and Miscellanies With One Hundred and Twenty Engravings, Drawn by George Cruikshank*. London: Hunt & Clarke, printed by: J. M'Creery et. al. 1827.

Hunter, David. 'Copyright Protection for Engravings and Maps in Eighteenth-Century Britain'. *The Library*, sixth series, 9, no. 1 (1987): 128–47.

Ivins, Jr., W. M. *How Prints Look: Photographs with a Commentary*. New York: Metropolitan Museum of Art, 1943.

Ivins, Jr., W. M. *Prints and Visual Communication*. Abingdon: Routledge and Kegan Paul, 1953.

Jardine, Lisa and Anthony Grafton. '"Studied for Action": How Gabriel Harvey Read His Livy'. *Past & Present* 129 (1990): 30–78.

Klancher, Jon. 'Wild Bibliography: The Rise and Fall of Book History in Nineteenth-Century Britain'. In *Bookish Histories*. Edited by Ina Ferris and Paul Keen. Palgrave Macmillan, 2009.

Kittler, Friedrich A. and John Johnston. 'There Is No Software'. In *Literature, Media, Information Systems*, 147–55. Routledge, 2013.

Lin, Tsung-Yi et al. 'Microsoft COCO: Common Objects in Context'. In *Computer Vision–ECCV 2014: 13th European Conference, Zurich, Switzerland, September 6-12, 2014, Proceedings, Part V* 13. Springer International Publishing, 2014.

Mak, Bonnie. 'Archaeology of a Digitization'. *Journal of the Association for Information Science and Technology* 65, no. 8 (2024): 1126–515.

Marsh, Christopher. 'Best-Selling Ballads and Their Pictures in Seventeenth-Century England'. *Past & Present* 233, no. 1 (2016): 53–99. https://doi.org/10.1093/pastj/gtw039.

McElligott, Jason. 'William Hone (1780–1842), Print-Culture, and the Nature of Radicalism'. In *Varieties of Seventeenth- and Early Eighteenth-Century English Radicalism in Context*, 241–60. Routledge, 2016.

McKenzie, D. F. 'Printers of the Mind: Some Notes on Bibliographical Theories and Printing-House Practices'. *Studies in Bibliography* 22 (1969): 1–75.

Mosley, James. 'Dabbing, Abklatschen, Clichage'. *Journal of the Printing Historical Society*, new series, 23 (2015).

Moss, Graham. *Thomas Bewick, Engraver & the Performance of Woodblocks*. Ashford: Florin Press, 2021.

Mullan, John and Christopher Reid, eds. *Eighteenth-Century Popular Culture: A Selection*. Oxford: Oxford University Press, 2000.

Nicolardi, Federica, Stephen Parsons, et al. 'Revealing Text from a Still-rolled Herculaneum Papyrus Scroll (PHerc. Paris. 4)'. *Zeitschrift für Papyrologie und Epigraphik* 229 (2024): 1–13.

Potten, Edward. 'Dating the Rylands Apocalypse Wood-block: John Bagford and the Earliest Facsimiles of Blockbooks'. *Journal of the Printing Historical Society*, third series, 3 (2022): 14–46.

Robinson, J. W. 'Regency Radicalism and Antiquarianism: William Hone's Ancient Mysteries Described (1823)'. *Leeds Studies in English* (1978): 121–44.

Rogers, Pat. *Literature and Popular Culture in Eighteenth-Century England*. Brighton: Harvester Press, 1985.
Raven, James. *The Business of Books*. New Haven: Yale University Press, 2007.
Raven, James. 'The Book as a Commodity'. In *The Cambridge History of the Book in Britain*, 83–117. Edited by Michael F. Suarez and Michael L. Turner. Cambridge: Cambridge University Press, 2009.
Savage, Elizabeth and Femke Speelberg, eds. *Printing Things: Blocks, Plates, and Other Objects that Printed, 1400–1900*. Oxford: Oxford University Press, forthcoming.
Schuster, Kristen M. and Sarah L. Gillis, 'Digital Humanities and Image Metadata: Improving Access Through Shared Practices'. In *Digital Humanities, Libraries, and Partnerships*, 107–23. Edited by Cheryl LaGuardia. Hull: Chandos Publishing, 2018.
Shannon, Claude E. 'A Mathematical Theory of Communication'. *The Bell System Technical Journal* 27, no. 3 (1948): 379–423.
Shepard, L. *John Pitts: Ballad Printer*, 63–4. London: Private Libraries Association; Detroit: Singing Tree Press, 1969.
Shillingsburg, Peter L. 'Text as Matter, Concept, and Action'. *Studies in Bibliography* 44 (1991): 31–82. https://site.pennpress.org/material-texts-2021/material-texts/ (accessed 5 November 2024).
Smith, Steven Escar. 'The Eternal Verities Verified: Charlton Hinman and the Roots of Mechanical Collation', *Studies in Bibliography* 53 (2000): 129–61.
St. Clair, William. *The Reading Nation in the Romantic Period*. Cambridge: Cambridge University Press, 2004.
Stoker, David. 'Another Look at the Dicey-Marshall Publications: 1736–1806'. *Library* 15, no. 2 (2014): 111–57.
Tanselle, G. Thomas. 'The Bibliographical Concepts of "Issue" and "State"'. *The Papers of the Bibliographical Society of America* 69, no. 1 (1975): 17–66.
Tattersfield, Nigel. *The Complete Illustrative Work of Thomas Bewick*. London: The British Library, The Bibliographical Society, Oak Knoll Press, 2011.
Thomson, R. S. 'Publisher's Introduction: Madden Ballads from Cambridge University Library'. Gale, 1987.
Uglow, Jennifer S. *Nature's Engraver: A Life of Thomas Bewick*. Chicago: University of Chicago Press, 2009.
Vetusta Monumenta, 1747–1906. Society of Antiquaries of London. http://vetustamonumenta.org.
Wakelin, Daniel. 'A New Age of Photography: 'DIY Digitization' in Manuscript Studies'. *Anglia* 139, no. 1 (2021): 71–93.
Warren, Christopher N., Avery Wiscomb, Pierce Williams, Samuel V. Lemley and Max G'Sell. 'Canst Thou Draw Out Leviathan with Computational Bibliography? New Angles on Printing Thomas Hobbes' Ornaments Edition'. *Eighteenth-Century Studies* 54, no. 4 (2021): 827–59.

Software

Abhishek Dutta, Joon Son Chung, and Andrew Zisserman, Traherne Digital Collator https://www.robots.ox.ac.uk/~vgg/software/traherne/https://www.robots.ox.ac.uk/~vgg/software/traherne/ and James P. Ascher and DeVan Ard, Pocket Hinman: https://pockethinman.net.
Prasanna Sridhar, Abhishek Dutta and Andrew Zisserman, VGG Image Compare. https://gitlab.com/vgg/image-compare.
Abhishek Dutta, Relja Arandjelović, and Andrew Zisserman. 2021. VGG Image Search Engine. https://www.robots.ox.ac.uk/~vgg/software/vise/.

Online Resources

Abhishek Dutta, Giles Bergel, and Andrew Zisserman, Visual Analysis of Chapbooks Printed in Scotland, https://www.robots.ox.ac.uk/~vgg/research/chapbooks/ for demos, data, code and documentation of both the chapbooks illustration detection and the visual matching tasks.

English Broadside Ballad Archive. https://ebba.english.ucsb.edu.

Léa Constantin, Pieces of Art: a Collection of engraved woodblocks, Rare Books and Special Collections at McGill. News, Acquisitions and Special Projects. https://blogs.library.mcgill.ca/rbsc/pieces-of-art-a-collection-of-engraved-woodblocks.

Taylor Berg-Kirkpatrick, Max G'Sell, Christopher N. Warren et. al, Print and Probability. https://printprobability.org/.

CHAPTER 4
FROM BOOKSHELVES TO BYTES
NAVIGATING THE DIGITAL TRANSFORMATION OF WRITERS' LIBRARIES

Anke Jaspers and Martina Schönbächler

Over the past two decades, an increasing number of digital editions of writers' libraries have been conceptualized and created. This chapter outlines the principal aspects of both the productivity and the challenges associated with such digital editions, while also recommending best practices that may serve as a foundation for further scholarly discourse.

The aims and characteristics of an edition extend beyond conventional archival and library practices. Besides the description, presentation and accessibility of a collection, editorial work also involves scholarly interpretation, selection, categorization, and contextualization of the material. The distinction between digital archives and digital editions, however, remains ambiguous (Van Hulle 2023), as every act of archiving requires a conceptual framework and a categorization of the material. Contemporary IT systems have reached a high level of sophistication, enabling the structuring, enrichment, and extensive interlinking of data, thereby facilitating their utilization or further development for editorial purposes, namely, the establishment of new data and the meaningful interconnection of existing datasets. Nevertheless, editions are ultimately shaped by practical, institutional, and scholarly objectives that differ from those of archives and libraries.

Editions of writers' libraries often originate from long-term, third-party-funded cooperative projects involving literary scholars, librarians, archivists, information designers, software developers, digital humanities specialists, and other experts. The diverse interests and differing conceptualizations of a 'digitized library' among the stakeholders involved, combined with the unique characteristics of each private library, necessitate that each member of a project team engages intensively with one another and with the experiences of others to shape their own edition. Consequently, the study and management of writers' libraries constitute a well-connected, transnationally active field that continues to thrive in both book history and literary criticism (see, e.g. Spedding and Tankard 2021). Despite, or perhaps owing to, this openness to experimentation and discussion, there remains a lack of comparative studies that would advance a better understanding of writers' libraries and their mechanisms as objects of research. Similarly, the digital projects dedicated to writers' libraries cannot yet be technically connected in ways that would allow their critical potential to be fully realized. However, in addition to a mindset facilitating the exchange among practitioners, scholarly experts, and institutional stakeholders, overarching institutional structures and financial resources would be essential prerequisites for compiling a critical inventory of existing editions, identifying best practices and developing international standards for the cataloging and digitization or the digital reconstruction of writers' libraries.

Catalogs of private libraries have a long tradition, traceable to the late Middle Ages. Most private libraries were not preserved; instead, like early modern scholars' libraries, they were typically dispersed through auctions shortly after their owners' deaths (Loh [1995–2017]). The auction catalogs produced for this purpose remain valuable, though often incomplete, sources for the study of writers' libraries. In cases where libraries, such as those of Goethe and Schiller, were preserved, catalogs like card indexes were eventually compiled and published, often with significant delay, for archival, library, and scholarly use. Beginning in the 1980s, technological advancements and the emergence of digital applications for data collection and processing (e.g. Excel, EndNote, and similar tools) led to the increasing establishment of digital databases of varying complexity. Today, Online Public Access Catalogs (OPACs) with different underlying systems have become standard in library services, providing options for searching and filtering metadata as well as linking catalog entries. In the course of this development, online platforms dedicated to writers' libraries have emerged, extending their scope beyond listing books and registering reading traces therein. Prominent examples include *Goethe Bibliothek Online*,[1] a digital (meta-)catalog of the 'extant' and the 'virtual' library (see below), with links to visualizations and to connecting collections; *Ludwig Tiecks Bibliothek*[2] or *Beckett Digital Library*,[3] which combines extant volumes from different collections and locations while integrating virtual entries, digital facsimiles, and lists of reading traces as well as links to Beckett's manuscripts; *Thomas Mann Nachlassbibliothek Online*[4] with its catalog, facsimiles, full texts, markup, and transcriptions of reading traces; and *Derrida's Margins*,[5] which edits and visualizes the 'library' of each published work. These examples illustrate the diversity of features and the varying degrees of editorial depth within the field of digital writers' libraries.

The editing of writers' libraries does not fully conform to the principles governing the critical editing of (other) textual sources. Various types of editions have become established for textual sources, differing significantly depending on their purpose and target audience; these range from reading and archival editions to historical-critical and genetic editions, many of which are now also available in digital formats. By contrast, the edition of writers' libraries has not yet been entirely embraced as a core area of textual scholarship (Van Hulle 2022), despite its origins in library and archival sciences *as well as* in scholarly editing (D'Iorio and Ferrer 2001). Beginning with simple listings and card

---

[1] https://opac.lbs-weimar.gbv.de/DB=2/.
[2] https://tieck-bibliothek.univie.ac.at/.
[3] https://www.beckettarchive.org/library/home/welcome.
[4] https://nb-web.tma.ethz.ch.
[5] https://derridas-margins.princeton.edu.

catalogs containing metadata, keywords, and additional information on provenance and reading traces of individual book copies, a spectrum of (proto-)editions or digital archives can be identified, extending to digital catalogs with structured data that facilitate various methods of filtering, networking, and visualization. The most conceptually and technologically advanced forms today incorporate digital facsimiles of book copies, full-text versions of printed materials, the transcription and markup of usage and reading traces according to editorial standards, as well as links to other elements of the *dossier génétique*, or visualization tools (see *Beckett Digital Library, Melville's Marginalia Online*[6] and *Fontanes Handbibliothek*[7]). At present, numerous digital editions of writers' libraries are regarded as model projects in that they represent significant advances in the field; others remain in progress (Hannah Arendt,[8] James Joyce,[9] Friedrich Nietzsche[10]), while a considerable number of projects are still in the planning stages.

With so many projects either completed or underway, it is time to pause and reflect on the productivity of digital editions, to raise awareness of both the challenges encountered and the successful practices established in the editorial process, and to articulate future perspectives on the digital edition of writers' libraries. In this chapter, we present our observations and considerations from the standpoint of two literary scholars in German Studies with expertise in digital humanities. While the advantages and disadvantages of editing a writer's library from the perspective of IT specialists and institutions can only be addressed briefly, it remains crucial to articulate the methodological affordances of undertaking this work in a digital environment. First and foremost, it is essential to clarify what we mean when referring to a writer's library.

A writer's library

For the subject at hand, the following working definition may apply: a writer's library is a collection consolidated under an author's or collective's label, comprising two overlapping yet conceptually distinct components: the 'extant library' (Van Hulle 2022, 77), a material corpus owned, used and read by (usually more than) one empirical person, and the 'virtual library' (Ferrer 2010, 15; Van Hulle 2022, 77), a partially preserved corpus of everything read by that writer or author, which is theoretically never fully reconstructable. This dual corpus can include a broad spectrum of media, ranging from books, journals, typescripts, and manuscripts to various inserts such as bookmarks, letters or newspaper clippings, digital text carriers, audiovisual materials, collectible items, and even the furnishings of library spaces (Wieland 2010).

---

[6] https://melvillesmarginalia.org/.
[7] https://uclab.fh-potsdam.de/ff/.
[8] https://blogs.bard.edu/arendtcollection/.
[9] https://www.uantwerpen.be/en/research-groups/centre-for-manuscript-genetics/projects/joyce-digital-library/.
[10] http://www.nietzschesource.org/.

Regardless of how conservatively or broadly this media spectrum is defined, the concepts of a writer's library are inherently shaped by notions of authorship. Although the English term 'writer's library' (German: 'Autor:innenbibliothek') refers to a person engaged in writing or, within a poststructuralist framework, the writer as a particular momentary entity of a 'scripteur' (Roland Barthes), what is considered a writer's library is closely tied to the concept of an author's (literary) work or œuvre. To put it briefly: what an author constitutes is a work (Spoerhase 2007, 290–93), and whoever is responsible for a work is an author (Lauer et al. 1999, 31 et seq.). Likewise, if an author owns and engages with books, other printed material or additional textual and non-textual media (as outlined above), these collectively form the writer's or author's library.

In archival and library practice, as well as in research, the terms 'writer's library', 'bibliothèque d'écrivain' and 'Autor:innenbibliothek' often remain polyvalent. They refer both to the books on the shelves of writing and publishing individuals and to collections with the character of a work in their own right (Wieland 2010; Werle 2018) like, for instance, the library of Aby Warburg (Raulff 1997). Therefore, research into writers' libraries concerns both the writer as an empirical person and the abstract author.

In German, the frequently used term 'Autorenbibliotheken' (authors' libraries) carries a gendered connotation due to its generic masculine form, referring predominantly to the libraries of men. To address the authorial function of the library itself or the author label under which it is assembled, a term like 'Autor-Bibliothek' (author library) would be more appropriate. Gender – beyond linguistic considerations – as well as other social factors play a constitutive role in the transmission of collections and thus influence what can be studied. The books collected and preserved in 'authors'' archives are remnants of private libraries and their complex 'life stories' (Gleixner et al. 2018). These collections were rarely assembled by individuals alone but rather by groups of people, sorted by descendants, curated by acquiring institutions, and expanded over time by various decision-makers according to shifting criteria (Jaspers 2020). Estate collections attributed with a certain cultural or scholarly significance tend to exert an increasing gravitational force, growing further even after their formal archiving.

As an abstract, material construct with a temporal extension, the writer's library as the foundation of writing is distinct from the archived library (Belin et al. 2018; Del Vento 2022). Its 'extant' part, all remaining units from an author's personal library, in most cases extends beyond the archived estate library (if indeed it has been preserved as a collection). Individual volumes may be dispersed across multiple institutions or private holdings. Even within an archive or (public) library, it can be challenging to distinguish 'genuine' estate books from those of different provenance. For example the volumes in the Thomas Mann Archive that were assigned to Mann's library despite having been written and published only after his death (Jaspers 2020, 159–61).

The writer's library also exceeds the mere sum of all books and media that once belonged to or were in the possession of a writer during their lifetime. Rather, its 'virtual' part encompasses 'a writer's reading' – books, texts – 'that can be reconstructed thanks to notes, diaries or letters' (Van Hulle 2022, 77). This includes publications and other documents a person may have only briefly handled or glanced at in passing, such as magazines, posters, or leaflets encountered in public spaces. The concept may extend even beyond the strictly textual, theoretically referring to interactions and influences that *can't* be identified or inferred.

This complexity and the difficulties it presents are repeatedly demonstrated by individual studies in the field, from the first attempts to catalog Goethe's library in the nineteenth century (Höppner 2022) to contemporary digitization and reconstruction projects of various book collections. For instance, *Ludwig Tiecks Bibliothek* digitally reunites dispersed volumes of Tieck's extant library by drawing on an auction catalog, physical identifiers within the books, and additional sources.[11] The boundaries of such corpora are determined differently in each case. Catalogs of extant and virtual libraries typically focus on 'books' or, more broadly, 'publications', but they can be enriched with information on inserts such as newspaper clippings, handwritten notes, or even letters found between the pages of private libraries. For a long time, archival practice dictated that these printed and holograph inserts did not belong to the library corpus and were instead classified as flat materials in the paper archive. This was and still is, on the one hand, a practical necessity, ensuring appropriate conservation and space-efficient storage. On the other hand, the categorizations in personal archives were shaped by principles developed in administrative archives, where hierarchical indexing plays a central role in managing extensive holdings (Messner 2018, 88 et seq.). Therefore, inserts removed from archived libraries have been categorized and separated under classifications such as 'work', 'correspondence' or 'life document'. The key question is, however, why writers' libraries warrant scholarly attention in the first place. Literary researchers are drawn to private libraries and marginalia to investigate a writer's reading and education, to identify sources and evidence for genetic criticism, and to explore the discursive background of a work. As a result, marginalia have become a recognized sub-field of study (Jackson 2001; Sherman 2008; Jaspers and Kilcher 2020; Spedding and Tankard 2021).

Similarly, the premises of current research into writing processes and genetic criticism do not align with the traditional archival categorization mentioned above. Their focus is on all written texts that are part of the genesis of a work, regardless whether they are found on and between book pages or in archival drawers; consequently, genetic dossiers and writers' libraries overlap and merge (Van Hulle 2016c, 45–8; D'Iorio 2017, 195–7). The interests of literary studies have never fully coincided with archival logic. But it is by focusing on the (writer's) library as an object of study in its own right and as an analytical category within literary studies (Wegmann 2000; Werle 2015) and its subsequent (digital) edition that this becomes a conceptual problem to be addressed.

Further challenges arise from the fact that a library is, in terms of medium, function, temporality, and space, far more than a collection of books and written texts kept on shelves. Firstly, in addition to paper products, various media that store textual and non-textual elements should be considered. Non- and semitextual structures, such as music,

---

[11] That is, certificates of book ownership, mentions of Tieck's reading in letters, his publisher's account books, and other historical sources such as the lending records of the University Library of Göttingen.

transmitted both materially and medially, might be preserved in the written form of scores or as specific musical interpretations stored on records, audio and video tapes, CDs, and other media. Such materials may belong to the writer's library just as well as photographs, paintings, and other artefacts from the private library space, including other artefacts that impact the reading and writing process.

Secondly, in order to expand or complete the genetic dossier, one should also consider oral texts that leave no written records but can be conceptually integrated. One might think of lectures heard or anecdotes recounted that inspire literary production, or even phrases overheard that find grammatical or phonetic representation in a literary text. However, impressions such as the view from a window or ambient sounds and conversations from a courtyard remain ephemeral, making the pragmatic decision to limit the conceptualization of the library to material media and stored materials understandable. But then again, this limitation is challenged when reconstructing the virtual part of the writer's library.

Thirdly, a library is also a spatial arrangement and, importantly, a system of order. The library's arrangement is shaped by its physical environment, particularly its furniture, which determines how the collection is organized and accessed. For this reason, original bookshelves are often archived to replicate a supposed 'final' order of the library. However, the notion of an ultimate and valid order of the material library comes fundamentally into question when it is transferred into a digital representation.

Ultimately, any project aimed at preserving, reconstructing, editing, and researching a writer's library requires a well-thought-out and, if necessary, individually tailored conceptual framework. It is therefore essential to consider the specific profile of each library, its history, the provenance of its individual items, the research interests and overarching goals of the edition, and – not to forget – its intended recipients (Rasmussen 2016). Key questions to address at the outset of a digital library project include: Which genres of texts and media should be incorporated? Should the focus be limited to materially transmitted items? Should the emphasis be on the (reconstructable) ownership of books and other media by one or several persons over a certain period? Or should the priority be on the (textual, medial, and ideological) interactions in the writing process?

Producing digital editions

The digitization of a writer's library involves various scientific, editorial, technical, and creative processes: the transformation from a card catalog to an electronic catalog of metadata, the recording of reading traces and inserts and the subsequent production of digital images, and the step from image files and OCR text to edited book pages with transcriptions and the markup of reading and writing traces. These activities entail more than transferring the material text collection into another medium. Digitization should not be understood solely as an act of reproduction or 'datafication', meaning the conversion of text and image into numerical values, or as a prerequisite for storing the generated image files. Rather, it must first be recognized as a scientific method

(Krämer 2018, 6), as a research approach to the library as an ideational, conceptual, critical, creative, social, and physical phenomenon. Beyond *addressing* conventional questions concerning a writer's 'sources' and the 'influences' on their writing, digitization can also *generate* interdisciplinary questions. The dematerialization and restructuring of the object, which makes us aware of its material construction and social conditionality (Wieland 2015, 148), initiates cognitive processes that might not have emerged without this shift in media. From the initial conception of a digitization project to the final stages of programming a user interface, theory and practice remain in continuous dialogue (Strobel 2021).

Hence, we wish to highlight that such projects can have a circular effect on cultural construction: The very existence and structure of a collection are facilitated by certain conceptual frameworks. In the process of analysing and editing a library, researchers inevitably derive findings that are informed by these same frameworks. This not only risks generalizing phenomena that are, in reality, highly specific to particular sociocultural contexts but also again influences which collections are made available for future research. Furthermore, researchers and editors bring their own background knowledge and biases – often aligned with or similar to those embedded in the collection itself – to their study of the library. Consequently, when a human (or artificial) intelligence, premoulded by the same assumptions and biases as the original corpus itself, now digitally structures and scientifically analyses the library, the effect of reproduction is further reinforced.

Once the corpus is identified, secured, cataloged, and enriched with structured metadata, it may be digitally represented in XML or other markup languages that are both machine readable and, at the same time, accessible to human researchers. Unlike in analog catalogs (e.g. Albina, Voronova and Manévitch 1979, 49; Grillparzer 1930; Richter, Alac and Badiou 2004), where the printed page and reading trace are separated, the facsimile preserves their unity. Given that data capacity is less of a problem in digital media, the library can, in theory, be displayed in its entirety and even linked to other catalogs and digital editions. Rather than presenting selected and abridged snippets alongside interpretative commentary, double page facsimiles allow researchers to examine and interpret reading traces within their full context, (relatively) free from editorial biases which might favor certain kinds of reading traces – for example annotations over inserts or markings (see Olsen-Smith 2022, 294 et seq.) – or, further still, marked over unmarked text. Additionally, the digital edition of a writer's library may be extended through citizen science initiatives, offering opportunities to expand or correct the dataset.[12] For instance, contributors could assist in transcribing marginalia, identifying ex libris and other bookmarks for provenance research, or locating books from the extant and titles from the virtual library.

---

[12] As has been done, for example, by the E-Pics Image Archive at ETH Zurich (https://ba.e-pics.ethz.ch/# 19.09.2024) or the digital edition of Hans Georg Nägeli's correspondence at the Zentralbibliothek Zürich (https://www.zb.uzh.ch/de/ueber-uns/citizen-science/freut-euch-des-lebens-naegeli-transkribieren 19.09.2024).

Secondly, the digital edition is something productive in and of itself. The sorting and filtering options of digital editions allow for a fast and clear formation of criteria such as topics, titles, names, dates, and more. Individual search queries generate new and meaningful connections, each producing distinct data outputs. These outputs are displayed on-screen as specific compilations of search results, fragmenting the unity of (material and digital) books by focusing on the edited page or trace. As a result, in the digital edition the boundaries of the book start to shift, as the text carrier – or reading unit – no longer functions as a 'material indication of completeness' (Hausendorf et al. 2017, 143). The physical book, enclosing its text between covers, conveys a sense of distinctiveness and closure, and demands to be treated as an independent unit. The same applies to other documents preserved in archival folders or even bound into booklets, such as manuscripts and typescripts assigned to the 'writer's library'.

The digital edition, however, constitutes a new form of hybrid text, integrating the printed text and its paratext, handwritten annotations, editorial markup, and possibly the metadata of the book and its digital copy in – potentially – a single text file or a series of files (Bamert 2021, 271). In this digital representation, a 'Ganzheitsbeweis' ('proof of wholeness') is still provided by the unified structure of a file and its linkages, ensuring the coherence of metadata, OCR text, and the markup of reading traces (Bamert 2021, 271). However, the delimitation of individual discrete units is made malleable by keyword and full-text searches, filtering and sorting options in ways that may not be apparent or possible in the material. Instead of providing the sum of its parts as separate texts, the library in its digital form becomes legible as a whole, revealing its very own patterns of inter- and hypertextuality (Schönbächler 2020, 312).

While the *archived library* (ideally) remains static, this does not correspond to the processual and 'living' nature of the *writer's library* and its evolving associations (as discussed above in relation to the question of ultimate order). In the digital sphere, it is thus revitalized – whereby all movable inserts, quite contrary to their (materially still) changeable character, undergo a final fixation in the digital edition (see below). Nevertheless, if all texts are 'fluid' in the sense of temporally changing stages or versions (Bryant 2002, 3 et seq.), then digital media and tools may offer a more nuanced representation of this fluidity than their relatively static print counterparts. Or, as Krista Stinne Greve Rasmussen has put it, the relationship between text and work can better unfold in the digital medium (Rasmussen 2016). In this analogy, the different expansions and configurations of the writer's library over its 'lifetime' can be understood as the changing versions of a fluid text. The hybrid (hyper-)text has qualities and potential significance that differ from those of its source material. At a higher level, the digital edition of a writer's library therefore constitutes what, following John Bryant, could be called a form of 'adaptive revision' of something that, even prior to its digitization, already existed as a 'fluid' (hyper-)text (Bryant 2002, 93).

Thirdly, the digital edition challenges established concepts of literary, archival, and bibliographical studies. It enables an engagement with the library that transcends conventional boundaries of genre, work, authorship, of text and paratext, of primary and secondary work. These categories not only shape our research questions but also inform the rigid hierarchical sorting criteria, which, as noted above, in personal archives often stem from material necessities and different archival logics – such as classification by provenance, genre, or materiality. In this sense, the digital edition not only preserves and provides access to (partially scattered) materials through full-text and metadata searching but also renders bibliographic classifications more dynamic, thereby deconstructing dominant notions of 'author', 'work' or 'originality' that traditionally govern the treatment of writers' libraries (see above). More significantly, it aligns the representation of literary texts (and works) with current scholarly conceptualizations of text, work and authorship. While libraries and archives rely on legal concepts of authorship and provenance to maintain practical and interoperable cataloging and metadata standards, the edition of a writer's library, which is based on these concepts on the one hand, but on literary and editorial theory on the other, raises the question of authorship anew. The hypertextual library produced through digitization exemplifies a form of complex, multiple authorship that encompasses not only the writers of the library books but also their annotators as well as the editors of the digital library (Schönbächler 2023b).[13]

Along with these aspects, a digital edition offers a platform for critical inquiry, for example by illuminating intertextual and interpersonal networks within a writers' library that manifest in dedications, book ownership records, or reading traces. Digital editions reveal the inherently networked nature of writers' libraries as dynamic hubs of material and intellectual connections. The added value lies particularly in the ability to reconstruct networks of annotations and intertextual linkages. For instance, Thomas Mann's library demonstrates, through the network of his marginalia, how he interwove his readings. By tracing these annotations and their reference texts, they can be conceptualized as intertextual reading networks, akin to a hypertext structure with interconnected links.

In a physical library, access is typically organized through author and title, and texts are generally read in a sequential or at least partially linear manner. By contrast, the systematic searchability of a digital catalog facilitates nonlinear reading patterns, allowing researchers to focus on specific annotated passages. The digital approach extracts these annotated sections from their original textual contexts, presenting them as equally significant fragments that can be reorganized and interpreted through various analytical procedures. While the study of reading traces was initially grounded in a positivist and material-focused methodology, systematic analyses of such networks can reveal the foundations of a writer's intellectual processes. Often enough, these networks do not only consist of reading traces stemming from the writer reading a text in the library but are based on the writer's own (published) work. In this sense, the intertextual networks in the library and in the literary works overlap (Schönbächler 2020; Jaspers 2022). The materialized connections that become visible and explorable in the digital

---

[13] Within the history of the book, the 'author' can also be reconsidered as a collective, transhuman subject or actor in the sense of ANT (Actor-Network Theory) of which the library is an active constituent (Schönbächler 2023a).

edition can, then again, prompt a reevaluation of archival principles (Messner 2018) and theoretical assumptions of the library.

Digital editions of reading traces, such as marginalia, serve a range of research interests, spanning from the analysis of individual sources for studies on influence and intertextuality research to quantitative approaches that rely on large text corpora and datasets. They render visible the intricate networks of people, books, knowledge, and discourses (see *Thomas Mann Nachlassbibliothek Online*). Moreover, the data can be visualized according to various research questions (see *Fontanes Handbibliothek*), for instance with regard to book exchanges, dedication records, or geographical information (see *Goethe Bibliothek online*). Additionally, data visualizations of fragmentary types of marginalia (see *Melville's Marginalia Online*) offer both comparative perspectives and a bird's-eye view of reading responses, facilitating thematic searches and browsing. Such comparative analyses of reading traces, book histories, and editions become possible across institutional boundaries, broadening the scope of scholarly inquiry.

This change of perspective then again can present challenges for modelling a digital edition. A digital edition that dismantles traditional hierarchies (author, title, genre) might create the impression that '(1) what is presented is all there is and that (2) all that is presented is of equal calibre' (Van Hulle 2016a, 237). Furthermore, the editorial markup of 'reading traces' risks reinforcing a positivist assumption that annotations indicate an annotator's heightened cognitive engagement with the text. While reading traces indeed represent an overlap between the real and virtual library, their significance must be evaluated case by case, considering the specific texts, books, and traces in question (Schönbächler 2024). When using a digitized library, it is therefore important to acquaint oneself with the physical library that underlies the digital edition, as well as the editorial principles governing the project. Such awareness fosters the critical sensitivity required for thoughtful source criticism and nuanced interpretation.

Editing a writer's library: Problems and practices

Digital editions are not only an asset for the preservation of archival material and the accessibility and interconnection of research resources. They also entail a loss of the material and sensory qualities of a library. Consequently, the editorial process is accompanied by a number of complex problems, requiring careful consideration of the corpus, its materiality, and the inherent biases that shape such projects.

Corpus

The material foundation of a digital scholarly edition of a writer's library must be defined according to the project's objectives, the library's collection, and the intended audiences and their expectations of editions. Those undertaking the editing of an estate library will need to access the book collection archived in one location, where they will encounter the traces of use and reading left by multiple individuals. In many cases, there is or was no single owner of the books, and a library is much more than just a collection of books in terms of its media, spatial, and social dimensions (see above). Conversely, those aiming to trace the writer's reading habits and history must look beyond the volumes preserved as the writer's library. As demonstrated by the Melville and Goethe projects, such an approach may include reading data derived from library borrowing records.

The transition to digital formats allows for the virtual consolidation of dispersed collections and the augmentation of analog library catalogs with entries from a writers' virtual library. Recent research in library and reading studies has enriched the positivist approach to material in writers' libraries by incorporating the reading biographies of their owners (Speer and Reuke 2020, 721–71; Anschütz et al. 2021). Reconstructing readings, that is, the virtual library, is, however, a highly demanding task. It requires provenance research across archives, libraries, and second-hand bookshops worldwide, as well as in estate materials like notebooks, excerpts, diaries, letters, and so on (Jaspers 2021 and 2024). The feasibility of such reconstructions is contingent upon the availability of financial and human resources. Because the process relies on interpreting the sources, Dirk Van Hulle proposes linking the corresponding research findings to an uncertainty scale (Van Hulle 2016b, 198–202). A purely virtual library, comprising only reconstructed readings without any original material, would then constitute a borderline case of a digital edition, as it lacks an extant corpus to be edited.

Equally time-consuming and costly is the effort to locate all extant volumes that were once part of a specific library but are now geographically and transnationally dispersed. The reconstruction of libraries whose histories have been shaped by war, exile, or division among multiple heirs can span decades (Höppner et al. 2021). Nevertheless, despite the considerable expense associated with their establishment and maintenance, sustainably managed digital catalogs and platforms offer substantial advantages over printed catalogs. They allow for the continuous updating of entries over long periods and ensure that new findings are made immediately accessible to an international research community. As paradoxical as it may sound: Increasing (online) accessibility to archive materials and their associated information – whether through digitization of a library catalog or the inclusion of provenance data into an existing OPAC – will, in fact, encourage researchers to work with the physical archives as well. This, in turn, enhances their usage and helps to secure the long-term existence of archival institutions.

Materiality, spatiality, corporeality

Reading digital texts and hypertexts differs significantly from reading material texts, both viscerally and cognitively (Mangen 2020). In analog libraries, access to content is initially physical: human bodies interact with material objects. In a digital edition, however, the material and spatial logics that guide, promote, hinder, and shape the reading experience in a physical library are no longer a given. Gone are the initial impressions of crowded bookshelves filled with volumes containing numerous inserts that invite readers to open them; the overwhelming sense of uncertainty when confronted with such a vast, complex collection; the surprise of encountering oversized volumes lying horizontally or those whose spines remain hidden, revealing only their edges; the tactile and visual allure of a well-worn reading copy; the serendipitous discoveries made while browsing the shelves and leafing through books; and the book neighbourhoods that are recognizable in a private library. A writer's library presented in its physical form therefore probably allows for more and different random discoveries and productive moments of disorientation than a digitally edited library, where search and retrieval are primarily structured through text-based research methodologies.

Designing a digital library, four levels should be considered: the individual reading trace, the (double) page, the item, and the collection as a whole (with potential additions). Regardless of their content, small, tightly printed paperbacks are read and annotated differently from heavy volumes and fragile texts, which becomes immediately apparent when handling them. When the tactile and sensory experience of these material objects is lost, so too is the practical understanding derived from interacting with them physically (Rautenberg and Schneider 2023). Accurately representing the format and weight of books in a digital environment presents a challenge, and so does conveying the colors of annotations and the writing utensils used – details that can be difficult to discern even in the physical artefacts due to ageing. For those reasons, access to the physical collection of a writer's library *as* a library should be ensured, *especially* in conjunction with a digital edition. Digital representation does not replace engagement with the physical material but rather complements it.[14]

Editorial determination

When printed texts, including reading traces, are to be digitally represented, the first step is to decipher and thus *interpret* the written traces. This involves *normalizing* them,[15] *determining* their scope and, in some cases, the function of markings made with pen or pencil ('Stiftspuren'). A classification based purely on formal criteria is hardly possible (Bamert 2021, 89–94). Thus, interpretative narrowing and fixation begin even before any markup is applied, as editors apply their theoretical and methodological assumptions as well as their own reading and hermeneutic skills to the analog object (see above). This critical process is also constrained by various pragmatic limitations. Markup in languages such as TEI-XML inevitably further restricts the ambiguity of meaning and imposes constraints on the potential interpretation of material phenomena. It

---

[14] See also Geoffrey Turnovsky's chapter in this volume for a similar discussion on diplomatics.

[15] Normalization always means that the diversity and ambiguity of forms are restricted, and thus information is destroyed. To ensure that the (specifically digital, i.e. machine-readable) usability of an edition is not compromised as a result, it is important to consider carefully which losses of information are acceptable and where categorization and the translation into standardized sign systems produce surplus and thus potentially 'false' information.

divides the text into a 'primär an die maschinellen Aktant:innen gerichtete Ebene mit maschinenlesbarem Markup und eine an die menschlichen Aktant:innen gerichtete Schriftoberfläche' (Nantke 2022, 45–9).[16]

To put it differently: Markup renders texts machine readable, but potentially minimizes or removes nuances that are essential to editing and close reading. It cannot translate formal and contextual ambiguities into machine-readable form, regardless of whether the markup itself can be filtered for searches. Inserts that, if not glued or otherwise fastened, would physically retain their mobility in the material text are, in the digital representation, fixed in a single location, such as in an XML file. Also, modelling XML presents significant challenges for encoding reading traces, as these often transcend hierarchichal structures and impose one structure (reading notes) on top of another (the corresponding text) (Estill 2016). At present, there are still no formalized guidelines for encoding such phenomena in TEI-XML (Bamert 2021, 34–7), but without established standards, data models will vary significantly, complicating efforts to integrate datasets across projects. This divergence is already evident in areas where TEI was originally implemented and where standards are in place: all forms of digital editing remain affected by the idiosyncratic nature of individual project guidelines, which arise from the vast diversity of material phenomena and the flexibility of the markup language itself. Such inconsistencies pose a challenge in the digital humanities, particularly for approaches that aim to analyse large textual corpora quantitatively.

Biases

For endeavors such as the editing of a writer's library, long-term international collaborations between reliable actors and institutions are essential, as vividly illustrated by the acknowledgements and link lists in publications on and digital editions of writers' libraries. Comparing projects highlights significant canonical-political differences: Whose library is archived? Which parts of it are preserved? Who makes these decisions? Who funds the digital edition of which library? And who finances, organizes, and sustains the edition in the long term (Ohge 2021, 109–18)? One of the major advantages of digitization is that it makes large volumes of data manageable, thereby reducing the impact of spatial limitations, which are often cited as the reason why archives and libraries of marginalized authors are not preserved. Instead of physically archiving libraries, which invariably also involves discarding duplicates, books without reading traces or other distinctive features, and supposedly 'uninteresting' materials (such as popular and functional literature, photo books, etc.), it is conceivable to preserve them digitally as entire corpora. Given that research on writers' libraries prioritizes the material itself, and because digital editions tend to deconstruct emphatic notions of authorship and the literary work anyway, it would be desirable to have digital projects dedicated to a

---

[16] A 'level primarily directed at machine actants with machine-readable markup and a surface in writing directed at human actants' (Translation: AJ/MS).

diversity of libraries, including those of writers who do not conform to the canonical image of authorship. Needless to say, such libraries should nevertheless be fully archived for future access and research, once again challenging the conventional practices and policies of archives and funding institutions.

Mediality

As mentioned above, the study of writers' libraries shows that it is possible for multiple media like audio and video recordings, artefacts, and furniture to accumulate and become part of a private library, all of which can become integral to the creative processes of reading (in its broadest sense) and writing. Again, depending on the conceptualization of what is conceived as the library but considering what would be possible in a digital edition, it might be advisable to include these multiple media into the digital representation. It would shift not only our traditional understanding of a library as a collection of books but also the focus on text in genetic criticism towards a more holistic understanding and (digital) representation of the creative process.

Perspectives

How and in what media environment we are reading is constantly changing in the digital age. Future projects concerning the libraries of contemporary writers will need to engage with hybrid (physical and digital) and born-digital libraries, involving a wide range of digital media and data formats, even when restricted to textual material. How can a digital edition of such a library adequately represent handwritten *and* digital annotations? Since these hybrid reading (and writing) practices have long been a reality, questions concerning adequate typologies and terminologies have become increasingly urgent, particularly if the goal is to establish editorial standards and guidelines.

Creating minimal editions with as little interpretation concerning the markup and leaving multiple options for users is common practice. But the development of authoritative editorial standards remains essential for producing high-quality and sustainable digital editions. Digital texts that have been read and annotated exclusively on-screen, without ever having been printed on paper, represent only the most immediate extension of the writer's library in the digital age. If, as mentioned above, research into writing processes continues to consider correspondence, the reading of everyday texts, and so on, then the digital forms of communication and media consumption today present a multitude of new challenges for personal archives. The preservation of emails in archival collections is already an area of concern. Further complexities are posed by SMS, chat histories and voice messages, all of which play an increasingly important part in communication and are received, processed, and sent on the same devices used for reading and writing texts. Contemporary text-genetic dossiers now include digital magazines, podcasts, and video essays, as well as the products of social media, such as blogs and vlogs. Consequently, the primary carriers of a writer's library will no longer be limited to bookshelves but will also include desktop computers, tablets, and mobile phones. The library itself will consist of an ever-changing variety of data formats.

For today's more conventional forms of library editions, it is essential to strive towards meeting certain minimum standards in terms of interoperability and comparability. At present, no consistent XML standards exist for writers' libraries, nor is there interoperability between library projects, an issue which includes the need for interfaces supporting protocols such as OAI and IIIF. In principle, however, these challenges begin with the production of reliable transcriptions and full texts, which remain highly labor-intensive. In this respect, there is hope in technological developments: improvements in OCR and HTR programs, as well as the potential application of AI not only to clean up image data, which improves OCR recognition itself, but also to correct OCR-read texts. XML files should, as far as the legal situation allows, be made publicly available. In short, it would be desirable for digital editions to follow the FAIR principles: ensuring findability through correct metadata and OCR text, (open) accessibility of the edition and its data files, interoperability as outlined above, and reusability. This also requires the highest level of transparency in communicating the editorial process and principles. As shown in many projects (e.g. the Beckett and Melville projects) and forums, there is an expressed need within the specialist community for commentary and discussion on the development of editorial guidelines. Often enough, they are the result not of purely theoretical and methodological considerations, but also of pragmatic decisions made due to limitations of time, personnel, financial resources, and technological capacity.

Something to consider in a long-lasting editorial process is not only the involvement of students in the digitization and marking of reading notes but also the integration of citizen science in generating content as noted above. Incorporating citizen and community science in edition projects would not only benefit from the collective knowledge of an author's transnational reader and research community but also help manage the masses of data, particularly in light of the financial and personnel restrictions that such projects often face.

The specifics of writers' libraries and more so their digital editions are still an object of specialized academic discourse. But first attempts have shown that including the work with writers' libraries into undergraduate education, across different disciplines, is highly effective. It provides students with opportunities to (re)engage with paper, books, and libraries, and encourages them to formulate innovative research questions within a research-based learning environment (Dahlke 2021). However, there is still a lack of didactic recommendations and models as to how studying and working with writers' libraries and their digital editions can be meaningfully integrated into existing curricula.

Future editions of writers' libraries will be confronted with increasing media diversity and growing editorial complexities, as well as the challenge of developing user-friendly interfaces that remain as intuitive and accessible as possible. As the technological possibilities for digital editions become more diverse and the TEI guidelines evolve to address existing gaps and become more comprehensive, it is equally essential to maintain an overview of the theoretical and conceptual prerequisites, the practical research aspects, and the target groups of future projects. The potential of these editions lies in their capacity to advance literary theory, enrich the didactic engagement with writers' libraries where social practices and the processual nature of (inter-)textuality become tangible, and contribute to research on specific authors' writings as well as the histories of individual books.

Bibliography

Selected Digital Editions of Writers' Libraries

Samuel Beckett Digital Library: https://www.beckettarchive.org/library/home/welcome
Jacques Derrida's Margins: https://derridas-margins.princeton.edu
Theodor Fontanes Handbibliothek: https://uclab.fh-potsdam.de/ff
Goethe Bibliothek Online: https://opac.lbs-weimar.gbv.de/DB=2.5
Hannah Arendt Personal Library: https://blogs.bard.edu/arendtcollection
James Joyce Digital Library: https://www.uantwerpen.be/en/research-groups/centre-for-manuscript-genetics/projects/joyce-digital-library (forthcoming)
Ludwig Tiecks Bibliothek: https://tieck-bibliothek.univie.ac.at
Melville's Marginalia Online: https://melvillesmarginalia.org
Nietzsche Source: http://www.nietzschesource.org (forthcoming)
Thomas Mann Nachlassbibliothek online: https://nb-web.tma.ethz.ch

Printed Sources

Albina, Larissa, Tamara Voronova and Susanna Manévitch. 'Einleitung'. In *Corpus des notes marginales de Voltaire*, tome I: A–B, 39–51. Edited by O. Golubiéva, T. Voronova and S. Manévitch. Berlin: Akademie Verlag, 1979.
Anschütz, Hans-Peter, Armin Thomas Müller, Mike Rottmann and Yannick Souladié, eds. *Nietzsche als Leser*. Berlin: De Gruyter, 2021.
Bamert, Manuel. *Stifte am Werk. Phänomenologie, Epistemologie und Poetologie von Lesespuren am Beispiel der Nachlassbibliothek Thomas Manns*. Göttingen: Wallstein, 2021.
Belin, Oliver, Catherine Mayaux and Anne Verdure-Mary. 'Introduction'. In *Bibliothèques d'écrivains. Lecture et création, histoire et transmission*, IX–XXIII. Edited by O. Belin, C. Mayaux and A. Verdure-Mary. Torino: Rosenberg & Sellier, 2018. https://books.openedition.org/res/1741 (26.09.2024).
Bryant, John. *The Fluid Text. A Theory of Revision and Editing for Book and Screen*. Ann Arbor: University of Michigan Press, 2002.
Dahlke, Birgit. 'Autor_innenbibliothek als Archiv? Die Privatbibliothek von Christa und Gerhard Wolf an der Humboldt-Universität Berlin'. In *Text und Kritik. Special Edition: Ins Archiv, fürs Archiv, aus dem Archiv*, 105–19. Edited by M. Töteberg and A. Vasa. München: Edition text + kritik, 2021.
Del Vento, Christian. 'Biblioteche private, biblioteche di scrittori, biblioteche d'autore. Postfazione'. In *Testi scientifici nelle biblioteche d'autore*, 253–60. Edited by M. Zanardo. Padova: Padova University Press, 2022.
D'Iorio, Paolo. 'Die Schreib- und Gedankengänge des Wanderers. Eine digitale genetische Nietzsche-Edition'. *editio* 31 (2017), 191–204.

D'Iorio, Paolo and Daniel Ferrer, eds. *Bibliothèques d'écrivains*. Paris: CNRS éd., 2001.

Danneberg, Lutz, Annette Gilbert and Carlos Spoerhase. 'Zur Gegenwart des Werks'. In *Das Werk. Zum Verschwinden und Fortwirken eines Grundbegriffs*, 3–26. Edited by L. Danneberg, A. Gilbert and C. Spoerhase. Berlin, Boston: De Gruyter, 2019.

Estill, Laura. 'Encoding the Edge: Manuscript Marginalia and the TEI'. *Digital Literary Studies* 1, no. 1 (2016). https://journals.psu.edu/dls/article/download/59715/59912?inline=1

Ferrer, Daniel. 'Bibliothèques réelles et bibliothèques virtuelles'. *Quarto. Zeitschrift des Schweizerischen Literaturarchivs* 30/31 (2010): 15–8.

Gleixner, Ulrike, Constanze Baum, Jörn Münkner and Hole Rößler, eds. *Biographien des Buches*. Göttingen: Wallstein, 2018.

Grillparzer, Franz. *Tagebücher und literarische Skizzenhefte VI von Ende 1856 bis 1870. Nr. 4149–4398 mit den Nachträgen Nr. 4399–4422 und dem Verzeichnis der Bibliothek Grillparzers*. Edited by R. Backmann, A. Hoffmann and R. Payer-Thurn. Wien: Schroll, 1930 (Sämtliche Werke. Historisch-kritische Gesamtausgabe 2. Abt., Vol. 12).

Hausendorf, Heiko, Wolfgang Kesselheim, Hiloko Kato and Martina Breitholz. *Textkommunikation. Ein textlinguistischer Neuansatz zur Theorie und Empirie der Kommunikation mit und durch Schrift*. Berlin, Boston: De Gruyter, 2017.

Höppner, Stefan. *Goethes Bibliothek. Eine Sammlung und ihre Geschichte*. Frankfurt (Main): Klostermann, 2022.

Höppner, Stefan, Caroline Jessen and Ulrike Trenkmann, eds. *Focal Point 'Der komplexe Faden der Herkunft: Provenienz'. IASL* 46, no. 1 (2021).

Jackson, Heather Joanna. *Marginalia. Readers Writing in Books*. New Haven: Yale University Press, 2001.

Jannidis, Fotis, Gerhard Lauer, Matías Martínez and Simone Winko. 'Rede über den Autor an die Gebildeten unter seinen Verächtern. Historische Modelle und systematische Perspektiven'. In *Rückkehr des Autors. Zur Erneuerung eines umstrittenen Begriffs*, 3–35. Edited by J. Fotis, G. Lauer, M. Martínez and S. Winko. Tübingen: Niemeyer, 1999.

Jaspers, Anke and Andreas B. Kilcher, eds. *Randkulturen. Lese- und Gebrauchsspuren in Autorenbibliotheken des 19. und 20. Jahrhunderts*. Göttingen: Wallstein, 2020.

Jaspers, Anke. '(Frau) Thomas Manns Bibliothek? Autorschaftsinszenierung in der Nachlassbibliothek'. In *Randkulturen. Lese- und Gebrauchsspuren in Autorenbibliotheken des 19. und 20. Jahrhunderts*, 141–65. Edited by A. Jaspers and A. B. Kilcher. Göttingen: Wallstein, 2020.

Jaspers, Anke. 'Stempel, Schilder, Signaturen. Exemplargeschichten aus der Bibliothek von Thomas Mann'. *IASL* 46, no. 1 (2021). *Focal Point 'Der komplexe Faden der Herkunft: Provenienz'*. Edited by S. Höppner, C. Jessen and U. Trenkmann: 264–82.

Jaspers, Anke. 'Digitalisierung als epistemische Praxis. Vom Nutzen und Nachteil der digitalen Katalogisierung und Erschließung von Autor:innenbibliotheken'. *Zeitschrift für Germanistik*. Neue Folge XXXII, no. 1 (2022): 133–54.

Jaspers, Anke. 'Bibliotheksphotographien'. In *Provenienz. Materialgeschichte(n) der Literatur*, 143–56. Edited by S. Gaber, S. Höppner and S. Hundehege. Göttingen: Wallstein, 2024.

Krämer, Sybille. 'Der 'Stachel des Digitalen' – ein Anreiz zur Selbstreflexion in den Geisteswissenschaften? Ein philosophischer Kommentar zu den Digital Humanities in neun Thesen'. *DCO* 4, no. 1 (2018): 5–11.

Loh, Gerhard. 'Verzeichnis der Kataloge von Buchauktionen und Privatbibliotheken aus dem deutschsprachigen Raum'. (1607–1834), Bd. 1–8. Leipzig: Loh, 1995–2017.

Mangen, Anne. 'Digitization, Reading, and the Body: Handling Texts on Paper and Screens'. In *A Multidisciplinary Approach to Embodiment*, 51–5. Edited by N. K. Dess. New York, London: Routledge, 2020.

Messner, Philipp. 'Eine offene Bibliothek. Der Nachlass des Marcel-Duchamp-Übersetzers Serge Stauffer an der Schweizerischen Nationalbibliothek'. In *Autorschaft und Bibliothek. Sammlungsstrategien und Schreibverfahren*, 82–94. Edited by S. Höppner, C. Jessen, J. Münkner and U. Trenkmann. Göttingen: Wallstein, 2018.

Nantke, Julia. 'Normalisierung als Bedingung von Schriftlichkeit am Beispiel digitaler Repräsentationen von Schrift'. In *Schriftlichkeit. Aktivität, Agentialität und Aktanten der Schrift*, 39–54. Edited by M. Bartelmus and A. Nebrig. Bielefeld: transcript, 2022.

Ohge, Christopher. *Publishing Scholarly Editions: Archives, Computing, and Experience*. Cambridge: Cambridge University Press, 2021.

Olsen-Smith, Steven. 'Books and Marginalia, Real and Virtual'. In *A New Companion to Herman Melville*, 283–96. Edited by W. Kelley and C. Ohge. Hoboken: John Wiley & Sons, 2022.

Rasmussen, Krista Stinne Greve. 'Reading or Using a Digital Edition? Reader Roles in Scholarly Editions'. In *Digital Scholarly Editing. Theories and Practices*, 119–33. Edited by M. J. Driscoll and E. Pierazzo. Cambridge: Open Book Publishers, 2016.

Raulff, Ulrich. 'Von der Privatbibliothek des Gelehrten zum Forschungsinstitut. Aby Warburg, Ernst Cassirer und die neue Kulturwissenschaft'. *Geschichte und Gesellschaft* 25 (1997): 28–43.

Rautenberg, Ursula and Ute Schneider, eds. *Das Buch als Handlungsangebot. Soziale, kulturelle und symbolische Praktiken jenseits des Lesens*. Stuttgart: Anton Hiersemann, 2023.

Richter, Alexandra, Patrik Alac and Bertrand Badiou, eds. *La Bibliothèque philosophique*. Paris: Rue d'Ulm, 2004 (La bibliothèque de Paul Celan).

Schönbächler, Martina. "[F]ehlerhafte[ ] Thatsächlichkeit'? – Thomas Manns Bibliothek als Medium seiner Poetologie'. In *Randkulturen. Lese- und Gebrauchsspuren in Autorenbibliotheken des 19. und 20. Jahrhunderts*, 293–314. Edited by A. Jaspers and A. B. Kilcher. Göttingen: Wallstein, 2020.

Schönbächler, Martina. 'Das Korpus der Autor*in. Die 'Autorenbibliothek' als Ort des Stoffwechsels'. In *'Ressource Schriftträger'. Materielle Praktiken der Literatur zwischen Verschwendung und Nachhaltigkeit*, 211–25. Edited by M. Bartelmus, Y. Mohagheghi and S. Rickenbacher. Bielefeld: transcript, 2023a.

Schönbächler, Martina. 'Marginalien in der digitalen Edition: Bemerkungen zu Text und Autorschaft am Beispiel von Thomas Manns Nachlassbibliothek'. *editio* 37 (2023b): 12–27.

Schönbächler, Martina. *Splitterpoetologie: Thomas Manns Gerda-Komplex zwischen Bibliothek, Frühwerk und 'Joseph in Ägypten'*. Göttingen: Wallstein, 2024.

Sherman, William Howard. *Used Books. Marking Readers in Renaissance England*. Philadelphia: University of Pennsylvania Press, 2008.

Spedding, Patrick and Paul Tankard, eds. *Marginal Notes. Social Reading and the Literal Margins*. Cham: Palgrave Macmillan, 2021.

Speer, Andreas and Lars Reuke, eds. *Die Bibliothek – The Library – La Bibliothèque: Denkräume und Wissensordnungen*, vol. 41. Berlin: De Gruyter, 2020.

Spoerhase, Carlos. 'Was ist ein Werk? Über philologische Werkfunktionen'. *Scientia Poetica* 11 (2007): 276–344.

Strobel, Jochen. 'A. W. Schlegels Korrespondenz – kollaborativ! Zu einer Theorie der Praxis digitaler Briefedition'. *editio* 35 (2021): 142–67.

Van Hulle, Dirk. 'A James Joyce Digital Library'. In *New Quotatoes: Joycean Exogenesis in the Digital Age*, 226–42. Edited by R. Crowley and D. Van Hulle. Leiden: Brill Rodopi, 2016a.

Van Hulle, Dirk. 'Digital Library History: The Virtual Bookcases of James Joyce and Samuel Beckett'. *Quærendo* 46, no. 2–3 (2016b): 192–204.

Van Hulle, Dirk. 'Modelling a Digital Scholarly Edition for Genetic Criticism: A Rapprochement'. *Variants. The Journal of the European Society for Textual Scholarship* 12–13 (2016c): 34–56.

Van Hulle, Dirk. *Genetic Criticism: Tracing Creativity in Literature*. Oxford: Oxford University Press, 2022.

Van Hulle, Dirk. 'Writers' Libraries in Genetic Editions'. *editio* 37 (2023): 1–11.

Wegmann, Nikolaus. *Bücherlabyrinthe. Suchen und Finden im alexandrinischen Zeitalter*. Köln: Böhlau, 2000.

Werle, Dirk. 'Literaturtheorie als Bibliothekstheorie'. In *Literaturwissenschaft und Bibliotheken*, 13–26. Edited by S. Alker and A. Hölter. Göttingen: Vandenhoeck & Ruprecht, 2015.

Werle, Dirk. 'Autorschaft und Bibliothek. Literaturtheoretische Perspektiven'. In *Autorschaft und Bibliothek. Sammlungsstrategien und Schreibverfahren*, 23–34. Edited by S. Höppner, C. Jessen, J. Münkner and U. Trenkmann. Göttingen: Wallstein, 2018.

Wieland, Magnus. 'Materialität des Lesens. Zur Topographie von Annotationsspuren'. In *Autorenbibliotheken. Erschließung, Rekonstruktion, Wissensordnung*, 147–73. Edited by M. Knoche. Wiesbaden: Harrassowitz, 2015.

Wieland, Magnus. 'Stell-Werk: Literatur im Bücherregal'. *Quarto. Zeitschrift des Schweizerischen Literaturarchivs* 30/31 (2010): 27–33.

CHAPTER 5
A GRAPH DATABASE APPROACH TO EDITING AND PUBLISHING INFINITELY RECOMBINANT DIGITAL TEXTS WITH OCHRE
Miller C. Prosser

As digital text editors, we aim for a computational editing platform that models all writing systems and all languages; allows for editorial observations at the grapheme, word, phrase and text level; integrates textual, image, audio, video, spatial and temporal data; compares manuscript editions of works; supports the implementation of well-known metadata schemas while allowing for customization where necessary; and allows for complex querying and publishing. Are these not reasonable requests? Further, the system must be accessible online, require no programming expertise, work across operating systems, support import and export of data, and come with institutional support. And then we require support for publication and maintenance. It is no wonder why a comprehensive computational text editing platform has been something of a white whale.[1]

The following essay weaves together three threads: (1) the dimensional complexity of text, (2) a few data modelling principles and (3) a new approach to digital publishing. These themes may strike the reader as nebulous, theoretical and intangible, but my goal is to triangulate among these topics to describe a specific, practical and tangible approach to digital text editing. Text is much more than a simple sequence of string characters. With textual dimensionality always front of mind, I emphasize a few principles of data modelling that respect this complexity and aim to meet the ambitious goals of digital text editing. I nod to the provocative futurism behind Ted Nelson's Xanadu project, reflect on Jerome McGann's call for a more serious approach to digital texts, and build upon Schloen and Schloen's work on a database approach to texts (Nelson 1974, 1987; Dechow and Struppa 2015; McGann 2014; McGann 2003; Schloen and Schloen 2014).[2] Each of these authors wrestles with the complexity of written text as a digital thing. In their own way, each also acknowledges that the practice of digital text editing includes something more than reproducing a version of the written text.

---

[1] In the analysis of texts, one would prefer the term *grapheme* to refer to the smallest meaningful unit of writing. However, in this discussion we consider the value of a graph database approach to texts; and the potential confusion introduced by the use of grapheme and graph seemed problematic in some instances.
[2] I have worked with the Schloens and with OCHRE for many years. The following is the author's own reflection.

New Directions in Digital Textual Studies

Texts contain multitudes

In the introductory textbook, *The World is a Text,* Jonathan Silverman and Dean Rader provide guidance for how to 'read and write about texts (movies, pieces of art, experiences, people, places, ideas, traditions, advertisements, etc.), in much the same way you would read and write about traditional texts' (Silverman and Rader 2018, 12). Readers of a digital humanities volume such as this are comfortable with the idea of reading various media as texts. When we talk about texts, many of us are talking about something more than the printed words on a page. While this essay focuses on written texts, we should remain cognizant of the fact that our analysis and interpretation take many different forms and require the integration of many different types of data. In his still relevant and challenging *Theories of the Text,* David C. Greetham reflects on the ontology of text. He considers the boundaries of where a text begins and ends and considers how the boundaries may be different for performance text: 'since a text is indeed woven of various strands, at both the physical and the conceptual level, how can we tell when the pattern is finished, the design complete?' (Greetham 1999, 27). As a starting point, I assert that 'the computer' must not be the limiting factor in determining when the textual pattern is finished. The task of defining the structures and boundaries of the text must lie squarely in the hands of the digital text editor.

Below I outline an approach to digital text editing that employs an upper ontology, which allows the editor to record any scholarly observation at any level of granularity or specificity and turns over to the editor the definition of 'the text'. The iterative performance of a text – and here also we must also consider the iterative hand copying of manuscripts before the print revolution – may challenge the definitional boundaries of when one text becomes another text. Where is the boundary of this slippery thing we call text? There is an often unappreciated and under-studied challenge that arises when we expand our definition of text to include the entire world of interpretive observation. The digital representation of text suddenly becomes a more complicated prospect, one that must meet the distant frontiers explored or proposed by textual and literary theory. Whether from the perspective of media studies, literary studies, or even archaeology, we read films, stage props, ancient architecture, and computer-generated art as text. Multiple texts bloom from these works – *they are large; they contain multitudes.* Just how deeply complex are these texts? In reworking a principle of quantum mechanics for the purposes of text analysis, Jerome McGann observes that '[i]n poetry every work carries the record of every previous interpretation it has experienced – in particular, that which created it – and in general it is impossible to reveal or evaluate this record' (2003, 15). McGann rightly contends that textual fields are n-dimensional, meaning that there is no theoretical limit to the network of worlds within a text. But if the entire world is a text, if we think beyond the literary work to include multimedia and physical objects, and if these texts are all n-dimensional, what hope do we have of representing this dimensionality as digital data, especially when the current state of digital text editing remains fixated on representing an overly simplistic view of text? Encoding at least a portion of the complexity inherent in a text requires a robust ontological landscape to capture the vast and intertwined network of texts, persons, objects, images, audio, and other readable textual fields that exist in the n-dimensional quantum space.

Digital aspirations

Textual studies, or the once and future field of philology, is the study of the interconnectedness of all things. Writing is a fundamental form of human expression by which we communicate our deeply intertwined thoughts. Persons and places, syntax and grammar, audio and visual, time and concepts – these are all present in text as interwoven threads of a complex tapestry, not to mention the integration of editorial intervention. McGann, again, summarizes the need for a more robust digital editorial practice in *A New Republic of Letters*.

> Could one develop a model for editing books and material objects rather than just the linguistic phenomena we call texts? . . . Could one develop a model for exposing and comparing relationships between phenomena that are radically discontinuous: different authors and their authorized texts, say, as well as the relations between various agents – individual as well as institutional – in an eventual field disposing more than just textual or bibliographical things? Could the model expose and examine relationships between phenomena – various works and their various agents – located in fields that are discontinuous in social time and space? Finally, could such machines be designed and actually built, the way the critical editions we inherit were designed and built? (McGann 2014, 24)

Ted Nelson famously championed a concept he coined as the neologistic portmanteau 'intertwingularity', the essential and unbounded interconnectedness of all humanistic expression and analysis. In the *Dream Machine* half of *Computer Lib/Dream Machine*, Nelson in 1974 reflects on the coming explosion in computer graphics and display, observing that '[i]t is usually hard to combine things: especially complicated technical things. Usually it takes infinite reconsiderations, finagling, modification, and intertwingling' (1974, D41). Further along, in a section called 'Everything is Deeply Intertwingled', where he considers the utility of hypertext and whether nuanced hierarchy is enough to represent text, Nelson has the hunch that 'all structures must be treated as totally arbitrary, and any hierarchies we find are interesting accidents' (1974, D45). Nelson's futurism involved hardware as much as software, with Xanadu being the system that was to address his observation that everything is connected in ways that transcend two-dimensional space. McGann's dimensionality and Nelson's intertwingularity, if we agree on the salience of these observations for humanistic research, must not be discarded in the practice of digital text editing.

Just beneath the seemingly ordered sequence of a text lies a complex network of ideas. A cursory analysis of any literary work reveals complexities beyond the linear representation of words on the page. For example, the moment we pause to consider the process through which a text reaches us, we realize that most texts are not stable but in fact have evolved through various forms and are composed of multiple strata. Whether it is the fluidity of Herman Melville's manuscripts (Bryant 2002) or the citational layers present in Piers Plowman and Shakespeare, texts are deep and complicated.[3] Some complexities are revealed only when multiple manuscripts of a work are compared. Consider a medieval manuscript of the Hebrew Bible collated with a Dead Sea Scroll dating some ten centuries earlier. By what process did versions of the Bible known to the Dead Sea Scrolls scribes – or to the editors of the Greek Septuagint and early Latin manuscripts for that matter – come to the medieval Masoretes? In many cases we observe the remarkable stability of the Hebrew Bible over this time, but even in this work we encounter variation that belies a complex textual history. A corpus that may rival the complexity of the Hebrew Bible is the Egyptian Book of the Dead, with the text of various spells being copied and recopied over millennia, a process that can be studied through the lens of assemblage theory and remix culture (Buchanan 2020; Scalf 2023).

Unless we are working strictly as epigraphers or paleographers to establish a reliable *editio princeps* (first published edition, which may include extensive editorial notes) of a newly discovered manuscript, we are interested in more than the simple task of reproducing a linear sequence of signs in a single text. We aim to compare multiple manuscripts, annotate graphemes, words and phrases with editorial observations, create glossaries and concordances, link to digital images, create maps, or generate social networks. I would argue that even in the case of an *editio princeps*, the digital editor ought to strive to produce a more richly described text edition. Thinking beyond the simple representation of the script act, the task of the (digital) editor is to communicate a message that might not be readily apparent to the reader. And alongside Peter Shillingsburg, '[t]he conventions of writing that make possible communication to audiences absent from the script originator are not simple' (Shillingsburg 2006, 50). The editorial task is complex. To achieve those goals, we must ask how the computer can be applied to the task.

We might also ask if our digital approaches to text editing result in an edition that is better than the printed version. Text can be represented in a linear sequence just as easily with ink on paper as in an XML file. The typical response to this question is that the computer makes our text searchable, reproducible, analysable and accessible in various forms not available to the printed page. The fact is that very few digital approaches to texts have accomplished much more than creating searchable versions of the printed text. As Christopher Ohge (2021, 10) observes,

> Editors and bibliographers must continue to push their thinking further by experimenting with computing and adopting a pragmatic view towards its

---

[3] For more on CEDAR, see <https://cedar.uchicago.edu/>.

principles. Unfortunately, the past twenty years or so of born-digital and hybrid print-digital editing have yielded few editions that do more than books can do. Many editors are still stuck in a document- and codex-oriented mode that expects book reading to translate into screen reading, even though studies have been suggesting that users of digital resources prefer basic and advanced searching for specific information over long-term browsing.

The following is a fairly noncontroversial observation, but it bears upon our understanding of digital text representation: What is it exactly that we are attempting when we encode a text digitally? We are likely attempting to record the text in a form that can be manipulated computationally: indexed, referenced, and annotated. Ultimately though – and this is the noncontroversial observation – most digital text editors require that the text be published for human consumption, at least in some form. This usually takes the form of a linear representation of characters.

Computers do not read texts in sequence

From early Mesopotamia, China, Egypt and Mesoamerica, through to Gutenberg, humans have reproduced the linear textual model in which we compose, edit and read texts as sequences arranged on a page or other support. This has been true for clay tablets to papyrus rolls to the codex (Woods, Emberling and Teeter 2010) and continues to be the case for computer screens. Humans require meaningful and communicative text to be represented as linear epigraphic and syntactic units. As a practice of communication, the text is composed as a complete, sequential thing. I imagine you are reading this sentence as a sequence of letters and words from left to right. Please accept this rudimentary syllogism: computers do not use human eyes and brains to read texts; therefore, computers do not need to encounter or store the textual thing as a complete linear, two-dimensional unit, as a sequence of letters and words in order. The failure to appreciate the significance of this fact has hindered the field of digital text editing. There can be little argument that the Text Encoding Initiative (TEI) is the reigning digital text editing standard, yet the TEI guidelines are based on the presumption that text must be represented in a one- or two-dimensional linear sequence. By committing to a linear sequence representation of text, scholars have gone to great lengths to devise inline and standoff markup strategies to accommodate the insertion of editorial observations in the text (see e.g. Spadini, Tomasi and Vogeler 2021). Or, as McGann and Buzzetti (2006, 59) observe in their lead up to discussing text markup, '[t]he linearity of digital text as a data type puts an immediate constraint on its semiotics.' This is not the place to rehash the history of scholarship on markup, SGML, the 'ordered hierarchy of content objects' (OHCO), and TEI. Instead I will stake my position, alongside McGann and Buzzetti (2006, 58–67) and Schloen and Schloen (2014, §§18–24), that a text is obviously not an ordered hierarchy of content objects. To that conclusion, I would add that markup of linear text is a problem only when we treat the linear sequence of text as the data storage model.

The foundational problem of overlapping hierarchical elements – a problem introduced by inline markup and insufficiently addressed by standoff markup – disappears when we represent text as discrete granular tokens and perform description of the data in that form. In other words, the limitation of an ordered hierarchical approach to text is solved if we implement TEI as a text publication schema and not as a text storage schema (see again Schloen and Schloen 2014). Text modelled according to the TEI guidelines can serve as the linear sequential document presented to the human reader or as a sharing format between computers, but this sequential composition should derive from a data storage model that treats the text as data according to established database principles (Prosser and Schloen 2021).

To reiterate, the core of the argument that follows is that a computer – or more strictly a database – does not require a text to be stored as a precomposed unit in sequential format. The argument extends one step further to assert that a computer should not store text as a fully composed linear sequence of characters, words, and clauses. As mentioned above, by starting with this presupposition, we find a practical approach for addressing the *n*-dimensionality of text. While expanding on Schloen and Schloen's (2014) proposal that digital text representation should move *beyond Gutenberg* and mixing in a healthy dose of Ted Nelson's intertwingularity, this argument also implements an extreme interpretation of E. F. Codd's (1970) principle of data normalization. Codd realized that a computer should not store tabular data in a precomposed, sequential model. He went so far as to make it a requirement that records in a relational data table must not be required to be stored in sequence. More on that below.

Why do digital text editors need to concern themselves with a concept like data normalization? For some inspiration, we travel back in time even further than Codd at IBM in the late 1960s. We return to 1945, when Vannevar Bush asked what new computational instruments might enter the domain of research. His starting point, of course, was electrical engineering in the context of US governmental policy and research, but he understood that computers would be applicable beyond their use as advanced calculators. Bush imagined an analogue machine consisting of switches, tubes, photocells and electron beams that could operate on principles of formal logic to process ideas in ways that machines had previously only processed numbers. Bush (1945, 106) described this future device as 'a sort of mechanized private file and library', and coined it 'memex'. The memex was to be a sort of universal thought-organizing appliance. A researcher reading through a book could create paths from that work through to other works with similar themes. These paths would be custom editorial interventions created by the reader and stored in a way as to allow the memex to select and retrieve them in a new editorial sequence. In this provocative thought experiment, Bush described the essence of scholarly investigation: interpretation of information recorded as editorial (or authorial) observation. Digital editorial practice involves essentially the creation of text editions supplemented by various pathways of integrated observations. These observations might take the form of an argument in favour of a specific reading, an excursus on form or rhetoric, or even illustration through digital imagery, 3D modelling or mapping.

Returning to the question of why a digital editor should be concerned with the database concept of normalization, to record the pathways imagined by Bush or the intertwingularity identified by Nelson, data must be recorded in a fashion that allows the computer to select and retrieve pieces of data that share common properties. So long as those pieces of information are stored as granular items, which are user-defined minimal meaningful parts, the computer can select, retrieve, and reconstruct a richly edited digital text. To do that we need a database.

What if not sequence?

The repeated reference above and below to Codd's seminal breakthrough in the late 1960s should not be taken as an endorsement of a relational database approach to texts. But some of the computational principles characteristic of the relational model can be lifted, modified and repurposed in a graph database model for the representation of textual data. And now we must reckon with the spirit of normalization. Whereas Codd asserted that tabular data should be normalized to remove repetition and then stored in tables joined by key fields, the following argument asserts that textual data should be atomized into granular minimal meaningful parts – words or graphemes, for example – with each part being stored as a separate node in a graph. Instead of storing similar records in a common table as in a relational data model, a graph database stores individual 'records' as discrete documents. The term 'record' does not sufficiently capture the potential granularity of textual data in a graph database. The term item more accurately describes the discrete nodes in the graph. An item can be something as small as a single word or grapheme. In Codd's model, a relational database joins data from various tables into a single recomposed unit for display while minimizing duplication and increasing data consistency. A properly configured relational database does not store a table of corporate employee data as a complete unit, for example. (See Figure 5.1.)

By associating tables using keyed fields, a relational database extracts fields from multiple tables to produce any number of derived views of the datasets. In other words, the form of the data we wish to read is secondary to and derived from the form in which the data is stored in the computer. A graph database can select thousands of discrete database items – words or graphemes – to produce a text edition in the linear sequence we require as human readers, deriving those items from an underlying semi-structured graph data model that minimizes duplication and increases data consistency. (See Figure 5.2)

When asked to reproduce a text version attributed to a specific editor, then, the computer retrieves all the word and grapheme items attributed to the editor in question and recomposes the text that represents that specific edition. Those same database items may participate in other versions of the text. Here I am thinking of the difference between a diplomatic facsimile edition versus a critical edition. According to the principle of normalization, words or graphemes that are common across two different text editions do not need to be duplicated.

PartyID	PartyName
1	Unaffiliated
2	Federalist
3	Democratic-Republican

UniqueID	LastName	FirstName	Party
e12345	Washington	George	1
e12346	Adams	John	2
e12347	Jefferson	Thomas	3
e12348	Madison	James	3

Figure 5.1 Simplified relational database schema tables recording U.S. Presidents and political party names in normalized tables. The use of primary and foreign keys to join data from the tables prevents duplication of string data in the database.

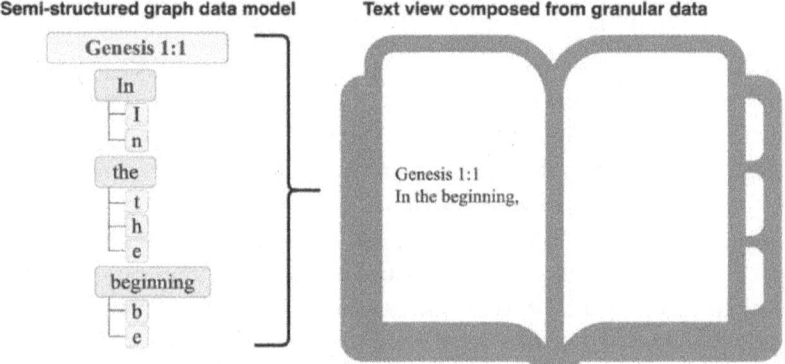

Figure 5.2 Schematic representation of a semi-structured graph database approach to texts. Each word and each letter are individual database items linked to other items. The database extracts the required items to produce a reading text.

When text is presented for public consumption, on the web for example, at that point TEI proves useful. The recomposed TEI-XML document can be displayed and shared using the well-documented and universally available TEI guideline. Again, TEI is useful for implementation as the data publication or sharing format for digital texts and not as the data storage model.[4]

---

[4] The TEI guidelines do not present it as a database model. However, it is often implemented as if it were.

More than books can do

Ohge, as quoted above, argues that digital texts should be able to do more than books can do. It remains then to define what more we want them to do and how digital editors can prepare them to achieve this end. What if we wish to analyse the evolution of a text from draft to manuscript, trace the recension history of a text over centuries, build a dynamic lexicon and concordance of an entire corpus, or create a visualization of the social network of persons named in our texts? For those tasks, we need a model that does more than replicate the printed text, and now we need to consider how to use the computer to accomplish the task. These are questions that were asked at the advent of digital editing but, from my perspective, have not been sufficiently answered.

Here we return to 'Beyond Gutenberg' (Schloen and Schloen 2014) and attempt very briefly to summarize the argument up to this point regarding the difference between a one- or two-dimensional approach to digital text on the one hand and an approach that atomizes text into minimal meaningful parts on the other. Schloen and Schloen call the former approach the document paradigm and the latter the database paradigm.

> In the document paradigm, the digital representation of information depends on the relative position of units of information in one or two dimensions. Information is represented by linear character strings or by tables consisting of rows and columns, as on a flat printed page. (Schloen and Schloen 2014, §1)

In contrast, then, the database paradigm 'is characterized by data structures that transcend the position dependent structure of predigital documents' (Schloen and Schloen 2014, §5). The core contrast between the two paradigms is the data storage principle implemented in each. In a database paradigm for texts, a digital editor identifies the minimal meaningful parts of the text. These tokens are each stored as separate, discrete items in the database management platform. Conceptually, in a graph data model, each of these items is a node connected to any number of other nodes by any number of edges. A word that appears in column one of a poem, for example, will be represented as an item in the database and will have an edge that specifies its relationship with another database item that represents column one.[5] The same database item that represents this word can be reused in editions of multiple text witnesses. If another witness of this poem does not contain columns, then the edge that represents the layout information of the word in this second witness would point to some other layout element, perhaps the page or manuscript surface.

In this way, a graph database approach to texts atomizes a text into many small entities, removing them from the sequential or hierarchical dependency of a document such as a

---

[5] Edge is a conceptual description of the relationship between these two nodes in the graph database. The strict implementation of this edge may be represented by a pointer, relationship, or whatever strategy is supported in the database schema.

TEI-XML file. The specific format and schema of the nodes in a graph database depend upon how the graph database is implemented. To be clear, a database approach to texts does not use inline markup, standoff markup, TEI, ordered hierarchies of content, or any of the other attempts that have been invented to solve the basic deficiency of the document paradigm.

In my view, the most powerful way to produce digital text editions that do something more than books is to implement a graph database approach to text. In the second half of this essay, I present the Online Cultural and Historical Research Environment (OCHRE) as a working example of this approach.

OCHRE

The Forum for Digital Culture at the University of Chicago supports the Online Cultural and Historical Research Environment (OCHRE) as a comprehensive research database platform in the humanities. For nearly two decades, OCHRE has been used by philologists working in a wide range of text domains, from ancient Elamite, Hittite and Ugarit to Biblical Hebrew, Greek and Latin to Modern and Early Modern English and more. Researchers using OCHRE pursue a wide variety of goals. Some integrate hundreds of thousands of digital images with their texts. Others build nuanced dictionaries with detailed text citations and richly articulated O.E.D.-style lemma definitions that closely resemble the Lexical Markup Framework (Francopoulo 2012). Some compare the development and evolution of texts over thousands of years, across different writing systems and languages. Others work to identify cultural features such as gender roles, power structures and economic networks discernible in texts.

OCHRE is a semi-structured graph database platform created to manage digital research. Digital text editing is only one small portion of what OCHRE supports, although it stands as a useful example to demonstrate the platform's ability to store, integrate, and publish digital research. The following approach is not theoretical, nor is it a proposal or a provocation for future researchers; rather, it is currently implemented in the Online Cultural and Historical Research Environment. The principles described below can be applied in other graph database platforms, of course, but I will demonstrate the approach to normalization, integration and digital text modelling in the OCHRE platform.

OCHRE employs an upper ontology called CHOIR to define the foundational data categories in the database.[6] An upper ontology, as opposed to a domain-specific ontology, is characterized by top-level classes meant to cover potentially all data. In OCHRE, every item that enters the database is an instance of an ontological class such as Person, Spatial Unit, Resource, or Text. An item in the Text category is composed of

---

[6] For more about the CHOIR ontology as implemented in OCHRE, see <https://corpus.uchicago.edu/platform/ochre-ontology/>.

items from other ontological classes, defined below. Beyond this high-level classification of data categories, the database is schema agnostic. In layman's terms, this means that OCHRE does not impose upon the user any specific metadata schema. Instead, OCHRE supports the implementation of any number of complementary metadata schemas. Dublin Core can be supplemented with an expression of the Europeana Data Model or with select fields from MADS or VBA Core, for example. For the purposes of this essay, we concentrate primarily on the implementation of the CHOIR text category in OCHRE (Schloen and Schloen 2012; Schloen and Prosser 2023).

In OCHRE, a text is composed of multiple overlapping hierarchies of database items. These hierarchies are of two types: epigraphic hierarchies and discourse hierarchies. Items organized in these two hierarchy types are called epigraphic units and discourse units, respectively. An epigraphic unit represents the scholarly interpretation of some observable feature of the physical layout of the text. Items in an epigraphic hierarchy may start at a high level with a page, an object *verso*, a line, or even a letter or punctuation. In the database ontology, these items are all in the epigraphic unit class and are arranged as a recursive hierarchy that represents a partitive relationship. The epigraphic unit for line 01 is a parent node that contains child nodes of all the graphemes in line 01, for example. Items in the discourse hierarchy represent interpretations of the meaning of the epigraphic units. Discourse units represent words but can then proceed up the hierarchy to create a stich, a phrase, a sentence and so on. Discourse units that represent words are linked to the epigraphic units (graphemes) that represent the constituent parts of the word. For example, a discourse unit for the word *montaigne* in the *passus primus* of Piers Plowman manuscript L is one discrete database item identified by a universally unique identifier. This database item is defined by links to nine discrete epigraphic units, one link per letter in the word. Each epigraphic unit is a discrete item in the database with a universally unique identifier. The relationship between the word and its constituent epigraphic units is already a small network. Extend this model to cover the full breadth of a text, and the result is an orderly network of individual nodes associated by labelled edges. To be clear, the OCHRE graph database does not store the epigraphic units in sequence or even in a strict hierarchical order. Properties of the epigraphic and discourse units in the database instruct OCHRE how to compose an editor's interpretation of sequence and hierarchy for a given text edition. Based on the choice of text witness and editor, OCHRE finds and retrieves the required database items to produce a text edition on the fly.

Beyond the use of epigraphic units, discourse units, and overlapping hierarchies to join the two, OCHRE does not prescribe anything else about a text. The identification and arrangement of epigraphic and discourse units is an act of scholarship attributed to an observer. The database does not assert any so-called true structure of a text. This is the work of the digital text editor. Epigraphic and discourse observations and every other editorial intervention are attributed to a scholar.

Everything is data

What digital editors think of as the textual content – words and graphemes – are stored as individual epigraphic or discourse units in a graph. But to be clear, the structure of the text is also recorded as data. For example, the *verso* of a manuscript or other support is a discrete database item, not an inline markup element in the text. By recording text and structure separately as highly granular database items, an editor can combine epigraphic or discourse units to create an infinite number of text editions, none of which is beholden to a so-called stable or authoritative edition.[7] Further, editorial observations are also recorded in the database. In OCHRE, this layer of observation would typically be recorded as metadata properties assigned to words or graphemes, but lengthy editorial comments may equally be associated with one or more database items, as might an image, video or map. In this approach, an editor possesses all the necessary tools to create infinitely recombinant multimodal digital editions: textual content can be combined and recombined, pulling content from within a text and across texts, including supporting and illustrative data and published for consumption as a multimodal digital product (McGann and Buzzetti 2006; McGann 2022).

Single edition versus manuscript comparison

McGann and Buzzetti state that 'Scholarly editing is grounded in two procedural models: facsimile editing of individual documents and critical editing of a set of related documentary witnesses' (2006, 52). OCHRE has been used for facsimile editing since 2008. Because the programme was developed first for use in Ancient Near Eastern studies, there are now tens of thousands of facsimile editions of cuneiform texts in the database. Scholars working on these types of texts are typically establishing the first edition of an unpublished document. They make detailed epigraphic notes, build dynamic dictionaries of the words found in the texts, identify persons named in the texts and record various other types of scholarly analysis.

As illustrated in Figure 5.3, OCHRE provides the editor with a summary view of the text. From left to right, the panes represent (1) a summary of bibliography, metadata properties, and notes about the text overall, (2) a sign-by-sign transliteration, (3) an epigraphic view using a font that resembles the native script, (4) a discourse view of the text word-by-word, (5) a translation and (6) a list of links to images, note cards, PDFs, maps, and any other supporting resources. The highlighted sections represent live links to other data in the project. Most notably, the words in the discourse pane link to grammatical entries in the project dictionary (not shown in this view), which

---

[7] I should clarify that projects not interested in commenting on a text letter-by-letter may opt to define a discourse unit as the smallest token in the database. Text editors are not required to atomize a text into individual graphemes. Furthermore, for some writing systems this level of atomization is not possible.

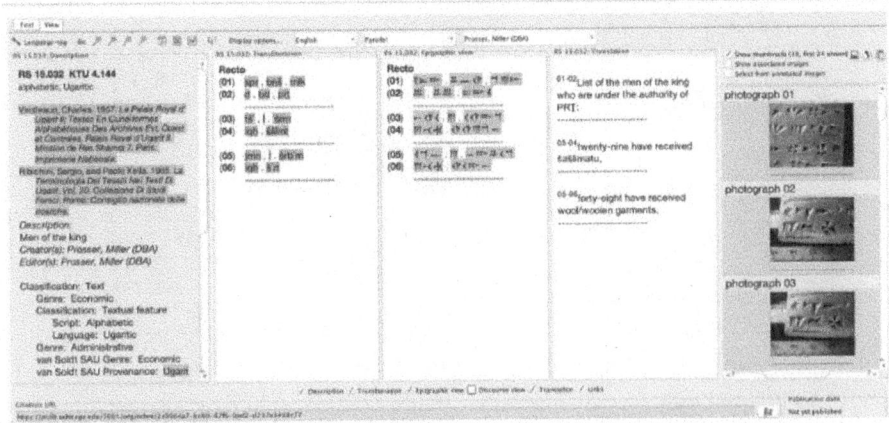

Figure 5.3 Facsimile text edition of an alphabetic cuneiform text from Ras Shamra (RS 15.032, Miller Prosser editor; photos by John Ellison; copyright PhoTEO).

is built dynamically from words attested in the texts. Note that the left pane displays the creator and editor of the text. OCHRE supports multiple text editions for any facsimile in case the editor wishes to record competing text collations. The view of a text is based on hundreds of discrete database items, including epigraphic units, discourse units, photographs, bibliographic entries and more. Any one of those items could be viewed and edited separately. The editor of the text may choose to add a long prose note explaining a translation, interpretation or anything else (Prosser 2018).

With the launch of the CEDAR project in 2017, researchers embarked on the ambitious task of demonstrating that OCHRE could be used to compare multiple editions of manuscripts, even across different languages and writing systems.

Figure 5.4 illustrates one view of a critical text edition created on the fly in the CEDAR Hebrew Bible project (see Yardney, Schloen and Prosser 2019 for colour images and further explanation). The text view is an interactive canvas. A click on any character, in this case the final letter in line 25, generates a panel showing where the manuscripts agree or vary at that point. The summary chart displays a list of the letters present in the manuscripts actively under examination and then also a list of letters present in other texts in the database but not currently being compared.

Very briefly, the CEDAR project achieves the comparison of multiple manuscripts by pushing the OCHRE graph data model in a new direction. Instead of treating each manuscript as independent and unrelated, composed of database items that occur only in that text, CEDAR editors begin by assembling a theoretical pool of all the epigraphic units that may occur in any version of a work. So, for Genesis chapter 1, the CEDAR Hebrew Bible team creates a collection of all possible items called the content pool. From this content pool, digital editors may build specific text editions. When two text editions share an agreement at the letter level, the two digital texts each reuse the same database item from the content pool. In the example from Genesis 1, the first letter of

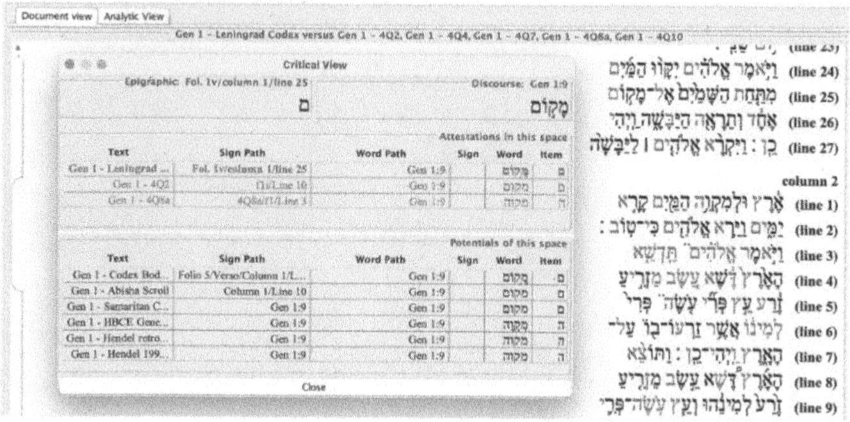

Figure 5.4 A comparison of multiple Hebrew manuscripts of the Book of Genesis, chapter 1.

the Hebrew Bible is a *bêt* which is typically translated as 'in' from the well-known opener, 'In the beginning.' The database item, an epigraphic unit, that represents the letter *bêt* in the specific Dead Sea Scroll manuscript called 4Q2 is reused in the digital edition of the Medieval Hebrew Leningrad Codex. Therefore, instead of asking the database to compare the differences between two TEI-XML documents, for example, a click on that letter asks the database to retrieve a list of all the texts in which a digital editor has reused the specific letter *bêt* from 'In the beginning'. CEDAR extends that logic to compare variations in the Piers Plowman manuscripts, Melville's *Typee*, the Egyptian Book of the Dead, and the Epic of Gilgamesh.

A literary machine

In the OCHRE model, the editor can intervene at every level, from highly detailed epigraphic observations of individual graphemes (lower criticism) to the identification of social phenomena appearing in the text (higher criticism) and at all points in between (McGann 2014, 27–8). The network of scholarly observations finds no limit in this hypergraph approach implemented in OCHRE (Yardney, Prosser and Schloen 2020). Objects, persons, concepts, time, images, audio, video, GIS – all are available to participate in the network as envisioned by the editor. Because the data is stored as extremely normalized granular tokens, they can be mixed and remixed to produce infinitely recombinant results.

With the Xanadu software, Ted Nelson wanted to make it possible to make new things out of old things. The idea was that 'all materials are in a shared pool of units' (Nelson 1987, 0/5). His conceptual 'xanalogical storage' system allowed for new things to be composed of a combination of new and old material. He explains that '[b]ecause the system is based upon one pool of storage which can be shared and organized in many ways, materials can be reorganized constantly without losing their *previous* organization' (1987, 0/7). To be clear, OCHRE is not a crystallized realization of Xanadu. In the practical implementation of data, there are probably more differences than similarities. I would not describe OCHRE as a hypertext/hypermedia platform, for example. But the spirit of the literary machine is present in the OCHRE platform. As I read Nelson on this point, the term 'literary' extends beyond digital text editing to include the representation of all human heritage (1987, 0/6). The team that supports and develops OCHRE sometimes uses the proverbial phrase, 'a place for everything and everything in its place' to describe the vast yet orderly nature of the platform. If a network graph of data strikes the casual viewer as too complex, it is in the ordered complexity that we find the value in this approach.

> The challenge here is to develop, with the aid of the new medium of computers, sites of textual complexity from which the beauty of complex coherence shines: where text and counter text, annotation and image, singularity and multiplicity of perspectives can serve readers upon whom nothing is lost. (Shillingsburg 2006, 24)

To date, OCHRE has been used for digital research in archaeology, text editing, lexicography, cinema and media studies, history of scholarship (astronomy, law, biological sciences) and more. Essentially, any domain area in which a researcher wishes to record observations about people, places, objects, time periods, and texts supplemented by images, audio, video, bibliography or prose can be modelled in OCHRE. By integrating these various types of data and by implementing foundational database principles such as normalization and reuse, OCHRE lives up to the spirit of intertwingularity and the literary machine.

Digital publishing

Academia must grapple with two concurrent issues. First, echoing Ohge again, is it not possible for digital texts to offer something more than print publications, and how can these digital publications be supported? Already in 2006, Peter Shillingsburg posited that 'the electronic representation of print literature to be undertaken in the twenty-first century will significantly alter what we understand textuality to be' (Shillingsburg 2006, 3). Even so, it seems we are still in a transitional phase where digital publications could become something more than PDFs. To this end, the Forum for Digital Culture at the University of Chicago is applying OCHRE to the task of producing digital publications. Specifically, the Chicago Online Research and Publication Service (CORPUS) serves as a digital research and publication venue, but not for linear prose, e-books or PDFs. CORPUS produces multimodal digital publications based on data modelled, stored, and curated in OCHRE. From this underlying data, researchers and CORPUS editors work together to decide which of various Web publication elements to add to their digital publication. Archaeology projects have access to powerful spatial analysis components, including maps and timelines. Long-form prose projects may choose to offer readers nonlinear pathways for navigating the publication. Digital text projects may publish text editions, dictionaries and concordances, each of which provides the reader with the type of unlimited navigation potential that is at the core of Nelson's discourse on intertwingularity. CORPUS publications are effectively networks of integrated data of all types supported by the OCHRE platform. The CORPUS initiative is currently in a nascent stage. But we are using a digital architecture that has been tested for over two decades for some very challenging textual studies projects. With the instantiation of the Forum for Digital Culture, CORPUS is now building various web publication components.

Among the other issues facing digital researchers – and also a feature of our point in history – academia is facing the potential loss of a generation of research because digital scholarly output has not been taken seriously and has not been saved in durable formats to be used by generations of future scholars. As an attempt to address this crisis, the Forum for Digital Culture and the University of Chicago Library have partnered in the development of UChicago Node, a digital architecture that is capable of storing digital research collections in a unified environment. When launched, Node will provide a public-facing interface for faceted discovery, display and delivery of digital collections.[8] Behind this search interface stands an archiving platform where digital research collections are deposited and maintained according to best practice. In this system, OCHRE serves as a federating clearinghouse where digital collections are described using standard open metadata schemas like Dublin Core and the Europeana Data Model and then published in various formats for discovery and display online.

Where Node addresses the problem of archiving and preserving digital collections, CORPUS achieves what both Nelson and McGann asked for: a mechanism for integrating any type of digital research and publishing it in stable, citable, and peer-reviewed volumes. CORPUS leverages OCHRE as the content management system and as the publication platform. But unlike so many content management system (CMS) publication platforms, data in CORPUS publications is stored in a semi-structured graph database as highly atomic tokens. While a publication with a DOI or other digital identifier will remain stable and citable, the individual scholarly observations that comprise that publication are free to be remixed to produce infinite outcomes. Data from various digital text projects can be recombined into any number of new digital presentations. And because CORPUS publications leverage the OCHRE ontology, they may include digital images, audio, and video making the publication multimodal in ways not possible in print. I acknowledge the aspirational nature of these goals. CORPUS,

---

[8] UChicago Node was initially supported and funded by the National Endowment for the Humanities, CHA-292055-24. Credit to my colleague Charles Blair, Director of the Digital Library Development Center at the University of Chicago, for the non-exhaustive list of the D's of digital collections management that will characterize UChicago Node: describe, deposit (sometimes delete), discover, display, and delivery.

within the context of the Forum and with the partnership of the University Library, is committed to this task.

Proposals to CORPUS are treated like proposals to traditional academic presses. A CORPUS editor shepherds the proposal through the approval process to contract, then the researcher and the editor work to bring the digital publication to life, a process that includes traditional blind third-party peer review if desired by the researcher. Publications will be made available free of charge through CORPUS and through UChicago Node. While we do not have the power to change instantly the perception of digital publications in academia, CORPUS intends to address some of the acknowledged deficiencies from which this form of publication has suffered. CORPUS editors will register the work as original, attributed to specific authors. Publications will be freely disseminated online through various portals and when allowable the data will be made available under open licences. By using OCHRE as the database back-end and by partnering with the UChicago Library, publications from CORPUS are guaranteed to be durable for the life of the University. Through attribution, certification, dissemination and preservation, CORPUS intends to fill the time-tested role of an academic press for multimodal digital publications.

Bibliography

Bryant, John. *The Fluid Text: A Theory of Revision and Editing for Book and Screen*. Ann Arbor: University of Michigan Press, 2002.
Buchanan, Ian. *Assemblage Theory and Method*. London: Bloomsbury Publishing, 2020.
Bush, Vannevar. 'As We May Think.' *The Atlantic*, 1945.
Codd, Edgar F. 'A Relational Model of Data for Large Shared Data Banks'. *Communications of the ACM* 13, no. 6 (1970): 377–87.
Dechow, Douglas R. and Daniele C. Struppa. *Intertwingled: The Work and Influence of Ted Nelson*. Springer Nature, 2015.
Francopoulo, Gil, ed. *LMF Lexical Markup Framework*. London: John Wiley & Sons, 2012.
Greetham, David C. *Theories of the Text*. Oxford: Oxford University Press, 1999.
McGann, Jerome. 'Editing and Curating Online.' *Textual Cultures* 15, no. 1 (2022): 53–62.
McGann, Jerome. *A New Republic of Letters: Memory and Scholarship in the Age of Digital Reproduction*. Cambridge: Harvard University Press, 2014.
McGann, Jerome. 'Texts in N-dimensions and Interpretation in a New Key [Discourse and Interpretation in N-dimensions]'. *Text Technology* 12, no. 2 (2003): 1–18.
McGann, Jerome and Dino Buzzetti. 'Critical Editing in a Digital Horizon.' In *Electronic Textual Editing*, 51–71. Edited by Lou Burnard, K. O'Brien O'Keeffe, Katherine, and John Unsworth. Modern Language Association of America, 2006.
Nelson, Theodor H. *Computer Lib/Dream Machines*. Chicago: Hugo's Book Service, 1974.
Nelson, Theodor H. 'Literary Machines: The Report On, and of, Project Xanadu, Concerning Word Processing, Electronic Publishing, Hypertext, Thinkertoys, Tomorrow's Intellectual Revolution, and Certain Other Topics Including Knowledge, Education and Freedom.' 1987.
Ohge, Christopher. *Publishing Scholarly Editions: Archives, Computing, and Experience*. Cambridge: Cambridge University Press, 2021.

Prosser, Miller C. 'Digital Philology in the Ras Shamra Tablet Inventory Project: Text Curation through Computational Intelligence.' *Digital Biblical Studies* (2018): 314. https://brill.com/view/book/edcoll/9789004375086/B9789004375086_012.xml.

Prosser, Miller C. and Sandra R. Schloen. 'The Power of OCHRE's Highly Atomic Graph Database Model for the Creation and Curation of Digital Text Editions.' In *Graph Data-Models and Semantic Web Technologies in Scholarly Digital Editing*, 55–71. BoD, 2021. https://kups.ub.uni-koeln.de/55226/.

Scalf, Foy. 'Assemblage Theory and Remix Culture in the Book of the Dead: A Case Study of Repeated Spells.' *Birmingham Egyptology Journal* 10: (2023) 1–21.

Schloen, J. David and Sandra R. Schloen. 'Beyond Gutenberg: Transcending the Document Paradigm in Digital Humanities.' *DHQ: Digital Humanities Quarterly* 8, no. 4 (2014). http://digitalhumanities.org:8081/dhq/vol/8/4/000196/000196.html.

Schloen, J. David and Sandra R. Schloen. *OCHRE: An Online Cultural and Historical Research Environment*. Winona Lake, IN: Eisenbrauns, 2012.

Schloen, Sandra R. and Miller C. Prosser. *Database Computing for Scholarly Research: Case Studies Using the Online Cultural and Historical Research Environment*. Springer, 2023.

Shillingsburg, Peter L. *From Gutenberg to Google: Electronic Representations of Literary Texts*. Cambridge: Cambridge University Press, 2006.

Silverman, Jonathan and Dean Rader. *The World is a Text: Writing About Visual and Popular Culture: Updated Compact Edition*. Peterborough: Broadview Press, 2018.

Spadini, Elena, Francesca Tomasi and Georg Vogeler, eds. *Graph Data-models and Semantic Web Technologies in Scholarly Digital Editing*, vol. 15. Norderstedt: BoD–Books on Demand, 2021.

Woods, Christopher, Geoff Emberling and Emily Teeter. *Visible Language: Inventions of Writing in the Ancient Middle East and Beyond*. Oriental Institute Museum Publications 32. Chicago: The Oriental Institute, 2010.

Yardney, Sarah, Miller Prosser and Sandra R. Schloen. 'Digital Tools for Paleography in the OCHRE Database Platform.' *TC: A Journal of Biblical Textual Criticism* 25 (2020) 129–43.

Yardney, Sarah, Sandra R. Schloen and Miller Prosser. 'New Digital Tools for a New Critical Edition of the Hebrew Bible.' *Open Theology* 5, no. 1 (2019) 80–94. https://doi.org/10.1515/opth-2019-0006.

CHAPTER 6
PRAGMATIC DIGITAL EDITING, DATA ANALYSIS AND CREATIVE-CRITICAL PRACTICES
THE CASE OF THE ANTI-SLAVERY ANTHOLOGY *THE BOW IN THE CLOUD* (1834)
Christopher Ohge

Digital methods and publishing have reinvigorated the discipline of scholarly editing and pushed its practitioners to rethink its core methodologies and publishing strategies. These new developments have also expanded the field to study textual phenomena that exist outside of the single-author-genius focus of much traditional textual editing. To demonstrate these issues, this essay examines my recent digital edition project on *The Bow in the Cloud* (1834), an anti-slavery literature anthology that was compiled and edited by the pioneering British abolitionist Mary Anne Rawson.[1] The digital edition aims to show how text encoding, text analysis and other data visualization tools are integrated into an edition that explores the nexus of manuscripts, book history and network analysis through critical and creative approaches.

Overview of the anthology and digital edition

The *Bow in the Cloud* is an anti-slavery anthology that was published in 1834 by the London firm of Jackson & Walford, in St. Paul's Churchyard. The anthology consists of eighty-six poems and prose pieces by a mixture of well-known and non-professional writers involved in anti-slavery societies throughout Great Britain. It was edited by Mary Anne Rawson, née Read (1801–1887), an activist from Sheffield who sought to create what she called in her preface to the anthology 'a structure of moral and literary architecture'. In 1826, Mary Anne Read, a young activist and secretary of the Sheffield Ladies Anti-slavery Society, encouraged by the example of her philanthropist parents, started compiling the anthology to influence public opinion. By 1834, Mary Anne, now married to George Rawson and still living in Sheffield, had shepherded *The Bow in the*

---

[1] The digital edition is available at https://antislavery-anthologies.org/books/bow-in-the-cloud/index. Its source data is accessible at https://github.com/cmohge1/bow-in-the-cloud-edition/tree/master.

Cloud into publication with a London publisher to commemorate the 1833 Slavery Abolition Act (which came into effect on 1 August 1834).

The Bow in the Cloud aimed to bolster various abolitionist movements throughout the world. The book was compiled during the period when slavery had been abolished in Great Britain in 1807 (but was still legal in the colonies) to when it was abolished in most of the colonies in 1833 but still alive in British territories owned by the East India Company and in many other parts of the world, notably the United States and Brazil (indeed Rawson's introduction took aim at the United States, 'that land of *boasted* freedom,' for its hypocrisy on the subject of liberty). The book had a print run of 500 copies and was sold for 12 shillings, which is about £50 in today's money. Put another way, it was about two days' pay for a skilled tradesman, or about the cost of a week's supply of butchered meat and tea. This was thus a middle-class product, on the edge of affordability.

The published book is 408 pages with about 20 prefatory pages. Its frontispiece was signed by H. Corbould (Edward Henry Corbould), who would enjoy a long career as a book illustrator. Like other gift books of the time, the volume in the John Rylands Library appears handsome: its foolscap octavo pages (at 6¾″ × 4¼″) were gilt on the edges and bound in turkey morocco with a gilded engraving on the cover. The publication's advertisement pamphlet called attention to its quality, which is true: the (blended) goatskin-based binding is sturdy, even if it was bound too tightly and has frayed at the edges (a higher-quality binding would not have frayed in that way). The foolscap pages themselves were also reflective of most publications of the time, so it was not an exceptional piece of craft. Instead, it was a quality production that was typical of early industrial-era nineteenth-century printing, which was combined with the new forms of the literary anthology and the 'gift-book' economy (Faxon and Winthrop 1912; Fee 2013; Onslow 2017; Thompson 1934).

Beyond its material characteristics, what requires further study is the nature of the enterprise itself: this anthology was edited by a pioneering woman with specific aims that were complicated to articulate, at a crucial time in history. Tom Mole argues that the dynamic cultural practices of 'selecting, abridging, excerpting, framing, and mediating' of texts show 'the power of anthologies to shape how their readers read' (Mole 2017, 188). Also, as Dr Fionnghuala Sweeney has shown in her work on abolitionist publishing histories, much can be learned by studying in detail the racial, gender, and religious intersections of anti-slavery social networks.

The *Bow in the Cloud* demonstrates unique practices for several reasons: it is an early example of the political literary anthology and a rather large one (over 400 pages) with some long pieces, and it features grassroots activists, politicians, and well-known literary writers (but no famous Romantic authors, although Rawson tried to commission work from the likes of Wordsworth, Southey, and Thomas Moore). This kind of eclectic book not only reflected growing literacy rates in the UK but also was the product of several decades of activity from various publishing movements, including the religious press, cheaper printing technologies, the expansion of the literary marketplace after the era of radical political publishing, and the gift books published by women's anti-slavery societies. Soon afterward, anti-slavery activists in the United States would publish similar anthologies, including William Lloyd Garrison's anti-slavery hymn book (1834) and the successful run of the *Liberty Bell*, edited by Maria Weston Chapman.[2] The *Bow in the Cloud* also comes with an under-researched manuscript collection of more than 600 items that is revealing – particularly so for an anthology of this kind, with so many contributors. It is unusual for a collection like this – that is, a nineteenth-century anthology – to have such a rich archive of surviving manuscripts. The reason for this is that Rawson saved almost everything she received during the project. She later collected the manuscripts into a two-volume scrapbook with quality bindings.

Most submissions to the anthology came with a covering letter (and some submissions have multiple letters spanning from 1826 to 1834). The scrapbook also includes photographs, artworks, engravings, or newspaper clippings with some submissions. This illustration below is a good example of the wealth of archival material in this collection: it is a watercolour illustration submitted by Ann Gilbert to accompany her poem 'The Mother' (the poem was published in the anthology, but not this accompanying illustration). (See Figure 6.1.) Some of those fair copies show evidence of Rawson's revisions to the pieces before she supplied a printer's copy to the publisher. Rawson also collected poems that she chose not to publish.

The entire manuscript collection, housed at the John Rylands Library (Eng MSS 414 and 415), was digitized in 2020 as part of a digital humanities start-up grant in 2018/2019.[3] The digital images of more than 600 surviving manuscripts total 818 high-resolution files, which are now available on Manchester Digital Collections – with extensive metadata of each item based on a thorough study of the manuscripts – as open-access images on an image viewer (Mirador IIIF viewer). A separate GitHub repository hosts all of the project data, including TEI-XML transcriptions of the published pieces, manuscripts and prosopography.

The Bow in the Cloud exemplifies the principle that each archival collection requires unique kinds of editorial treatment. The edition employs a complementary method of text encoding as text analysis, as well as pragmatic theories of intentionality and creative-critical approaches (Ohge 2021). As Sarah Connell aptly put it, in relation to her work on the Women Writers Project's edition of *The History of Mary Prince*, 'when we approach our analysis with care and critical attention, the friction between complexity and abstraction becomes not paralyzing but generative, opening up new readings and supporting urgent research inquiries' (Connell 2025, 202). The primary purpose of the edition of the *Bow in the Cloud* is to show how the anthology was constructed based on

---

[2] *A selection of anti-slavery hymns, for the use of the friends of emancipation.* Boston: Garrison & Knapp, 1834. *The Liberty Bell* was an abolitionist annual published between 1839 and 1858. *The Liberty Bell* was sold at the National Anti-Slavery Bazaar headed by the Boston Female Anti-Slavery Society.

[3] This project first received financial support from the John Rylands Research Institute and Library, University of Manchester (2018/19). The project then received an NEH-Mellon Fellowship for Digital Publication in 2023/24 (FEL-289788).

Figure 6.1 Digitized facsimile of Ann Gilbert's illustration to accompany her poem 'The Mother' (John Rylands Library, Manchester).

the surviving documentary evidence. There are three parts to the edition: the published version of the anthology (along with the attendant manuscripts from the scrapbook relating to each piece); a selection of important unpublished material, including poems that were submitted but not published in 1834, letters from authors who declined to contribute to the anthology, and letters from contributors who offered thoughts on the anthology; and text analysis, network analysis and mapping tools to demonstrate the social and semantic networks, as well as the geographical clusters, of the people associated with the anthology.

Attending to these neglected documents makes it possible to discern Rawson's rationale for connecting with her readership. This also aims to facilitate research into how her choice of material mediated anti-slavery rhetoric at a crucial time when the British government was passing the 1833 Slavery Abolition Act and the American abolitionist movement, led by William Lloyd Garrison, was ramping up its publication activity. *The Bow in the Cloud*, as published, was representative of the abolitionist movement at this time, featuring religious leaders, politicians, non-professional writers and writers of repute. Among those who declined, however, are prominent names such as William Wordsworth, Robert Southey, Thomas Moore, Thomas Babington Macaulay and one of the founders of the British abolitionist movement, Thomas Clarkson. As F. S. Aird has shown, female anti-slavery societies in Newcastle and Darlington organized local meetings with prominent anti-slavery campaigners and spearheaded regional and national discourses about abolition and wider discussions about race and slavery. Books like *The Bow in the Cloud* offer a case study in these kinds of networks of rhetoric and influence, but it was based in Sheffield and connected to other English womens' anti-slavery societies.

The publisher, Jackson & Walford, was best known as the publisher of the nonconformist, progressive magazine *Eclectic Review* as well as the *Congregational Year Books* and other ecclesiastical books. One of the contributors to *The Bow in the Cloud*, Josiah Conder, had since 1813 been the owner and editor of the *Eclectic Review*, which also featured a substantial and laudatory review of *The Bow in the Cloud* in its July 1834 issue. This review was significant, since the *Eclectic Review* was one of the most prestigious literary periodicals of its time, one that published not only prominent romantic authors but also American authors such as Washington Irving. It was not long after the publication of *The Bow in the Cloud* that American abolitionists William Lloyd Garrison and Frederick Douglass visited Rawson and several of her peers, illustrating the significance of Rawson's stature and her noble attempt to influence public opinion through the force of literature and transatlantic networks.

Rawson's publication intersects with the moment in 1834 when, as Richard Huzzey has argued in his book *Freedom Burning* (2012), the British started to use 'anti-slavery' as a national credo that projected moral superiority over other civilizations. Yet Rawson's anthology, and the cache of unpublished material she decided to save, shows that she was aware that such posturing was far from altruistic or compassionate, as new forms of violence and economic exploitation of colonial possessions continued to be central to British foreign policy and British allies.

Rawson's work on the anthology shows her as an active editor, organizer, and writer. Rawson relied on her social network of anti-slavery activists, not only through the Sheffield Ladies Anti-Slavery Society but also in London and elsewhere. The details can also be rendered as data and statistics that aid researchers, and that is the guiding principle of producing this digital edition.

Rethinking editorial theories

The focus on Rawson's editorial rationale presents challenges to textual scholars. Some of these are met with different kinds of digital tools, including a linked biographical index, an annotated map of placenames, and demographic statistics. But other editorial issues can be met by using pragmatic and creative-critical approaches, including enhanced revision narratives, open annotation, and digital storytelling tools.

Another editorial crux involves the status of the scrapbook itself. As Eleanor Bird suggests, 'The scrapbooks are a collection in their own right and can be understood not only as Rawson's attempt to store her papers relating to the gift book but also to preserve a record of her relationships and a memory of her writing project' (Bird 2021). It is an open question as to whether an intimate circle of Rawson's family and friends circulated the *Bow in the Cloud* scrapbooks instead of the printed gift book and whether some of those manuscript copies were made before or after the anthology was printed. Several of Rawson's fair copies of manuscripts precede the printed book. This can be demonstrated by the fact that many of Rawson's fair copies differ from the final published version, suggesting that further revisions were made in a printer's copy that is not known to survive. But other pieces of evidence show that many of these copies preceded the publication and were used as preparatory copies for a printer's copy. For instance, on the top of the first page of Thomas Burchell's missionary narrative (English MS 414/60b), Rawson wrote in pencil, 'To follow Knibb's Persecuted Missionary' (which is also written by a missionary). Examples like this suggest that many (if not all) of these manuscripts were first part of the editorial enterprise before they were scrapbooked. Bird concludes:

> By presenting these voices wholesale, Rawson connected to a moment of national reflection on the legacy of British colonial slavery in 1833–34 and placed her own abolitionist ideas and activism within this wider context. The scrapbooks therefore not only preserve the contributions and letters but collate a vaster archive that represented a wider social network than was involved in the printed version. (Bird 2021)

It is the goal of this edition to evince this 'vaster archive' with digital tools.

The edition adopts a pluralistic approach that is indebted to Peter Shillingsburg and John Bryant's theories – Shillingsburg's digital pluralism and Bryant's 'fluid text' theory in particular. This edition's focus on Rawson's editorial rationale therefore employs aspects of several editorial approaches, including the historical-documentary, genetic text and social text theories, yet it also adopts a principle of Rawson's editorial intentions using a logic similar to a critical editor's. It also follows Dirk Van Hulle's important proposition that by knowing how a text was made, we can understand *how* and *why* it works (Van Hulle 2022). Instead of focusing on the authorial intentions of the writers in the anthology, I follow Rawson's editorial judgements as the anchor for textual decision-making. The fact that the book is a multi-author literary anthology also presents new challenges to an editor, but the aim is to show how the book was made and why she and her collaborators made their decisions. At the same time, the documentary and book's historical focus requires attention to meta-textual information about what Van Hulle (2024) calls the 'ecologies of writing' – the conditions under which the book was edited and disseminated. Yet textual editors still need better models for how to evince such important theoretical ideas in the space of digital technologies and web infrastructures.

The best way to ensure sustainable and understandable digital textual work is not to produce the best websites or interfaces but to focus on creating sustainable data models and the curation of FAIR data. As such, the FAIR XML-encoded documents that comprise the digital edition are accessible on GitHub and available for download. These documents consist not only of poem and prose fair copies (many of which were revised by Rawson) but also of the original submissions with their contributors' cover letters. Encoding these unpublished documents gives researchers a sense of the varieties of work and information exchange that went into the publishing of this anthology, as well as the connections among the documents that form the basis of network analysis tools. For example, there are at least three versions of the preface that Rawson collaboratively wrote: two drafts and the published version. But there is one striking unpublished note evidently intended for the preface that reveals Rawson's struggle to justify her role before the public:

> The Editor of this little volume is not placed in the awkward predicament of many original writers, who feel it necessary to make an apology for (appearing before the public) or (for adding to the number of books already before the public). She has no apology to offer – nay – so far from feeling one needful and pleading for indulgence, she is enabled to take far higher ground – she feels that she has conferred a favour on the public especially the junior part of it, and she can unhesitating[ly] say, that she considers [these] a most valuable & rare collection of original papers. (English MS 415/199a/1)[4]

Rawson chose not to sign her preface in the published version, so her 'role' was as an anonymous editor from Wincobank Hall, Sheffield. Her name does not appear anywhere in the published book.

Thinking of digital editing as a pragmatic method of encoding and analysis facilitates experiences through the anthology's wider social connections not only to other archival materials but also to other anti-slavery activists (Ohge 2021). For example, the sanguine verse that started to appear between the British 1807 Slave Trade Act and the 1833 Slavery Abolition Act, such as Montgomery's *The West Indies and Other Poems* (1823), came with a less celebratory tone in *The Bow in the Cloud*. Montgomery's Moravianism is an under-explored strand of the transatlantic religious map of British abolitionism. He connects to European and US anti-slavery through the poetry of Lydia Huntley Sigourney, who published a collection of poems about the Moravian Count Zinzendorf in 1835. In 'Leonard Dober', Montgomery narrates the Moravians's first evangelical mission to the West Indies, in 1732, to convert Black enslaved people. Montgomery is a guiding light in this collection in other ways, too, for many of the contributors were friendly with him or had worked with him (as was the case with Rawson). In one of his letters to Rawson, he advises her on how to edit some poems in the collection. There are other important

---

[4] https://antislavery-anthologies.org/books/bow-in-the-cloud/editioncrafter-view-of-the-notes-to-the-preface?path=preface#/ec.

examples of collaboration, such as from the Reverend J. W. H. (Joseph William Henry) Pritchard (English MS 414/63, 414/64, and 414/67), who also offered editorial advice on some submitted poems and the preface; Jeremiah Holmes Wiffen (English MS 414/33), who provided ideas for the title of the anthology; and Richard Cecil (English MS 415/181), who contributed language for the book's advertisement and preface that Rawson adopted.[5]

Data analysis

The digital edition of *The Bow in the Cloud* has rendered the 408-page printed anthology and (as of this writing) thirty-four unpublished manuscripts into machine-readable XML data that can be used for various analytical purposes. These data analyses can offer the user of the edition different methods of discovery and research in ways that can be more effective than reading texts or annotations.

The published anthology is roughly 73,000 total words, with 9,917 unique word forms, and averages 25.1 words per sentence. Its vocabulary density is 0.135; readability index, 10.340.[6] The fourteen most frequent substantive words are also revealing:

Term	Count
shall	247
god	204
slave	191
man	159
free	152
slavery	122
love	114
slaves	107
negro	107
men	104
heart	98
liberty	97
day	92
lord	86

---

[5]See the edition's Selected Unpublished Pieces section at https://antislavery-anthologies.org/books/bow-in-the-cloud/selected-unpublished-pieces.
[6]Vocabulary density refers to the ratio of the number of words in a document to the number of unique words in the document. Readability index measures how difficult a text is to read, based on factors such as word length, sentence length and syllable counts.

Fuzzy searches of these top terms also suggest some critical interpretations: slave* 443 times; free* 279; god* 219; liber* 124. From a content perspective, enslaved people and the institution of slavery far outweigh the notion of God or godliness; freedom is privileged over liberty.

Among the unpublished texts featured in the edition, the word 'work' has a high frequency (thirty-two times); 'think' and 'hope' both appear twenty-five times. It might be surprising that a heavy word like 'blood' appears eleven times, but it also appears sixty-two times in the published version.

The published anthology features fifty-nine writers. As the People Mentioned page of the edition shows, all but four authors (A. H. Smith, J. R., Elizabeth Jones and one who is anonymous) could be identified. Of the fifty-nine published writers, forty-three could be identified as male authors and fourteen as female (see also Peter Webster's chapter in this volume for a similar analytical approach to quantifying text, disambiguating names and critically positioning religious affiliation within approaches to printing and readership). In some cases, the anthology did not name the author of a piece, but they have been identified through the analysis of their manuscripts. One of the tasks of curating this data was to undo the evident patriarchal elements of the book. The most prominent example is the Preface, which was authored but not signed by Rawson (again, she is not named anywhere in the book). There are other examples of name standardization: 'The Slave Ship,' by 'S.', was written by Mary Sterndale; 'The Martyred Missionary's Grave,' by 'T. R. T.', was written by Thomas Rawson Taylor; 'The Lot of the Slave,' by 'R. C---l', was written by Richard Cecil; and 'The Hope of the Slave', by 'E.', was written by Elizabeth Walker. One important feature too is that authors' names are made consistent in the edition: for example, in the book Miss Dinah Ball is also Dinah Townley (Dinah Ball married James Townley while the book was being compiled); 'Mrs Josiah Conder' is labelled Eliza Conder; and 'Mrs. Henry Walker' is Elizabeth Walker.

The religious affiliations are interesting: fourteen authors were Congregationalists (which is not surprising because Rawson was a Congregationalist), fourteen Anglicans (many of whom were evangelicals, but some were not), eight Quakers, four Methodists, four Baptists, three Unitarians, two Presbyterians, one Moravian and one Spiritualist (or Swedenborgian). (See Figure 6.2)

Religious affiliations were determined through biographical analysis and secondary sources that could identify church membership. Admittedly, this is a difficult designation. In some (unambiguous) cases, authors were open about their affiliation and some were employed within a particular church. In other cases, religious affiliations could be inferred through baptism records, burial records, and associations with a particular milieu. It is also impossible in some cases to ascertain whether religious feeling was strong or whether it was social. While these latter cases may seem tenuous, it is still worthwhile to consider how the religious context of a writer may have affected their views and rhetoric on slavery.

Scholars may wonder what kind of narrative shape and sentiment value may be applied to this book. As a 'commemoration', does the book have a narrative arc? According to

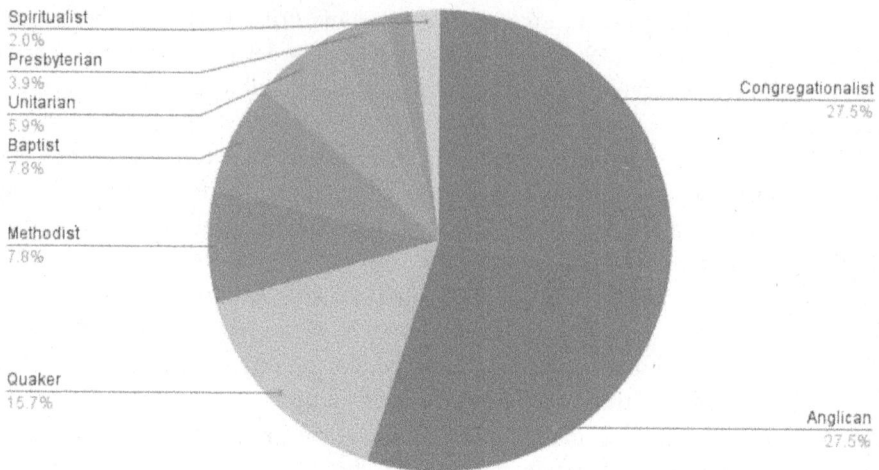

Figure 6.2 Religious affiliations for contributors published in *The Bow in the Cloud*.

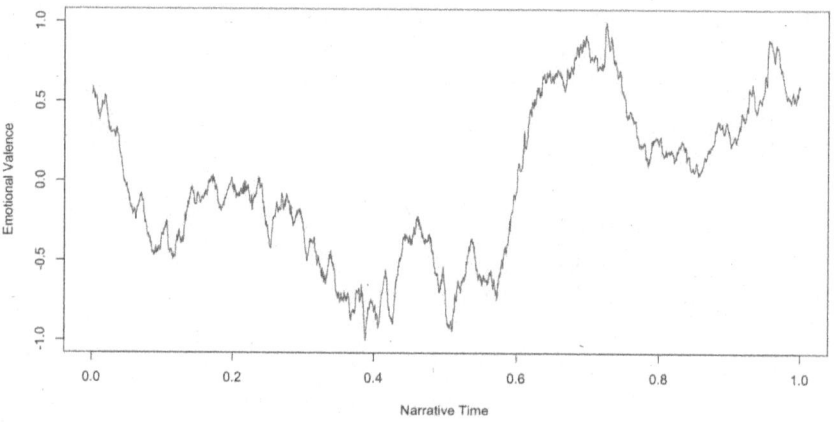

Figure 6.3 Sentiment values in *The Bow in the Cloud* (published text, 1834), with Rolling Means.

sentiment scores, the book does show a 'happy ending', with a dark middle period.[7] (See Figure 6.3)

The overall sentiment score of the published book is -89.95. This is less negative than the two other prominent narratives of slavery from this era, Mary Prince's (-96.3) and Olaudah Equiano's (-120.25). The narrative shape of Rawson's anthology is also different from Prince and Equiano's.

---

[7] These sentiment results were generated from the syuzhet package in R, developed by Matthew Jockers (https://cran.r-project.org/web/packages/syuzhet/vignettes/syuzhet-vignette.html).

These data analysis tools are meant to emphasize different reading experiences of this edition and to facilitate new research questions and methods of discovery: for example, how might narrative shape be different in an anthology? How would that affect the reading experience?

Such dynamic aspects of meaning and textual production can be enhanced with detailed TEI-XML encoding of the published text and manuscripts, yet, as Sarah Connell has argued, that work is very time-consuming and sometimes takes away from the work of narrative building and other important aspects of textual analysis (Connell 2025, 207). While the markup is important, this editorial project is more than the sum of its bibliographical facts or its data model – the networks of the archive, the data and their statistical valence, as well as the inclusions and omissions surrounding Rawson's editorial vision, also merit consideration. *The Bow in the Cloud* edition is pragmatic because the material suggests a focus on the book's genesis as well as the data connected to the publishing of a physical book – the nodes of which can be illustrated, analysed and networked with computation and digital publication.

Creative-critical revision narratives and 'data stories'

The previous methods covered in this essay concern some older elements (transcription) and newer elements (data analysis and visualization) of digital textual scholarship. However, digital media also open up editing to creative-critical approaches that centre the creativity and aesthetic potentials inherent in scholarly editing (Nabugodi and Ohge 2022; Ohge 2025).

One approach is to expand John Bryant's idea of the revision narrative. A revision narrative is meant to complement (or replace) the traditional (and print-based) *apparatus criticus*, which conveys a list of variants in an edition but which does little to expand on the critical or aesthetic significance of the revision(s). While it is true that many printed editions had separate sections for 'textual notes' to attempt such narratives, they were still often placed in the back of the book, and it was usually impossible to see those revisions in high-quality images of their original documents. For example, in James Montgomery's letter to Mary Anne Rawson (English MS 414/81), he offers suggestions for revising James Townley's sermon 'The Abolition of Slavery' in the anthology.[8] He indicates in the letter, 'The sentence respecting Buxton certainly does read awkwardly [. . .] After the word "Senate," you might omit the "and," place a semicolon after the former word, and read thus: "Senate; where eventually, his great" &c. Then remember to strike out a "eventually" in the last line [. . .] of the paragraph.' The edition offers two layers of revision narrative and creative-critical apparatus: the first is a public annotation with Hypothes.is, prompted by my open-ended question, 'Why is Townley's original phrasing

---

[8] https://antislavery-anthologies.org/books/bow-in-the-cloud/letter-from-james-montgomery-to-mary-anne-rawson-english-ms-41481.

awkward? Does the suggested revision improve the piece?' to which users can respond; the second is a revision narrative note explaining that Rawson followed Montgomery's suggestions while offering more information about the versions of the piece.

Another revision narrative demonstrates again the collaborative nature of the anthology as well as the potential for juxtaposing multiple versions of texts. The edited text of the Reverend J. W. H. Pritchard's letter to Rawson (English MS 414/63) explains that he suggested dropping the first three stanzas of Sarah J. Williams's poem 'Voice from the Land of Bondage', as well as offering other minor revisions.[9]

Another approach employs a kind of guided tour through manuscripts to effect a 'data story'. I experimented with this idea in the edition with 'Compensation for the Slave', written by the prominent abolitionist, Quaker and MP Thomas Buxton. Buxton's submission came in a 6 October 1833 letter to Rawson at the end of which Buxton admits, 'you are of course at liberty' to include and amend the contribution. The printed first line is not the same as the extract in his letter. In her fair copy of his extract, Rawson proceeded to revise sections of it and added some pencil revisions towards the end of the process. Yet she was evidently not satisfied with it. On the back of the last page of her fair copy of Thomas Pringle's poem 'The Wild Forester', she copied the first half of Buxton's letter extract in pencil and added further revisions, which were adopted in the published version. The opening of the published version of Buxton's letter extract appears to have been rewritten by Rawson.

Buxton's published letter extract therefore has four material versions: the original letter, Rawson's fair copy (with her revisions), Rawson's rewritten opening of the extract, and the published version. An editor might use an apparatus and notes to convey this complicated transmission, and perhaps a digital editor would be able to present all four versions in the edition. While I opted for the latter option, I still realized that the narrative glue was missing. While presenting this project at the *Out of Practice* creative-critical studies seminar at the Institute of English Studies, in London, the artist Emily Orley asked me why I didn't use digital storytelling to convey this information. It reminded me of Brett Barney's attempt to animate Walt Whitman's revisions using a combination of TEI encoding and video animation (and, as Wim Van Mierlo shows in Chapter 9 of this volume, we could do better at 'unlocking literary heritage' with digital storytelling). Then, Huw Jones, the Digital Scholarship coordinator at Cambridge University Library, introduced the IIIF-based storytelling tool Exhibit (https://www.exhibit.so/) while guest lecturing for my London Rare Books School summer school course on the Book Historian's Digital Toolkit. I decided to use this tool to guide users through the four versions of Buxton's letter extract in a 'data story'. (See Figure 6.4)

Animation, storytelling, and other forms of interactive revision narratives could enhance the experience of users of digital editions. Such experiences combine elements of editing, curation and creative-critical approaches to situate users within the scholarly and aesthetic possibilities of working with texts.

---

[9]https://antislavery-anthologies.org/books/bow-in-the-cloud/a-voice-from-the-land-of-bondage.

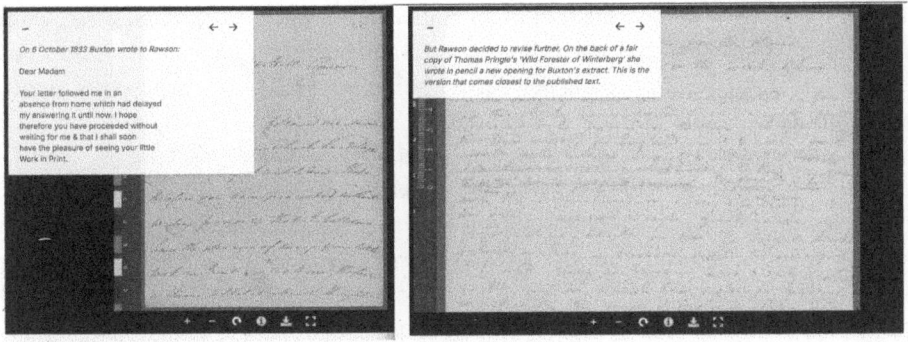

Figure 6.4 Data story (two screenshots): Thomas Buxton's 'Compensation'.

Conclusion

The Bow in the Cloud expands on unique manuscript evidence to draw attention to the editor of the anthology, her collaborators and the nature of the book as a significant publishing event within networks of anti-slavery print culture. Rawson's example illustrates the shift from what editing *is* to what it *does* in the digital age, as it is not solely object-based but rather activity-based: it focuses on various roles of authors, editors, works and readers existing within complex information networks involved in publishing an anthology in the 1830s.

Digital editors are also well aware of the problems of sustainability for innovative projects. Yet it must be emphasized that the methods proposed here come out of a distributed open data model: that is to say, all of the edition's source data is FAIR (findable, accessible, interoperable, and reusable) and therefore portable. Some projects might also combine FAIR data with the CARE principles, which are appropriate for neglected collections and those involving ethnic minority and indigenous groups.[10] With respect to CARE principles, responsible digital editing can extend into community awareness and ethics. The interfaces of the current edition are the product of multiple FAIR data formats (txt, xml, html, json) in a computational pipeline; as such, any of the data sources could be used to create alternative interfaces. In theory, an AI tool might be able to access this open data and generate a data analysis tool or interface. Rather than privileging the final edition – like editors were forced into doing when printed books were the only option – digital textual scholars can curate FAIR data that could proliferate in many different ways for many different experiences. Just to underline this point, a collection of digital facsimiles with substantial metadata, or something like the Exhibit 'data story', demonstrates how connecting digital facsimiles with narrative

---

[10]CARE stands for Collective Benefit, Authority to Control, Responsibility and Ethics, emphasizing the importance of ethical data use and Indigenous self-determination. For more on CARE principles, see https://www.gida-global.org/care.

can be as effective a knowledge tool as an edited transcription. Tools like these, when complemented with text analysis, network graphs and maps that show their connections, are also significant for discovering new ideas – some of which do not necessarily require transcriptions to be effective.

The edition of this anthology aspires to model a digital museum of archival experience. Through a digital reconstruction of encoded texts from a large archive and a broad consideration of literary, archival and socio-political networks, this curated experience starts with an annotated reading text based on the published book and moves through an exhibition of facsimiles of archival materials in a complex network of information. The information can take the form of subject tags, maps, dendrograms, library catalogue data, data stories, as well as the standard reading text. Yet the edition is also designed to optimize nonlinear exploration through various analysis tools, freeing up the user to engage with the text in different ways. As an archival recovery project of a publishing event, *The Bow in the Cloud* digital edition illustrates a model for scholars to move beyond the constraints of single-author editions, presenting new opportunities for experimentation with a greater diversity of texts in our archives.

Bibliography

Aird, F. S. 'Workers, Wives and Radicals: Women and Abolitionism in the North-East of England, 1792–1865'. *Slavery & Abolition* (January 2024): 1–21. https://doi.org/10.1080/0144039X.2024.2303061.

Barney, Brett. 'TEI, the Walt Whitman Archive, and the Test of Time'. *TEI: Journal of the Text Encoding Initiative*, 13 (2020). https://doi.org/10.4000/jtei.3249.

Bird, Eleanor. 'A Woman of Letters: Mary Anne Rawson's Letter Collection and her Compilation of the Anti-Slavery Gift Book *The Bow in the Cloud*, 1826–1834'. *Nineteenth-Century Gender Studies* 17, no. 2 (Summer 2021). https://www.ncgsjournal.com/issue172/bird.html.

Bryant, John. *The Fluid Text: A Theory of Revision and Editing for Book and Screen*. Ann Arbor: University of Michigan Press, 2002.

Carey, Brycchan. *From Peace to Freedom: Quaker Rhetoric and the Birth of American Antislavery, 1657–1761*. New Haven: Yale University Press, 2012.

Clapp, Elizabeth J. and Julie Roy Jeffrey, eds. *Women, Dissent & Anti-Slavery in Britain and America, 1790–1865*. Oxford: Oxford University Press, 2011.

Connell, Sarah. 'The History of Mary Prince and Digital Humanities'. In *The Cambridge Companion to Mary Prince*, 201–18. Edited by Nicole N. Aljoe. Cambridge: Cambridge University Press, 2025.

Faxon, Frederick Winthrop. *Literary Annuals and Gift Books: A Bibliography with a Descriptive Introduction*. Boston Book Company, 1912.

Ferguson, Moira. *Subject to Others: British Women Writers and Colonial Slavery, 1670–1834*. London: Routledge, 1992.

Fritz, Meaghan M. and Frank E. Fee Jr. 'To Give the Gift of Freedom: Gift Books and the War on Slavery'. *American Periodicals*, 23, no. 1 (2013): 60–82.

Halbersleben, Karen. *Women's Participation in the British Antislavery Movement 1824–1865*. Lewiston, NY: Edwin Mellen Press, 1993.

Harris, Katherine D. *Forget Me Not: The Rise of the British Annual, 1823–1835*. Columbus: Ohio University Press, 2015.

Hulle, Dirk Van. 'Creative Ecologies: The Complete-Works Edition in a Digital Paradigm'. In *Futures of Digital Scholarly Editing*. Edited by Matt Cohen, Kenneth M. Price, and Caterina Bernardini. Minneapolis: University of Minnesota Press, 2024.

Hulle, Dirk Van. *Genetic Criticism: Tracing Creativity in Literature*. Oxford: Oxford University Press, 2022.

Huzzey, Richard. *Freedom Burning: Anti-Slavery and Empire in Victorian Britain*. Ithaca: Cornell University Press, 2012.

Levy, Michelle. *Family Authorship and Romantic Print Culture*. London: Palgrave Macmillan, 2008.

Levy, Michelle. *Literary Manuscript Culture in Romantic Britain*. Edinburgh: Edinburgh University Press, 2020.

Midgley, Clare. *Women Against Slavery: The British Campaigns 1780–1870*. London: Routledge, 1992.

Mole, Tom. *What the Victorians Made of Romanticism*. Princeton: Princeton University Press, 2017.

Nabugodi, Mathelinda and Christopher Ohge, eds. Special Issue: 'Creative-Critical Provocations'. *Textual Cultures* 15, no. 1 (2022). https://www.jstor.org/stable/e48511031.

Ohge, Christopher. 'Beyond Representation: Some Thoughts on Creative-Critical Digital Editing'. In *Twenty-First Century Digital Editing & Publishing*. Edited by James O'Sullivan, Michael Pidd, Bridgette Wessels, Michael Kurzmeier, Órla Murphy, and Sophie Whittle. Edinburgh: Scottish Universities Press, 2025.

Ohge, Christopher. 'The Making of an Anti-Slavery Anthology: Mary-Anne Rawson and *the Bow in the Cloud*'. *John Rylands Research Institute Blog*, 24 April 2019. https://sites.manchester.ac.uk/jrri-blog/2019/04/24/the-making-of-an-anti-slavery-anthology-mary-anne-rawson-and-the-bow-in-the-cloud-part-1/.

Ohge, Christopher. *Publishing Scholarly Editions: Archives, Computing, and Experience*. Cambridge: Cambridge University Press, 2021.

Onslow, Barbara. 'Gendered Productions: Annuals and Gift Books'. In *Journalism and the Periodical Press in Britain*, 66–83. Edited by Joanne Shattock. Cambridge: Cambridge University Press, 2017.

Prince, Mary. *The History of Mary Prince*. Edited by Thomas Pringle. London, 1831. Women Writers Online, Women Writers Project, Northeastern University. www.wwp.northeastern.edu/texts/prince.history.html.

Shillingsburg, Peter L. *From Gutenberg to Google: Electronic Representations of Literary Texts*. Cambridge: Cambridge University Press, 2006.

Thompson, Ralph. 'The *Liberty Bell* and Other Anti-Slavery Gift Books'. *New England Quarterly* 7, no. 1 (1934): 154–68.

Turley, David. *The Culture of English Antislavery, 1780–1860*. London: Routledge, 2004.

Twells, Alison. *The Civilising Mission and the English Middle Class: the 'Heathen' at Home and Overseas, 1792–1850*. London: Palgrave Macmillan, 2009.

CHAPTER 7
EXTRACTING FOR EXPERIENCE
MATERIAL ANNOTATION AND ITS AFFORDANCES IN TEXTUAL STUDIES
Mary Erica Zimmer

'Only Connect!' engaging encyclopaedic narrative

Amid the ebb and flow of daily experience, the ability of artistic works to lend shape to existence remains a truism – a point gestured towards by E. M. Forster's oft-quoted epigraph to *Howard's End*, a text itself advanced in an age of fragmentation. Yet while Forster's novel highlights the sense of orientation that works of art may provide, the sheer scope of some texts – whether verbal or visual – can impact the terms of encounter they offer.[1] Here, Edward Mendelson's concept of the 'encyclopedic narrative' captures the dual challenge that a select few, including *Moby-Dick*, present: to be understood fully, they must be approached in 'terms . . . both historical and formal' (Forster 1910; Mendelson 1976). Those who seek to support readers' engagement with the challenges such works pose must consider both informational and aesthetic 'gaps' they may involve. Without appropriate support for the simultaneously broad and deep reading required, 'encyclopedic' texts can convey vastness and obscurity at once – a combination potentially paralyzing to even the most enthusiastic of audiences (Mischke 2022). Providing appropriate 'handles', through annotation, for readers to take hold of the textual 'bundles' these works present is thus vital.

Might extraction, properly understood, pave the way for recalibrating perspectives? In general, the negative connotations of 'extraction' arise from the word's use in contexts linked to exploitation and environmental degradation – yet delving into the nuances of the term sheds light. Within a wider argument distinguishing extraction from extractivism, Jeffery Insko echoes this insight, contrasting 'material' with 'literary' extraction as follows:

> The former, of course, is violent, exploitative, instrumentalist, and we now know all too well, unsustainable and ultimately self-defeating. The latter, by contrast, is (relatively speaking, at least) playful, generous, generative, and renewable – and finds its apogee, I think, in the 'Extracts' that Melville assembles and presents as preface to *Moby-Dick*. (Insko 2023, 73–87)

---

[1] Edward Mendelson terms such works, including *Moby-Dick*, 'encyclopedic narratives' (Mendelson 1976).

Counterpoising the two allows Insko to consider actions such as 'copying, excerpting, borrowing, and reproducing': all practices retaining some connection to contexts in which desired items or passages arise (Insko 2023, 73).

How one's own multifaceted perspective might be brought to bear on a topic is a question that gains force in light of John Dewey's insight that 'the actual work of art is what the product does with and in experience' (Dewey 1934, 3). At first glance, this view seems to chime with Melville's working to shape material from his own year and a half at sea (as well as his own extensive reading) into the novelistic forms of *Moby-Dick* (Bryant 2007). Yet Dewey's words also suggest the importance of offering multiple modes of engagement through which readers may develop their own registers of connection with potentially obscure entities the novel contains. Doing so creates conditions of possibility to enrich one's sense of these objects' 'general significance' in contexts from which they are drawn (Dewey 1934, 3). As well, such work sets the stage for readers' registering how these named objects may figure in the narrative. By inviting participation and reconsideration, strategies of this kind encourage readers to revisit foundations upon which the novel's narrative draws, then leverage their deepened perspective as they revisit the potentially alienating aesthetic 'wall' of the text itself (Dewey 1934, 3).

As we shape editions to meet readers' potential needs, our annotations should provide points of entry into an evolving aesthetic conversation through support that is minimally interventionist but of maximal impact. Yet fine-tuning an annotation's pitch can prove challenging. As Samuel Johnson once noted, it remains the editor's task 'to correct what is corrupt, and to explain what is obscure' (Johnson 1745). Insofar as new audiences inevitably grow more distant from a text in time and experience, however, anticipating and addressing their needs becomes increasingly complex. As against Johnson's eighteenth-century editorial confidence, one might place William Empson's twentieth-century concern that the desire to annotate tactfully may itself prove vexed as spheres of knowledge grow more specialized (Empson 1987). Might encouraging annotation in a new register help widen interpretive horizons (Hanna 1991, 78)? Exploring the insights that tactile engagement can bring evokes Michael Polyani's sense of 'tacit knowledge' as an 'embodied' realm of expertise. Annotations drawing on this register would – echoing his words – 'know more' than they can immediately 'tell', while expanding what Hans Robert Jauss might term readers' 'horizons of expectations' about the object and its operations (Polyani 2009; Benzinger 1967).

What follows is a framework for engaging the 'book' of *Moby-Dick* digitally through both computational techniques and haptic points of entry. Such approaches can help audiences work 'against the grain' of fictionalized experience. Carried along by an overarching narrative, readers may well tend to elide or deprioritize terms that initially seem unfamiliar, especially in works as substantial as this one. Yet the cumulative effect of unfamiliarity can be alienating. Using material annotation provides touchstones through which those new to a novel can recalibrate and recontextualize their sense of relation to less familiar entities therein. Since these objects can also prove more broadly resonant within the whole, pausing to reorient oneself through experiences of tangible connection holds the potential to intervene even more deeply in one's understanding (McGowan, Hoffstaedter and Creese 2022; Norouzinia et al. 2022).

Grappling with immensity: The body of the whale

Viewing the 'body' of *Moby-Dick* in terms of its encyclopaedic nature and concomitant lexical bounty is nothing new: within the Digital Humanities, using an introductory 'word cloud' strategy brings forward both the novel's scope and its verbal range (see Figure 7.1):

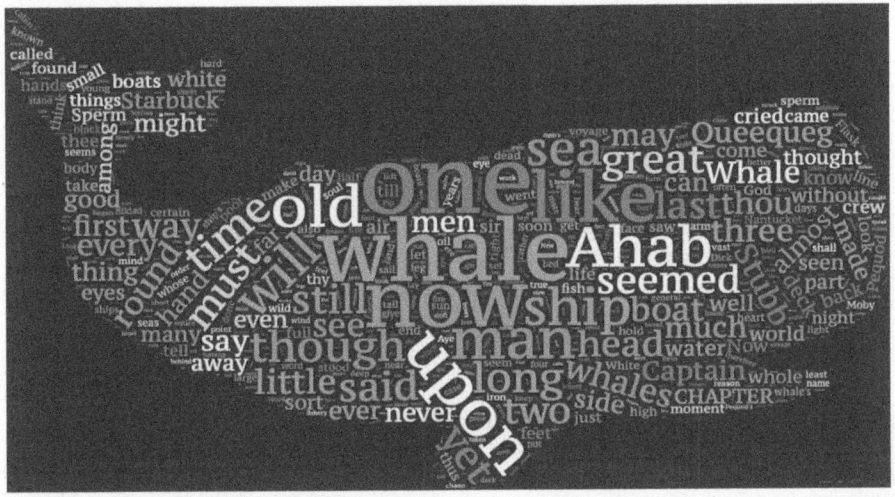

Figure 7.1 Text of *Moby-Dick*, represented through word cloud software. Created in 2021 using https://www.wordclouds.com.

Here, the largest terms within the image convey the most frequent substantive word forms in the text; size is a reflection of number. In itself, this visualized verbal density proves a starting point for exploration. As a single novel, *Moby-Dick* has 16,950 word 'types', or forms, and 218,385 'tokens', or instances of the same. By contrast, the complete works of Shakespeare (as edited through the Folger Digital Texts) contain 24,483 types (978,678 tokens); the novels of Jane Austen, 15,386 types (783,763 tokens). In tandem with this lexical richness, *Moby-Dick*'s use of multiple discourses specific to worlds of whaling can lead contemporary readers to experience objects and dynamics depicted therein as obscure, despite the narrative's being only a few hundred years removed from them in time.[2]

---

[2]For *Moby-Dick* and Shakespeare, counts were obtained through AntConc's 'Word List' function: https://antconc-manual.readthedocs.io/en/latest/word_list.html; for Jane Austen, through Voyant: https://voyant-tools.org/?corpus=5d96f342c0e227eab60e3d6a6082034d&view=DocumentTerms.

Yet while this visualized verbal composite may be pleasing, the light it sheds on the significance of individual terms is limited, since the underlying algorithms used to create it give greatest prominence to words already likely to be perceived as vital – a point that digital humanities research often highlights. Relying solely on the perspective such a lens provides under-reads the potential of less common terms to serve as powerful points of connection (Froehlich 2019).

Cognate with *Moby-Dick*'s verbal plenitude are visually variegated texts like Jos Sances's *Or, the Whale*: a 51-foot scratchboard mural – the size of a female sperm whale – that inscribes within the body of its subject a host of extractive industries, as manifested in the history of the United States and more broadly. As Tim Drescher explains in his *Catalogue Key to 'Or, the Whale'*:

> The mural's title, which is the subtitle of Herman Melville's epic 1851 novel, *Moby-Dick*, immediately draws attention to the relationship between the mural and the novel that inspired it, but it is important to distinguish between the two. The novel is about whales, whaling, adventure, myth, labor. . . . The mural is about the consequences of capitalism, of our actions or inactions seen against visions of the future we are leaving our children and grandchildren. It is also about whales. For example, the scratches visible on the whale's snout typically come from sperm whales' ingesting giant squids, whose tentacle hooks scratch the animals as they are eaten. This art work is a metaphorical scratch on capitalism's snout. (Drescher 2021) (See Figure 7.2)

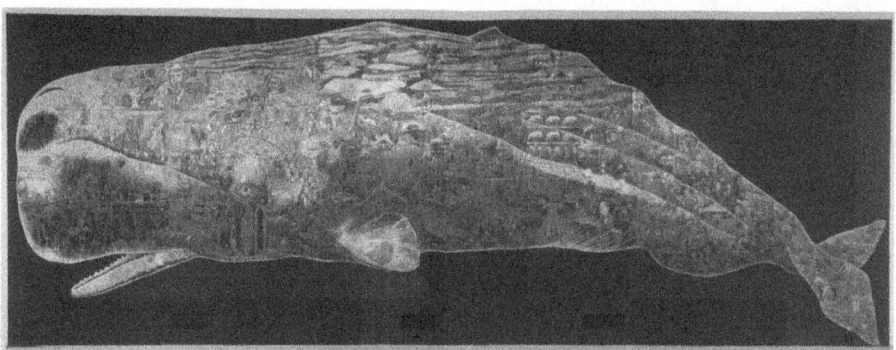

Figure 7.2 'Or, the Whale,' by Jos Sances (2020–1). Image from Drescher, *Catalogue Key*, 3. See also the time-lapse install linked through Sances' website at https://josart.net/.

Engaging the complexity of this visual text also shows the effects and power of scale upon perspective: at a distance, those viewing the work tend to register its outline, given the contrast of the whale's brightly inscribed body against the scratchboard's dark background. As one moves closer, however, details of individual industries and images emerge, as do connections suggested by these elements' spatial arrangement. (See Figures 7.3a and 7.3b) Such movement is modelled through 'Or, the Eye', a StoryMap created

Extracting for Experience

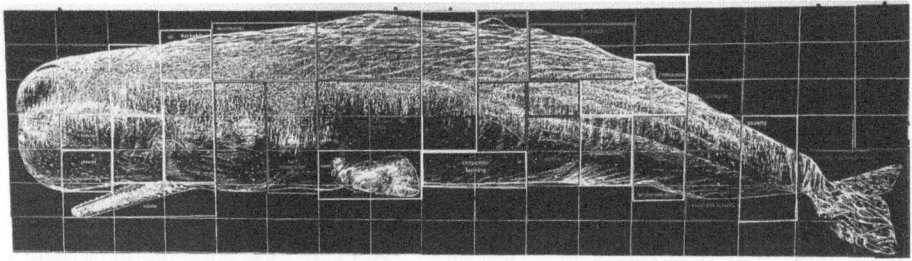

Figure 7.3a 'Or, the Whale,' with section headings (credit: Jos Sances, 2020–1). For a zoomable colour view, see https://tinyurl.com/2n2296cp.

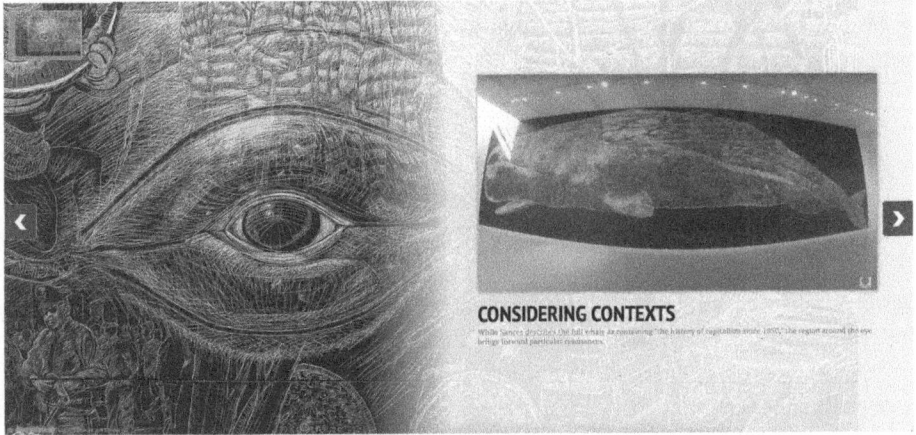

Figure 7.3b Detail from 'Or, the Eye' StoryMap (credit: Erica Zimmer and Jeff Peterson, 2021). For the 'Or, the Eye' StoryMap created by Erica Zimmer and Jeff Peterson, see https://uploads.knightlab.com/storymapjs/8614707ce8a6fbbbd2abadf1af0113d6/or-the-eye/index.html.

for Sances by Erica Zimmer and Jeff Peterson that provides support for grappling with the whole's complexity by affording users the opportunity to 'zoom into' one particular region: the visually dense area surrounding the whale's eye, where images rendering the human toll of exploitation and misrepresentation are densely packed. While these constituent images grow more obscure with each passing year, the vivid, troubled places many still hold in cultural memory – such as the chained bodies of the Scottsboro Boys, seen immediately above the whale's pupil – continue to compel viewers to appreciate the thrust of Sances's commentary.

Metaphorically, the ability to engage and reflect at multiple levels upon this visual whole chimes with the support necessary for reading *Moby-Dick* in any edition. What follows is a meditation upon a programme of annotation that might initially appear extractive, given its goal of bringing forward unfamiliar keywords as touchstones for their immediate contexts. Specifically, I will show how such an approach supports readers' exploring the significance of individual entities, then re-engaging contours of the broader narrative along lines that depend for the assistance they provide upon accumulated, evolving experiences with the objects in question.

Captioning and contexts: Models from museum theory

Visiting the world of museum theory provides context for this approach to annotation. As discussed by Beverly Serrell and Katherine Whitney in 2024, contemporary theories of creating museum exhibitions emphasize the importance of encouraging visitors to connect personally with contexts from which the objects displayed have come (Serrell and Whitney 2024). Such a view evokes John Dewey's sense of the 'actual work of art' as an entity that refines and extends lived experience. However, the status of such a work *as* art becomes comprehensible only insofar as it is recontextualized amid its conditions of creation. As Dewey observes:

> In common conception, the work of art is often identified with the building, book, painting, or statue in its existence apart from human experience. Since the actual work of art is what the product does with and in experience, the result is not favorable to understanding. (Dewey 1934, 3)

Dewey's attention to how works of art intervene 'with and in experience' connects the realms of visual art and museum studies to the curated 'worlds of whaling' that readers are invited to enter through *Moby-Dick*. Honouring Dewey's sense of artworks as crystallizing potentially lived trajectories is Serrell and Whitney's 2024 discussion of 'interpretive exhibitions', which they cast as seeking to 'tell stories' and 'contrast points of view'. Such exhibitions, they observe, 'give visitors an opportunity to become engaged in the exhibit environment' while finding 'personally meaningful connections' with entities within the same (Serrell and Whitney 2024, 15; McNeil 2023). In recent years, many museums and cultural heritage institutions have reworked their approaches to providing context – drastically, in some cases. In this vein, Serrell and Whitney urge those charged with writing exhibit labels to 'offe[r] provocation beyond simply presenting information', while leveraging the capacity of exhibitions to 'tell origin stories, envision the future, and give a sense of continuity and purpose', in part through the 'real objects and real people' that their carefully curated spaces feature.

Thinking of narration as provided through curation of an exhibition space, however, overlooks the degree to which artefacts tend to involve their own arguments, especially if one understands 'argument' in the sense of 'angle'. Yet choices made in the novel's characterization, representation, and revision all inflect the reader's sense of how to interpret fictionalized scenes in which these objects feature.

Understanding the novel's own textual trajectory as context allows us to reflect upon the stakes of 'extracting' particular objects from it for consideration. In *The Art of Museum Exhibitions* (2016), Leslie Bedford calls attention to Steven Conn's 1998 account of museums as 'sites of intellectual and cultural debate where the prevailing cultural ideas and assumptions of American society [have been] put on display and where changes in those assumptions [are] reflected' (Conn 1998, 22). Novels such as *Moby-Dick* function in cognate terms: by presenting narratives that recontextualize artefacts of cultural history, they provide powerful means of reflecting and meditating upon the same. To this end, I outline below an approach to 'material annotation': that is, the use of 3D printing and other forms of engagement with hands-on media to augment readers' sense of connection with unfamiliar named objects and entities a novel may feature, prior to re-engaging trajectories of fictionalized experience in which these entities appear. Such an approach enables a dual form of enrichment: one that looks forward and back, at once clarifying readers' sense of the discrete entities featured therein, while allowing them to serve as 'handles to get hold of the bundle' a text may present. Encouraging readers to widen their horizons of expectation through tangible experiences of connection supports diving back into the text with renewed perspective.

Qualitative emphases: Keywords and points of entry

Keywords occurring in chapter titles provide the most obvious means of facilitating augmented experience.[3] As noted above, Melville's own practical and readerly experience with 'worlds of whaling' informs the novel throughout. Of the novel's 135 chapters in its first American edition, a substantial number are 'glossed' at their outset through named objects that feature prominently in episodes that follow. Chapter 118, 'The Quadrant,' gives a vivid example. As a specialized navigational instrument (able to measure up to 90 degrees, hence the name), this object and its physical properties may well prove opaque to readers even if its function is contextually clear. Since the term occurs only eight times in the novel, the contextual glossing provided by its specific instances is likewise limited. Occurring primarily within its eponymous chapter (where six of eight instances are found), the significance of the device's features comes forward through depiction of its use. To wit: observing the sun through the quadrant's 'coloured glasses' prompts Ahab to register the overweening ambition this instrument's navigational capacities might support, prompting him to destroy both the object and its 'heavenly' power of triangulation (Chapter 123, 'The Musket'). Crushed beneath Ahab's own 'ivory heel', the quadrant's 'copper-sight tubes' become useless, yet later chapters show aspects of the device's function as approximated through an act of nautical cleverness in which Ahab 'recasts' the points of two cruder instruments (a pair of lances) as compass points for navigation, prompting the crew's awe and wonder at his near-devilish human skill (from Chapter 124, 'The Needle').

---

[3] I am grateful to the 2024 'Teaching Melville' Institute participants for this 'glossing' insight. Echoing Dennis Mischke, one might note here a reminder of the text's 'literariness' in the move between qualitative and quantitative markers for attention (see also Mischke 2022, 300).

One need not have a physical quadrant to hand to appreciate the metaphor's power. Yet attending to how the chapter title presents its object as central to the episode it precedes highlights the degree to which possessing a physical manifestation of the same might encourage readers to register the entity's broader resonance within the narrative. (See Figure 7.4)

Figure 7.4 3D-printed quadrant (credit: Mirkoengineer, on Thingiverse). For the quadrant's CAD files, context, and further materials, see https://www.thingiverse.com/thing:2540410.

Even this streamlined contemporary model suggests the instrument's capacity for nuanced calculation.[4] While it does not display all features found in Melville's description, working tangibly with a reproduction such as this could cultivate significant engagement. Insofar as models such as the one above are available, one's own sense of wonder at the captain's actions may well grow, given the perspective the printed object provides on the complexity of the instrument destroyed, as well as the relative simplicity of those accoutrements eventually taking its place (Ohge 2022).

That the 'glossing' tendency of chapter titles may be found throughout the novel argues the degree to which Melville's meditations on personal experience with whaling and its implements should be understood to infuse the whole. Roughly forty of *Moby-Dick*'s chapters are titled through generically named objects that feature prominently in the chapters themselves: of these, just under twenty could benefit from material annotation. Here, nautical accoutrements are strongly represented: monkey-ropes (Chapter 72), try-works (Chapter 96), 'log and line' navigation (Chapter 125), and life-buoys (Chapter 126), to name a few. Yet not all are necessarily unfamiliar: in some cases, such as 'The Pipe' (Chapter 30), contexts invoked through Melville's narrative make the

---

[4]The 3D-printed object is designed to be functional.

commonplace more strange. Further objects throughout the novel could also be selected through strategies this chapter explores.

In the case study that follows, one group of highly motivated readers took up related strategies for reading, connecting, and reflecting on their engagement with the novel, along lines further unpacking Dewey's insight regarding the bases of aesthetic experience.

'Worlds of Whaling': Connecting with 2024's Melville Summer Institute

Taking a moment to probe contemporary theories mobilizing Dewey's insight helps to set the stage for the impact that material annotation may have. Writing in 2014 on how exhibitions might transform 'how visitors understand a particular set of ideas', Bedford casts Dewey's sense of aesthetic experience as involving 'work in the subjunctive mood': that is, as taking place under conditions that encourage viewers, readers, and other audiences to use their imaginations to move into the realm of the possible, asking 'what if?' they, from their own perspectives, were to enter the refined and curated experiences that artistic works offer (Bedford 2014, 13–16)? Recast slightly to apply to works of narrative fiction, one might view Bedford's account as an equation: *story + imagination = aesthetic experience*, if 'story' = a novel's 'narrative' and 'imagination' = the horizon of prior experience readers bring to it. Understood in this light, material annotation's ability to recalibrate readers' perspectives depends on selecting highly resonant objects as points of entry into the narrative. While approaches to this selection could vary, what follows are several possibilities suggested through activities begun during the Summer 2024 National Endowment for the Humanities (NEH) Institute *Moby Dick and the World of Whaling in the Digital Age*.

What *was* the Institute? As articulated through NEH promotional materials, this three-week hybrid experience – now in its third iteration and directed by Tim Marr, Wyn Kelley, and Mary Bercaw Edwards – was designed to 'empower' its participant-teachers 'to journey boldly and immersively with their students into *Moby-Dick*' while dramatizing the 'value of the humanities as an essential force of social revitalization'.[5] Throwing the group in headfirst, as it were, served as a prompt to transformation. Multiple aspects of this intense (and intensely collaborative) experience expanded the interpretive horizons on which its determined members might draw in bringing Melville's 'worlds of whaling' back to their classrooms across the country.

Distinct among the 2024 Institute's emphases was its commitment to the value of material cultural analysis – an angle re-emerging strongly alongside the digital pedagogies and computational tools that defined the 2021 version.[6] Yet in each instance,

---

[5]For the NEH overview, see https://www.neh.gov/programinstitutefellowship/moby-dick-and-world-whaling-digital-age. For more on the Institute, see https://www.teachingmelville.org/institute-overview.
[6]For a sampling of digital approaches informing the 2021 Institute, see https://www.teachingmelville.org/2021-teacher-presentations.

this multi-week institute has offered a range of strategies allowing educators to make richer, more intimate contact with the environments and objects populating 'the dynamic worlds of *Moby-Dick*'. Convened through the Institute were twenty teachers of varying backgrounds, interests, and levels of experience with the novel: their student populations ranged from grammar school to high school. Throughout their three weeks together, they underwent a powerful shared experience that was at once highly intellectual and deeply personal. After an initial online week of reading and conversation, the Institute reconvened in person for two further weeks of presentations, discussion, activities, and educational travel. Not only did its members develop a distinct chemistry, but its composition also underscored the value of bringing diverse intellectual and personal backgrounds to the text.

Establishing interpersonal trust through the experience of reading together appears to have primed participants for deepened connections in person. Beyond site-specific experiences such as whale watches, a group climb of Monument Mountain, and visits to both Nantucket (where the initial chapters are set) and Arrowhead (Melville's western Massachusetts residence where he composed *Moby-Dick*), the group benefited from meeting amid the resources of the New Bedford Whaling Museum, in whose classrooms the majority of the Institute's sessions were held. Here, the physical environment served as catalyst to conversation. Entering the museum beneath enormous whale skeletons suspended in the main hall, the group daily encountered a host of exhibited objects that characterized the nautical and maritime environments with which the novel's fictional trajectory was in dialogue.[7] Inevitably, curiosity sparked conversation: often regarding the very objects by which the group was surrounded, given the roles many of these played in the massive whaling narrative.

Artefact analyses

Near the end of the second week, participants undertook a form of artefact analysis developed by Marr and the NEH Institute faculty team. Conducting this activity *after* the initial week of reading allowed the novel's trajectory and implicit arguments to serve as a special form of shaping context. Prior to each's selecting a single artefact for commentary from the museum's displayed collections, all participants were encouraged by Marr and others to reflect broadly, as directions distributed for the analysis indicate:

> One might begin with a revealing or puzzling reference in the novel and then locate a conjunctive item in the museum or elsewhere in New Bedford. A corollary investigation would begin with a found artifact itself and explore how it resonates with moments in the book. Think of how you might locate and define a revealing

---

[7] For the New Bedford Whaling Museum's ongoing 'Skeletons of the Deep' exhibition, see https://www.whalingmuseum.org/research/research-resources/whale-science/biology/skeletons-of-the-deep/.

Extracting for Experience

station in the development of a *Moby-Dick* tour of New Bedford (the museum or its environs) at which the place and object dialogue productively with the text and you supply the informed conversation.

This sense of bringing 'place and object' into 'dialogue' with the text proved highly productive for Institute participants – all the more so, given the multiple registers of resonance they were encouraged to explore. Such flexibility was designed to afford these educators the opportunity to consider personal as well as professional significance in making their choices. (See Figures 7.5a and 7.5b)

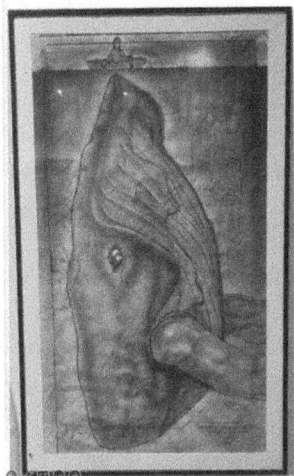

"Whale Peace Offering" (2022)
Nelson Andrews (Mashpee Wampanoag)
Painted over 1877 map of Mashpee, MA

How does this contemporary Wampanoag art-object respond to Melville and write into *Moby-Dick*?

How does this work interrogate and challenge our cultural narratives of indigeneity, colonization, whaling, Melville, and the New Bedford Whaling Museum?

How might Melville already explore and enact similar critiques within *Moby-Dick*?

- Wampanoag people indigenous throughout Eastern RI and Southern MA at time of colonial encounter
- Decimated, including in King Philip's War (1675-6)
- Throughout 19C, changing legal rights for Wampanoag people in Mashpee, MA, including:
  - 1834: state recognition of limited sovereignty
  - 1870: Mashpee incorporated into MA; sovereignty stripped
- Mashpee Wampanoag people granted federal recognition in 2007

Wilson Taylor

Figure 7.5a 'Artefact Analysis' slides. (Credit: Wilson Taylor.)

Pequod, you will no doubt remember, was the name of **a celebrated tribe of Massachusetts Indians; now extinct as the ancient Medes.**

("The Ship," 64)

But this is not all. New Zealand Tom and Don Miguel, after at various times creating great havoc among the boats of different vessels, were finally gone in quest of, systematically hunted out, chased and killed by valiant whaling captains, who heaved up their anchors with that express object as much in view, **as in setting out through the Narragansett Woods, Captain Butler of old had it in his mind to capture that notorious murderous savage Annawon, the headmost warrior of the Indian King Philip.**

("The Affidavit," 163)

In a sense, Nelson Andrews is painting against empire while claiming the whale, and the natural world, as a postcolonial symbol.

Andrew's form of the palimpsest—layering the cetacean and human figures over and against a legal map—aestheticizes processes of historical inquiry and reclamation while centering and celebrating the natural world, enacting an ethic of mutual coexistence rather than colonial conquest.

Such an approach echoes Melville's generic blending and anticolonial imaginary in *Moby-Dick*; Andrew's style also perhaps references Matt Kish's multimedia engagement with Melville's text.

Andrew's savvy appropriation of archival, colonial sources (such as maps) allows him to enact a historical and contemporary critique of colonialism, genocide, and Native erasure, including that performed and reinforced by aesthetic representations as well as archives, historical records, and museums.

"Whale Peace Offering" further engages a discourse already animating *Moby-Dick* through Melville's own historical reclamations, critiques of settler-colonialism and white supremacy, and critical elisions of colonial violence with cetacean violence.

Wilson Taylor

Figure 7.5b 'Artefact Analysis' slides. (Credit: Wilson Taylor.)

In the slides above, Institute participant Wilson Taylor raises a series of probing questions and quotations to this end, along lines echoing and leveraging the exercise's framing. His work serves as a salient example of the cognate work done by many in the group, which reflected on the interventions particular objects and artworks might make in, and as part of, a wider interpretive conversation. In discussing objects selected for analysis, those presenting tended either to immediately invoke passages from the novel or – in tandem with context provided by the museum's exhibits and their own research – to conclude by bringing an interpreted form of the object back into dialogue with Melville's narrative.[8] In either case, the selected images and entities served as touchstones through which participants were able to read with *and* against the text's grain.

Building on this activity, participants undertook a two-part 'digital' extension – one through which, on one hand, they could computationally identify further contexts from the novel where key terms related to their item of interest appeared; or alternately, they could take the opportunity to work with linoleum blocks to carve images that were related to the text yet had been selected for reasons of personal significance, while reflecting on their reading of the novel as a whole. Although time constraints limited the degree to which all could pursue both options, the activity's overall design honoured multiple ways that unfolding registers of related experience could enrich, reinforce, and even re-inflect one's engagement with the text.

Since many of the teachers chose carving, I have presented the 'extractive' computational option in summary below, followed by speculation as to how modified forms of that activity might support a wider programme of material annotation. To conclude, I then turn to the latter 'digital' extension, inscription – a practice whose means of encouraging readers to consider and comment upon their experiences with the novel proved surprisingly profound.

Digital material(ism): Strategies for selection

Acutely aware that in-person connections are not, in general, available to a geographically dispersed population, museums are increasingly considering means by which 3D-printed versions of their rare and distinctive objects may enable such experiences 'at home': that is, by being additively manufactured in contexts far from those in which the physical items are held.[9] Such a vision of expanded access is emblematized by the Smithsonian 3D Digitization programme, whose framing underscores the 'virtual light' its work

---

[8] On 'interpretive labels' in museums, see Serrell and Whitney 2024, 15–22.
[9] See, for instance, resources shared by the Smithsonian at https://3d.si.edu; see also Google's 'Scan the World' project archive, available at https://artsandculture.google.com/story/scan-the-world-scan-the-world/egWRnanxkLB0zg?hl=en.

stands poised to shed on the 99 per cent of collections currently not on display. Here again, benefits are phrased in terms of enabling fresh narratives: these 'digital assets', the Smithsonian curators observe, 'will allow not just the Smithsonian, but the world at large, to tell and share new stories about the familiar – and the unfamiliar – treasures in [its] collections.'[10] While it is true that individual programmes of 3D printing remain cost-prohibitive for many, the expense involved pales in comparison to that of acquiring actual historical objects, and the technology's increasing availability through makerspaces and design labs supports the realization of this cultural heritage dream – one similarly espoused by many major institutions, as well as advanced through libraries of 3D models being developed to this end. What follows is one possible approach to leveraging these emerging resources' power.

How one might go about working at 'encyclopedic' scale to select items for printing is a challenge. Of course, it remains the case that any audience could simply read through a text, marking terms and concepts its members find either less familiar or more in need of contextualizing. Such qualitative paths can complement strategies I am advocating. Yet working in tandem with digital tools can bring forward further keywords, and even registers of language, likely to benefit from increased attention. Attempting to articulate principles and practices that would enable such work at scale sets the stage for a programme of annotation that could extend throughout the novel and beyond.

Selecting qualitatively

During the Institute's version of the 'material annotation' activity, each participant was encouraged to focus on a single term or image that he or she had found personally significant during the group's time together. As briefly noted above, this focus – which could be verbal or visual – was then explored with either digital or manual tools. Those who chose to explore key terms computationally worked with Voyant and AntConc's 'concordance' features to collate contexts throughout the novel in which their selected terms appeared.[11] Figures 7.6a and 7.6b give one example:

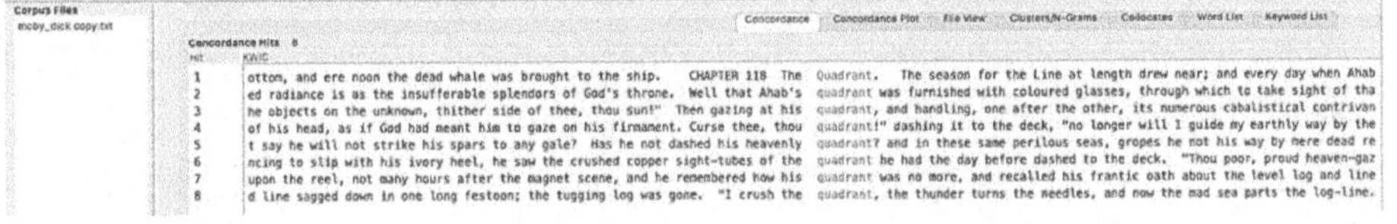

Figure 7.6a Concordance view of 'quadrant' in *Moby-Dick* (AntConc).

---

[10]For Smithsonian 3D resources, see https://3d.si.edu/.
[11]For AntConc's 'concordance' feature, see https://antconc-manual.readthedocs.io/en/latest/concordance.html (AntConc); for Voyant's 'Contexts', see https://voyant-tools.org/docs/#!/guide/contexts.

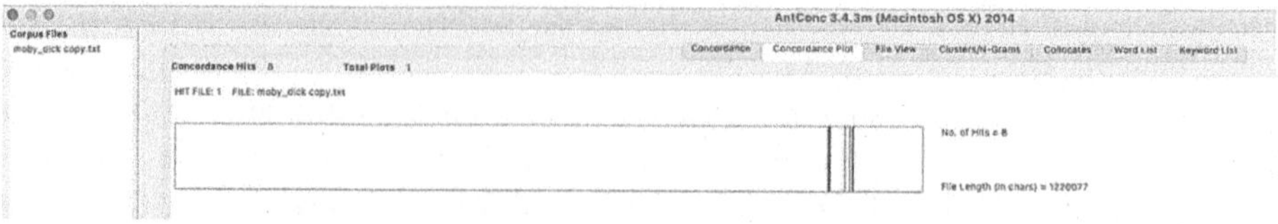

Figure 7.6b Concordance plot of 'quadrant' in *Moby-Dick* (AntConc).

Together, the images above expand the 'quadrant' case discussed earlier, while illustrating Dennis Mischke's insight regarding the usefulness of computational reading strategies in developing perspective on *Moby-Dick*'s immensity (Mischke 2022, 300–3). Using these tools brought forward for reconsideration both the object's features (i.e. its 'coloured glasses' and 'copper-sight tubes') and its contexts of use and destruction (i.e. its 'handling' and being 'dashed to the deck'). In doing so, these verbal visualizations helped to underscore its significance in the narrative while creating a rapid imaginative sketch of its operations. Placing the contexts thereby convened into dialogue with a 'plot' of the term's appearances highlights the terms of encounter the story provides, while allowing parallel passages to serve as a form of internal annotation that calibrates one's sense of the object while suggesting its resonance in the arc of the whole.

These anatomized interpretive moves might at first appear mainly relevant for literary study. Yet promising agendas for annotation also developed in relation to non-literary subjects that Institute participants taught. In cases such as these, entities to annotate materially could be selected through teachers' professional sense of connections likely to most profoundly impact students' horizons of experience in their specific educational contexts. For instance, Institute participant Elizabeth Sobkiw-Williams, who currently teaches fine arts at the Belmont Public Schools' Butler Elementary, is working to assemble 'tactile portfolios' of the whale species noted in Chapter 32: 'Cetology.' (Here, Melville's use of book formats to classify whales also might merit annotation in a book historical context.) While Melville's descriptions are often whimsical – and, in several cases, make reference to persons real but unnamed – the chapter's encyclopaedic approach (initially almost echoing the opening 'Extracts' in miniature) makes desirable an organized presentation of the species detailed therein. Particularly if the specimens were created at a form of scale to one another, students could compare and contrast them, with an eye to registering how each articulated type might be considered figuratively as well as literally.

Selecting algorithmically

Intriguingly, key terms may also be 'extracted' on a wider scale through tools, techniques, and statistical measures used to explore digitized textual corpora. Here, the novel's expansive aspirations become computationally tractable once chapters are converted into text files (.txt) able to be processed with corpus linguistics software often used for digital humanities research. Two readily available programs, AntConc and Voyant, allow users to rapidly count instances of a discrete word-form's appearance throughout the novel: for more advanced AntConc work, lemmatizing and part-of-speech (POS) tagging are also available.[12]

Using selected points of entry to focus and extend readers' engagement with the text provides an orientation to certain episodes that is both tailored and more tangible. As discussed above, this experience of deepened connection holds the potential to increase appreciation of key terms' resonances, both in contexts proximate to the term and in relation to the broader narrative. What follows is speculation regarding strategies through which one might select terms throughout the novel that are likely to reward annotation. Such an approach could present an initial 'pass' of possibilities that qualitative curation could then refine.

One might begin from the premise that a novel's relatively rare words are often less immediately familiar to many audiences – an insight directing our attention to the 'long tail' of *Moby-Dick* as corpus. Within a table tracking the frequencies of 'a large sample of words used', Zipf's Law holds that 'the frequency of any word is inversely proportional to its rank' (Zipf 1936, 1949). Figure 7.7a presents the conventional graph for this principle:

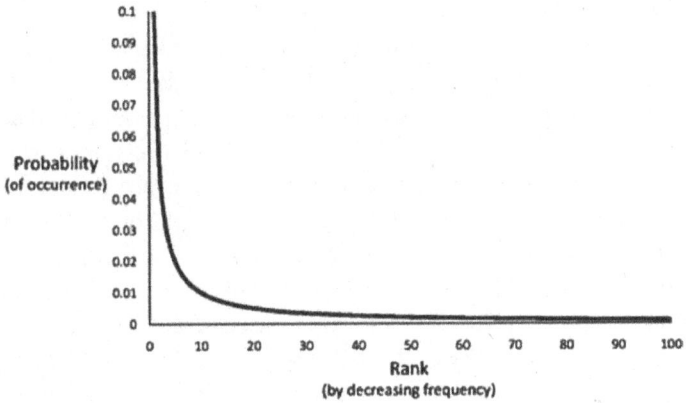

Figure 7.7a Zipf's Law, visualized. Image from Froehlich 2019.

Yet moving beyond a text's (relatively few) most frequent words causes the picture to change rapidly, since the 'long tail' containing a corpus' far less frequent terms does not obey this governing condition. As one moves along the graph's flattened 'tail', the number of words in each range interval *increases* as the number required to qualify for that interval declines. (See Figure 7.7b, which shows the expanding number of words

---

[12]For the most recent version of Laurence Anthony's AntConc, see https://www.laurenceanthony.net/software/antconc/; for the browser-based version of Stefan Sinclar and Geoffrey Rockwell's Voyant, see https://voyant-tools.org/.

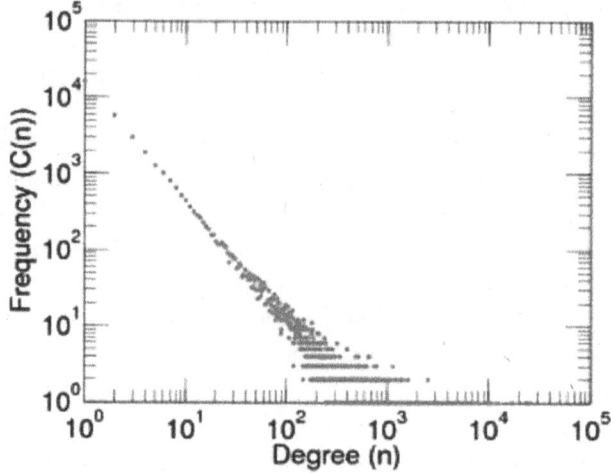

Figure 7.7b Distribution plot for corpus following Zipf's Law. For discussion of the distribution plot and its contributions to visualization, see https://networkscience.wordpress.com/2013/06/02/how-to-visualize-skewed-distributions/ and https://towardsdatascience.com/data-centric-security-threat-hunting-based-on-zipfs-law-50ad919fc135.

clustered at each 'value', or number of instances, for a corpus following Zipf's Law.) By implication, any word in the 'tail' might prove a strong candidate for material annotation, since one envisioned benefit of the practice is the increased perspective that thoughtful selection of relatively rare key terms could have upon smaller sections of the novel.[13]

From the tail's list, one might simply select terms qualitatively. Yet reflecting on ways algorithmic approaches could assist this selection sheds light on further qualities that strong candidates for annotation might possess. For instance, to gauge a word's potential resonance from its immediate contexts, one might choose those with high term frequency-inverse document frequency (tf-idf), since this measure indicates a term's appearing prominently in one 'document' (here, 'chapter') and low statistical likelihood of appearing in others. Combining high tf-idf scores with a preference for words occurring in positions of narrative prominence (i.e. chapter titles) or leveraging the perspective provided by their parts of speech (here, common nouns) could yield further subgroups of *Moby-Dick* terms likely to repay material attention. Making use of probabilistic strategies would also increase the speed with which these lists of potentially promising terms could be generated.

Keeping these factors in mind may make exporting a novel's 'wordlist' (i.e. its full list of terms, ranked by frequency of appearance) a valuable exercise in itself. In the case of *Moby-Dick*, using such a list to bring forward terms appearing near the end of *Moby-Dick*'s statistical 'tail' confirms that a register likely to repay material annotation

---

[13] For quick views of this measure, Voyant's 'Corpus Terms' tool can be useful. See https://voyant-tools.org/docs/#!/guide/corpusterms. (For *Moby-Dick*, see https://voyant-tools.org/?corpus=c22fe073cb511596f7c29d6213abe9df&view=CorpusTerms.)

emerges among terms occurring a small, but not the smallest, number of times in the novel. Within *Moby-Dick* as a corpus, these words are frequently drawn from nautical vocabularies: broadly, this maritime register includes specialized *functions* ('steersman' [7], 'yarman' [7], 'bowsman/bowsmen' [9]), *actions* ('pitchpoling/pitchpoled' [with 'pitchpoler', 8]), and *environments* ('archpelagoes' [6], 'gangway' [6], 'gam' [7], 'inland' [with 'inlander'/'inlanders', 8], 'bowsprit' [8]), as well as the *objects* ('oakum' [5], 'schooner/ schooners' [6], 'jib' [with its hyphenated combinations, 6], 'handspike/handspikes' [8], 'quadrant' [8], 'albatross/albatrosses' [10], 'quohog/quohogs' [10]) with which this essay is concerned. Intriguingly, a significant number of the novel's chapter titles are also concentrated in the 5–10 instance range, with a distinct spike in the 8- and 9-occurrence group where 'quadrant' is found. Patterns emerging through this overview suggest that work along these lines may shed light on dynamics of individual chapters while bringing forward further points of resonance to consider as the novel's plot unfolds.

Again, the technique's productiveness depends in part on Melville's 'materiality': that is, his tendency to present the objects, stages, components, and processes of a whaling journey in light of senses of significance one might assign to these entities' properties and operations in fields of human action. Such near-poetic connections are a hallmark of Melville's style. While this feature makes *Moby-Dick* particularly ripe for material annotation, articulating the novelistic tendency argues that strategies detailed above could be adapted for wider use: not only with further nineteenth-century texts, but also beyond this temporal and generic context.

Moving forward, materially

Once desired entities are chosen, their material referents may be established: here, visual models found through online archives such as Thingiverse, Prusa Printables, Cults3D and MyMiniFactory can prove valuable, as can working with programs and technologies designed to create models directly from scans or images of museum artefacts.[14] While 3D models have for some time been built through photogrammetry, which involves stitching together multiple photos to capture an object 'in the round', evolving AI technologies have also introduced tools that begin the work of 3D modelling by developing depth within a snapshot.[15]

Although online libraries of 3D models are idiosyncratic in their coverage, resources in this area are growing, and as noted previously, collection-specific tangible corpora are

---

[14] For Thingiverse, see https://www.thingiverse.com; for Prusa Printables, see https://www.printables.com; for Cults3D (which, as of this writing, supports automatic imports of Thingiverse-shared files), see https://cults3d .com/; for MyMiniFactory (previously, MyMiniVerse), see https://www.myminifactory.com.
[15] While this technology remains under development as of this writing, free accounts can be obtained from https://3d.csm.ai/; for one introduction to photogrammetry (a technique of 'stitching' photos together which itself requires training), see https://www.instructables.com/Turning-Your-Photos-Into-a-3D-Model/; see also the excellent resources shared by the University of London's 3D Summer School (credit: Gabriel Bodard and Valeria Vitale) at https://github.com/SASDigitalHumanitiesTraining/3D?tab=readme-ov-file.

increasingly being created by museums themselves. (Within the world of book historical scholarship, this trend is also notable, as indicated by recent initiatives supporting the 3D printing of specialized artefacts peculiar to the printing trade.[16]) Such moves follow the mid-2010s trend towards digitization in archives and special collections. During that time, libraries and major cultural institutions found that enhanced digital access appeared to correlate with increased in-person traffic and greater overall engagement, as measured by their collections' being more extensively cited and used overall. There is little reason to think a programme of 3D annotation would not help to cultivate the same (Hirtle 2002). Ongoing access to versions of a museum's objects could serve as both invitation and *aide-mémoire*: in each case, the tangible creations would stand poised to catalyse further insights.

It is true that the charm that 3D-printed objects hold for some audiences could lead to such annotations' devolving into 'souvenir sets' of distinct and unusual material entities. Yet such an outcome is not necessarily to be criticized, especially if one keeps in mind the etymological sense of a *souvenir* as a memento of a journey – fictionalized or otherwise. Indeed, the line between the desire to possess a tangible object and material clarification thereby facilitated might well be fine. Extended dialogue with Institute participants also confirmed a range of state and national learning goals as addressed by this annotative approach – and the current importance of teachers' explicitly addressing curricular standards in their class planning constitutes a further argument for the technique's value to pedagogy.

Inscription as postscript

Yet such means of making are not the only haptic path to deepening engagement. While the productive extraction that underlies 'material annotation' helps orient readers to a text's less familiar vocabularies, bringing keywords (of any frequency) from the text together with images related to the same can constitute its own form of meditation upon how the one may deepen and enrich the other. Particularly when undertaken tangibly, such selection and arrangement can also inscribe perceived connections ever more strongly into readers' consciousnesses.

Evidence of inscription's power as an editorial strategy can emerge in surprising ways. Within the world of *Moby-Dick* fandom, the desire to inscribe is often seen through tattooing – and the practice is widespread. Choosing to make selected words and images, separately and in combination, more permanent upon the writing surface of one's own body suggests this practice as evidencing a personal sense of connection. Echoed in this practice is Melville's presentation of the same, as seen in Ishmael's careful rationing of

---

[16] For 3D-printable resources designed to enhance book history instruction, see, for instance, Jet Jacobs, Kevin M. O'Sullivan, and Marcia McIntosh's 3Dhotbed Project (https://www.3dhotbed.info/project), and Martin Schneider and Dominik Schmitz's Open Press Project (https://openpressproject.com/).

Extracting for Experience

the space his body presents for creative inscription. Explaining his choice not to capture there the 'odd inches' found in measuring a whale's skeleton, he argues that his few remaining 'untattooed parts' were better preserved as a 'blank page' for 'a poem [he] was then composing' (Bryant and Springer 2007, 397). In essence, on a personal canvas 'crowded for space', only that deemed most significant is to be recorded – not least, given the 'indelible impression' (a phrase from Melville's *Typee*) that such work constitutes (Bryant and Springer 2007, 397).

Whether Institute participants took up this more immediate form of the practice remains unknown. Yet modified means of the approach were explored, and these further 'digital' forms of engagement exerted their own form of power. Using linoleum blocks provided for the purpose, participants produced (and reproduced) a range of images: the main guideline was simply to choose a visual emphasis reflecting an aspect of the novel they had found personally significant. While many, unsurprisingly, focused on the whale, seeing varied realizations of this theme side by side suggested a form of implicit commentary on the experience of reading itself (see Figure 7.8):

Figure 7.8 Whale images carved by participants Elizabeth Sobikw-Williams and Alicia DeMaio.

Immersion, breaking through, diving in headfirst: among those who chose to represent the whale in some form, variations in the same suggested how participants saw themselves as having come to terms with the novel's immensity. Since the group had been encouraged throughout their time together to consider visual and verbal modes as being in dialogue with one another – most notably, during sessions led by Institute faculty member Robert Wallace and when engaging the work and perspective of *Moby-Dick in Pictures: One Drawing for Every Day* creator Matt Kish – having the opportunity to reflect artistically near the Institute's close may also have helped bring together and consolidate that experience.[17] The hands-on technique of carving may well have created its own sense of grappling: here, the resistance – even recalcitrance – presented by materials themselves could have set the stage for the subsequent, if implicit, commentary.

Extending this activity beyond the Institute suggests ways its metacognitive aspects might be made more explicit. Students might either be given a key term or quotation or be asked to select one; images then chosen to accompany the text could be designed to serve as commentary on the same, and students could then be encouraged to reflect upon combinations thus crafted. Potential uses of material annotation might also prove whimsical. During the Institute's concluding presentations, several participants discussed how resources, strategies, and insights developed by the group might support more recreational reading experiences: here, the extensive, detailed planning of Laura Gallinari provides a substantive example. Within the context of her 'Leviathan Book Club', completing the text earns students a badge of honour: in this light, 3D-printed whale accoutrements such as key fobs, articulated models, and more could sustain a sense of connection with the text at hand.[18]

Object-based keywords are not the only elements of the novel that can be 'remixed' to leverage the support they may provide for further aesthetic experience. Beloved by the group and played 'after hours' during the Institute's final week was *Moby-Dick; Or, the Card Game*, a tabletop gaming experience that 'extracts' sailors from the novel to form crews that deploy these figures' strengths and special powers during chapter-based episodes that are punctuated with battles against whales similarly 'reshuffled' from their original contexts. While the whales, like the sailors, are removed from their immediate chapters of reference, the game's means of indicating strength, age, and other distinctive qualities ensures that the powers of both character types remain alive in its environment. Yet while 'Melville mode' may be used to shape the game's unfolding in a way closely mirroring the fictionalized narrative, its creators eschew visual representation of the culminating leviathan, electing instead to configure the final battle through only an increase in the adversary's powers and a series of rule shifts 'tipping the balance' to players' doom. What is more, cards bringing *Moby-Dick* to the field of play present only Melville's language, which asserts, through dark text on a white background, this ultimate adversary's ultimate defiance of representation. Lack of graphic reference supports greater imaginative connection with any memory players may have of the novel's framework: as a prompt, those concluding the chase meditate only on 'the whiteness of the whale'.

---

[17] For one sample of Matt Kish's work, see https://www.matt-kish.com/moby-dick/2016/4/8/moby-dick-page-550.

[18] For the Leviathan Book Club, see https://www.fenwickfriars.com/list-detail?pk=211299.

Conclusion

Insofar as points of engagement with the novel can be extracted and extended, their use can spark continued conversation. Such dynamics may be best understood as a form of dialogue with 'archives' of language, memory, and experience. Using multiple digital approaches to explore key objects and points of entry helps to shed light on how these entities' conditions of creation and curation lend a sense of significance to the same. Anticipating the benefits of such approaches, the *Melville Electronic Library* (MEL) is working to incorporate text analysis as part of its platform; *Melville's Marginalia Online* (MMO) already features a bespoke interface based on Voyant Tools. Ultimately, calling attention to, and even challenging, these curatorial practices encourages readers to bring materials of Melville's life together with the novel's narration, thereby deepening and strengthening their appreciation of the text as an aesthetic experience.

Bibliography

Anthony, Laurence. *AntConc*. https://www.laurenceanthony.net/software/antconc/ (accessed 5 November 2024).

Bedford, Leslie. *The Art of Museum Exhibitions: How Story and Imagination Create Aesthetic Experiences*. London: Routledge, 2014.

Bodard, Gabriel and Valeria Vitale. '3D Training Activities at the School of Advanced Study, University of London.' [GitHub site]. https://github.com/SASDigitalHumanitiesTraining/3D?tab=readme-ov-file (accessed 5 November 2024).

Conn, Steven. *Museums and American Intellectual Life, 1876–1926*. Chicago: University of Chicago Press, 1998.

CSM. *Cube*. https://3d.csm.ai/ (accessed 5 November 2024).

Cults3D. *Cults* [3D Modelling Marketplace]. https://cults3d.com/ (accessed 5 November 2024).

Dewey, John. *Art as Experience*. First given as the 1932 William James Lecture at Harvard. New York: Minton, Balch & Company, 1934.

Drescher, Tim. *Catalogue Key to 'Or, the Whale'*. 2021. Online at https://issuu.com/lawrenceartscenter.org/docs/jos_sances_gallery_guide.

Empson, William. 'Obscurity and Annotation'. In *Argufying: Essays on Literature and Culture*, 70–87. Iowa City: University of Iowa Press, 1987.

Empson, William. 'Note on Notes'. In *The Complete Poems of William Empson*, 112–13. Edited by John Haffenden. Gainesville: University of Florida Press, 2001.

Forster, E. M. *Howard's End*. London: Edward Arnold, 1910.

Froehlich, Heather. '*Moby-Dick* is about Whales, or Why We Should Count Words'. 2019. https://hfroehli.ch/2019/09/27/moby-dick-is-about-whales-or-why-should-we-count-words/ (accessed 5 November 2024).

Gallinari, Laura and Nicoline Shoffer. *Leviathan Book Club*. Fenwick High School. https://www.fenwickfriars.com/list-detail?pk=211299 (accessed 5 November 2024).

Google. *Scan the World Project*. https://artsandculture.google.com/story/scan-the-world-scan-the-world/ (accessed 5 November 2024).

Hanna, Ralph. 'Annotation as Social Practice'. In *Annotation and its Texts*, 178–84. Edited by Stephen Barney. Oxford: Oxford University Press, 1991.

Hirtle, Peter B. 'The Impact of Digitization on Special Collections in Libraries'. *Libraries & Culture* 37, no. 1 (2002): 42–52. Special Issue: The Infinite Library.
Holmes, Mikaela. 'Turning Your Photos into a 3D Model'. In Autodesk's *Instructables*. https://www.instructables.com/Turning-Your-Photos-Into-a-3D-Model/ (accessed 5 November 2024).
Inscription: The Journal of Material Text – Theory, Practice, History. Edited by Gill Partington, Simon Morris and Adam Smyth. https://inscriptionjournal.com/.
Insko, Jeffrey. 'Resource Extraction and Melville's Extracts'. *Leviathan: A Journal of Melville Studies* 25, no. 1 (2023): 73–87. https://10.1353/lvn.2023.0008.
Jacobs, Jet, Kevin M. O'Sullivan and Marcia McIntosh. *3Dhotbed Project*. https://www.3dhotbed.info/project (accessed 5 November 2024).
Jauss, Hans Robert. *Literaturgeschichte als Provokation de Literaturwissenschaft* (Konstanz, 1967). Republished in *Literaturgeschichte als Provokation* (Frankfurt, 1970); published in English as 'Literary History as a Challenge to Literary Theory'. Translated by Elizabeth Benzinger. *New Literary History* 2, no. 1 (1970): 7–31. https://www.jstor.org/stable/468585.
Johnson, Samuel. *A Proposal for Printing a New Edition of the Plays of William Shakespeare*. London: E. Cave, 1745.
Kish, Matt. *Moby-Dick in Pictures: One Drawing for Every Page*. Portland, OR: Tin House Books, 2011.
McGowan, Glenys, Gerhard Hoffstaedter and Jennifer Creese. 'Object Based Learning in the Social Sciences: Three Approaches to Haptic Knowledge Making'. *Teaching Anthropology* 11, no. 2 (2022): 97–107.
McNeil, Timothy J. *The Exhibition and Experience Design Handbook*. London: Rowman and Littlefield / American Alliance of Museums, 2023.
Melville, Herman. *Moby-Dick; Or, the Whale*. With an introduction by John Bryant. Edited by John Bryant and Haskell Springer. New York: Longman, 2007. An updated digital edition is available on the *Melville Electronic Library*, https://melville.electroniclibrary.org/how-to-use-the-edition-moby-dick.
Melville Electronic Library: A Critical Archive (MEL). Edited by John Bryant, Wyn Kelley and Christopher Ohge. https://melville.electroniclibrary.org (accessed 5 November 2024).
Melville's Marginalia Online (MMO). Edited by Steven Olsen-Smith and Peter Norberg. https://melvillesmarginalia.org (accessed 5 November 2024).
MyMiniFactory [3D Modelling Library]. Previously *MyMiniVerse*. https://www.myminifactory.com (accessed 5 November 2024).
New Bedford Whaling Museum. '2024 Institute'. *Teaching Melville: Resources for Educators*. https://www.teachingmelville.org/institute-overview (accessed 5 November 2024).
New Bedford Whaling Museum. 'Skeletons of the Deep'. https://www.whalingmuseum.org/research/research-resources/whale-science/biology/skeletons-of-the-deep/ (accessed 5 November 2024).
Mendelson, Edward. 'Encyclopedic Narrative: From Dante to Pynchon'. *MLN* 91, no. 6 (1976): 1267–75. https://doi.org/10.2307/2907136.
Minnis, Alistair. *Medieval Theory of Authorship*. Philadelphia: University of Pennsylvania Press, 2010.
Mischke, Dennis. 'Counting (on) Melville: *Moby-Dick*, Computational Literary Studies, and Dictionary-Based Readings'. In *A New Companion to Herman Melville*, 297–312. Edited by Wyn Kelley and Christopher Ohge. John Wiley and Sons, 2022. https://doi.org/10.1002/9781119668565.ch24.
National Endowment for the Humanities. '*Moby-Dick* and the World of Whaling in the Digital Age'. https://www.neh.gov/programinstitutefellowship/moby-dick-and-world-whaling-digital-age (accessed 5 November 2024).

Norouzinia, Farzaneh, Bianka Dörr, Mareike Funk and Dirk Werth. 'Haptic Learning and Technology: Analyses of Digital Use Cases of Haptics Using the Haptic Learning Model'. In HCI International 2022 Posters. HCI 2022. *Communications in Computer and Information Science*, vol. 1582. Edited by Constantine Stephanidis, Margherita Antona and Stavroula Ntoa, 72–79. Cham: Springer, 2022. https://doi.org/10.1007/978-3-031-06391-6_10.

Ohge, Christopher. 'Computation and Dead-Reckoning'. In *A New Companion to Herman Melville*, 313–28. Edited by Wyn Kelley and Christopher Ohge. John Wiley and Sons, 2022. https://doi.org/10.1002/9781119668565.ch25.

Polyani, Michael. *The Tacit Dimension*. Chicago: University of Chicago Press, 2009.

Prusa. *Printables* [3D Modelling Library]. https://www.printables.com (accessed 5 November 2024).

Schneider, Martin and Dominik Schmitz. *Open Press Project*. https://openpressproject.com/.

Serrell, Beverly and Katherine Whitney. *Exhibit Labels: An Interpretive Approach*. London: Rowman and Littlefield, 2024.

Sinclar, Stéfan and Geoffrey Rockwell. *Voyant Tools*. https://voyant-tools.org/.

Smithsonian Institution. *Smithsonian 3D* [3D Modelling Library]. https://3d.si.edu (accessed 5 November 2024).

Ultimaker. *Thingiverse* [3D Modelling Library]. https://www.thingiverse.com (accessed 5 November 2024).

Zimmer, Mary Erica and Jeff Peterson. 'Or, the Eye' StoryMap. https://uploads.knightlab.com/storymapjs/8614707ce8a6fbbbd2abadf1af0113d6/or-the-eye/index.html.

Zipf, George K. *Human Behavior and the Principle of Least Effort*. Cambridge, MA: Addison-Wesley, 1949.

Zipf, George K. *The Psychobiology of Language: An Introduction to Dynamic Philology*. Boston: Houghton-Mifflin, 1936.

CHAPTER 8
READING THE EDITED COLLECTION, DISTANTLY
SOME TRENDS IN BRITISH THEOLOGICAL PUBLISHING IN THE TWENTIETH CENTURY
Peter Webster

Introduction

Even though digital means of representing and analysing the cultures of academic publishing have been at hand for some years, historians of the humanities have so far been slow to embrace their use. Such disciplinary histories as have appeared have taken several shapes and have often focused on the shifting content of the discipline – the periods and subjects under examination – and on the development of scholarly method. A landmark study of theology and religious studies in the UK, published by the British Academy, was itself an edited collection, organized by subject; John Kenyon's classic *The History Men* is more chronological (Kenyon 1983; Nicholson 2003). Publishers too have their historians, most notably the multi-volume histories of the university presses of Oxford and Cambridge (Eliot 2013). These volumes, often focused on the technology and economics of publishing, have been usefully supplemented by studies of particular journals: their evolving sense of their own purpose and the editorial decisions that flow from it (Fyfe et al. 2022). However, relatively few studies in the humanities have conceptualized journals as containers of networks, of authors, of peer reviewers and of citations (Colavizza and Romanello 2019; Spinaci, Colavizza and Peroni 2022).

If the journal-as-network remains an under-investigated part of the history of the humanities, the edited collection of essays is more obscure still. Among the reasons for this neglect, possibly the most salient is the brute inconvenience of obtaining the data to begin with. Except for those collections published in recent years, publishers have not tended to itemize the contents of such volumes in sales catalogues and delivery systems, and neither (in general) have library cataloguers. As a result, while the tables of contents of a digitized journal can relatively easily be extracted for use, no such base data exists for the edited collection, except for the subset that was noted in subject bibliographies, which cover only some of the disciplines and only for more recent years, and from which (being proprietary) the data are not so easily extracted. So far, then, the edited collection as a format has received practically no scholarly attention, although there is an abundance of more informal, present-centred reflection on its affordances (Webster 2020). Yet the very existence of that kind of reflection points to the importance of the format in many (though by no means all) disciplines, and particularly in the humanities. In the 2014 Research Excellence Framework (REF) exercise in the UK, 99.5 per cent of items submitted to Main Panel A (medicine and biological sciences) were journal articles. Yet, despite this, more than 9,000 edited collection chapters were submitted to the REF as a whole. In history, one chapter was submitted for every 1.7 journal articles; in theology and religious studies, the figure was 1.2; in classics, the number of chapters submitted was greater than the total number of articles (Webster 2020, 57–8).

I define the edited collection here in technological terms: as a printed codex, containing signed works by several hands, brought together by one or more editors, which is printed, distributed and marketed by a publisher, then acquired, catalogued and made available by libraries to readers, and (in some cases) acquired by readers directly. As so defined, there might appear to be no clear difference between an edited collection and an issue of a scholarly journal. However, I make a distinction, which is one not of format but of identity. An edited collection, as defined here, will have been conceived as a single entity; it will have been titled and described as a distinct object and (in terms of the codex itself) designed, printed, marketed and distributed as such, in a way that goes beyond the journal special issue. It is also likely to make greater claims for itself in terms of comprehensiveness than the special issue. In recent years, online delivery has made this distinction less clear, but in earlier periods (such as the one in question here, the twentieth century), it holds well enough.

This chapter, then, uses digital methods to explore the particular critical possibilities afforded by viewing edited collections as an object of analysis *en masse*. It examines some aspects of one network graph in particular, of contributors to edited collections published in Britain between 1918 and 1999 in the fields of theology and divinity, broadly defined. It is offered as the first instalment in a larger project exploring the particular characteristics of this graph, examining in particular the geographical, personal, denominational, institutional and sub-disciplinary patterns formed in different parts thereof. This chapter focuses on three observable overall trends over time in the whole graph, in relation to gender, nationality, and institutional type. It is offered as a case study in the changing shape of one discipline in the twentieth century and as a provocation to other scholars to position other disciplines in comparison to it.

Why theology?

The focus on theology in particular is a natural progression from my own previous work as a historian of the twentieth-century churches in the UK and from a short book on the pasts, present and futures of the edited collection as a format, in which one of the narrative case studies was theology (Webster 2020, 14–19, 23–4). But the discipline of theology as practised in the UK also had specific features of note with regard to gender, nationality and institution.

The first women to be awarded degrees by the University of Oxford received them in 1920; those at Cambridge had to wait until 1948. But by 2019, women significantly outnumbered men in the UK undergraduate population – a remarkable reversal of the balance, though one that did not occur immediately (Mead 2023). Social expectation and economic necessity slowed that transition in general, but particular factors in theological publishing acted as an additional drag. Probably most salient was the exclusion of women from ordained ministry. Of the denominations most well represented in the data, it was the Methodist church that ordained women the earliest, in 1974; the Church of England followed suit only in 1994, at the very end of the period covered; others have to this day not done so, notably the Roman Catholic and Orthodox churches (Gill 1994, 232–67). As such, opportunities for theological publishing for women were constrained by the fact that they could not write from the position of specialist authority that ordained ministry conferred.

In terms of its international profile, theological publishing was shaped by the same general internationalization of higher education as other disciplines. At the same time, the wider readership for theological work was configured in distinctive ways. Most of the major denominations, and supremely the Roman Catholic Church, were shaped by leadership and collective deliberation at international levels, over and above layers of debate and decision-making at national and local levels. The ecumenical movement for the reunion of separated churches, at its zenith in the twentieth century, certainly involved efforts of cooperation between churches in the UK, but these interacted with and were shaped by contact between Anglican and Roman Catholic, or Catholic and Orthodox, at a global level. The growth of former colonial churches (particularly in the global South) to self-governance and (over time) to a greater assertion of parity was also reflected in the printed literature. The threat of nuclear war, conflicts such as that in Vietnam and the apartheid regime: these were all issues debated by Christians both locally and internationally (Webster 2015, 119–27). The discipline, then, developed both by its own intrinsic intellectual logic and also in response to external stimuli that were in significant part international.

Finally, the discipline of theology, and its sister biblical studies, also had an institutional existence and professional composition that are quite distinct from those in other disciplines. At one level, there were a great many similarities: professional scholars were employed in departments of theology, divinity or biblical studies in the universities; they taught undergraduate students and supervised others for higher degrees; they organized and attended conferences; and published their work in monographs, journals and edited collections (Inman 2014). As such, scholars in these disciplines were subject to similar institutional, economic and technological forces to those in history, literature or philosophy. What marks theology out, however, is a particular relationship between the discipline and other, non-university institutions. All the main Christian denominations maintained independent training institutions, in particular for their ministers but also for laypeople, as well as training colleges for schoolteachers. The histories of these foundations are by and large yet to be written, along with the story of their changing relationships with the universities. (For two such studies, see Chandler 2013; Chapman 2004). But they were staffed by scholars who quite often wrote and published their work in the same channels as those in the universities. As well as these, many ordained people whose main role was as a local minister or as a senior leader of their church also maintained a scholarly life and published its fruits. There was significant mobility within and between these various institutions. There were also others from a vast range of secular occupations who contributed to this literature. Accordingly, the occupational background of those in the network was unusually diverse when compared to other disciplines.

The data: principles of inclusion

At an early stage it was necessary to decide what the precise scope of the data was to be and (in particular) to distinguish (and choose) between a history bounded by a set of publishers, on the one hand, and the history of a discipline in a particular country, on the other. The latter option was preferred, which dictated certain decisions. First of these was to include volumes that were published elsewhere, but only those that clearly originated in the UK. A collection was included if at least one editor was domiciled in the UK and at least 20 per cent of the essays were by scholars similarly resident at the time of publication. By dint of the method of data collection (described shortly), there is not comprehensive coverage of volumes that fall into this category; they tended to be discovered in passing. However, they are included in this analysis since they function in the same way as a representation of a discipline in a place. Correspondingly, volumes noted along the way that were published in the UK but clearly originated elsewhere (by the same criteria of editorial and authorial residence) are excluded as being the product of a different milieu. Finally, in the cases where a volume was published simultaneously in the UK and elsewhere, either by a single publisher with operations in both countries or by two presses in partnership, it was included here when the UK edition was clearly the principal edition.

My definition of the discipline of theology was consciously inclusive. As well as the classic stuff of the discipline, such as systematic and dogmatic theology and the study of the Bible, included were works on the philosophy of religion when emerging from a Christian frame (the kind of work usually described as natural theology or philosophical theology). As well as this, all kinds of more applied work were also included: works on the practical ordering of church government and worship, along with Christian ethics, social and economic critique, and the very active ecumenical movement. Also included were works devoted wholly to the history of the churches. Excluded were volumes of what became known during this period as comparative religion, in which Christian subjects were only one part of an explicitly comparative exercise in relation to other faiths. The object was to capture a picture of both church and academy, reasoning both together and separately, on the state and prospects of Christianity in particular.

The edited collection also served a greater number of distinct functions for theology than was typical among the humanistic disciplines. Certainly there were areas of textual biblical scholarship or the philosophy of religion that were of interest primarily to specialists. But the fundamental stuff of theological scholarship – Christology, soteriology[1] – was at certain times at the centre of vigorous debate in the churches themselves and indeed in the public sphere more generally; so too were matters of theological ethics, the conduct of worship, the ecumenical relationships between the churches, and a great deal else besides. As such, publishers published some edited collections aimed at very specialist audiences, some at the churches, and others again for the educated public at large. And many scholars, from different types of institutions, published equally readily in different kinds of collections. As such, my policy was inclusive, taking in volumes of essays written by experts but intended principally for a non-specialist audience. In practice, an exclusive policy would have been difficult to follow, since university-based scholars contributed to these more 'popular' volumes, while local clergy and others contributed to more traditionally 'academic' volumes, as defined by subject matter (which itself is period- and context-sensitive in any case), or by tone, style, the presence of a full critical apparatus, and so on. Additionally, a number of publishers operated in both markets, and so a clear publisher division into 'academic' and 'trade' was too difficult to implement in a meaningful way.

A further set of distinctions was made, in order to define the nature of the edited collection more tightly as the container of dateable nodes in a network of contemporary scholarly activity. I omitted volumes that consisted wholly or mostly of writing that had previously been published, although volumes containing a small proportion of such chapters alongside new material were admitted. Routinely included were collections containing a significant proportion of chapters that had been written prior to the conception of the volume, such as selections of papers given at annually recurring conferences. While difficult to verify, it is likely that a good proportion of such work existed in draft form before contact was made between author and editor to negotiate its inclusion in a volume. However, a certain time frame was imposed, such that only collections of essays written within the previous few years were included; in a handful of cases, volumes drawing together unpublished work spanning much longer periods were included in part but not whole. This rule had the effect of excluding the posthumous work of deceased scholars, except those whose death had occurred during the formation of the volume.

One of the confounding difficulties in the study of the edited collection at scale is the availability of the data. As such, the dataset was compiled in an iterative and cumulative manner, since it was not possible to establish a definitive list of volumes before the data collection began. A partial list was extracted from the British National Bibliography, although (due to the varying cataloguing practices in that data) the identification of a volume as an edited collection had often to be inferred from certain title words or the

---

[1] Certain key doctrines have tended to be the focus of the task of dogmatic theology – the defining of individual doctrines – and systematic theology has been concerned with the interrelations between them. Christology – the study of the person and work of Jesus Christ – is thus interrelated with soteriology – the understanding of human salvation – as well as the nature of the Church (ecclesiology), and much else besides.

naming of an editor, since they are not otherwise identified. An additional start was made with the significant number of volumes on the author's own shelves and on the open shelves of the most accessible library, that of the defunct Chichester Theological College, now dispersed among the wider collections of the University of Chichester. The bibliographies of these volumes were checked, and the details of further volumes harvested. The set includes a considerable number of Festschrift volumes, which often contain lists of the publications of the dedicatee; these too were scrutinized, and additional volumes were noted for pursuit. There eventually came a point at which the flow of new volumes being found by these methods slowed to a trickle (though without running completely dry); at this point, a decision was taken to close the dataset and begin the analysis.

The manner in which the data was collected has, then, some implications for the strength of the conclusions drawn here. Firstly, I can make no claims as to the perfect completeness of the set of volumes compiled. A number of volumes have certainly not been included. Some of these seem not to have survived in any library for which an online catalogue is available; others survive only in those libraries to which I did not have easy access. There will also be further volumes that were simply not yet discovered at all. However, I would claim to have inspected a sufficiently large proportion of those volumes that would be in scope to be able to plot some high-level trends. Those volumes that were not seen are unlikely to be sufficiently different (as a group) in their gender, occupational, and geographical composition that their omission materially skews the analysis here.

More significantly, it is conceivable that both my existing research specialism (in the Anglican church in particular) and the reliance on the library of Chichester Theological College in the early stages may have led to a fuller coverage of volumes emanating from Anglican circles and a corresponding under-representation of Roman Catholics, Methodists, or Baptists. In the absence of definitive lists, this is hard either to show or to discount. However, it is likely that the relative overweighting of Anglican voices in the data in fact reflects the profile of the volumes published, being at least as much a function of the numerical and institutional strength of the Church of England and the greater presence of Anglican scholars in the universities as it is of lacunae in the data itself.

The data

To be included, volumes had to bear a publication date within the eight decades that began in 1919 and ended in 1999. This periodization was more firmly bounded at the beginning (by the end of the First World War) than at the end. By the millennium, several trends were altering the terms of trade for academic publishing, including the growth in the numbers of students in the UK universities (and thus of academic staff to teach them), the developing framework of formalized national research assessment in the form of the Research Assessment Exercise, and the growth in both e-books and e-journals. In truth, other dates in the late 1990s or early 2000s might equally as well have been selected as a terminal point, since these interlocking trends cannot all be shown to reach an inflection point all at once. 1999 serves well enough for my purposes, but to have chosen (say) 1997 instead would not have materially changed the analysis.

Within that eight-decade period, three shorter periods were marked out as a means of understanding change over time. The first extends from 1919 until 1945, the end of the Second World War and the constraints on book production it entailed. The second begins in 1946 and runs until 1974, apparently a fallow year in the publication of edited volumes, possibly due to a situation of crisis in the British economy as a whole and the consequent rapid rise in the price of paper and other raw materials. The third then extends from 1975 until the period ending in 1999. Thus divided, the data shows a very marked increase in the number of edited volumes being published. In total the dataset included the contents of some 482 volumes. Seventy-four of these appeared between 1919 and 1945, 15 per cent of the total. A further 181 appeared between 1946 and 1974; between 1975 and 1999 the figure was 227, almost half of the whole, in the shortest of the three periods. It is beyond the scope of this article to establish the causes of the increase and to distinguish such causes as were unique to the genre (though some suggestions are made below) from those forces tending towards a growth in book publishing in general. Several factors are likely in play, including technological advances in relation to publishing, printing, marketing and transport (Thomson 2005).

Gender

I noted earlier the additional drag on the entry of women into academic publishing (when compared to other disciplines) caused by their exclusion from ordained ministry for much of the period. The effect of this is quite clear in the data if we consider the proportions of authors who were ordained or otherwise recognized as ministers of their churches. Those authors who were identified as being in active Christian ministry, as ministers or priests (depending on the denomination) or their bishops and other overseers, are recorded as such in the data. However, it is certain that a great many others, often those employed in the universities, were also ordained, but the convention was often to identify their academic status alone. Only about 60 per cent of chapters in the data have any ordination status associated with them, whereas that figure is much higher for gender, nation and institution. Among the authors of that 60 per cent, those who were ordained outnumber those who were not by three to one, meaning that nearly half of all the chapters were certainly written by ordained people, and this is probably a significant underestimate.

Examined in this light, then, the graph shows an unsurprising but nonetheless stark imbalance between male and female voices. It was possible to record a probable gender for 96 per cent of the data points (i.e. for 5,718 chapters of the 5,930 that were in scope). Of these, some 390 were written by women (just under 7 per cent), while the remaining 93 per cent (5,328 chapters) had male authors; fewer than one in sixteen were written by women. It is also likely that this is, in fact, an overestimate of the true proportion, since most of those whose gender could not be determined were identified by their initials, a convention that seems to have been applied most often to men. When the data is considered in three time series, the picture that emerges is one of an expansion from a state of almost complete absence to one merely of gross under-representation. (See Figure 8.1)

In the period between 1918 and 1945, just over 2 per cent, or about one in fifty chapters, were written by women (21 in total over nearly three decades); the appearance of such a chapter was a less-than-annual event. These are few enough to be considered individually. To inspect the list is to be struck by the presence of women with a certain marginality, or at least disconnection from institutions. Two names present are the novelist and playwright Dorothy L. Sayers and the spiritual director Evelyn Underhill, both of whom were conscious in their lifetime of being on the fringe and (in Sayers's case) quite protective of that status (Webster 2010, 570–3; Shaw 2018, 15). The Anglican suffragist and campaigner for the ordination of women, Maude Royden, moved so far to the margin as to found (and preach in) a wholly new ecumenical congregation, an almost unprecedented venture. Only one of the authors in the data before 1945 held a university teaching position, and that was indeed in history, not divinity: the medieval historian Margaret Deanesly, of the University of London.

From 1946 until 1974, the proportion of women in the graph became large enough to be visible on the chart, at least; a figure closer to one in thirty (3 per cent). In this period the data show an increasing number of women working in universities, but at least as often in other disciplines such as history, literature, or philosophy. The first woman I have been able to securely place in a university department of theology or religious studies was Margaret Thrall (Bangor), in 1970. The first two women to appear in the data while at one of the theological colleges were the Anglican Mollie Batten and the Baptist scholar Gwenyth Hubble, both in 1958. Between 1975 and 1999, the balance shifted somewhat. Between this period and the post-war one, the total number of chapters published (for which a gender can be assigned) had risen by 71 per cent; meanwhile, the growth in the number of chapters by women had far outstripped the general growth, increasing

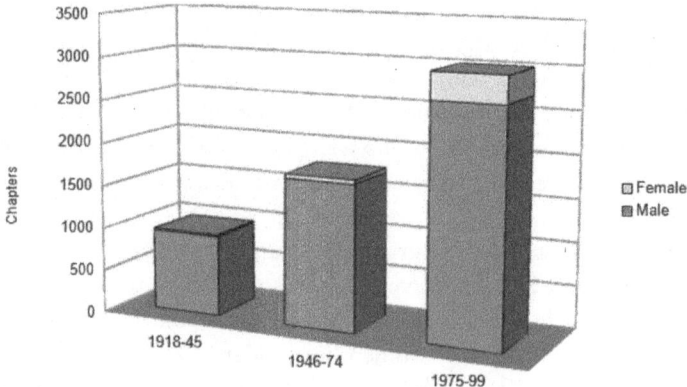

Figure 8.1 Authorship and gender.

by a factor of six, from 51 to 318. However, a vast imbalance still remained. For all the growth in absolute numbers, it remained the case that female authors accounted for only just over one in ten of the chapters published in the later period (for which an authorial gender can be determined).

Institutions

I have already noted the peculiar mixed institutional economy of theological learning in twentieth-century Britain. But it was an economy in flux, as both the vitality and size of each part shifted as the period progressed. The caricature of the leisured country rector (a largely, if not quite uniquely, Anglican figure) was never universally applicable; between the wars the Church of England began to address the great divergences in the size of parochial endowments that pertained between different parishes and different parts of the country: an imbalance of resources that allowed some incumbents a great deal of leisure for study while others were greatly overworked (Chandler 2006, 64–88). As the century progressed, and the size of congregations dwindled and parochial incomes shrank, such niches that allowed leisure to read and write became fewer. Although the changing working lives of Christian ministers remain largely unstudied, it seems likely that sustained theological scholarship increasingly became the preserve of the particularly gifted or well-organized among the working clergy.

The situation in the universities was also shifting, first expanding and then (by the millennium) shrinking again. In 1918 theology was conducted mostly in a small number of older institutions: in England, at Oxford, Cambridge, Durham and the (relatively new) King's College London, and University of Manchester; in Scotland, at the similarly ancient foundations of Aberdeen, Edinburgh and Glasgow. University College London had been founded in the nineteenth century on an explicitly secular basis and therefore had no place for theology. The same could be said for most of the new institutions of the 1960s, such as Sussex, East Anglia, and Essex. But after the Second World War there was a significant upswing in theological provision in the civic universities of the nineteenth and early twentieth centuries. Sheffield instituted its Biblical Studies department in 1947, in response to the Education Act of 1944 and its institution of compulsory religious instructions in schools (Rogerson 1990, 19–23); the theology department at Nottingham dates from the same period. The Old Testament scholar Roy Porter moved from Oxford to take up a new chair of theology at Exeter in 1962; the Cambridge theologian Howard Root became the first professor of theology at Southampton in 1966 (Brewer 2018, 12–13); a new department was founded in Bristol in 1965. By the end of the period, however, a cold wind of contraction had set in: the Southampton theology degree was short-lived, ceasing in the early 1980s; since celebrating its fiftieth anniversary in 1995, the department in Sheffield has been drastically cut. But the full effects of this contraction fall outside the scope of the present chapter. From 1918 until the mid-1990s, the overall picture is one of expansion.

The same cannot be said for the many institutions of learning that the churches maintained themselves for the education of both clergy and laity. Some of these were located close to the universities, particularly in Oxford and Cambridge, such as the Anglican institutions of Wycliffe Hall or Cuddesdon College, or the Congregationalist Mansfield College. The organization of the Church of England around small cathedral towns meant that many Anglican clergy trained in Chichester, Ely, Lincoln or Wells. Never very large in size (when compared to the universities), they nonetheless were home to scholars of considerable note: Lincoln Theological College was staffed by the Anglican theologians E. L. Mascall and Michael Ramsey in succession in the 1930s, two of the most significant of their generation. Few of these institutions, however, escaped the effects of a marked collapse in the number of candidates for ministerial training in the 1960s. This effect is most well documented in the Anglican case, where the early 1970s saw a drastic programme of closures and amalgamations, including the college at Ely (Welsby 1984, 143–6). The contraction continued, however, and by the 1990s both Chichester and Lincoln had gone the same way. Taken overall, then, the church colleges, while never very prominent, were greatly denuded by the mid-1990s.

Such, in outline, was the shifting institutional pattern of theological work in the twentieth century, although the narrative is only lightly integrated into the wider history of the period, and much of its details remain almost entirely unstudied. Space does not allow a full working-out of the degree to which the data supports or undermines this narrative. But overall it appears to be compatible with it. As already observed, the period saw a considerable expansion in the overall number of collections being published. Consequently, there was an absolute increase in the volume of work being published by scholars in all three situations – clergy, seminary and university. The volume of work from the clergy was 24 per cent greater in the period after 1975 than it had been between the wars; work produced within the theological colleges nearly trebled in volume over the same period. Even if the numerical strength of both active clergy-scholars and staff in the church colleges was falling, it would appear that the increase in publishing capacity and the ease of production was sufficient to offset the effect. At the same time, however, the volume of work being produced within the universities grew by a factor of more than eight. As such, the proportions within each time period attributable to each group show a shift in the centre of gravity, as visible in the chart below. (See Figure 8.2)

Between the wars, the proportion of chapters attributable to the working clergy was more than 40 per cent; by the post-1975 period, it was less than 20 per cent. In the same interwar period, authors here categorized as Other accounted for another 20 per cent of the total. This included a small number of missionaries, members of the religious orders, and chaplains in non-university institutions but was predominantly the work of writers from a myriad of secular occupations and from among the leisured classes. By the later period, though the absolute volume had again grown, the proportion had shrunk from 20 per cent to 14 per cent. This trend, which might be characterized as a squeezing of the space available for the interested amateur, was matched by a massive expansion of the proportion of work that was produced within the universities. Between the wars, slightly fewer than one in four such chapters were written by university-based scholars; between

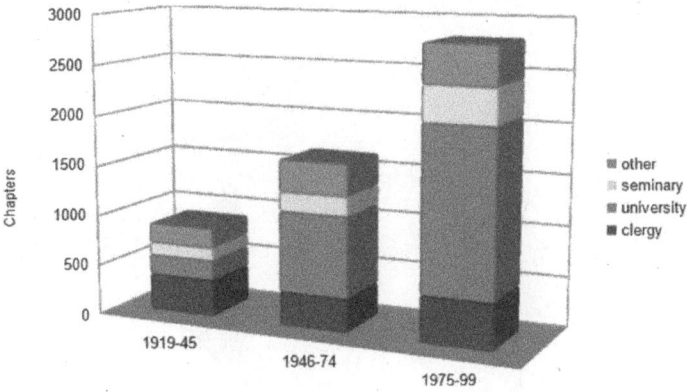

Figure 8.2 Chronological proportions: Authorship by professional status.

1975 and 1999, it was well over half (58 per cent). Add to this the work emanating from within seminary contexts (the proportion of which remained broadly similar across the period), and the proportion produced by professional scholars was 70 per cent, when between the wars it had been a little over half that. To an extent, then, theology had become, if not more professionalized (since that is a question of practice and attitude), then certainly more dominated by professional scholars.

Nations

The third significant shift observable in the data relates to geography, that is, the domicile of authors contributing to volumes that (according to my earlier definition) emanate principally from a British milieu. A great deal of research remains to be done on the circulation patterns of English-language monographs and periodicals and what those patterns would indicate in regard to the existence and nature of an Anglophone community of readers in theology. Such understanding as there is of this is most often to be found in studies of individual scholars and their patterns of citation. Leaving that aside, it is certainly the case that the period saw a significant growth in opportunities for theologians to travel internationally and meet fellow scholars. This was to a degree a matter of technology and economics. The Anglican philosopher Eric Mascall, who in 1910 as a small boy learned of the death of Edward VII while seated on the upper deck of a London horse-bus, was in the 1970s and 1980s to be a visitor and lecturer in the United States, travelling by commercial aeroplane, probably the single most important catalyst of the growth of international conferences (Mascall 1992, 19, 333). The increase in speed in communications technology, notably the fax machine in the 1970s and then email in the 1990s, would certainly have made the business of assembling a volume much faster and easier. Whether these advances served to create a global community or simply to bring a community that already existed into more regular contact (or to a degree

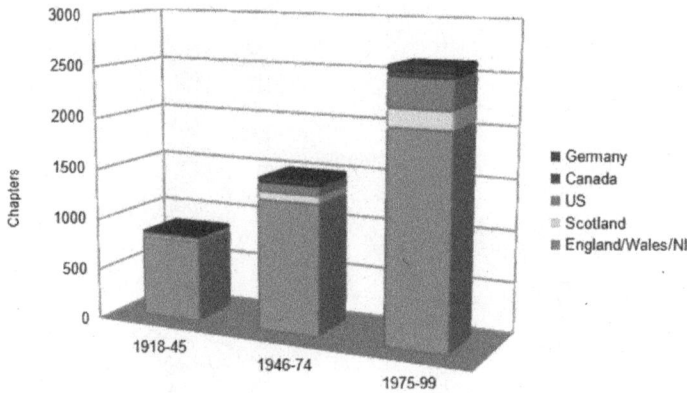

Figure 8.3 Geographic proportions.

both), the edited collection data examined here indicates a growth in participation of international scholars.

Of the 5,930 chapters in hand, 91 per cent (5,421) had a country of residence recorded for its author. Sixty-one unique countries are represented in that body of work, but 4,993 (92 per cent) were from the UK, North America or Germany, with the next most represented nations being Australia, France, Switzerland, and the Netherlands. The chart above shows the proportions originating in the most significant countries. (See Figure 8.3)

As shown in previous sections, the absolute growth in publishing activity over the period is clearly visible. Most striking, however, is the proportional growth of the involvement of international authors. In the interwar period, forty-five such chapters were recorded from North American or German authors as opposed to 803 from England, Wales, and Northern Ireland combined, a ratio of 1:18.[2] In the period from 1975, that ratio was nearer 1 to 5. There was one chapter from the United States alone for every seven from authors in England, Wales and Northern Ireland. Recalling, finally, the chapters from the many other nations represented in the data but not shown in this chart, it is clear that the period saw a marked internationalization of the contents of edited collections that originated in the UK.[3]

---

[2]In general the output from scholars based in Wales and Northern Ireland is so small that they have been grouped with the vastly preponderating volume from England.

[3]The chart also shows the rising prominence of Scottish authors – most particularly associated with the universities of Aberdeen and Edinburgh – in proportion to the rest of the UK. I intend to examine the reasons for this elsewhere.

Conclusion

This chapter has shown that between the ending of the First World War and the turn of the millennium, British theological publishing shifted in significant ways. Firstly, the volume of edited collections themselves increased significantly: three times as many such volumes were published in the last segment of the period than in the first. Most importantly, the profile of the contributors shifted in three different ways. The proportion of women increased significantly, but from such a low base that even by the end of the period they remained vastly under-represented. By the end of the period, the institutional location of authors was much more weighted towards those who earned their living in scholarly practice, either in the theological colleges or (in particular) in the expanded university sector. Though the absolute volume of work produced by each kind of scholar had increased, the role played by the parish clergyman or the independent scholar was proportionately diminished. Finally, the period saw a marked internationalization of these volumes, even though they were originated by British scholars and still predominantly populated by British authors.

Much research remains to be done, however, not least to establish a relationship of causation rather than the apparent correlation between this data and the broader narrative of the period in the historical literature to date. The precise interactions between the strategic moves and economic constraints of publishers and the scholarly impulses of editors are as yet relatively unexplored, yet they condition this particular causal chain fundamentally. As well as that, there are a great many small networks within the nearly five hundred edited collections from which the dataset is derived. Some represent the attempts of groups within the academy and church to define and police boundaries around doctrine and practice; others reflect the deliberate attempt precisely to transcend boundaries and bring opposing viewpoints into dialogue. Some reflect the histories of individual institutions; others, not least the large number of Festschrifts, are a kind of documentation of scholarly careers and the interconnections that they generate. These I have begun to explore elsewhere and plan to further through the lens of this network graph of a discipline instantiated in its edited collections (Webster 2022).

For now, however, I hope to have achieved three broad aims. Firstly, for my fellow religious historians, and historians of theology in particular, I have tried to set up a broad narrative framework within which subsequent studies may examine particular corners of the discipline. To what degree might histories of journals, publishers or editors, not to mention institutions or individuals, corroborate or contradict it? Secondly, I hope to provoke historians of the book, of publishing, of twentieth-century higher education, and of the other humanities disciplines alike to pursue comparative study of edited collections in other contexts (with or without digital methods) to determine what elements of this demographic and structural analysis may be generalized and what is unique to British theology of the twentieth century. The third is to suggest to specialist historians of the book (one of whom I have not hitherto considered myself) the potential offered by the study of edited collections not merely as printed objects or as individual, self-contained representations of a specific research topic at a point in time, but as objects of book historical study at a collective scale using digital methods.

The analysis of these volumes as containers of groups of nodes in larger networks is largely impossible without the kind of graph visualization applications that are now available. Even the simple analysis of individual chapter contributors in terms of such characteristics as those considered in this chapter, while not strictly impossible in an analogue world, would be prohibitively laborious without the routine power of computers to filter and count. The invocation of the notion of distant reading in my title, then, is intended to be allusive rather than strict, yet meaningful nonetheless. The digital allows the conceptualization and characterization of groupings of texts at scale and the analysis not (in this case) of the words on the page, but of the constellations of authors, editors and publishers that produced them.

Bibliography

Brewer, Christopher R., ed. *Theological Radicalism and Tradition: 'The Limits of Radicalism' with Appendices*. Abingdon: Routledge, 2018.

Chandler, Andrew. *The Church of England in the Twentieth Century: the Church Commissioners and the Politics of Reform, 1948–1998*. Woodbridge: Boydell, 2006.

Chandler, Andrew. *The Latter Glory of this House: A History of Two Christian Commonwealths in Modern Britain, 1828–1980*. London: Darton, Longman and Todd, 2013.

Chapman, Mark, ed. *Ambassadors of Christ: Commemorating 150 Years of Theological Education in Cuddesdon, 1852–2004*. Aldershot: Ashgate, 2004.

Colavizza, G. and M. Romanello. 'Citation Mining of Humanities Journals: The Progress to Date and the Challenges Ahead'. *Journal of European Periodical Studies* 4, no. 1 (2019): 36–53. https://doi.org/10.21825/jeps.v4i1.10120.

Eliot, Simon, ed. *The History of Oxford University Press*, four vols. Oxford: Oxford University Press, 2013–17.

Fyfe, Aileen, Noah Moxham, Julie McDougall-Waters, and Camilla Mørk Røstvik. *A History of Scientific Journals: Publishing at the Royal Society, 1665–2015*. London: UCL Press, 2022.

Gill, Sean. *Women and the Church of England from the Eighteenth Century to the Present*. SPCK, 1994.

Inman, Daniel. *The Making of Modern English Theology: God and the Academy at Oxford, 1833–1945*. Minneapolis: Fortress Press, 2014.

Kenyon, John. *The History Men: The Historical Profession in England since the Renaissance*. Oxford: Weidenfeld and Nicolson, 1983.

Mascall, E. L. *Saraband: The Memoirs of E. L. Mascall*. Leominster: Gracewing, 1992.

Mead, Daniel. 'The Gender Gap in University Enrolment: Evidence from Subjective Expectations'. *Education Economics* 31, no. 1 (2023): 54–76. https://doi.org/10.1080/09645292.2022.2027877.

Nicholson, Ernest ed. *A Century of Theological and Religious Studies in Britain*. London: Oxford University Press, 2003.

Rogerson, John W. 'Biblical Studies at Sheffield'. In *The Bible in Three Dimensions: Essays in Celebration of Forty Years of Biblical Studies in the University of Sheffield*, 19–23. Edited by David J. A. Clines, Stephen E. Fowl, Stanley E. Porter. Sheffield: Journal for the Study of the Old Testament, 1990.

Shaw, Jane. *Pioneers of Modern Spirituality: The Neglected Anglican Innovators of a 'Spiritual but Not Religious' Age*. London: Darton, Longman and Todd, 2018.
Spinaci, Gianmarco, Giovanni Colavizza and Silvio Peroni. 'A Map of Digital Humanities Research across Bibliographic Data Sources'. *Digital Scholarship in the Humanities*, 37, no. 4 (2022): 1254–68. https://doi.org/10.1093/llc/fqac016v.
Thomson, John B. *Books in the Digital Age*. Cambridge: Polity, 2005.
Webster, Peter. *Archbishop Ramsey: The Shape of the Church*. London: Routledge, 2015, 21–36, 119–27.
Webster, Peter. 'Archbishop Temple's Offer of a Lambeth Degree to Dorothy L. Sayers' (edition and introduction). In *From the Reformation to the Permissive Society*. Edited by Melanie Barber, Stephen Taylor, and Gabriel Sewell. Woodbridge: Boydell and Brewer, 2010.
Webster, Peter. *The Edited Collection: Pasts, Present and Futures*. Cambridge: Cambridge University Press, 2020.
Webster, Peter. *Visualising English Theology in Edited Collections*, 2022. https://peterwebster.me/2022/12/13/visualising-english-theology-in-edited-collections/.
Welsby, Paul A. *A History of the Church of England, 1945–80*. Oxford: Oxford University Press, 1984.

PART II
INTERDISCIPLINARY REFLECTIONS

CHAPTER 9
UNLOCKING LITERARY HERITAGE
FROM CABINETS OF CURIOSITIES TO DIGITAL STORYTELLING
Wim Van Mierlo

A visitor who walks into the Science Museum in London or the Museum of Science and Industry in Manchester encounters sumptuous spaces in which the wonders of technology are showcased and unlocked, often supported by digital technologies, in a way that is illuminating and educational for the widest possible audience. If that person then travels to see the visitor galleries at The British Library (BL) or The John Rylands Library, they mostly encounter an array of traditional display cabinets with books, papers and interpretive labels. I do not wish to suggest at all that the BL or the Rylands are poorly curated – quite the contrary – but there is a striking difference in approach that says something about how these institutions view their collections. The 'meaning' of the literary artefact, not least when that artefact is a manuscript, is still viewed as 'inherent', rather than 'situated and contextual' (Macdonald 2006, 2).

As a literature scholar, I want to have for our written and literary heritage what scientists have for physics, chemistry, and engineering.

Why does this difference exist? The simple – and probably cynical – answer is that in the popular imagination STEM is more important to society than the arts and humanities, and consequently attracts more funding. But that is not the whole answer. There is something about books and literature that makes them serious and highbrow. In this, they are no different from other cultural artefacts like paintings and antiquities. But at least art, sculpture, Greek vases, and Anglo-Saxon jewellery are beautiful to look at. The written word, by comparison, can be quite plain. Famous examples excepted – the likes of the Book of Kells (good for up to 1,000,000 visitors per year) or the Kelmscott Press *Canterbury Tales* – most books and manuscripts, even those from the Middle Ages, are actually quite nondescript. Their primary function is to be carriers of text and information; any aesthetic attributes are extra. Creating resonance and wonder (to use Stephen Greenblatt's [1991] famous terms) from our literary heritage therefore poses a challenge. A first edition of a Virginia Woolf novel, with cover art by her sister Vanessa Bell, or an original manuscript in the hand of John Keats, is evocative. But how do you display the 'novel'? Or 'creativity'? In other words, how can you meaningfully replicate the wonder that comes from creating a poem or work of fiction as well as the effects of those creations on past and present readers?

In untangling these questions, this chapter seeks to pinpoint what literary heritage is before turning to a brief analysis of current curatorial practices. Relying on affect theory, its precept is that the imagination is both the subject of and the driving force that makes literary heritage engaging. Literary heritage has a tangible presence in the artefacts that are the product of literary creation (the books and manuscripts) and life writing (letters, diaries, marginalia, but also in the 'association' objects that once were in the writer's possession (pens, typewriters, desks, clothing, locks of hair, and other paraphernalia). At the same time, the 'true' nature of literary heritage is the creative work itself – the ideas, words, characters, plots, rhymes, and cadences that sprang from the writer's mind whose abstract forms are difficult to capture and represent in a museum or exhibition. Can digital technology help with this task? Certainly – but not, as I will argue, as a panacea.

In the last decade or more, digital curatorship has made significant inroads in the museum and heritage sector, at first through multimedia displays, interactive devices, and (as Ellen Charlesworth and Claire Warwick show in Chapter 12 of this volume) social media, but now museums are also increasingly employing augmented reality (AR) and virtual reality (VR). The benefits are self-evident: the interactivity can lead to richer, more in-depth, and personalized visitor experiences (Cheng 2024). However, there is scepticism in the sector as well in that digital technologies can be seen as intrusive or intimidating (Wieneke, Weiß and Geelhaar 2005). It is key therefore that these technologies are tied to the visitor experience, complementing and enhancing the emotional and intelligent connections with the objects on display and the curatorial narrative in which they are placed (see Geismar 2021).

The number of case studies on digital curation that have appeared over the last decade has been substantial. By comparison, little attention has been devoted to the role and impact of digital media in literary heritage specifically. The reasons are, first, that a clear theoretical and methodological framework is still lacking for literary heritage as a field: despite some very valuable work relevant to literary heritage (Booth 2016; Watson 2020; Sutherland 2022). Second, the fledgling digital practices in archives and literary house museums, especially in the UK, have not yet led to the same kind of technological revolution that we find elsewhere in the heritage sector. Why this is owes as much to the status of literary heritage in the wider field as to the limitations on resources needed for digital technologies to work effectively and efficiently. The potential for effective use of digital technology is possible precisely because the digital straddles the same liminal gap between materiality and immateriality as the in/tangibility of literary heritage (Kirschenbaum 2002). Digital screens, it is true, are a poor substitute for the physicality of the artefact, but they do possess other useful affordances. While you cannot touch or smell the object – which are rarely possible in a heritage setting anyway – with a digital surrogate, you can rotate, zoom, and look inside the object in a way that you cannot with the original. The crucial point, however, is what we might call the phenomenology of seeing with computers. As a window through which you look at 'stuff', the interface is both a display tool that is strictly functional and a discursive tool that mediates whatever data and data processes that exist within the system and offers these it up to users for exploration, interrogation, and interpretation (Drucker 2016; Van Mierlo 2022).

With this in mind, this chapter provides, on the one hand, an overview and assessment of what digital practices already exist and, on the other, a reflection and a blueprint of what is possible. A good point to start, however, is by expounding what literary heritage entails and why it is unique and different from other forms of heritage.

What is literary heritage?

In case a definition is needed, literary heritage is the literary past viewed as a public good. Literary heritage thus manifests itself as any type of commemoration or celebration of the life and writing of the nation's poets, playwrights, novelists, essayists and memoirists, from statues and blue plaques to 'Shakespeare in the Park'. But it also concerns itself with the preservation of the memory and legacy of these writers as well as the artefacts that they have left behind. For the purposes of this chapter, I am looking at the preservation practices undertaken by literary house museums and heritage centres and the public institutions that look after literary archives.

What makes literary heritage special, however, is that more than other forms of heritage it is concerned with both tangible and intangible heritage. As objects, Elizabeth Gaskell's writing table (on display in the Gaskell House in Manchester), Agatha Christie's typewriter (owned by the Christie Archive Trust), and Charlotte Brontë's miniature manuscripts (in the collections of the Brontë Parsonage, Haworth) bear testimony to the creative life of the writers. The cerebral life of the imagination, however, only exists in the mind. While both the act of writing and the act of reading do reveal external traces, the acts themselves remain hidden from observation. The artefacts, in other words, stand at one remove from those processes. That is the case even with a writer's manuscripts which, although they are the closest we can ever get to the creative process, do not give us direct access to the processes of the creative mind (Van Hulle 2014; Van Mierlo 2013). From a curatorial point of view, literary heritage's double nature presents a particular challenge – though not necessarily one that is insurmountable. Good design, imaginative curatorial practice, and innovative digital technology can leverage rich interpretations and affective responses to an otherwise contingent set of circumstances.

The theory of affect has for a long time been an important component in museum and heritage studies. The affect is the emotional and psychological response to a historical artefact or place; as a subjective experience, it is immediate and undefined, but nonetheless the museum visitor recognizes a power and value that emanates from that place or artefact – from its *authenticity* – that renders it an important stepping-stone for meaningful engagement. Visitors' first encounter with objects is through the senses, not language. The experience of viewing the object, as art historian Jules David Prown (1980, 201, 207) contends, is 'visceral' and instinctive rather than intellectual, and thus very unlike any interaction with written sources. Greenblatt explains these emotional, and in many ways automatic and unconscious, responses in terms of 'resonance' and 'wonder' associated with the artefact whose 'arresting sense of uniqueness' can 'evoke an exalted attention' in the viewer and elicit a sense of critical curiosity (1991, 42). I use the word 'critical' here in the sense of *acuteness*. I do so in part to deconstruct Greenblatt's privileging of 'resonance', which stimulates the intellect more intently than the pleasurable experiences of 'wonder' (44, 51). Yet the affect, as it has been conceived in museum and archive studies since Greenblatt, focuses more clearly on the critical thresholds of emotion elicited in the visitor by the artefact. To be meaningful, the encounter with the authentic object creates an authentic experience that does not – or should not – lead to rational engagement with its meaning. Yet one hopes of course it might.

Greenblatt was thus an early exponent of what would become known as the affective turn in cultural studies, which contends that 'affects, emotions, and feelings are legitimate and powerful objects of critical scholarly inquiry' (Cifor and Gilliland 2016, 2). The affect, however, is more than a lens for scholarly research. Especially in museum and archives studies, the affective turn has made significant inroads. Affective curatorship has transformed museum practice that has shifted away from the traditional top-down approach, in which the knowledge and information are provided by specialists, to a visitor-focused approach that focuses on environment and design to leverage emotions and feelings across different 'social, sensory, and emotive registers'; the aim is to contextualize the display to realize new understandings and relationships (Varutti 2023; Fisher and Reckitt 2015, 361–2). In these 'affective encounters' involving the interpolation of the visual, the textual, the material, and the imaginative, the digital is by no means the only – or even the best – way to generate emotion, but it certainly plays its part (Varutti 2023, 62). In literary and archive studies, too, the affect is seen as a way of offsetting traditional critical concerns with the production of meaning. The very act of reading for pleasure is predicated on literature's ability to resonate and enchant across time and space (Felski 2008). With respect to archives, the affect can take different forms: the testimony of emotions recorded in the archives (Cifor 2016), the emotional attachment to the records and memory documents (Halilovich 2016), or the affective response deriving from the sensory encounter with the sight, smell, and touch of the archive (Lee 2016). Maryanne Dever likewise speaks about the 'aura' (in Benjamin's sense, when the object takes possession of us) that emanates from the documents in respect of the archives of a number of women artists and writers she analyses. In particular, she writes about 'the circuits of emotion and feeling' that exist within and without the documents – in what the documents speak about and in the way they were lovingly created, handled, and preserved. Archival documents, therefore, are not 'inert' but 'moving' (Dever 2019, 41–2, 103). However, while these affects are undeniable, a difficulty arises from Dever's account, too. As she is well aware, hers is a privileged encounter. The 'affective intensity' that she experiences as a scholar is mostly denied to ordinary people who lack the credentials that allow them the same direct, sensory and bodily encounter with primary source materials. When moved behind glass, the archive becomes inert again, tangibly out of bounds. Please do not touch.

The digital display cabinet

Digital technologies have been a game changer for the display of rare books and manuscripts. To be sure, digital screens are no substitute for the original: that still cannot be touched. But they can significantly enhance access and exploration as well as simulate affect. The fact is, books and manuscripts are difficult to put on display. Of a book, one can at most show two pages at the time; the back of a document is always hidden from view when it lies flat in the exhibition case. Furthermore, reading what it says on the page is not always easy, especially when the print is small and the handwriting dense, unfamiliar and messy.

In the early 2000s, Armadillo Systems developed Turning the Pages, a digital display cabinet, in partnership with The British Library (https://ttp.onlineculture.co.uk). Predating the Apple iPad and iPhone, Turning the Pages' touch-screen technology was revolutionary. On a standalone kiosk, visitors to the public areas of the BL could browse a small selection of valuable books and manuscripts from the collections, including the Codex Arundel, containing notes and writings by Leonardo da Vinci, and a notebook with draft poems and drawings by William Blake. Swiping the screen with their fingers, users could leaf through digital facsimiles of the artefact as if they were turning the actual pages.[1] The advantages of this technology are apparent. Not only do the digital reproductions permit exploration of the book or manuscript as a whole, but various aids also enable an in-depth engagement: image rotation, a zoom function or overlay magnifying glass that floats across the page, and a switch to bring up a transcription. Furthermore, users can bring up contextual information, the equivalent of the traditional museum label, explaining the artefact's history, provenance, and significance.

In the case of the BL, Turning the Pages allowed the public to see rare items that are not normally accessible to members of the public. In other instances, the kiosks are used alongside the original books or documents on display in the gallery. The permanent exhibition of 'Yeats: The Life and Works of William Butler Yeats' at the National Library of Ireland (NLI), for instance, uses several screens with drafts of Yeats's most famous poems so that visitors can trace for themselves Yeats's creative process alongside the aura of the authentic document. As a dynamic, interactive device, Turning the Pages is thus quite effective in creating resonance and wonder in a way that allows the user to get 'into' the artefact through three-dimensionally simulating the look and feel of the original.

The system also has its drawbacks, however. While the developers put great effort into replicating the behaviour of the page when it is turned according to the weight and size of the original, the inorganic hardness and coldness of the screen cannot really capture the experience of touching (or for that matter cases smelling) the actual object. Variable processor power furthermore can lead to the system lagging or being unresponsive, which further detracts from the authenticity of the simulated experience. Then there is also the cost of purchasing and maintaining the tool. Without doubt, Turning the Pages provides value for money, yet its high price tag makes it unaffordable for all but the biggest institutions. Its value, nonetheless, is proven by the fact that twenty years on

---

[1] The kiosks have since been withdrawn.

some of its design ideas are common features in state-of-the art digital scholarly editions such as the Samuel Beckett Digital Manuscripts Project (beckettarchive.org).

Digital opportunities

Despite its limited use, it is fair to say that Turning the Pages remains a gold standard in written heritage technology. No other system has since emerged to rival Turning the Pages in its technological innovation, effectiveness, and user experience. Concomitantly, the heritage sector itself still sits on the fence when it comes to embracing digital technology. Institutions generally recognize the added value of innovation, but there is also doubt as to whether it is right for them. The reasons for this are understandably varied, with questions ranging from suitability to affordability. A common worry among museum professionals, for instance, is that screens are distracting, drawing attention away from displays (Miano and Borsotti 2023, 12; Paschou and Papaioannou 2023; Nikolaou 2024, 1787). The biggest threshold, however, is cost. The initial acquisition is usually only one factor; there are also costs associated with training, support, and maintenance to consider that can be prohibitive especially for small- or medium-sized organizations (Nikolaou 2024). It should come as no surprise then that, in the UK at least, the digital revolution has yet to affect curatorial practices in penetrating literary heritage in any significant way. Yet literature's unique properties, consisting as they do of both tangible and intangible elements, make it uniquely suitable for different forms of digital mediation and interpretation.

No archive or literary house museum remains completely untouched by the digital sphere. From back-end systems (catalogues, content management etc.) to social media, literary heritage institutions use digital technologies as part of their day-to-day workflow (Paschou and Papaioannou 2023). Social media in particular are a popular, effective, and low-cost way to engage with the public and share digital images from the collections, as are websites. Few UK archives and literary houses, however, unlike their American counterparts, offer substantial digital collections through the web or via third-party platforms like Flickr. Large institutions such as The British Library, the National Library of Scotland, the National Library of Ireland (NLI), and Balliol College, Oxford, are notable exceptions. Wordsworth Grasmere was an early adopter with *From Goslar to Grasmere, William Wordsworth: Electronic Manuscripts* (2007), a digital edition for specialists and educators developed in collaboration with the University of Lancaster that presented digital facsimiles and transcriptions of selected manuscripts for *The Prelude* and *Home at Grasmere*.[2] Likewise, the National Art Library at the Victoria & Albert Museum (NAL) experimented with digital facsimiles of its Charles Dickens manuscripts in the 2010s, when the library had conserved and rephotographed its holdings for the Dickens

---

[2] The website is no longer maintained, but is still available in deprecated form at https://collections.wordsworth.org.uk/GtoG/home.asp?page=FrontPage.

bicentenary. The project did not come to fruition, owing to technical impediments; the proprietary page-turning software that the V&A was using proved difficult to implement. The NAL, however, has since continued working on the online presentation of Dickens's manuscripts. It has migrated its images to an IIIF-compliant image server and has made a substantial selection of individual manuscript pages publicly accessible.[3] Linked with this, is the *Deciphering Dickens* project, an interactive online archive that will enable users to explore Dickens's creative process from the comfort of their home (Dodds 2018, 229–88; https://www.vam.ac.uk/research/projects/deciphering-dickens).

When *Deciphering Dickens* is completed, this will undoubtedly be a fantastically useful resource. But like *From Goslar to Grasmere*, its impetus is editorial rather than curatorial – the difference being that the digital editorial projects remediate rather than curatorially contextualize and interpret the original artefacts. Although digital editorial projects make the originals easily available, owing to their size, depth, and structural complexities, these editions also impose thresholds on access on use (very often not least for users with disabilities). Therefore, they are implicitly geared towards expert users, such as students and scholars. By comparison, 'dumping' loads of images online has no curatorial value at all.[4] Many organizations, however, actively create online exhibitions in various forms and guises.

The majority of online exhibitions are the digital counterpart of temporary exhibitions held in situ; most are very simple webpages with text and some images that do not attempt to replicate the exhibition as such. The National Library of Scotland's *200 years of 'Pride and Prejudice: From Austen to Zombies'* (2013), for example, furnishes a descriptive survey of what was on display together with a handful of images of the objects accompanied by a brief commentary.[5] By comparison, *Childhood in Dickensian London* (2020) at Senate House Library, University of London (2020) is more exhaustive in its approach in that, in terms of images and layout, the online exhibition replicates the design and original displays of the exhibition.[6] Online exhibitions can help organizations reach wider audiences – which is why some literary heritage institutions also create online-only exhibitions to showcase their work, or create bespoke micro-exhibitions that would be costly to mount in situ.[7] But in each of the above cases, the impetus is to counter the inevitable ephemerality of exhibitions by creating a digital version for posterity. The NLI likewise made a version of their Yeats exhibition for the web before it was originally set to close, but went one step further by creating a virtual copy of the

---

[3] The International Image Interoperability Framework (IIIF) is an open-source standard for delivering images over the web.
[4] The BL's *Discovering Literature* pages are in that respect an example of good practice.
[5] https://www.nls.uk/exhibitions/treasures/pride-and-prejudice/.
[6] https://www.london.ac.uk/about/services/senate-house-library/exhibitions/childhood-dickensian-london.
[7] For good examples of online, 3d and virtual exhibits, see https://wordsworth.org.uk/online-exhibitions/, and https://www.19thc-artworldwide.org/autumn18/webster-on-a-digital-recreation-of-the-lenox-library-picture-gallery.

exhibition space.⁸ Using Adobe Flash Player, users could 'walk through' a map of the exhibition, visiting each of the sections; by clicking on icons, they could zoom in on individual displays and artefacts, and read the original captions. Navigating the tour could be a bit cumbersome, because Flash (now deprecated) used a lot of bandwidth and could put a strain on CPU usage (not ideal for users with slow internet connections or older computers); but the tour offered the most complete digital experience of the original exhibition's curatorial narrative.

When it comes to on-site use of digital media in literary house museums and exhibition galleries, the picture is, as I have already indicated, less developed. Nonetheless, it is clear that there are a lot of opportunities for integrating innovative digital technologies into curatorial practice. Not all of them, moreover, need to break the bank. In the following paragraphs, I will survey some tools and technologies that range from simple and affordable to the more advanced.⁹

- **QR codes.** Without doubt, QR codes are the simplest and cheapest technology that can encourage visitors to explore the artefact or display in greater depth on their mobile phones. At the Charles Dickens' Birthplace Museum in Portsmouth, for example, QR codes in each room direct visitors to museum's website where they can read more about the room in question: its use, the contemporary furniture on display, and its decorative features (https://charlesdickensbirthplace.co.uk/what-to-see-do/displays/). The Elizabeth Gaskell House in Manchester installed QR codes for children on their garden trail that link to 'fun facts' and games, as well as tips about ecology and wildlife protection that can be applied at (https://elizabethgaskellhouse.co.uk/about/). The blended experience that QR furnishes can replace intrusive interpretive panels in the physical space.

- **Audiovisual technology.** Screens provide another simple form of blended experience. Whether for video or slideshow loops, flatscreens installed around the exhibition space can display supplementary photo-visual material, videos or text. The advantage is that these can run from a flash drive, using Powerpoint files converted to images or video. Content in other words can be easily and quickly updated. More sophisticated AV solutions are touch screens, CAVE projection screens, and holographic screens.¹⁰ Named for Plato's allegory, CAVE stands for Cave automatic virtual environment and consists of multiple projectors pointed at walls, the floor, or one or more rear-projector screens. Holographic screens are a simpler version of full 3D holographic projections that produce light diffraction using laser technology or electromagnetic resonators; also using rear-projection, the holographic screens render a 2D image on a

---

⁸The 360° Virtual Tour was launched in 2008 and withdrawn in 2021, when Adobe ended its support of the Flash Player.
⁹See especially their series of six case studies at https://advisor.museumsandheritage.com/features/technology-in-museums-making-the-latest-advances-work-for-our-cultural-institutions/.
¹⁰For further information, see prodisplay.com, a UK company specializing in projection technologies.

semi-transparent surface, thus replicating the ghostly appearance of the object or person.

- **Digital museum guide systems.** Personal digital assistants (PDA) or smartphone apps using location-based activation can be used for text, audio, and images as the visitor walks through the museum or exhibition space. The Wieland Museum in Oßmannstedt, near Weimar, dedicated to the German poet Christoph Martin Wieland (1733–1813), who lived in the house and surrounding estate, have experimented with a PDA system as an unobtrusive but effective way for visitors to explore Wieland's life and work. Wieneke, Weiß and Geelhaar (2005) describe how the 'Digitales Osmantinum' system is adapted to the 'modalities of the site', and through its use of GPS technology it offers an experience that is unique for each visitor. Quite deliberately, not all content is available all at once. To arouse the sense that the museum visit is an embodied experience, the visitor has to physically move through the space to get to new information. Additionally, integrated in the PDA is a RFID reader (which stands for Radio-Frequency Identification Device that is commonly used as a contactless payment device) which picks up a signal when the device is pointed at a marker next to specific artefacts which guides visitors to further information.

- **Interactive and 'gamification' tools.** I am not aware of any such tool currently in use at literary house museums and archives, but this is an area where there is considerable potential, especially for archival material; several developments in the field of the digital literary studies field can offer inspiration. Under the influence of the impact agenda, research in digital scholarly editing has yielded interesting practices are user engagement and co-production. These practices can be easily adopted for gallery use. Taking their cue from citizen scholarship, projects like *Transcribe Bentham* (http://transcribe-bentham.ucl.ac.uk/td/Transcribe_Bentham) and From the Page (https://fromthepage.com/digital_scholarship) have developed relatively simple tools and interfaces by which members of the public or students undertake the laborious task of deciphering and transcribing unpublished, handwritten documents (Pierazzo 2015, 21–5).[11] The interface automatically transforms the text into TEI-XML, the standardized encoding system developed by the Text Encoding Initiative (https://tei-c.org), that renders the text machine-readable. In the exhibition gallery, visitors could test their ability to decipher handwritten material using a similar interface on a computer terminal or tablet. A more experimental approach is suggested by the theoretical possibilities of 'using game mechanics in a non-game context' (Pierazzo 2015, 32). The idea stems from research into dynamically displaying manuscripts within the digital edition, moving away from the static 'one page equals one image' towards a more interactive, processual visualization.

---

[11] https://janeaustens.house/news/frank-austen-transcription-project-underway/.

Pierazzo (2014; 2015, 31–2), for instance, developed a prototype for a Proust manuscript where the user could choose to view the draft either in the order of its inscription, capturing the sequence in which Proust added the word on to the page, or in the sequence in which they, following further revision, finally appeared in the published text (Barney 2020). Extending this idea, one can easily envisage an interface in which digital objects can be dragged around the screen in the way online jigsaw puzzles work. In an exhibition or gallery, for example, visitors could view a manuscript on display and then turn to a terminal in which they are tasked to arrange different versions or revisions of the text in the correct sequence.

The preceding list should not be considered definitive and exhaustive; in any case, digital curatorship is a rapidly evolving field. What is important to reiterate, though, is that these tools and technologies are curatorial aids, not an end in themselves. In order to add value, the technology needs to be integrated functionally and holistically in the larger design. This is where the concept of digital storytelling comes into play.

Digital storytelling

Simply put, digital storytelling is the method of creating stories using digital means, whether this is through video, image, text, or a combination of all three. The elegance of digital storytelling is that it is largely platform-independent. Content can be created, edited, and shared on a smartphone; as well as using more sophisticated online platforms and toolkits.[12] Because of its democratizing effect, digital storytelling, therefore, has become a popular vehicle at grassroots level in conducting oral history, community projects, citizen journalism, education, autoethnography and self-branding (Spurgeon and Edmond 2015; Copeland and de Moor 2018; Henrickson, Jephcote and Comissiong 2022). Digital storytelling has also already made its entry into heritage, too (Underberg-Goode 2017; Paiva and Cardoso 2023). It provides a connection and opportunity, too, for the narrative-based concerns in literary heritage. In this final section, however, I want to slightly expand digital storytelling as a concept to explore its usefulness in eliciting the affect. In a heritage context, digital technologies do not operate independently of the context in which they are used; they should not be an 'add-on', but need to be integrated with and carry forward the larger curatorial narrative.

The reason why digital technologies require this performative function is that their – perceived – properties signal immateriality and inauthenticity, the exact opposite of what heritage is about (Nikolaou 2024, 1786–7). Digital technologies, in other words, do not self-evidently elicit affect, which is why visitors can experience them as distracting and intrusive. Yet, paradoxically, digital technologies can be effective in conveying

---

[12]See, for example, https://www.intractive.app/post/best-interactive-storytelling-software-tools.

meanings from intangible phenomena, which make them very suitable for literary heritage, in a blended experience that is seamlessly incorporated into the exhibition space or museum. What is also true for both – but especially the house museum – is that it is not only the individual objects that are authentic, and capable of the affect, but also the environment itself. The affective properties of the museum's space and design have long been acknowledged. The effect of these properties is 'atmosphere', an 'emotional state' that is an aspect of the museum's multi-sensory content (Paschou and Papaioannou 2023, 2, 7; Varutti 2023). Immeasurable, yet real and perceptible, atmosphere impacts in significant ways on the visitor experience (positive or negative) and thereby is instrumental in eliciting affect alongside and complementary to the artefacts on display in that environment. Bringing in digital technologies, when done sympathetically and coherently, can mediate and enhance the experience (Paschou and Papaioannou 2023, 7–8; Miano and Borsotti 2023).

Once again, in current practice, digital technologies do not yet have a significant presence in literary heritage. Nonetheless, we can find some interesting examples of digital storytelling practices that elegantly integrate audiovisual media with the overall curatorial narrative. In each of the following two case studies the presence of these digital media is non-intrusive (and, in fact, quite minimalistic in the first case); combining information with ambience, their use also blends effectively with the materiality of the artefacts on display.

Wordsworth Grasmere probably counts as one of the best and most fascinating instances of atmosphere in the way environment, space, and content intermingle. The site comprises three buildings: Dove Cottage, the home of William and Dorothy Wordsworth from 1799 to 1808; a museum gallery with permanent and temporary exhibitions; and the Jerwood Centre library and archive. The archives and reading rooms are usually off limits to visiting tourists, but the space is used for an extensive educational and outreach programme that often involves handling of objects and manuscripts from the collections (Cowton 2023). The archives' 'aura', however, possess an extraordinarily quality, not only because of the vast number of drafts, fair copies, letters, journals and notebooks compiled and composed by William, Dorothy, Wiliam's wife, Mary, but also because the site's foundational collections have never left the Lake District. Produced at Dove Cottage and other houses in Grasmere and Rydal, the Wordsworth papers travelled after his death no further than Carlisle, where the poet's son, Gordon Graham Wordsworth, resided; at the end of his life Gordon bequeathed the papers to the Wordsworth Trust and they returned to Grasmere.[13] Central to Wordsworth Grasmere's ethos is the lived experience of the Wordsworths: 'At this site, uniquely, we can read an author's own words about a place, composed in that very place, on the very paper on which these words first were transcribed. People, poetry, place, and the collections which embody their lives and work, is the essence of The Wordsworth Trust' (Cowton 2023, 247). This ethos translates

---

[13]See https://www.romanticism.amdigital.co.uk/introduction/user-guide.

into a well-considered and intimate approach to the way the space is curated. At the time of writing, visitors typically start with Dove Cottage itself. Before entering the Grade I-listed cottage, visitors watch a video which relates some of the history of the dwelling and its connection with the Wordsworths, but mainly tells an evocative story of life in Dove Cottage and its influence on Wordsworth's creativity. The digital storytelling is thus quite minimalistic, but nevertheless captures well the mood of the site, preparing the visitor for the main house. Inside the furniture and items on display (several of them authentic) creates an atmosphere which is very much 'the way the Wordsworths knew it'. None of the furniture is cordoned. Instead, visitors can sit down at the kitchen table and various other places and pick up and peruse some of the books and manuscripts, reproduced three-dimensionally in facsimile, that are strewn across the table. This 'interactive' approach is very effective in representing the day-to-day domesticity, a hive of activity, conversation, and creative energy, as one may know from reading Dorothy Wordsworth's famous journal. After seeing Dove Cottage and its famous gardens, the visitor can find their way to the museum, where they can see first editions and manuscripts written by the Wordsworths and their circle, including an extensive display with original drafts that relates the history of the long gestation of *The Prelude*, Wordsworth's autobiographical poem begun in 1798 and published posthumously in 1850.

The second case I want to discuss is the Museum of Literature Ireland (MoLI). Opened in 2019 in Newman House on Dublin's St. Stephen's Green, the museum is a collaborative venture of University College Dublin and the NLI, drawing on both institutions' vast printed and archival collections. The building itself is of historic interest. Built in 1738, Newman House became the site of the Catholic University of Ireland in 1854 and was named after its first rector, John Henry Newman. The poet Gerard Manley Hopkins had rooms in the building when he taught classics there from 1884 and 1889. But Newman House's most famous literary association is no doubt James Joyce, who was a student at the University from 1898 to 1902. The historic Georgian building is therefore part of MoLI's layered visitor experience, which includes the 'Physics Theatre', the location of a crucial scene in *A Portrait of the Artist as a Young Man* in which Stephen Dedalus, Joyce's fictional counterpart, politely spars with the Dean of Studies over language and Irish identity. Unsurprisingly, Joyce's life and work are a prominent feature.

The main exhibition starts with an immersive audiovisual installation, called 'A Riverrun of Language' with a nod to Joyce's *Finnegans Wake*, that celebrates the diversity of accent and voice in Ireland and how its writers from the earliest times to the present have used language to celebrate and express its magnificence as well as the historical trauma and tribulations that characterize and define Irish identity and experience.[14] The digital installation, combining sound with word projections, creates an interesting moodscape that brings Ireland's rich literary legacy and the country's continuing deep engagement with the written word to life. The galleries then open up into the analogue

---

[14] https://moli.ie/exhibitions/riverrun-of-language.

part of the museum. Downstairs, this includes 'Dear Dirty Dublin', a 3D model of the city and detailed timeline with important moments from Joyce's life; upstairs is reserved for other Irish writers and temporary exhibitions. The space includes an audio section with digital recordings of contemporary writers talking about their creative process; it also has an actual reading nook, accentuating that literary heritage is as much about writers from the past as readers in the present. The final section of the top-floor gallery is again devoted to James Joyce's writing, displaying first editions, notebooks, and draft manuscripts. On the whole, MoLI is a true celebration of creativity and the written word in Irish literature, tastefully encapsulated in a well-designed, stimulating, sensory environment that is aesthetically, affectively, and intellectually engaging.[15] Even a visitor who is not well versed in James Joyce or the work of other Irish writers comes away stimulated and curious for more.

Conclusion

At the time of MoLI's opening in 2019, *The Irish Times* reported that 'literary visitors' who visit Dublin want to find the traces of the 'literary greats' that Ireland has produced; they come to MoLI hoping to 'find some substance to the intangible thing that we call inspiration' (Tipton 2019). This is as good a definition of the dual nature of literary heritage as any. Like other types of heritage, literary heritage strives to elicit an affective experience in the visitor, but to reach from the tangible artefacts (books, manuscripts, association objects etc.) to the intangible fundament of literature itself (inspiration, beauty, narrative, cadence etc.) is not a self-evident action. Digital technology can play the role of intermediary, no doubt because the digital itself straddles two spheres: while manifestly real and tangible, the digital nonetheless also has an unreal quality to it, most notably lacking texture and smell that are defining features of all other artefacts; yet the discursive power of the digital interface is well suited to mediate the affective qualities and meanings of literary heritage in interesting and effective ways. In current literary heritage practice, however, digital technology shows great potential that is only just beginning to be realized and implemented.

Bibliography

Barney, Brett. 'TEI, the Walt Whitman Archive, and the Test of Time'. *Journal of the Text Encoding Initiative* 13 (2020). https://doi.org/10.4000/jtei.3249.

Booth, Alison. *Homes and Haunts: Touring Writers' Shrines and Countries*. Oxford: Oxford University Press, 2016.

---

[15]Images that visitors have posted on Tripadvisor and elsewhere provide good visual evidence of MoLI's exhibition space and design.

Cheng, Mofan. 'Analysis of Digital Curating in Museums'. *Interdisciplinary Humanities and Communication Studies* 1, no. 5 (2024).

Cifor, Marika. 'Affecting Relations: Introducing Affect Theory to Archival Discourse'. *Archival Science* 16 (2016): 7–31.

Cifor, M. and A. J. Gilliland. 'Affect and the Archive, Archives and Their Affects: An Introduction to the Special Issue'. *Archival Science* 16 (2016): 1–6.

Copeland, Sarah and Aldo de Moor. 'Community Digital Storytelling for Collective Intelligence: Towards a Storytelling Cycle of Trust'. *AI & Society* 33 (2018): 101–11.

Cowton, Jeff. 'Poetry that 'will live and do good': Fulfilling Wordsworth's Hopes for His Work Through Interpretation and Outreach at Dove Cottage in Wordsworth 250.' *European Romantic Review* 34, no. 2 (2023): 243–54.

Dever, Maryanne. *Paper, Materiality and the Archived Page*. London: Palgrave, 2019.

Dodds, Douglas. 'From Analogue to Digital: Word and Image Digitization Projects at the V&A'. *Journal of Victorian Culture* 23, no. 2 (2018): 222–230.

Drucker, Johanna and Patrik Svensson. 'The Why and How of Middleware'. *Digital Humanities Quarterly* 10, no. 2 (2016). https://www.digitalhumanities.org/dhq/vol/10/2/000248/000248.html.

Felski, Rita. *Uses of Literature*. Malden, Mass. and Oxford: Blackwell, 2008.

Fisher, Jennifer and Helena Reckitt. 'Introduction: Museums and Affect.' *Journal of Curatorial Studies* 4, no. 3 (2015): 1–2.

Geismar, Haidy. 'Museum + Digital =?' in *Digital Anthropology*, 264–87. 2nd ed. Edited by Haidy Geismar and Hannah Knox (London: Routledge, 2021).

Greenblatt, Stephen. 'Resonance and Wonder'. In *Exhibiting Cultures: The Poetics and Politics of Museum Display*, 42–56. Edited by Ivan Karp and Steven D. Lavine. Washington: Smithsonian Books, 1991.

Halilovich, Hariz. 'Re-imaging and Re-imagining the Past after 'Memoricide': Intimate Archives as Inscribed Memories of the Missing'. *Archival Science* 16, no. 1 (2016): 77–92.

Henrickson, Leah, William Jephcote and Rhys Comissiong. 'Soft Skills, Stories, and Self-reflection: Applied Digital Storytelling for Self-branding'. *Convergence: The International Journal of Research into New Media Technologies* 28, no. 6 (2022): 1577–97.

Kirschenbaum, Matthew G. 'Editing the Interface: Textual Studies and First Generation Electronic Objects'. *Text: An Interdisciplinary Annual of Textual Studies* 14 (2002): 15–51.

Lee, Jamie A. 'Be/longing in the Archival Body: Eros and the 'Endearing' Value of Material Lives.' *Archival Science* 16 (2016): 33–51.

Macdonald, Sharon. 'Expanding Museum Studies: An Introduction'. In *A Companion to Museum Studies*, 1–12. Edited by Sharon Macdonald. Oxford: Blackwell Publishing, 2006.

Miano, Alessandra and Marco Borsotti. 'Experiencing Authenticity of the House Museums in Hybrid Environments'. *Multimodal Technologies and Interaction* 7, no. 7 (2023): 72.

Nikolaou, Polina. 'Museums and the Post-Digital: Revisiting Challenges in the Digital Transformation of Museums'. *Heritage* 7, no. 3 (2024): 1784–1800.

Paiva, Odete and Paula Cardoso. 'Digital Storytelling in Museums: The Power of Communication.' In *Combining Modern Communication Methods With Heritage Education*, 134–45. Edited by Lia Bassa. Hershey, Pennsylvania: IGI Global, 2023.

Paschou, Sofia and Georgios Papaioannou. 'Exploring the Digital Atmosphere of Museums: Perspectives and Potential.' *Technologies* 11, no. 5 (2023): 149. https://doi.org/10.3390/technologies11050149.

Pierazzo, Elena. *Digital Scholarly Editing: Theories, Models and Methds*. Farnham, Surrey: Ashgate, 2015.

Pierazzo, Elena. 'Of Time and Space: A New Framework for Digital Editions of Draft Manuscripts'. *Variants: The Journal of the European Society for Textual Scholarship* 11 (2014): 53–71.

Prown, Jules David. 'Style as Evidence.' *Winterthur Portfolio* 15, no. 3 (1980): 197–210.

Spurgeon, Christina and Maura Edmond. 'Making media participatory.' *Media International Australia* 154, no. 1 (2015): 53–6.

Sutherland, Kathryn. *Why Modern Manuscripts Matter*. Oxford University Press, 2022.

Tipton, Gemma. 'First Look Inside the New Museum of Literature Ireland', *Irish Times*, 14 September 2019. https://www.irishtimes.com/culture/books/first-look-inside-the-new-museum-of-literature-ireland-1.4009173.

Underberg-Goode, Natalie. 'Digital Storytelling for Heritage Across Media'. *Collections* 13, no. 2 (2017): 103–14.

Van Hulle, Dirk. *Modern Manuscripts: The Extended Mind and Creative Undoing from Darwin to Beckett and Beyond*. London: Bloomsbury, 2014.

Van Mierlo, Wim. 'The Archaeology of the Manuscript: Towards Modern Palaeography.' In *The Boundaries of the Literary Archive: Reclamation and Representation*, 15–29. Edited by Carrie Smith and Lisa Stead. Ashgate, 2013.

Van Mierlo, Wim. 'The Scholarly Edition as Digital Experience: Reading, Editing, Curating.' *Textual Cultures: Texts, Contexts, Interpretation* 15, no. 1 (2022): 117–25.

Varutti, Marzia. 'The Affective Turn in Museums and the Rise of Affective Curatorship.' *Museum Management and Curatorship* 38, no. 1 (2023): 61–75.

Watson, Nicola J. *The Author's Effects: On Writer's House Museums*. Oxford: Oxford University Press, 2020.

Wieneke, Lars, Tobias Weiß and Jens Geelhaar. 'Digitales Osmantinum: Digital Media Integration for a Literature Museum'. *Digital Culture and Heritage: Proceedings of ICHIM05*, Paris, 2005. https://www.museumsandtheweb.com/biblio/bauhaus_university_weimar_germany_digitales_osmantinu.html.

CHAPTER 10
FOLKLORE ARCHIVES IN THE DIGITAL AGE
Karoline Strittmater

Folklore archives can come in a variety of sizes and types. They also serve several different purposes, both for professionals and the communities they represent. Primarily, they require space to store their collected items but also need to provide access to diverse materials that are important to the given culture from which they are collecting. Because of the somewhat delicate nature of many folklore materials, folklorists in different archives have devised ways to safely store and share folklore materials.

Most individual folklorists cannot afford to create and maintain an archive in private spaces. Because of this, many are funded by various public institutions. These include universities, historical societies, anthropological museums, and websites such as the American Folklore Society, universities like the Indiana State University Folklore Archives, the Archives of Northwest Folklore at Oregon University, the Maine Folklife Center archives, and cultural institutions such as the Royal Danish Libraries Folklore Archives. These archives range in sizes from a single filing cabinet to entire buildings. For example, the University of Oregon holds the Archives of Northwest Folklore. The size of this particular archive is one large room with an expanding number of filing cabinets. Each contains various collections, critical papers, dissertations, theses, newspapers, published books, journal letters, books, related subjects, an atlas of Oregon, file cards and a few small artefacts. However, it does not accept larger objects, as it has no safe facility for storing them safely (Toelken 1996). Many countries see the folklore collections and study to be directly connected to the development of a national, cultural and/or ethnic identity. While it is beyond the scope of this chapter, some examples include the extensive and well-financed facilities for folklore studies, such as the Estonian Folklore Archives (EFA), that emerged after the Second World War or the fall of the Iron Curtain and helped connect the nation to its own identity (Toelken 1996).

Aside from physical space, folklore archives also provide care and preservation of their materials and approach these materials as delicately and respectfully as possible. They offer, of course, physical protection, such as filing, maintenance and so on, but they also have ethical considerations such as decorum, ritual secrecy, and adherence to data privacy and copyright laws (Toelken 1996). Folklorists must always be aware not to embarrass, offend, or otherwise hurt the culture to which the archive is connected (Bronner 2009, 22-3). Respect and communication between folklorists and any given culture are key, especially in folklore archives. An anecdote from folklorist Jim Griffith provides a prime example:

I arranged for an African-American quilter to show her work to a gift-shop purchasing committee without preparing either party for what to expect. The result in this case was failure: The quilts were rejected as 'not traditional,' and the elderly quilter was hurt and puzzled. I should have put my warm body in the middle of that situation, and have tried to do just that ever since. (Griffith 2022)

Griffith goes on to emphasize the need for respecting others in the field, and the ability of folklorists to 'bridge cultural gulfs'. This respect carries over to folklorists' archives. As will be discussed in this chapter, archives of all sizes are developing storage and retrieval systems with the aid of digital technology. Many of these digital projects have the added benefit of becoming part of a larger worldwide system that creates greater access for all.

A brief history and evolution of folklore archives

The earliest modern folklore studies were more focused on collecting for the sake of collecting and displaying eclectic materials than consciously building collections with a coherent focus (Jones 2017, 110). Before the early nineteenth century, folklore was rarely collected in a 'proper context' ('proper context' being the collection of things that have quantitative values; that is a process that classifies and categorizes items in a collection using quantitative methods, and that can create depth and breadth for a collection). Early folklore collecting by students was encouraged, but there was a substantial lack of published scholarly information on the purposes or methods of such collecting. At a minimum, an early folklore scholar had to document the collection, informant, place, and date (Halpert 1958, 1). These early folklore archives' priority was to preserve a specialized body of knowledge, while the collections themselves were in constant flux (Kolovos 2004, 20). As time moved forward, it became clearer that materials needed to be recorded in their full context.

In the late nineteenth century, American folklorists called upon the ideas of the English 'amateur gentleman scholar' (or antiquarian) and the German philologist's textual accuracy and historical annotation (Stone 2019, 2). While these early folklorists were more focused on scholarship, they often found the so-called 'lower classes' unimportant and that the rich cultures and traditions that certain groups created were unappreciated by their originators[1] (Halpert 1958, 2). These types of folklore collections had much in common with natural history collections and were often filed along with taxonomical objects. In this manner, early folklore archives were more like scientific classifications than anything else. Each item was categorized with folkloric equivalents of genus and species. Along with subgenres and other dissections, they were collected in files, folders, envelopes and transcribed on index cards. Additionally, the provenance was maintained

---

[1]Although this statement may seem to disregard the self-identity of native cultures, it is beyond the scope of the chapter to discuss this issue at length.

by the collector. Materials were organized by the collector's name, their original order, and then indexed in great detail. These archives were made by folklorists, for folklorists, and so were shaped to serve the needs of the folklorist 'collector' and not necessarily for the people/culture those objects came from (Kolovos 2004, 21).

By the 1950s, folklorists began to understand that the context of any given materials was vitally important, and was required in good indexes, notes, and dictionaries. One example is Stith Thompson's Motif-Index of Folk-Literature, which categorizes folklore motifs and is often used in analysis (Thompson 1955–1958). These folklorists also tended to avoid colourful language and excessively descriptive prose, as they felt it did not add to understanding the importance of the person or community that was being studied (Halpert 1958, 4).

The late 1960s–1970s saw massive changes[2] owing to a major shift in how folklorists defined themselves and their profession. Instead of identifying themselves as scholars of comparative folklore texts, they began to see themselves as ethnographers that studied artistic communication and cultural documentation (Kolovos 2004, 25). Concurrently, trends in archives management – subject file documents, working bibliographic files, reports from academic folklore archives and folklore classification systems – all came together and became codified during the creation of digital collections for public use (Georgitis 2015).

Before digital archives were even dreamed of, it was common for folklorists and similar scholars to engage in independent contract work or work with small nonprofits to maintain index card files. Early personal computers gave folklorists the ability to create computerized tables and databases with contact information, ethnographic content, and other forms of documentation. Then came the rise of word processing software and mailing lists. This, in turn, eased classifying and cataloguing material and fieldwork files. As Georgitis states, 'While we certainly did not use the term metadata at the time, we applied the concept in our folk artist reporting forms, media logs, folk artist lists, and organisations' (Georgitis 2015, 105). It was a chaotic time of a do-it-yourself operation, of making up standards as they went along, long before they were formalized. As with many digitization processes, folklore archives began the practice of enhancing the conditions for both the preservation and storage of materials as digitization grew and evolved. Digitization was a boon to access; but, as stated previously, not at the cost of any culture's respect and community values. However, folklorists did not evolve alone, as their relationship with professional archivists would play a consistent role in their continued development.

---

[2] While it is likely that this change in thought in folklore archives was at least partially due to the various movements of the 1960s, that subject goes beyond the scope of this paper.

Folklore archives

All archives have a hierarchical system for cataloguing their materials. Many archives create simple systems with broadly defined areas so that researchers can retrieve and make their analytical judgements for their projects. Folklore archives do not differ in this fundamental way. This is often because archives housed in universities or special collections have conformed to similar organizational standards. Online systems for folklore archives, such as Indiana State University Folklore Archives, differ little in setup or use from other online archives, like for example Eaton College's Collection of Science Fiction and Fantasy.

One example that gives insight into the purposes and benefits of digital folklore archives as a whole, particularly in terms of digitized archives, comes from the Plateau Peoples' Web Portal. This Web Portal is a collaboratively curated site for the cultural materials of the Native American cultures in the Arizona area. This site is both a management system and a community-built digital archive, using Mukurtu, a minimalist (i.e. low cost and low maintenance) content management system developed specifically for indigenous archives and folklore. It was built to cater to the needs of all indigenous people across the world by being a part of the larger digital stewardship ecosystem, which includes access to and preservation of archival materials. Additionally, it doubles as an educational website for indigenous cultural heritage (Davis 2018, 8). As the director Dr Kim Christen states, it is startling 'how things can get erased in our landscape' (Davis 2018, 9). From physical objects being broken or worn down to languages being lost for any multitude of reasons, archives such as these are key to preserving that would otherwise be lost. Christen further urges an understanding of not just the 'archive' as such but the functions it can serve. The site can be both a place for remembrance, but also can be a place of beginnings, urging the next generation to both preserve their heritage while also using said heritage as a platform to expand new ideas and projects. These sites are 'creation(s) of knowledge', 'constructions of memory', and are cornerstones of the origin of a people (Davis 2018, 11). In this way, these sites are not passive, immovable things, but rather active places of furthering knowledge and creation. Content management systems like Mukurtu also illustrate the importance of creating low-cost digital infrastructure for archives that can reach Indigenous communities as well as the Global South.

Archivists, particularly those from folklore archives, are no longer simply custodians or guardians. By digitizing and making collections and material available, archivists are getting away from the idea that the material object is what has value, and moving towards what they (and users) do with a 'thing' that is valuable using new media. The days of taking an object simply to preserve it have come to an end, making it important to find a balance between respecting individual cultures and increasing access and connection. Because folklore is such a complex, multidimensional amalgamation of media, ethical considerations must be made especially when their digital platforms are community driven.

Folklorists and archivists

Before discussing the digitization projects and processes that folklore archives have been a part of, it is necessary to consider various case studies from archivists, folklorists, their efforts in the field of digitization, and the interplay between the two professions.

As Kolovos states in *Contextualising the Archives*, archivists and folklorists do differ. Archivists see that their records 'do not exist in a cultural vacuum but rather emerge from a variety of individual, social, cultural and institutional contexts, and have been fundamental to professional practice since the middle of the 19th Century' (Kolovos 2004, 19). Folklorists, on the other hand, tended to be focused on the theoretical context of the folklore and saw said folklore as a 'context situated event'. By this we mean folklorists tend to see folklore within the lens of that particular culture; that the individual culture was the context in which any aspect of said folklore could be viewed (Kolovos 2004, 19).

Nathan Georgitis describes the efforts of archivists and folklorists at the University of Oregon and their use of archives management tools – both their successes and struggles. Their main goal was to improve student access to the University's folklore fieldwork collections. They wanted to use archives management tools and practices to better present the folklore collections within the library's databases and digital collections for both research and public access. They created what they called a 'hybrid practice' that pulled from both folklore and archives practices (Georgitis 2015, 85). The main digital tool used was the Archives Toolkit (AT) because it followed descriptive standards for the collection and would help with collection development, and because it also used the descriptive practices of folklorists. Such descriptions included the classification of folklore items using terms from the folklore Ethnographic Thesaurus. AT was a free and open-source data management system that was built 'for archivists by archivists' (Georgitis 2015, 90). This 'hybrid practice' of folklore archives management successfully compiled the theory, methods, and tools of both disciplines. The tools of the archivist were modified to fit the needs of the folklore archives, much like the ways that archives management tools have improved book catalogues (Georgitis 2015, 92).

While folklorists have begun to receive professional archive training and therefore are starting to be exposed to digital models, many public folklorists are not as well versed in archiving documentation, as they have primarily focused on fieldwork and public programming. Another challenge is the ever-changing nature of digital technologies. J. C. Gilmore found many different struggles between archivists and folklorists during their careers (Gilmore 2015, 108). During the American Folklore Society's Archives and Libraries Section meeting in 1996, Gilmore found that there was resistance by both veteran archivists and new folklore-archivists for having 'a necessarily imperfect choice' between one codified standard and several competing systems (Gilmore 2015, 110). In short, American folklore archives often mirror whatever institution they are a part of because American folklorists usually have many different points of view about things such as methods of collection, data collection, and the meaning of the folklore for the people of a particular culture (Gilmore 2015, 111).

However, Gilmore often found that even if students and professionals in libraries and archives were available to perform the work, they often needed additional training and orientation in folklore and, more specifically, a better understanding of public folklore materials in general. For many digitization projects, the preparation of the materials and productions were often time-consuming, exacting, and had the additional problem of organizing content into online formats. The public folklorists of Gilmore's project did not understand the metadata and content management systems. Meanwhile, they found that terminologies that the public folklorists used were not useful to the digital models used by the archivists and librarians (Gilmore 2015, 113).

Gilmore continues with their struggles with digital archiving, stating that archivists and their public folklorists have detailed item-level descriptions for several collections for a variety of reasons, most importantly for future events, and they needed details for submitting to external partners such as contractors. Gilmore advocates for more detail rather than less because they found that having more information aided in indexing and flexibility. This method aims to abandon item-level description and instead uses general descriptive information about a collection (Greene and Meissner 2005, 216). However, Gilmore does concede that this level of detail takes time and that this process can quickly become counterproductive (Gilmore 2015, 125). Although Gilmore does find terminologies, structures, and interpretations vexing, they also see that both sides are working with each other for the greater goal of making collections accessible to the public (Gilmore 2015, 126).

Even if folklorists and archivists often quibble over the details, communication and interdisciplinary training lead to great successes, as both professions have similar goals in mind. What these issues of training show is the way that digitization is now embedded in folklore archives.

Digitization of folklore archives: case studies

Digitization of folklore archives primarily aims to improve public access to them; individual archives often have secondary goals such as preservation, community and global engagement, and empowerment of cultures. Digital tools in the folklore profession provide ways to innovate and improve representations of culture and communities. Folklorists can use a variety of tools, from simple tactics like online surveys on social media, to more complex technologies such as recording software for oral traditions, and content analysis software. However, they also require methodical, proven strategies to preserve and provide digital access (Bogdanova et al. 2008, 183). Case studies help us to understand the variety of goals digitization of folklore can take.

Digital recordkeeping is vital because records can be combined into one cohesive collection guide, while maintaining the respect *des fonds*[3] of each collection that makes up its part in the larger united collection (Gilmore 2015, 118). As a cornerstone of traditional archiving, the combination of the respect *des fonds* with the digitization of archives creates a sense of stability and familiarity for the archivists who work with these collections. Digital collections are also a safe solution for presenting valuable cultural items. Digital archives are an effective way to store, access, search, filter, maintain, annotate and index digitized collections (Rangochev 2008, 21). Digitizing folklore archives does also come with both opportunities and challenges, such as classification, indexing, and user experience. While this does create a learning curve for many, it also allows researchers to create their own classifications and boundaries for their questions (Tangherlini 2016, 7).

There are now hundreds of folklore and heritage archivists who are working on digitization. The Dorothy Howard Collection in Australia offers a great example and overview of the overall goals of digitizing folklore archives. Following the 'general goals' that almost any archive can have, archivists working on the Dorothy Howard Collection have used documentation systems, visualizing tools and other technologies to enhance collections; made collections more available to both researchers and wider users; provided a foundation for future researchers to more easily analyse the relationships between things like creators, themes, and places; and pushed to drive relationship-building and collections development.

In particular, this project uniquely used the 'extraction and curation of data from museum and archival documentation (collection metadata) in a systematic manner that would enable digital humanities scholars and other researchers to use existing visualisation tools to study the collection' (Jones 2017, 102). These goals were further compounded by their databases and their document-level descriptions, contextual research images, keywords and cross-references. Those working with the Dorothy Howard collection found that folklore was an ideal source for researchers who wanted to analyse the interplay between documents and cultural context and found that these digitization projects were ideal for exploring such analyses (Jones 2017, 105). The items in the Dorothy Howard collection, such as play party songs from Swan Meadow school and quilting squares, were placed so that one could understand both its sociocultural context and its archival relationships with other documents. With the aid of computational folklorists, these documents and images can now be used to analyse the interconnected data in what Jones calls the 'folklore macro-scope' (Jones 2017, 110).

The Folklore Institute at the Bulgarian Academy of Sciences (BAS) digitized multimedia folklore objects, focusing primarily on new ways to develop, analyse, and secure born-digital folklore archives. They started with a web-based client/server system

---

[3]Respect *des fonds* is a part of archival theory. It proposes to group collections of archival records according to their *fonds*, or according to the entity by which they were created or from which they were received

and embedded text-secure watermarks[4] into the system data. This data was used to produce identification codes that would remain even after decryption processes. They also used improved digital tools and algorithms to further analyse their databases. From there, the BAS was divided into two types of folklore information systems: database text/electronic indexes and searching systems adapted to work specifically with folklore objects (Bogdanova et al. 2008, 183). The Organization of the database was created to give greater flexibility in searching and adding information (Bogdanova et al. 2008, 198).

Two years later, the BAS furthered its digitizing processes and security. This was broken down into different methods for securing both the intellectual property and author rights of any particular object, including watermarking and error-correcting codes, and describing the process of both the creation and organization of the digital folklore item that 'contains' the object's digital image with their metadata and security data (Bogdanova, Todorov and Noev 2010, 335). BAS notes that care must be taken, as many objects that are in line to be digitized are exceedingly fragile and that digitization may be their only hope for preservation (Bogdanova, Todorov and Noev 2010, 336).

BAS provides access for persons with disabilities, new opportunities to work with material funds, the ability to copy, multiply and forward objects and information, full-text searches, and ease of metadata information compilation (copyright, creation date, identification number) (Bogdanova, Todorov and Noev 2010, 335). BAS was also concerned with security measures. They want to protect their information from unauthorized distribution and have been researching more effective methods of security (Bogdanova, Todorov and Noev 2010, 338). Unlike the Dorothy Howard collection, the BAS was focused primarily on their algorithms and database organization on a technical level. While the Dorothy Howard collection was not devoid of such issues of information organization, its primary focus was on usability and access.

The Romanian Academy's folklore archive also has an ongoing digitization project that includes investigating solutions for long-term digital preservation. The Academy's archive includes pieces based on theatre or dance; these materials proved to be fascinating because the people performing the dance are not presenting as individuals, but rather as a collective representing their heritage. It became a matter of great importance that the public could access these recordings (both audio and video), not only from a cultural heritage standpoint but also for personal and emotional reasons (Pop 2015, 3). However, the Academy found issues with planning long-term digital repositories, because digital archives need more maintenance and attention than physical archives. For example, a physical paper document could be left alone in a file cabinet with little interaction to keep it viable. Meanwhile, digital versions need to be checked regularly, backups made and distributed to different locations, files have to be transformed, documents that have migrated need to be converted or emulated, and, more frustratingly, digital copies may become obsolete when newer, better quality technologies come along (Pop 2015, 4).

---

[4] A text-secure watermark is a faint design that identifies the maker that is used to protect digital content like documents, images and videos.

Despite these potential issues, the archivists at the Romanian Academy are already seeking to create a network of communities that have both direct and partial access to copies of the archive. They have already created a website for their archive but have added onto it by planning to place a public object in a physical space to access the archive. The idea is to create a kind of 'memory box' that acts as a kiosk to access the archive via WiFi (Pop 2015, 8). While the idea of a physical object to connect to a larger network is interesting, the idea of a handful of kiosks seems highly individualized to this specific scenario. It is unlikely that such an idea will be scalable. Other archives see the need for consistent attention in digital archives as a boon, as its flexibility allows for more routine maintenance and updates to even closed collections when information changes or comes to light (Gilmore 2015, 120).

Along with European archives, the United States has been making strides in digital folklore preservation. One of the most famous folklore archives in the United States, the Archives of Northwest Folklore at the University of Oregon, has also been working on managing their digital folklore archives. Like many other folklore archives, the University of Oregon (OU) Folklore and Public Culture Program envisions a threefold purpose for their archive: as a public resource, an academic collection, and a place for professional archival training (Georgitis 2015, 87). To facilitate this purpose, their primary reason for digitizing their collection was to move away from 'longitudinal and cross-cultural studies of textual folklore forms' and towards an 'emphasis on relationships between folklore materials and the social, political, and economic contexts from which they emerge' (Georgitis 2015, 89). In doing so, the university incorporates its collections into their academic research tools, which then act as a way to further accessibility and integration in campus communities.

The team in charge of the digitization project adapted the Dublin Core metadata schema, so that the records could include images from survey records as well as student field work collections (Georgitis 2015, 92). Collection creators primarily influence the collection management decisions, as they are the ones who contribute the most to the collection for both research and instruction. Many of these creators are young researchers delving into sensitive topics, so the project team made finding aides to label the collection by creator name, not by title or topic (Georgitis 2015, 93). This method aids those who use the collections most frequently; however, there is no indication of how others who have access to these collections feel about this management. By using the archive management tools at their disposal and the descriptive standards, OU was able to convert their physical copies of their master sheets and card catalogues into digital forms that could be easily used as research tools for researchers of all kinds, particularly students at OU. Overall, this was done through the implementation of database and keyword searching instead of the time intensive redoing of the entire index system and subject vocabularies (Georgitis 2015, 96).

Other cultural heritage organizations in Oregon are also dealing with the successes and problems brought on by digitization processes, such as the Oregon Heritage Commission (OHC). The OCH created a survey of several Oregon institutions to gather information on how digitization would be done throughout the state. Firstly, they prioritized the items they wanted to digitize, as they saw digital collections as a means to preserve their value to the general public. Secondly, they observed that staff and volunteers needed training, as most of them had limited training in the digitization process. Thirdly, they gathered their needed equipment – a scanner and photo editing software, access to digital storage, hard drives, servers, and cloud storage. This leads them to their end goal to create online access to collections statewide (Dehn 2018, 42).

The primary issue the OHC found from their surveys of several heritage organizations was that they depended on the revenue from selling their digital images and therefore did not want to share free images. Despite this, most organizations responded positively to collaborative digitization projects and providing online access. Additionally, most were in favour of implementing a loaning system for digitization equipment, which would save money for many of these under-resourced or self-funded institutions (Dehn 2018, 45).

Many folklore collections, and indeed archives in general, are not 'born digital' but contain physical objects with a physical, real-world presence that are then digitized to be seen and accessed online. However, with the rise of digital culture, this is no longer the case. The Web Cultures Web Archive (WCWA) and the Webcomics Web Archive (WWA), created by the American Folklife Center at the Library of Congress (LC), are just two examples of online archives that contain born-digital folklore collections. These collections will, eventually, feature memes, GIFs, image macros, webcomics, and other internet phenomena that are found in online pop culture. These collections follow the Library of Congress' mission to 'preserve and present American folklife', in this case, the creations from the Internet age (Peet 2017, 14). In particular, the webcomic collection originated in 2001, as an agreement between the LC and the Small Press Expo (a convention of comic art and its creators).

Getting permission from creators was of utmost importance for this collection, as online pirating and theft of digital works have been a near-constant issue since the early 1990s. The process for archive work is as follows: recommendations are entered into LC's curatorial tool DigiBoard, which automates collection activities and creates metadata. The item is reviewed, and then, if approved, the LC will ask for the owner's permission to archive said item. If permission is granted, then LC gets into contact with the Internet Archive (IA). They then use the Heritix web crawler tool to capture the site. The site is then archived in snapshot form because the archive wishes to present how a page looked at a certain date (Peet 2017, 18). As digital media pages are subject to constant ongoing change and improvement, selecting and representing a specific date is vitally important to the integrity of the archive.

Through all of these studies, there is one thing that becomes strikingly clear: these folklore archives are digitizing to allow further availability and access to wider, geographically dispersed audiences. Community members, scholars, and even those with simple curiosity can all have access to many different sources and archives. Many proponents of the post-custodial movement are advocating for digitization and digital surrogates to make them widely available, but are clear in that the keepers do not 'own' the collection. This parallels the current movement in libraries and publishing advocating for Open Access. Archivists are moving away from the idea that it is the object that has value, and moving towards the notion that it is the people and culture they embody that is important (Davis 2018, 12).

It is for this reason that some folklore archives are employing more people who are not necessarily archivists but who are doing archiving, such as software engineers, literary scholars, designers, anthologists, creative writers and community members that are coming together to solve multi-layered problems (ethical considerations, technological obsolescence, differences between folklorists and archivists) in digital folklore archives. Digital archives are becoming multidisciplinary and interfacing with creative communities (Rangochev 2008, 22). They are also employing new methods of analysis and dissemination. This is particularly evident in the development of new areas of study in digital folkloristics and 'algorithmic folklore' (De Seta 2020), in addition to the recent digital projects ALGOFOLK (https://algofolk.substack.com/p/algorithms-folklore) and Project StoryMachine (https://storymachine.iisys.de/). These relationships with other professions take time, money and energy to fully develop; however, even as the digital revolution has created more access to our archives, professions have been opened up to meet these digital problems collaboratively.

Conclusion

While the organization and aims of various archives may differ, the underlying message that ties all these disparate institutions together is the idea of access and availability for all. Folklore – and, even more broadly, culture and heritage – is not something that can be held in the palm of your hand in its entirety. It is something ephemeral but also ineffable. However, these folklore archives allow as many people as possible to engage with that one piece of culture that they may not have known existed. As archives move away from the idea of owning a folklore object of culture (much like a book) to sharing its data, digital approaches facilitate newer kinds of engagement with the value of these objects, cultures and people.

Bibliography

Blank, Trevor J., ed. *Folklore and the Internet: Vernacular Expression in a Digital World*. University Press of Colorado, 2009.

Bogdanova, Galina, Todor Todorov and Georgieva Tsvetanka. 'New Approaches for Development, Analysis, and Security of Multimedia Archive Folklore Objects'. *Computer Science Journal of Moldova* 16, no. 2 (2008): 183–208.

Bogdanova, Galina, Todor Todorov and Nikolay Noev. 'Digitalization and Security of "Bulgarian Folklore Heritage" Archive'. In *Proceedings of the 11th International Conference on Computer Systems and Technologies and Workshop for PhD Students in Computing on International Conference on Computer Systems and Technologies*, 335–40, 2010. https://doi.org/10.1145/1839379.1839438

Bowker, Geoffrey C and Susan Leigh Star. *Sorting Things Out: Classification and Its Consequences*. MIT Press, 2000.

Bronner, Simon J. 'Digitizing and Virtualizing Folklore'. In *Folklore and the Internet: Vernacular Expression in a Digital World*, 21–66. Edited by Trevor J. Blank. Utah State University Press, 2009.

Davis, Leslie, Zachary Griffith and Jacob Neely. 'Traditional Knowledge and Digital Archives: An Interview with Kim Christen'. *Investigación y Desarrollo* 27 (2018).

Dehn, Beth. 'Surveying Oregon's Digital Heritage Collections'. *OLA Quarterly* 24, no. 4 (2018): 41–7.

De Seta, Gabriele. 'Digital Folklore'. In *Second International Handbook of Internet Research*, 167–83. Edited by Jeremy Hunsinger, Matthew M. Allen and Lisbeth Klastrup. Dordrecht: Springer, 2020. https://doi.org/10.1007/978-94-024-1555-1_36.

Dodds, Douglas. 'From Analogue to Digital: Word and Image Digitization Projects at the V&A'. *Journal of Victorian Culture* 23, no. 2 (2018): 222–30.

Georgitis, Nathan. 'A Case Study in Folklore Archives Management: The Randall V. Mills Archives of Northwest Folklore at the University of Oregon'. *Journal of Folklore Research: An International Journal of Folklore and Ethnomusicology* 52, no. 1 (2015): 85–98.

Gilmore, Janet C. 'Filling "An Immense Brain with Very Little in the Brain" for "Perpetual Memory": Folklore Archiving New and Old'. *Journal of Folklore Research: An International Journal of Folklore and Ethnomusicology* 52, no. 1 (2015): 99–138.

Greene, Mark A. and Dennis Meissner. 'More Product, Less Process: Revamping Traditional Archival Processing'. *The American Archivist* 68, no. 2 (Fall/Winter 2005): 208–63.

Griffith, Jim. 'Respect Is the Core of Caring'. *Borderlore*, Southwest Folklife Alliance, 2022. borderlore.org/thinking-like-a-folklorist-respect-is-the-core-of-caring/.

Halpert, Herbert. 'Folklore: Breadth versus Depth'. *The Journal of American Folklore* 71, no. 280 (1958): 97–103. Retrieved from https://www.jstor.org/stable/537679?seq=1-.

Hakamies, Pekka, Anne Heimo and Suomalainen Tiedeakatemia, eds. *Folkloristics in the Digital Age*. Suomalainen Tiedeakatemia, Academia Scientiarum Fennica, 2019.

Johns, Adrian. *Piracy: The Intellectual Property Wars from Gutenberg to Gates*. Chicago: University of Chicago Press, 2019. https://doi.org/10.7208/9780226401201.

Jones, Mike, Kate Darian-Smith, Deborah Tout-Smith and Gavan McCarthy. 'The Dorothy Howard Collection: Revealing the Structures of Folklore Archives in Museums'. *Archives and Manuscripts* 45, no. 2 (2017): 100–17. https://www.tandfonline.com/doi/abs/10.1080/01576895.2017.1328695.

Kolovos, A. *Archiving Culture: American Folklore Archives in Theory and Practice*. Doctoral dissertation. Indiana University, 2010. https://scholarworks.iu.edu/dspace/handle/2022/9696.

Kolovos, A. 'Contextualizing the Archives'. *Folklore Forum* 35 (2004): 18–28. https://scholarworks.iu.edu/dspace/bitstream/handle/2022/2448/35(1-2)%2018-28.pdf?sequence=1.

Lourdi, Irene, Christos Papatheodorou and Mara Nikolaidou. 'A Multi-layer Metadata Schema for Digital Folklore Collections'. *Journal of Information Science* 33, no. 2 (2007): 197–213.

Pavlov, Radoslav, Galina Bogdanova, Desislava Paneva-Marinova, Todor Todorov and Konstantin Rangochev. 2011. 'Digital Archive and Multimedia Library for Bulgarian Traditional Culture and Folklore'. *International Journal "Information Theories and Applications* 18, no. 3 (2011): 276–88. Retrieved from http://www.math.bas.bg/moiuser/~todor/papers/CSJMol.pdf.

Peet, Lisa. 'Technology LC's New Born-Digital Archives'. *Technology and Culture* (2017): 14–16.

Pop, Liviu. 'Open Source Folklore Archives–Disseminating Small Memory Boxes'. *Review of the National Center for Digitization* 26 (2015): 47–52. http://poincare.matf.bg.ac.rs/~ncd/NCD_2627_2015/StariFajlovi/29_LiviuPop/liviu_pop_open_source_folklore_archives.pdf

Rangochev, Konstantin, Dessislava Paneva and Detelin Luchev. 'Data and Functionality Management in a Folklore Digital Library'. In *the Proceedings of the International Conference-Slovo: Towards a Digital Library of South Slavic Manuscripts*, 21–26. 2008.

Ruthven, Ian and Gobinda G. Chowdhury, eds. *Cultural Heritage Information: Access and Management*, vol. 1. London: Facet publishing, 2015.
Shifman, Limor. *Memes in Digital Culture*. Cambridge, MA: MIT Press, 2013.
Stone, Duncan. 'Deconstructing the Gentleman Amateur.' *Cultural and Social History* 18, no. 3 (2019): 315–36. https://doi.org/10.1080/14780038.2019.1614284.
Tangherlini, Timothy R. 'Big Folklore: A Special Issue on Computational Folkloristics'. *Journal of American Folklore* 129, no. 511 (2016): 5–13.
Thompson, Stith. *Motif-Index of Folk-Literature: A Classification of Narrative Elements in Folktales, Ballads, Myths, Fables, Mediaeval Romances, Exempla, Fabliaux, Jest-Books, and Local Legends*. Indianapolis: Indiana University Press, 1955–1958.
Toelken, Barre. *Dynamics of Folklore*. Boulder: University Press of Colorado, 1996.

CHAPTER 11
TEACHING TRUMAN WITH HYPERTEXT METHODS
PROJECT WHISTLESTOP OVER TWO DECADES

Ashney V. Randle, Logan F. Thompson, Renee M. Jones and Sarah A. Buchanan

---

As the first library established under the 1955 Presidential Libraries Act (PLA), the Harry S. Truman Presidential Library & Museum was dedicated on 6 July 1957 in Independence, Missouri, the hometown of the thirty-third president of the United States (Harry S. Truman Library & Museum 2023). Harry S. Truman (1884–1972), who served two terms as president from 1945 to 1949 and 1949 to 1953, preserved his papers upon leaving the presidency in January 1953, and moved them carefully to multiple locations in the Independence area until they could be made accessible in the Truman Library. The voluminous quantity and variety of media in the Truman archival collections reflect the wide-ranging 'historical atmosphere' (Niekrasz 2015) of his presidency – from ending the war in Europe and initiating the United Nations ratification to transitioning America's domestic policy to a peace economy and expanding civil rights during a second term brought about by the success of Truman's 'Whistlestop' campaign during the US presidential election of 1948. Those historical events and more are documented in the millions of manuscript pages, photographs, sound recordings, moving images, objects, and books comprising the primary source materials at the heart of Project Whistlestop, a two-decade-long collaborative educational research effort, originally funded by a five-year, $1.9 million US Department of Education grant. Its website, Whistlestop.org, was developed to digitize primary source materials and make them available on the then-fledgling World Wide Web for teachers and students to engage in project-based learning. The site's data were migrated to Trumanlibrary.org at the end of the grant in 2001. The Truman resource remains distinctively multimedia among peer works that create digital archives and editions of presidential papers (e.g. the papers of George Washington, https://washingtonpapers.org/; James Monroe, https://monroepapers.com/; Abraham Lincoln, https://papersofabrahamlincoln.org/; and those of other presidents at the Library of Congress).

The PLA legislated for the first time in the United States the preservation and public availability of presidential papers. Though the PLA was followed in later years by related laws regulating presidential papers and their public ownership in 1978 and 1986 (U.S. NARA 2023; Hackman 2006), the Truman Library was the first to be dedicated after (bipartisan) passage of such law; currently there are fifteen such libraries (from

Hoover to Trump). Scholarship about the system considers the strategic storytelling practised in its public displays (Wilson 1991) and the 'necessary' preservation-facilitated interdisciplinary research each namesake makes possible (Wolff 1989).

Today Project Whistlestop offers enduring insights on project-based learning for secondary school and university-level pedagogy. As expressed by Swain (2003: 140), 'the practical use of oral history to supplement or explain information in existing archival collections' has been a long-standing tool in archival-based research. Our contribution incorporates oral history interviews with the principal project investigators and interprets both an archival collection and the digital library as it appeared at Trumanlibrary.org in 2018, before it migrated to Trumanlibrary.gov/library/online-collections, where it is accessible today. In considering the linkages between bits of archival information, our methodological approach is thus a higher-order analysis of hypertext and its reflexive capacities. Key educational insights are highlighted from each collaborator, followed by reflections on Project Whistlestop's successes, theoretical implications, and lasting legacy as a resource supporting multimodal scholarship. Oral histories here are crucial resources for contextualizing archival collections that are complex in many ways (content quantity, the multiple media formats enclosed, and a lengthy time period of formation) in Project Whistlestop's case.

Presidential library context and origins

Project Whistlestop was started by a consortium of schools in the Independence (Missouri) School District and the Truman Library, who applied for and became one of twenty-four recipients of the Technology Innovation Challenge Grant (TICG) in 1996 (U.S. Department of Education 2009). The TICG was created by the US Department of Education to encourage schools to 'use technology to improve learning, and to help their students achieve high academic standards being set by states and districts nationwide' (Carroll 1997). The TICG goal was to have 'every classroom and every library in the entire United States by the year 2000' equipped with 'computers and good software and well-trained teachers' (Pelavin Research Institute 1997: 5). The Missouri consortium's goal was to create a website that would become a 'virtual community of teachers and students engaged in inquiry-based learning projects, supported by primary source materials of the Harry S. Truman Presidential Museum and Library' (Seago 2003: 7). Viewing and accessing primary sources from a distance, via the digital archive, was intended to help connect teachers, librarians, and archivists and extend the study of Truman's presidency to all those unable to visit in person. The Truman presidency was thus presented online in the project's 1997 collections drop-down via 'official documents' in seven major topics (The Decision to Drop the Atomic Bomb, The Recognition of Israel, The Marshall Plan, The Truman Doctrine, Truman's Personal Files, Desegregation of the Armed Forces and 1948 Campaign); by the 2001 table of contents, three added categories were The Berlin Airlift, NATO and The Korean War (Whistlestop.org 2001a).

Information scientists' contributions

To create the project website, the school district and the Truman Library turned to the University of Missouri (MU). Faculty in the School of Library and Informational Science (SLIS) had been creating a digital library for computer science teachers in the Kansas City area, and they accepted the consortium's offer of a portion of the grant funding to support SLIS classes in exchange for providing web design and maintenance. Dr Thomas Kochtanek, recently appointed a SLIS department chair, had experience in creating and maintaining websites and was chosen to work with the consortium on building the project website (Tom Kochtanek, personal communication with first author, 19 March 2020). From its inception, Kochtanek recalls that the project's aim was to provide primary source materials to K-12 educators at five schools in the Kansas City metropolitan area (Tom Kochtanek, personal communication with second author, 3 December 2018), though that grew in scope, as the team realized through a hit counter soon added that people from all over the world were accessing the site for many purposes outside of teaching in schools (SISLT 2017). Of the initial funding of $1,900,000 over five years, $30,000 per year was allotted by the project advisory board for digitization and website-building equipment; the majority of project funds went towards building computer labs for the schools, establishing networks for internet access, and an evaluation team, which was paid $50,000 a year to monitor their progress and efficiency. The project promised novelty and innovation in the teaching realm, while also creating a general foundation for libraries to support online pedagogy and digital archives.

With the University of Missouri responsible for website creation, it became the faculty's responsibility to figure out where to host the site. Dr Kochtanek secured permission from SLIS to have space set aside on the school server in Columbia, thus avoiding the need to pay for a server out of the allotted $30,000. That enabled the hire of one part-time employee to assist him in programming for the website and the purchase of initial equipment to build the site. Kochtanek recruited students to volunteer and receive course credit. The allotted funds primarily supported the employee and their training to learn the programming skills necessary to meet the desired standards of the Truman Library and the consortium (Whistlestop.org 1998).

Jim Borwick served as the site administrator through 2008 (Borwick, personal communication with third author, 15 September 2017). His work generated some paper holdings that he expertly referenced as documentation sources. For that rediscovery one can credit Borwick's successor in the role, Bennett Magnino, who discovered 'an awful lot of stuff piled into cabinets' (Magnino, personal communication with third author, 28 September 2017), organized by the SLIS Department of Information Science into distinct file categories: grants and administrative documents, digital standards, on-site backups, and promotional materials. All of the items date back to the project's beginnings, and the arrangement suits the chronicle of Project Whistlestop's first five years. We use the four-part arrangement in our archival analysis below.

Hired by Kochtanek as a graduate research assistant in early 1997, Borwick came to Project Whistlestop armed with basic coding knowledge and the desire to learn more.

Borwick remembers those early days as 'intimidating', in part because of where their work was being completed on campus. The Center for Technology Innovations in Education (CTIE – renamed The Allen Institute in 2001), founded by Dr James Laffey and Dr Dale Musser in the fall of 1995, had moved into 8,000 square feet of unrenovated space in London Hall. The site had previously been a vocational education building. CTIE's mission statement was 'To conduct research to reform teaching and learning methods through innovative applications of technology. These technologies are created with the purpose of supporting people's learning through active and enthusiastic engagement in interesting, fun, and meaningful tasks' (CTIE 1998). It was an R&D centre brimming with spirited computer science and engineering students. A handful of meeting notes from the mid-2000s labelled 'CTIE Project-by-Project Update', which mention Project Whistlestop, are preserved in SISLT records in the MU University Archives (University of Missouri 2003).

According to Borwick, the proximity of CTIE students or 'hackers' and their passion for programming and gaming at all hours of the night made those initial days on Project Whistlestop exciting. 'The space was inviting. Big windows. Wide open. There was an expectation of sociability. Bean bag chairs. Nerf guns. Fishing tank. You could bring your dog to work' (Borwick, personal communication with third author, 15 September 2017). It was under those creative conditions that the Project Whistlestop team, which included fellow MU Master of Library Science students Heather Tunender and Seong-Mo Kim as Research and Implementation Assistants, began their work (Whistlestop.org 1999).

Project Whistlestop differed from other CTIE endeavours in that it was production-driven, rather than research-based. Borwick remembers that his original workflow involved a steady volume of email correspondence between him and Kathleen Vest, who served as the liaison between the grant-affiliated school teachers and SISLT. Those first few years also involved Vest snail-mailing disks full of teachers' lessons to MU for conversion to HTML. Borwick's job was in making the materials web-ready and transferring the site-bound files to the server. Given the modest computing power of the 1990s, digitizing documents on a flatbed scanner was time-consuming and involved 'judgement calls'. Decisions had to be made as to what file format would be used and for how long or if masters should be kept. Because typical network connection speeds were 56K dial-up in 1997, 'balancing visual quality with speed of download' was vital (Borwick, personal communication with third author, 30 September 2017). Handwritten letters by President Truman needed to be legible on-screen to be useful to students.

Schoolteachers' contributions

Before a website could be built, SLIS needed content, and that was in abundance at the Truman Library, where archivists and teachers from the school district soon made their mark. Between 500 and 1,000 documents from the Truman Administration, each listed by previous archivists in the late 1980s, were selected 'to make archival research easier and more approachable for high school and undergraduate students' (Tammy Williams,

Archivist & Social Media Coordinator, personal correspondence with second author, 9 November 2018). Physical copies of those documents were already assembled in boxes, intended for on-site use by visiting students (Mark Adams, personal correspondence with second author, 7 November 2018). Those provided a logical starting point for the first batch of documents included in Project Whistlestop, and they make up much of the *Research Files* subsection discussed below (Williams, personal correspondence with second author, 9 November 2018). Their presence avoided the need for *staff* to re-select materials. It is most important to note the connection here between robust in-house archival practices and the development of an efficient, collaborative workflow between archivists, public services staff, and teachers. Project Whistlestop was a trailblazer of digital library practices, proving that a fully-realized analog archival tradition is capable of digital transition.

Teacher training to create new digital resources, which use new media for age-appropriate historical research (further contextualized in a section below on hypertext), was unique to the project. At a two-week training camp in the summer of 1996, teachers brainstormed together the types of activities and lesson plans they wanted to provide on the website (each received a $1,200 stipend, per Kochtanek, personal communication with first author, 19 March 2020), while the archivists shared documents, photographs, film reels and audio file examples as inspiration and assisted teachers in finding additional resources they might need. Once teachers completed their lesson plans and archivists digitized the relevant content, both were sent to Kochtanek, where he and his team at SLIS uploaded their creations to the website. Within the first two years of the project, they had digitized 5,000 documents (Kochtanek et al. 1999). The website went live on 5 December 1998 (see Figure 11.1) in time for President's Day school activities in 1999 (Martin 1998) and was noted by the agency as the only project then under the Challenge Grant Competition that had a functioning website (personal communication with first author, 19 March 2020). After creating a hit counter within 6 months of the website going online, the team discovered that thousands of domestic and international users were visiting the website. The numbers demonstrated that there was a genuine interest beyond the initial target audience. In 2017, the team recorded over seventy million hits from users viewing their records. The project, and its faculty-student presentations and published findings about the site search engine performance (Kochtanek and Laffey 1998; Kochtanek et al. 1998b; Kochtanek et al. 1998a), showcase the value of Information Science skill sets, through collaborators' ability to creatively work with technology and build collaborative networks that sustain both research and teaching infrastructures.

After the grant ended in 2001, the Truman Library continued SLIS' hosting of the website and merged it that year with trumanlibrary.org (as presented in Adams and Kochtanek 2002; Kochtanek 2002). They retired the domain in 2010. The collaborative team comprised two people at MU SLIS dedicated to the hosting – Kochtanek and an 'i-Net Administrator' (Kochtanek, personal correspondence with second author, 3 December 2018) – and from the Truman Library, Mark Adams, Director of Education, has largely acted as the web administrator, with archivist colleagues having also

Figure 11.1 Screenshot of the Project Whistlestop homepage on 5 December 1998. https://web.archive.org/web/19991012034516/http://whistlestop.org/.

contributed and selected some content for inclusion (Adams, personal correspondence with second author, 7 November 2018).

Project Whistlestop archives: A four-part content review

Key themes thus far introduce the value of collaborative work for innovative digital projects, the importance of long-term planning to maintain digital resources, and the opportunities of hypertext in digital/presidential archives projects. Multimedia archives elucidate Project Whistlestop's key progressions from 1996 to 2019, among them SLIS' adoption of its new name of SISLT in 1996 (Niederberger, Buchanan and Allen 2022) and the contributions of Bennett Magnino, who joined the school and the project as site administrator in 2014.

1. Whistlestop grants and administrative documents

The original grant proposal for Project Whistlestop, which predates SISLT, was authored in part by Professors Timothy B. Patrick and Jim Laffey, and Jim Andrews, the co-director of CTIE. On the website's earliest pages, those original MU contributors are referred to as the Whistlestop Pilot Project Team. Kochtanek was enlisted to take the helm when SISLT was established in late 1996, which coincided with the awarding of the grant. A close inspection of specific grant documents titled 'Project Whistlestop Abstract', 'Consortium Partners' and 'Project Whistlestop Activities Timeline' provides an abundance of details, including the who, what, why, where, and how the project was designed to work. CTIE's role is explained as, 'the university connection will create the electronic database needed for searching as well as connections to their undergraduate teacher education program' (Project Whistlestop Abstract p. 1, in Project Whistlestop Archives 1996). Kochtanek, Borwick, and Magnino each separately explained how designing a searchable online database of digitized media was the key accomplishment that made Project Whistlestop noteworthy.

Records show that the majority of the initial grant funding was allocated to the district schools to purchase computer equipment, upgrade the network, and install faster T1 lines and classroom Internet connections. On SISLT's end, volunteer graduate and practicum students transferred teaching units to the web (Kochtanek, personal communication with third author, 7 September 2017). The folder also contains several letters written to and from a variety of stakeholders in support of the project. One to Truman Library Director Larry Hackman from the Executive Director of the Franklin and Eleanor Roosevelt Institute (itself newly partnered with the FDR Library, IBM, and Marist College in the NEW Deal Network), John F. Sears, pinpoints further how a peer recognized the unique contributions of the project: 'I am particularly impressed by the kind of partnership into which the library and schools have entered' (Sears 1996; original in Harry S. Truman Library, Project Whistlestop Collection 1996).

Digitization initiatives in the late 1990s were unusual and progressive enterprises. As late as 2001, when a study of the use of technology and digitization activities in libraries and museums nationwide was first conducted, the numbers were quite small. The Institute of Museum and Library Services, which led the survey, found that just 32 per cent of museums were digitizing any of their materials and of those who were, just 47 per cent provided public access to their digital collections (IMLS 2002). Magnino suggests that 'Altogether, this folder betrays the excitement and anxiety of everybody involved in the early days of the project' (Magnino, personal communication with third author, 28 September 2017), which we have attempted to best capture through the remembrances of Jim Borwick above.

2. Digital standards

A second large file of collected papers illustrates how the early era of digital libraries and the objects held within them was a confusing time in terms of metadata and standards. The documents show that Truman archivists, including Ray Geselbracht, attended the 1996 Society of American Archivists (SAA) annual meeting in San Diego. At the conference, they encountered a variety of cutting-edge information pertaining to Encoded Archival Description (EAD), metadata standards, document scanning, and archival best practices. Upon his return, Geselbracht submitted a report to Director Hackman that expanded his awareness of the ambiguities Project Whistlestop faced in terms of those concerns. In a memo addressed to Kathleen Vest, Tim Patrick and Doug Allen, all key figures involved in Project Whistlestop at Truman Library, Hackman discussed how 'rapid changes in technology, information standards, and the Internet' created 'many unsettled issues' for the project. Hackman added, 'I suspect some of the challenges we face in making materials accessible are beginning to come through to all of you' (Harry S. Truman Library, Project Whistlestop Collection 1996).

That the file folder contained copies of Janice E. Ruth's pivotal 'Encoded Archival Description: A Structural Overview' 1997 article and the 1998 'NARA Guidelines for digitising Archival Materials' (Project Whistlestop Archives 1996) further confirms how Truman and SISLT staff explored and contributed to best practices in digital libraries. Handwritten notes on the NARA paper, ostensibly scribbled by a Truman archivist, ask the questions, 'If ours were a true archive, how would finding aids be set up? What are finding aids + their functions? Do we use any?' (Project Whistlestop Archives 1996). Those jottings indicate how digital libraries were mysterious things in the late 1990s, and the parties involved were perhaps wrestling with the concept of Project Whistlestop as an archive. Further discussions with Magnino revealed that the Truman team follows NARA guidelines for metadata elements, which are adapted from the Dublin Core Metadata Initiative (DCMI) and encoded in XML.

3. On-site backups

Items in this folder are primarily CDs and ZIP disks of early digitized Truman Library materials in numerous formats. The backups were kept in case something happened to the in-house CTIE Linux server. The site's server moved later to MU's data centre, administered by their IT team. Analogue cassette tapes of audio recordings of President Truman's speeches are also stored. Magnino explained that an audiovisual archivist at the Truman Library in the 1990s was eager to maintain content not dependent on computers (Magnino, personal communication with third author, 28 September 2017). Cassette, CD, and ZIP formats bring into question the real concern of other eventual hardware obsolescence: according to McCargar (2005), 'Every new data storage format signals the end of its predecessors'. Obsolescence reveals the challenges of media formats and positions archivists and librarians to negotiate their strategic uses. Consistent documentation practices shape project sustainability.

Throughout the summer of 1997, a training institute was held in which a cadre of district teachers (Whistlestop.org 1998) developed lessons and the definitions for Show Me Learning, a combination of Missouri 'Show Me Standards' and project/inquiry-based learning. Described as 'boot camps' (Kochtanek, personal communication with third author, 7 September 2017), the workshops produced teacher lessons, quizzes, and games – based on such complex subjects as 'Desegregation of the Military', 'The Decision to Drop the Atomic Bomb' and 'The Recognition of Israel' – that are still available for school projects and personal use on the Truman Library website and on the backup storage disks. Arguably the most significant lesson plan introduces students to the 'Three Branches of Government' (TrumanLibrary.gov. 2023c). One of the first lessons on the site, it was developed by Library staff member Kathleen Vest for Grades 5–8 and, according to Magnino, is 'by far the most popular part of the site'. As late as 2017 it was the first hit retrieved from a Google search for 'three branches of government'. A second key project activity is 'The Spy's Dilemma' (Trumanlibrary.gov 2023b), an interactive Cold War lesson in which the player assumes the role of a Soviet spy rifling through Truman's office, and a rare exemplar of its genre, having been recognized in the 'InfoTech' column of *Teacher Librarian* just in June 2015 (Lamb and Johnson 2015). A collaborative effort between CTIE and Truman Library staff, the game debuted on the site in late 1998 and presently exists on the Truman site in upgraded and mobile-friendly form (recently without Adobe Flash, which became obsolete in 2020). Finally, the most innovative of Project Whistlestop's educational tools is a 'Daily Presidential Appointments Calendar' (Trumanlibrary.gov 2023a), a searchable tool that allows visitors to access President Truman's schedule during his entire term of office. The transcribed calendar content is stored on a database table and retrieved using PHP and SQL scripts written by Rafee Che Hassim, then a PhD student in SISLT, whom Borwick credits for enabling crucial steps toward making the site more dynamic.

4. Promotional materials

Printed informational brochures comprise the final category of preserved documentation maintained by SISLT. Four different pamphlets are reviewed here. One is for the Truman Library itself. The second was produced to promote a temporary exhibit at the Library. Two others showcase Project Whistlestop: one is from the perspective of the consortium that started the project, and the other showcases a variety of CTIE projects.

For the first years of Project Whistlestop, its pages were accessed almost entirely by in-house users at the Truman Library, the schools, or SISLT, as Kochtanek had expected. However, the SISLT team noticed a significant uptick in visitors, and Kochtanek realized the increase in visitors could be attributed to several positive scholarly reviews (Reagan 2002; McCoach 2002; Whistlestop 2001b) as well as external publicity. At a time when there were roughly 100,000 total websites in 1996 (Pingdom 2008) the project's notice in *USA Today* on Tuesday, 21 July 1998 (Meddis 1998) generated a surefire traffic increase, as did its selections for the Yahoo Pick of the Day Award, the Internet Scout Award, the Britannica Internet Guide Award, the Study Web Academic Excellence Award, and on shortlists by Homework Central and Learning in Motion (Whistlestop 2001b). Kochtanek and his team began using Project Whistlestop statistics for research into search engine retrievability (personal communication with third author, 7 September

2017). Their work resulted in co-authored scholarly articles beginning in 1998 and archived in the collection (Kochtanek et al. 1998b; Tunender and Ervin 1998). The project's efforts to digitize multiple media created opportunities to improve digital strategies. Truman librarians and archivists curated analogue resources for faraway access, while Information Science scholars innovated digital archives performance and educators introduced new lessons to students of all ages.

Trumanlibrary.org (2001-2019)

In 2001, post-grant, Kochtanek then turned to the Truman Library Institute (formerly Truman Library Foundation) to fund and upgrade the website infrastructure. The Institute agreed, and the team successfully reapplied for support every year for fifteen years, after which NARA provided support. Although annual amounts have varied between $80,000 and $100,000 (Kochtanek, personal correspondence with second author, 3 December 2018), the project's continuous funding since its inception allowed for its continual expansion, refinement, and a dynamic prioritization process over the years. Continued funding allowed for the project's scope to expand alongside the user base: before long, the focus changed to digitizing series and file units in their entirety, regardless of their importance. Those efforts are now reflected in the website's two other main subsections, *Collections with Online Content* and *Other Online Collections* (Trumanlibrary.org 2018c; Williams, personal correspondence with second author, 9 November 2018). Digitization efforts have also been responsive to materials in high demand from scholars or those that have high intrinsic value (e.g. documents with handwriting from Harry and Bess, per Williams, 9 November 2018). Exhibit and social media use factor into the decision-making process and the discretion of the archivists. As Mills (2015: 165) states, 'Organizations cannot exclusively rely on user-based selection, as they risk assembling haphazard digital collections that do not support institutional missions and goals.' In our case archivists endeavour to balance the needs of users along with the needs of the whole institution and real-world constraints when selecting materials and providing them online.

Trumanlibrary.org (2002) provided a 'site integration map' that pointed website visitors in the right direction to find relocated content: for example, under Research and 'Multimedia: Digital Archives', 'Official Documents' could now be accessed with Photos and Speeches, while the Student Guide largely migrated intact, and a 'Truman Kids Page' housed the two former 'WhistleStop Interactive' pages ('Harry's Hall of Games' and 'Truman 4 Primary Kids'). Over time, the above new content changed as the priorities of the project shifted and its resources became incorporated into the main website. SLIS student volunteers continued to tag and create metadata for the digitized materials which were uploaded primarily to the *Online Documents* section of the website. The *Online Documents* section (which we discuss below) also presented materials added separately from Project Whistlestop, such as items processed by Truman Library volunteers and archival interns – thus the section is a result of effective project collaboration.

Review of the digital library's 'Online documents'

The Truman Library made its 'Online Documents' webpage available in 2018, which had evolved from earlier components in Project Whistlestop. Its addition, informed by selection criteria and research potential, reflects newer approaches to linking across media within a digital archive. The digital strategy at work here is informed at a lower order by the archival principles of organizing by hierarchical levels and transparent sourcing of materials when gathered from dispersed locations.

Research files

The *Research Files* section consists of collections regarding the large topics and events surrounding Truman's presidency (such as the Marshall Plan and desegregation of the armed forces). Each collection has been assembled around a topic, and those are subdivided by individual tabs (*documents, photographs, lesson plans* and *other resources*). Digital objects are then embedded within each tab, albeit in slightly different formats. For the *documents* tab, links to the objects are provided within a timeline. For example, the collection *Harry Truman's World War I*, includes a timeline spanning from 1917 to 1970. Whenever possible, years are further broken down into month spans – but the documents included are not always that specific with date. A brief description of the object is included within the timeline, with just enough information to catch one's eye without being cluttered.

The *photographs* tab has many thumbnails of the photos embedded, with links to the full records; they are also sorted chronologically by year whenever possible. The *lesson plans* tab includes links to lesson plans, including worksheets, handouts, songs, videos and presentations for K-12 students. They are in line with the original aims of Project Whistlestop: to provide educational resources to teachers and students. The *other resources* tab includes a variety of audio links, museum object links and external resource links.

The *Research Files* section conveys that archival records were chosen for project digitization because of how they provide direct evidence of prominent events during Truman's presidency or his life story. For example, records from the Nuremberg Trials, which held Nazis accountable for their war crimes, are included in *The War Crimes Trials at Nuremberg and Tokyo, 1945-48* collection. Records on the creation of NATO are found in the collection *Establishment of the North Atlantic Treaty Organization*. Those events are of historical importance and play an important role in modern international politics, so they are of much interest to researchers, politicians and educators. Such ongoing importance gives the particular documents a high evidential value, making them a high priority for digitization efforts. Taking into consideration the above two factors (relevance and size of audience), future efforts could seek out examples of high-relevance, small-audience documents as well as low-relevance, high-audience documents within the archival collections. Both sorts of materials have tended to mark the cut-off point for digitization efforts, as they may not be relevant to everyone, or they are of low importance in general. Those of the lowest general importance could be subject to deaccessioning.

Collections with online content

The *Collections with Online Content* section is divided mostly into the papers of Truman and those of his associates and family members. The collections are further divided into series and subseries specific to each collection. For example, the Papers of Harry S. Truman Pertaining to Family, Business, and Personal Affairs is arranged into four series (family correspondence file, general file, military file, and publications file) with a total of six subseries (four under family correspondence and two under military) (Trumanlibrary.org 2018b).

Each collection is presented as a digital finding aid. Each might include an overview about the collection, administrative data (such as size and access), a biographical sketch, a description of the collection, a series and subseries outline, and a list of box contents (folders). The folders within a box are listed, and if they have been digitized already, a hyperlink is given. However, not all of a given collection, or even a given box, is digitized yet. If a folder is not digitized, it is still listed so that a user is aware of its existence – they will just have to view it in person. If it is digitized, clicking on the hyperlink will take that user to a page for the documents contained within.

Other online collections

The *Other Online Collections* section includes photographs, audio, maps and political cartoons. As there is a heavy emphasis on manuscripts and written works in the other sections, this section attempts to counterbalance those by adding materials from a variety of formats. Materials in this section are also organized in a manner different from the other two. The photographs and maps have their own dedicated search engines, while the audio section is sorted chronologically by year, and the political cartoons are sorted topically (Trumanlibrary.org 2018a).

The image search engines offer several filters. One can search by keywords and sort by relevance or date. It is also possible to use a date range when searching. Several of the metadata fields, including subjects, description and accession number, are also searchable.

Formats, metadata and accessibility

Overall, the digital objects included on the Library website tend to be PDFs for documents or JPEGs for images. Audio files are typically presented in the Real Audio Metadata (.ram) format, which saves a great deal of server space by providing access in lower-quality, lossy formats even while higher-quality copies are digitized and preserved offline.

Descriptive metadata is included at various points, although they vary somewhat across objects, material type, and collections. For example, from the aforementioned First World War collection, some correspondence written in cursive has a typed transcript next to it, promoting legibility. Likely those documents were perceived by archivists to have a higher intrinsic value and were therefore given more staff time. Others, which were originally typescript or which were more legible to begin with, do not include transcripts. The records for photographs tend to include fields such as description, date, subject(s), keywords, and usage rights.

Organizing materials in multiple ways increases the accessibility of materials for end users. All three major sections utilize a different method of retrieval and serve different purposes. *Research Files* sorts topically and then chronologically – only including those documents deemed important by archivists. *Collections with Online Content* uses the classic archival finding aid in a digital realm. Finally, search engines make photographs and maps within *Other Online Collections* findable. That diverse approach is superior to one providing just one method of access. Rather than leaving the important documents, maps, and photographs within their respective collections, their work to highlight certain content makes the collections more accessible to novice users.

Coverage, past and future

Years on from the scope expansion from single document to series-level digitization mentioned above, there are still many documents not yet made available online: perhaps on the order of fourteen million pages. Those of lower intrinsic value and lower relevance also comprise a lower priority for digitization, which again expands and attracts new audiences to the core innovative, accessible, and usable project elements pursued by its collaborators. A collection-level archival analysis also indicates other types of materials that are unavailable, difficult, or time-consuming to put online (e.g. bearing copyright or other use restrictions, or accessioned at a later date), apart from their value and relevance.

Partner educational contributions and theoretical implications

One of the valuable takeaways from this project is the importance of project management skills among information professionals. While Dr Kochtanek is not an archivist, after the Challenge Grant ended in 2001 and he secured funding through the Truman Foundation, he became the principal investigator of Project Whistlestop, and he coordinated with the archivists in maintaining the site and ensuring they had their needs met. With a small budget to work with for a project of this scale, Dr Kochtanek was able to find cost-effective solutions to issues as they arrived so that when he did ask for something that was allowable under the grant, such as an assistant, he had the full support of administration. He received several requests from school officials and archivists asking for features that might have been good to have but could not be afforded or provided the manpower. Working as closely as he did with the consortium and the archivists allowed for the building of trust, and Kochtanek explained what could and could not be achieved to stakeholders (personal communication with first author, 19 March 2020).

The Project Whistlestop experience mirrors current trends in the archival field, with more collaborative projects taking place and archivists asked to manage digitization activities. Horine (2017: 289) notes that current business trends show individuals becoming more 'likely to deal with cross-functional, cross-cultural, or virtual environments' as many try or are compelled to do more work with less resources. Rarely is a professional project manager still hired to handle such projects, and so archivists have taken on that role to further advance the purpose of their institutions: providing access to records. Archivists find in working across environments that they are in the unique position of representing their archive and acting in an advocacy capacity. Archivists must be able to build positive relationships with other groups for an archive to succeed, as such projects can bring in new users who otherwise would not have heard of the collection. Thus, a key part of being a project manager is being an effective communicator.

Along with effective communication, records management is an essential activity in project management. During the initial five years under the Challenge Grant, little to no documentation was made for sharing, and no project management software was used. Few notes on how the programmers wrote the code or documentation of meetings and such held with the schools and the Library were saved: like for other web pages, 'the process of creation is largely undocumented' (Winters 2017: 243). Still, Project Whistlestop's data, in terms of uploaded Truman materials, resided on the in-house SISLT-built database, did include metadata, and was maintained by one individual. The few secondary sources (Reagan 2002; McCoach 2002; and Tunender and Ervin 1998) and original data still available about the project mostly pertain to its renewals over fifteen years from the Truman Foundation. Upon completion of the Truman Library's contract with MU in early 2019, the National Archives and Records Administration (NARA) took over Project Whistlestop in June 2019 and relaunched it on the Harry S. Truman Library and Museum website on 3 July 2019 (see Figure 11.2). Only then did the Truman Library website have a .gov designation, instead of the .org it had been since the 1990s (Adams, personal correspondence with second author, 7 November 2018). When the NARA assumed control of the project, they assigned a new team to run and maintain the website, which offers improved administration and better performance, though only Kochtanek was able to assist them in the transfer of data to a new server. Kochtanek ensured the server continued to function and provided transitional programming support, and remembers the painstaking difficulty of migrating Project Whistlestop's database to the Truman site, because it was proprietary (personal correspondence with third author, 7 September 2017). In broader context, the earliest websites generally resembled static pages with useful metadata attached to digital objects to support discovery (per Leetaru 2015, the first homepage snapshot of CNN.com, which was first launched in September 1995, was taken in June 2000). Since 2019, Truman Library archivists and a dedicated special media team primarily add content and upload to the site.

Teaching Truman with Hypertext Methods

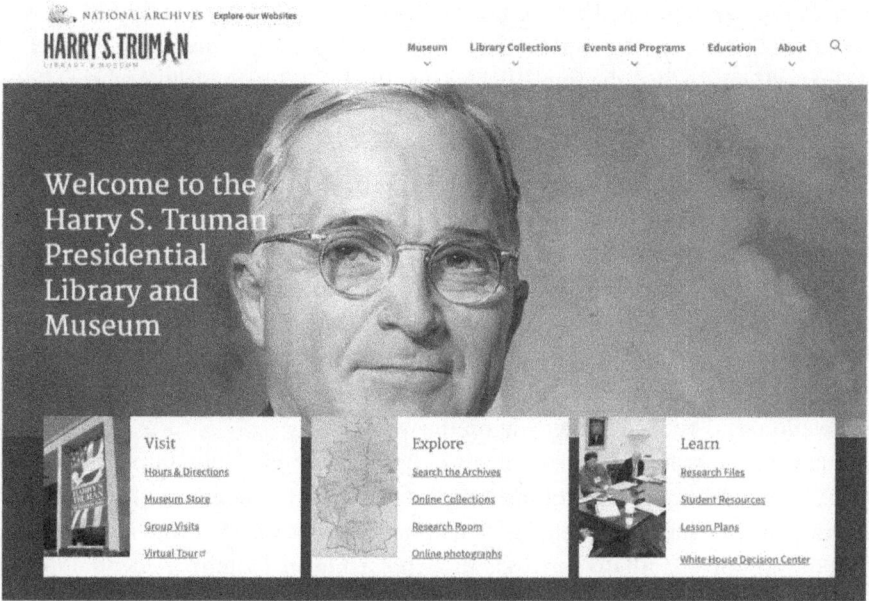

Figure 11.2 Screenshot of the Truman Presidential Library & Museum website on 16 May 2020. https://www.trumanlibrary.gov/.

Such ongoing changes to the website may influence changes to the physical exhibits, which were renovated and reopened in July 2021 (Macchi 2020). However, the website's content will likely follow the exhibits, which do factor into archivists' selections for the digital collection (Williams, personal correspondence with second author, 9 November 2018). From an aesthetic view, the former Trumanlibrary.org website had room for improvement and modernization, though its simplicity and ease of use should also persist for those seeking information and those making high usage of the digital materials.

Hypertext supporting digital curation and storytelling

Digital infrastructures enable historical research as well as public engagement with book history and histories of print. Hypertext has enabled digital and digitized collections to evolve. Amidst the genealogy of digital humanities, hypertext is a major practice characterizing our 1980s and 1990s period when the field's focus shifted from mastery of corpus to the construction of problems (Dalbello 2011). When Project Whistlestop began, the scholarly community included 'distinct sub-communities working both on hypertext as a knowledge tool and hypertext as digital literature', which altogether support hypertextuality studies (Millard and Hargood 2021; Hayles 2002; Hines 1998). In the former tradition, navigation across media became the focus of problem-solving by web designers working with a multiplicity of source material. Hypertext systems such

219

as Project Whistlestop contain structural trails, virtual documents, and links, of which the latter are by far the most emblematic. Project Whistlestop emerged in parallel with electronic editions such as the Rossetti Archive (1992–), William Blake Archive (1995–), and other digital narratives (Page and Thomas 2011) that helped textual studies survive in a time of upheaval. Contending that 'form and materiality' became foundations of the new digital literary studies, Earhart (2012) provides a complementary perspective on the great, deep value scholars ascribed to digital tools: their flexibility, new forms of presentation, and pathways for collaboration with source authors. Still, some book editors who pummel 'the digital' for its instability deal with such issues by privileging visual (over textual) media (Shillingsburg 2009; Puglisi 2015) and might appreciate the extensive 'value added' to the photographs, audio, and video clips within Project Whistlestop by experts who curated, with hypertext, specific items for digitization, interpretation, and public engagement on the website.

Along with the technical developments of hypertext, digital humanities in the 1990s were located in 'multiple forms of institutional presence' (Flanders and Mylonas 2009). Academic libraries' support for digital humanities centres coincided with rising technical capabilities around quantitative analysis and scholarship, including presidential speeches and historiography (Deluca and Pallitto 2018; Bay-Cheng 2016). Digital humanities' collaborative and cooperative emphases and use of tools and datasets to accomplish research goals suggest a convergence with the work of academic library professionals (Zhang, Liu and Mathews 2015; Hartsell-Gundy, Braunstein and Golomb 2024). In particular, project documentation, partnerships, and infrastructure-building have become central features of successful digital humanities centres under – in part or whole – library umbrellas (Rosenblum and Dwyer 2016). Looking back to Project Whistlestop, its focus on digital storytelling through authentic presidential material mirrors efforts undertaken by developers and instructors based in libraries, especially those who make existing space and infrastructure fit to purpose (Yee and Stevens 2019). As digital access intensifies, we might observe commonalities between the flexibility of digital humanities work in academe and the growing number of models for Presidential Library governance in light of the Obama-era digital-first corpus (Evans 2018). Project Whistlestop offers librarians valuable insights on ways to engage and collaborate to advance access to texts and enhance digital humanities practices.

Conclusion: A resourceful legacy

Project Whistlestop started with the goal of making primary source documents at the Truman Presidential Library available to five school districts. As the project developed, its user base boomed, and the project took on new, ambitious goals. It jump-started the Truman Library's website as we see it today, and it was one of the first digital collections of archival materials online. In contrast to most late-1990s websites, Project Whistlestop ushered in a more interactive, dynamic web experience. Not just its innovations, but its collaborations – as this paper has documented by means of archival records, website snapshots' review, and interviews – support future investigations into the history of digital libraries (of texts) by celebrating the achievements of early web pioneers. Ideally, our glimpse into the early years of Project Whistlestop and its enduring value will serve as a springboard for further exploration into its subjects and ensure permanent retention of the rare archival materials relating to it.

One legacy of Project Whistlestop will be its impact on the Truman Library's digital collections and the innumerable research products completed by its thousands of global visitors. Project Whistlestop has also impacted many students, the Truman Library, and the works of humanities scholars. Biographer David McCullough, for example, dedicated over thirty years of his career to ensuring the success of 'some of the most transformational times in the library's history', speaking at the Truman Library's fiftieth anniversary celebration in 2007 and appearing at events there through 2018 (Burnes 2022). Historians lauded its value 'for teachers from the elementary to the university level' of United States and world topics alike (Patrick 2004). Truman archivists' selection of materials for inclusion in the digital collection at first developed organically from those important topical materials already selected for students. Later, and as funding continued, the focus of the digitization efforts shifted away from the 'most important' documents to entire collection series. While certain portions are prioritized for digitization – largely based on the needs of users, the exhibits, and social media – the end goal is for the entire collection to go online. Archivists at the Truman Library have made selections based on sound appraisal practices – and therefore, the major aspects of Truman's life are represented in the digital library.

Project Whistlestop exemplifies two digital humanities methods: effective project management and records management. While often overlooked, project management plays a direct role in how archivists end up managing records, as record retention schedules are built by studying how a record series is used and referenced in a department or organization. Such schedules are common practices that libraries, archives, and museums engage in more often as processes are streamlined, and information professionals take on additional duties in response.

Project management and recordkeeping courses are essential offerings in library and information science programmes, as a 2018 study found that between 1950 and 2015, '41% of contemporary librarians hail from a disciplinary background in the humanities' (Clarke and Kim 2018: 186). Another example shows this to be a global issue in the field, as Complutense University in Spain found through a survey that 'most academic librarians stated they had taken a non-LIS program' (Cobo Serrano and Arquero Avilés 2018: 129), which resulted in many of the librarians learning project management and recordkeeping skills either on the job through offered training or by taking courses outside of work.

Further research into project management in book history projects and archives could reveal implications deeper than keeping a project organized, as it is through project management that the first steps in working with external cultural groups take place. How collaborators manage projects and communicate their needs and capabilities can lead to building positive relationships that can bring attention to the archive and demonstrate the worth of the professional work. Project management may not be more than a gesture compared to the content it supports, but it is the starting foundation that makes many forms of content-based outreach possible.[1]

Bibliography

Adams, Mark and Tom Kochtanek. 'Interface Design for Integrating Disparate Web Sites.' Mini-Workshop at Museums and the Web 2002, Boston Park Plaza, Massachusetts, 19 April 2002. https://www.archimuse.com/mw2002/abstracts/prg_160000668.html

Bay-Cheng, Sarah. 'Digital Historiography and Performance'. *Theatre Journal* 68, no. 4 (2016): 507–27. https://doi.org/10.1353/tj.2016.0104

Burnes, Brian. 'Inside David McCullough's Relationship with the Truman Library'. *Flatland*, 22 September 2022. https://flatlandkc.org/arts-culture/inside-david-mcculloughs-relationship-with-the-truman-library/

Carroll, T. G. 'Challenge Grants: Bringing Schools into the Information Age'. *Principal* 76 (1997): 26–8.

Clarke, Rachel I. and Young-In Kim. 'The More Things Change, the More They Stay the Same: Educational and Disciplinary Backgrounds of American Librarians, 1950–2015'. *Journal of Education for Library & Information Science* 59, no. 4 (2018): 179–205. https://doi.org/10.3138/jelis.59.4.2018-0001

Cobo Serrano, Silvia and Rosario Arquero Avilés. 'Project Management Techniques at the Complutense University: Academic Librarians' Perceptions'. *New Review of Academic Librarianship* 24, no. 2 (2018): 124–35. https://doi.org/10.1080/13614533.2017.1406378

CTIE: Center for Technology Innovations in Education. 'History.' University of Missouri website, 12 December 1998. https://web.archive.org/web/19981212024126/http://www.ctie.missouri.edu:80/

Dalbello, Marija. 'A Genealogy of Digital Humanities'. *Journal of Documentation* 67, no. 3 (2011): 480–506. https://doi.org/10.1108/00220411111124550

Deluca, Lisa and Robert Pallitto. 'The Contemporary Presidency: Digital Resources to Support Quantitative Scholarship in Presidential Studies'. *Presidential Studies Quarterly* 48 (2018): 537–51. https://doi.org/10.1111/psq.12474

Earhart, Amy E. 'The Digital Edition and Digital Humanities'. *Textual Cultures* 7, no. 1 (2012): 18–28. https://doi.org/10.2979/textcult.7.1.18

Evans, Meredith R. 'Presidential Libraries Going Digital'. *The Public Historian* 40, no. 2 (2018): 116–21.

Flanders, Julia and Elli Mylonas. 'Digital Humanities.' In *Encyclopedia of Library and Information Sciences*, 3rd edn. Edited by M. J. Bates and M. Niles Maack. Boca Raton, Florida: CRC Press, 2009.

Hackman, Larry J. 'Toward Better Policies and Practices for Presidential Libraries'. *The Public Historian* 28, no. 3 (2006): 165–84. https://doi.org/10.1525/tph.2006.28.3.165

Harry S. Truman Library, Project Whistlestop Collection. 'L. J. Hackman, December 5, 1996[a], Document access challenges,' [Letter to K. Vest, T. Patrick and D. Allen]. 'J. F. Sears, December 10, 1996[b], Congratulations' [Letter to L. Hackman]. Independence, Missouri. 1996.

---

[1] The authors gratefully thank Professor Tom Kochtanek, SISLT staff Bennett Magnino and Jim Borwick, MU archivist Gary Cox, and Truman Library staff Mark Adams and Tammy Williams for their generous contributions to this work.

Harry S. Truman Library & Museum. 'History of the Truman Library & Museum'. 2023. https://www.trumanlibrary.gov/about/history

Hartsell-Gundy, Arianne, Laura Braunstein and Liorah Golomb. *Digital Humanities in the Library, Second Edn.* Chicago: Association of College and Research Libraries, 2024.

Hayles, N. Katherine. *Writing Machines.* Cambridge, Massachusetts: MIT Press, 2002.

Hines, Susan. 'What Hypertext is Not Bound to Do: Digital Decisions in the Literary Humanities.' Presented at CUMREC Conference, 1998. Conference, 1998. https://library.educause.edu/resources/1998/1/what-hypertext-is-not-bound-to-do-digital-decisions-in-the-literary-humanities

Horine, Greg. *Absolute Beginner's Guide to Project Management*, 4th edn. Indianapolis: Pearson Education, Inc., 2017.

IMLS: Institute of Museum and Library Services. *Status of Technology and Digitization in the Nation's Museums and Libraries 2002 Report.* Washington, D.C., 2002. https://www.imls.gov/sites/default/files/publications/documents/2002report_0.pdf

Kochtanek, Thomas. 'Interface Design for Integrating Disparate Web Sites'. Presented at InfoToday 2002, New York Hilton & Towers, May 14–16, 2002. https://www.infotoday.com/it2002/nationalonline.htm

Kochtanek, T. and J. Laffey. 'Project Whistlestop: Design Considerations for Information Retrieval Performance in an Image Database'. In *Proceedings of the 19th National Online Meeting, New York, 1998.* Medford, New Jersey: Information Today, 1998.

Kochtanek, T., J. Laffey, J. Ervin and H. Tunender. 'Project Whistlestop: An Evaluation of Search Engines on the Web'. In *Proceedings of the 19th National Online Meeting, New York, 1998*, 211–21. Edited by M. E. Williams. Medford, New Jersey: Information Today, 1998a.

Kochtanek, T., J. Laffey, H. Tunender, J. Ervin and J. Borwick. 'Project Whistlestop: An Evaluation of Search Engines on the Web'. In *Proceedings of the 17th Integrated Online Library Systems Meeting*, New York, 1998b.

Kochtanek, Thomas R., Jim Borwick, Seong-Mo Kim and James Laffey. 'Project Whistlestop: An Analysis of Visitations to a Digital Library Web Site'. Presented at 20th Annual National Online Meeting, May 1999. https://www.infotoday.com/nom99/nomprogram.htm

Lamb, Annette and Larry Johnson. 'Rethinking President's Month Projects through Presidential Library Websites'. *Teacher Librarian* 42, no. 3 (2015): 64–8. https://hdl.handle.net/1805/8584

Leetaru, Kalev. 'How Much of the Internet Does the Wayback Machine Really Archive?' *Forbes*, 16 November 2015. https://www.forbes.com/sites/kalevleetaru/2015/11/16/how-much-of-the-internet-does-the-wayback-machine-really-archive/#7c4189694469

Macchi, Victoria. 'Sneak Peek: The Truman Library, Reimagined and Redesigned'. *National Archives News*, 16 December 2020. https://www.archives.gov/news/articles/truman-library-renovation

Martin, Edeen. 'Project Whistlestop Web Site Offers Interactive Learning about President Harry Truman'. *Truman Library*, 15 December 1998. https://web.archive.org/web/19990913204824/https://www.trumanlibrary.org/news/wstop.htm

McCargar, Victoria. 'Following the Trail of the Disappearing Data'. *Seybold Report* 4, no. 21 (2005): 7–14. http://www.loc.gov/standards/premis/TSR-0209.pdf

McCoach, D. Betsy. 'Using the Web for Social Studies Enrichment'. *Gifted Child Today* 25, no. 3 (2002): 48. https://www.thefreelibrary.com/Using+the+web+for+social+studies+enrichment.-a090162398

Meddis, Sam V. 'Hot Sites'. *USA Today*, 30 December 1998. https://web.archive.org/web/19990427111030/http://www.usatoday.com:80/life/cyber/chb0721.htm

Millard, David E. and Charlie Hargood. 'Hypertext as a Lens into Interactive Digital Narrative'. In *Proceedings of Interactive Storytelling: 14th International Conference on Interactive Digital*

Storytelling, ICIDS 2021, Tallinn, Estonia, December 7-10, 2021, 509–24. Cham, Switzerland: Springer, 2021. https://doi.org/10.1007/978-3-030-92300-6_51

Mills, Alexandra. 'User Impact on Selection, Digitization, and the Development of Digital Special Collections'. *New Review of Academic Librarianship* 21, no. 2 (2015): 160–69. https://doi.org/10.1080/13614533.2015.1042117

Niederberger, Erin, Sarah A. Buchanan and Hali Allen. 'Mary F. Lenox: Library and Information Science Connector and Poet of Justice'. *Libraries* 6, no. 1 (2022): 187–210. https://doi.org/10.5325/libraries.6.1.0187

Niekrasz, Emily. 'The Harry S. Truman Presidential Library: The 30-Year Journey'. *Pieces of History: A Blog of the U.S. National Archives*, 2015. https://prologue.blogs.archives.gov/2015/10/13/the-harry-s-truman-presidential-library-the-thirty-year-journey/

Page, Ruth and Browen Thomas, eds. *New Narratives: Stories and Storytelling in the Digital Age*. Lincoln: University of Nebraska Press, 2011.

Patrick, Sue C. 'Truman Presidential Library Digital Archives, Project WhistleStop' Review'. In *Teaching Difficult Legal or Political Concepts: Using Online Primary Sources in Writing Assignments*, 2004. https://www.historians.org/teaching-and-learning/teaching-resources-for-historians/teaching-and-learning-in-the-digital-age/the-history-of-the-americas/teaching-difficult-legal-or-political-concepts/truman-presidential-library-digital-archives-project-whistlestop

Pelavin Research Institute. *Investing in School Technology: Strategies to Meet Funding Challenge*. Washington, D.C.: 1997. https://eric.ed.gov/?id=ED415577.

Pingdom. 'The Web Back in 1996-1997'. 16 September 2008. https://www.pingdom.com/blog/the-web-in-1996-1997/

Project Whistlestop Archives. 'Project Whistlestop Abstract' in Whistlestop Grants & Administrative Documents file. 'NARA Guidelines' in Digital Standards file. Columbia, Missouri, 1996.

Puglisi, Paola. "'The Day Has Not Yet Come...": Book-Jackets in Library Catalogs'. *Cataloging & Classification Quarterly* 53, nos. 3–4 (2015): 368–81. https://doi.org/10.1080/01639374.2015.1017783

Reagan, Patrick D. 'Project WhistleStop: Truman Digital Archive Project http://www.whistlestop.org' (Web Site Review). *Journal of American History* 88, no. 4 (March 2002): 1631. https://doi.org/10.2307/2700771 and https://historymatters.gmu.edu/d/4922/

Rosenblum, Brian and Arienne Dwyer. 'Copiloting a Digital Humanities Center: A Critical Reflection on a Libraries-Academic Partnership'. In *Laying the Foundation: Digital Humanities in Academic Libraries*, 111–26. Edited by J. W. White and H. Gilbert. West Lafayette, Indiana: Purdue University Press, 2016.

Seago, Dale A. 'Evaluation of a Multi-year Teacher Professional Development Program to Improve Teacher Instructional Practices: A Case Study'. EdD diss., Saint Louis University, USA, 2003. https://www.proquest.com/docview/288340240/B849C77CD96E4FDBPQ/1

Shillingsburg, Peter. 'How Literary Works Exist: Convenient Scholarly Editions.' *Digital Humanities Quarterly* 3, no. 3 (2009). https://www.digitalhumanities.org/dhq/vol/3/3/000054/000054.html

SISLT: School of Information Science & Learning Technologies. 'Harry S. Truman Library Project Receives Additional Funding through 2018'. 11 May 2017. Formerly at http://sislt.missouri.edu/2017/05/harry-s-truman-library-project-receives-additional-funding-through-2018/

Swain, Ellen D. 'Oral History in the Archives: Its Documentary Role in the Twenty-first Century'. *The American Archivist* 66, no. 1 (2003): 139–58. https://doi.org/10.17723/aarc.66.1.9284q6r604858h40

TrumanLibrary.gov. 'Daily Appointments of Harry S. Truman'. 2023a. https://www.trumanlibrary.gov/calendar
TrumanLibrary.gov. 'The Spy's Dilemma: A Problem in Intelligent Choice and a Matter of Life and Death'. 2023b. https://www.trumanlibrary.gov/whistlestop/applications/dilemma/
TrumanLibrary.gov. 'Three Branches of Government'. 2023c. https://www.trumanlibrary.gov/education/three-branches
TrumanLibrary.org. 'Project WhistleStop: Site Integration Map'. 2002. https://web.archive.org/web/20020225225301/https://www.trumanlibrary.org/whistlestop/index.htm
TrumanLibrary.org. 'Online Documents: Truman Library & Museum'. 2018a. https://web.archive.org/web/20181003170046/https://trumanlibrary.org/online-collections.htm
TrumanLibrary.org. '[Collections with Online Content: Truman Papers:] Papers of Harry S. Truman Pertaining to Family, Business, and Personal Affairs.' 2018b. https://web.archive.org/web/20180922115649/https://www.trumanlibrary.org/hstpaper/fbpa.htm
TrumanLibrary.org. '[Collections with Online Content:] Bess W. Truman Papers.' 2018c. https://web.archive.org/web/20190606124008/https://www.trumanlibrary.org/hstpaper/trumanbw.htm
Tunender, Heather and Jane Ervin. 'How to Succeed in Promoting Your Web Site: The Impact of Search Engine Registration on Retrieval of a World Wide Web Site'. *Information Technology and Libraries* 17, no. 3 (1998): 173–9.
University of Missouri. 'CTIE Project Update'. In *SISLT Centers and Research Projects, 1997-2013*, C:8/27/2. Box 1 – 040720, University Archives, University of Missouri. Columbia, Missouri, 8 April 2003.
U.S. Department of Education. 'Technology Innovation Challenge Grant Program: 1996 Challenge Grant Awards.' 2009. https://www2.ed.gov/programs/techinnov/awards.html
U.S. National Archives and Records Administration (NARA). 'Presidential Records: Laws and Regulations.' 2023. https://www.archives.gov/presidential-records/laws-and-regulations
Whistlestop.org. 'Project WhistleStop Team and Partners'. 1998. https://web.archive.org/web/19981202004502/http://www.whistlestop.org:80/team.htm
Whistlestop.org. 'MU Design Team'. 1999, February 9. https://web.archive.org/web/19990209162145/http://www.whistlestop.org:80/design.htm
Whistlestop.org. 'Project Whistlestop.' 2001a, November 27. https://web.archive.org/web/20011127182247/http://whistlestop.org/
Whistlestop.org. 'Project Whistlestop's Awards.' 2001b, December 1. https://web.archive.org/web/20011201162609/http://www.whistlestop.org:80/awards/awards.htm
Wilson, Don W. 'Presidential Libraries: Developing to Maturity.' *Presidential Studies Quarterly* 21, no. 4 (1991): 771–9.
Winters, Jane. 'Coda: Web Archives for Humanities Research – Some Reflections.' In *The Web as History: Using Web Archives to Understand the Past and the Present*. Edited by N. Brügger and R. Schroeder. London: UCL Press, 2017.
Wolff, Cynthia J. 'Necessary Monuments: The Making of the Presidential Library System.' *Government Publications Review* 16, no. 1 (1989): 47–62. https://doi.org/10.1016/0277-9390(89)90043-5
Yee, Perry and Elliott Stevens. 'Digital Storytelling.' In *Culture of Digital Scholarship in Academic Libraries*, 83–100. Edited by R. Chin Roemer and V. Kern. Chicago: American Library Association, 2019.
Zhang, Ying, Shu Liu and Emilee Mathews. 'Convergence of Digital Humanities and Digital Libraries.' *Library Management* 36, nos. 4/5 (2015): 362–77. https://doi.org/10.1108/LM-09-2014-0116

CHAPTER 12
DIGITAL PUBLISHING PRACTICES IN MUSEUMS
OLD HABITS, NEW PLATFORMS
Ellen Charlesworth and Claire Warwick

The emergence of digital and online technologies proved disruptive to established publishing practices. As Kurt Andersen argued in the *New Yorker* in 1997, 'With a computer and a phone line, anyone can become his own publisher/commentator/reporter/anchor, dispatching to everyone everywhere credible-looking opinions, facts, and "facts" via the Internet' (1997, 40). This blurring between consumer and producer rapidly transformed the media landscape (Bødker 2016; Kaplan and Haenlein 2010). As Jay Rosen has argued, control of the 'printing presses' changed hands with the advent of the Internet; blogs had undermined the 'old-style, one-way, top-down media consumption', and in doing so had irrevocably transformed the balance of power between producers and audiences (Rosen 2012, 13).

However, it is debatable to what extent this shift in power presented a radical departure from previous modes of publishing. Interactivity, although more evident on social media, is not unprecedented. In Stuart Hall's *Encoding/Decoding*, he notes that production is not a 'closed system' and that 'circulation and reception are, indeed, "moments" of the production process in television and are reincorporated, via a number of skewed and structured "feedbacks", into the production process itself' (1980, 164). As Henrik Bødker noted, 'Hall's observation that consumers of information are also its producers has only found greater expression in social media' (2016, 3). Not only do most consumers also produce posts themselves, but the number of 'feedbacks' within the publishing process has significantly increased. Comments, likes, shares and replies are all mechanisms through which social media users can evaluate the reception of their posts – although they remain 'skewed'.

As useful as Hall's writing is for understanding new media, it is far from the only theoretical framework that has been applied to the new modes of publishing. Much of the current research on social media is indebted to earlier work on the mass media of the twentieth century. Prominent examples include the adaptation of Erving Goffman's presentation of self (Hogan 2010), Pierre Bourdieu's information capital (Ignatow and Robinson 2017), and Bruno Latour's actor-network theory (Chadwick 2017; Ngai, Tao and Moon 2015). However, the reliance on pre-digital theory has been criticized by Ralph Schroeder, who notes that 'theories that were suited to mass media and interpersonal communication are no longer suited for digital media – since new media often have elements of both' (Schroeder 2018, 324).[1]

This chapter explores how elements of these theoretical frameworks can be used in parallel with other approaches to provide a more holistic view of social media practices. Using a case study of UK museums' social media as a methodological foundation, we draw together large-scale data analysis, interviews and case studies to provide a more holistic view of social media practices. We consider the practical and theoretical difficulties new media analysis presents and propose a set of six questions to guide researchers new to the field.

While museums may not seem an obvious starting point, the radical transformation of communication norms in the sector over the past twenty years provides fertile ground for an analysis of publishing practices. The first half of the chapter explores *what* museums have been publishing online, providing a brief overview of changing attitudes and strategies within the sector. We then detail our own methods and reflect on the applicability of twentieth-century media theory, focusing on Hall's 'encoding/decoding' model. The final section then discusses our findings, combining different forms of analysis to explore *why* museums' publications have taken the form that they have.

Museums online

With its increased levels of peer-to-peer interaction, the 'social web' shifted publishing practices towards a 'participatory culture' in which anyone can publish and disseminate texts (Lievrouw 2010; Jenkins 2009; Shirky 2008). It was this potential for new media to facilitate a dialogue that had first excited museum professionals and academics (Walker 2016); George MacDonald and Stephen Alsford (1997) were just a few of the many voices in the 1990s arguing that digital technologies would transform the way museums communicate with their audiences. It was believed that by embracing digital technologies, museums could realize a more participatory approach that shifted the focus from their collections to their visitors – creating an 'audience-driven museum' (Hooper-Greenhill 1992; 1994; Falk and Dierking 2000). But to what extent has the radical potential of the 'social web' been realized?

While some museums with the resources and expertise embraced the opportunities presented by the World Wide Web, the sector as a whole was resistant to change (Giannini and Bowen 2019; Bowen 2010). The radically democratized communication of the internet challenged notions of expert authorship integral to museums' existing modes of publishing, and many struggled to adapt (Fransen-Taylor and Narayan 2018; Deodato 2014).

In his seminal article, published in 1997, Peter Walsh described the hesitancy of institutions to adapt to the norms of online communication, arguing that they propagated institutional authority by adopting the 'Unassailable Voice'. This voice – which delivers

---

[1]This chapter is the result of research supported by the Arts and Humanities Research Council, grant number: AH/R012415/1.

'polished, endless monologues' – assumes that 'museums have the knowledge and then benevolently dole it out to the comparatively ignorant public' (Walsh 1997, 78–9). This somewhat patronizing approach is the antithesis of the plurality of voices found online and the new democratized modes of communicating (Rabinovitch and Alsford 2002). Jennifer Trant summarized the issue, describing museums as facing 'an onslaught of interpretations of culture from an incredible number of sources, and forced into an awareness that they are no longer the sole interpreters of their collections' (1999, 107).

However, in the intervening decades museums have shaken this hesitancy. This is partially attributable to new funding pressures (Belfiore 2015), as well as an increase in engagement with postmodernist and postcolonial criticism that has seen museums refashion their relationship with their audiences (Speight 2016; Falk and Dierking 2000; Hooper-Greenhill 1992). These factors, alongside the eventual ubiquity of social media, have contributed to the significant shift, or 'digital pivot' over the last twenty years (Wong 2011; Parry 2010).

Publishing on social media is now common practice. Jamie Larkin et al. estimated that 77 per cent of all museums in the UK have a Facebook account (Larkin, Ballatore and Mityurova 2023, 634). A percentage that is higher than the 60 per cent of accredited museums that are estimated to use their own websites as a publishing platform (Charlesworth, Beresford, et al. 2023, 10). A Nesta survey found that social media use was on the rise, despite the falling number of museums 'maintaining a blog, and publishing to a website' (2017b, 11). Social media has emerged as a free 'potential substitute', usurping websites as the primary place audiences can learn more about a museum (Nesta 2017b, 11). The apparent transformation of attitudes within the sector and rapid rate of change provide fascinating insights into the appeal and challenges of new media.

Methods

The prevalence of social media platforms, even amongst museums with little digital expertise, means that there is enormous variety in museums' digital publishing practices. While case studies can provide an insight into the advantages and difficulties of an individual organization, it is difficult to extrapolate wider sector trends from a handful of examples. However, the ability to access the data collected by companies like Meta and Google via application programming interfaces (APIs) provides vast quantities of information. This has enabled researchers to use machine learning and AI to analyse broader trends in the sector through a 'distant reading' of the texts museums publish online (Underwood 2016; Gooding, Terras and Warwick 2013). By looking beyond individual case studies, we gain new knowledge of systems – such as topics, themes and trends – at the expense of some of the complexity and richness an in-depth 'close reading' of an individual text can provide (Bode 2018). Like with any methodology, the results can be limited by unrepresentative sampling or an uncritical approach (Da 2019). However, at its best, 'distant reading' is able to describe *what* is happening over a large corpus – although, it does not necessarily give us an explanation as to *why*. This kind of insight requires additional context provided by subject experts. As such, to understand museum publishing practices, our approach combines data-led research with interviews to help explain the trends in the data and investigate why they are occurring.

Our research primarily draws from two datasets. The first looks at the online presence of a representative sample of 315 UK museums, spanning across five different social media platforms and museum websites (Charlesworth, Beresford et al. 2023). The other, collected by the Mapping Museum Project team at Birkbeck and King's College London, collates the Twitter and Facebook data of every museum in the UK over the course of three years (Larkin, Ballatore, and Mityurova 2023; Ballatore and Candlin 2023; Candlin and Larkin 2020).[2] These two datasets are combined with interviews of staff and volunteers from ten museums, which were chosen for having social media presences that were representative of wider trends in the sector. This sample helped us explore the publishing strategies of a range of organizations of different sizes and specialisms. We included four small, three medium, and three large museums that represent a diverse array of collections. The anonymized descriptions of participants' roles and their organizations are specified in Figure 12.1.

An apparent failure

We first began our inquiry to track the dramatic changes in museums' online publishing strategies during the Covid-19 lockdowns of 2020. Museums' attitudes towards social media changed enormously over the course of the pandemic. A report by the Network of European Museum Organisations (NEMO) found that 73 per cent of their respondents had increased their social media use in the early months of the pandemic (2020, 15). Yet, while the Twitter and Facebook data shows a large increase in museums online publishing during the initial national lockdowns, it declines to pre-pandemic levels by the end of 2021 (Larkin, Ballatore and Mityurova 2023). As one of our participants summarized:

> I think social [media] really came into its own with COVID, obviously, but it's completely fallen off now. (P2)

The reduction in posting as museums reopened is perhaps unsurprising; teams were able to dedicate more time to digital content while their sites were closed.

> There was no one in, we've not got any communications going on internally, everyone's on furlough… so, we had a lot more time on our hands. (P5)

---

[2] As the Twitter datasets underpinning this research were collected prior to the re-branding and the interviewees and existing scholarship also refer to the site as Twitter, the original name has been kept for consistency.

Participant (P)	Participant Role	Collection	Size	Area description
1	Digital resources manager	Science	Large	Cosmopolitan
2	Marketing and communications officer	Industry	Medium	Sparse Welsh countryside
3	Treasurer (volunteer)	Social History	Small	Scottish countryside
4	Trustee (volunteer)	Local History	Small	English countryside
5	Communication coordinator	Industry	Large	English region with manufacturing legacy
6	Experience and engagement lead	Fine Art	Large	University town/ city
7	Site manager	Local History	Small	Costal region with aging population
8	Marketing and communications manager	Religion	Medium	English university town/ city
9	Curator (interim)	Archives	Medium	Scottish countryside
10	Collections manager	Transport	Small	Affluent English rural region

Figure 12.1 A table of interview participants including details of their museum's collection, size and area. Additional information on museum size and descriptors of demographic area were drawn from the data set created for the Mapping Museum Project (Candlin et al. 2019).

Yet the influx of posting to social media during museum closures did not result in any significant increase in the size of online audiences (Charlesworth, Beresford, et al. 2023, 13). The diversity of audiences also remained the same. Despite initial hopes that online texts would reach beyond museums' traditional visitors, an 18-month survey of the UK cultural sector – conducted by the Audience Agency – found that online audiences mirrored those of museums' physical sites (Walmsley et al. 2022, 68; The Audience Agency 2021; Noehrer et al. 2021). For the majority of museums, then, the democratiing promise of social media has not been realized.

It has been argued that social media is a useful tool for engagement. Well-loved and successful museum social media initiatives include the Grant Museum of Zoology's 'Glass Jar of Moles' – which featured in the first #MuseumMascot day – and more recently Adam Koszary's viral tweets for the Museum of English Rural Life, which garnered thousands of interactions (Deakin 2021; Douglas and Koszary 2018; Warwick 2013). However, these accounts are not representative of the sector. The data indicates a gulf between the most innovative accounts and the majority of organizations; 90 per cent of interactions with museums on Twitter – this is all likes, retweets, replies or quotes – were directed at just 25 per cent of the accounts (Larkin, Ballatore and Mityurova 2023).

This highlights the first issue facing researchers working on social media, and that is sampling bias. What are you looking at, and what are you missing? This question is equally important when studying either publishing practices or audience reception.

> *Q1. What are the limitations of your data? Who/What is missing?*

Monologues and sales pitches

Why have museums struggled to materialize the diverse possibilities of social media? The contributing factors have been divided into the following three sections: an outdated mode of communication, a lack of resources and the technological underpinnings of the social media platforms.

The fact that museums have continued to disseminate information much as they did with traditional print publishing has been a long-running criticism of their online publishing strategies. When studying the US museum sector in 2012, Adrienne Fletcher and Moon Lee concluded that, 'For the moment, museums are mostly involved with one-way communication strategies using Facebook and Twitter to focus on event listing, reminders, reaching larger or newer audiences by increasing the number of fans and promotional messaging' (2012, 518). This mono-directional mode of communication is the antithesis of the interaction and potential for dialogue that had initially drawn museum professionals to social media. This strategy has also since proven to be ineffective; posts that promote what is happening within the museum receive far less engagement than the posts about museum collections (Arnaboldi and Diaz Lema 2021). Yet, among our participants, posts about events and ticket sales – in short, marketing – continue to make up the vast majority of their online texts.

> We use Facebook as our most explicit marketing platform; it's what we put our digital budget into. It's where we post about big sales, the store, behind-the-scenes events, buying tickets . . . (P5)
>
> [We use social media] on occasion, we only use it to support sales of our events. (P8)

The majority of our participants – except for the smallest institution – predominantly used their social media to advertise museum events, but they were well aware of the disjoint between what they were posting and the type of posts that gained traction on the platform.

> It's particularly museum artefacts or museum collection photos, they seem to generally be the winners in terms of getting a lot more recognition . . . [I post most about] our latest events, our talks, our art workshops, our family events, evening event, you know, that sort of thing. Generally, that's what I use it most for, but I know that actually what gets the most recognition is the other stuff. (P7)

To return to Hall, the 'feedbacks' are resolutely ignored by museums. One participant noticed the shift in response they received when they were able to move away from marketing when their site was closed during the pandemic.

> [Over the course of the pandemic] we weren't like *we* – the Royal *we* – as content creators, we weren't doing our normal thing of 'please buy this ticket'. We had all this extra time to invest in creating a kind of a digital community that celebrates our kind of specific arts heritage organisation. . . . But now we have moved back into the, 'oh also, we have a museum tour'. So, we've gone from very much 'sales with a little bit of story', to 'all story', and now we're trying to do a little bit of both. (P5)

This juxtaposition of the 'royal *we*' with a more authentic, story-based experience speaks to Peter Walsh's notion of the 'Unassailable Voice'. In order to maintain a consistent organizational voice, some interviewees were subjected to much greater managerial oversight – 'posting by committee' as one participant called it. This practice mirrors Walsh's description in 1997 of the 'vaguely evasive tone of a text created by committee . . . [that] merely mouths words of a disembodied, anonymous authority' (1997, 78). While he was writing about museum publishing practices before the advent of social media, his description still summarizes their approach twenty-five years later.

Therefore, it is questionable to what extent the majority of museums' digital communication strategies have adapted their publishing approach to new media platforms.

> *Q2. How do the texts you are working with conform – or not, as the case may be – to conventions of the medium? What does this reflect about the priorities of the text's author?*

An issue of resources

Amongst the ten museums we chose to interview, it was the one with the largest online following that had thought most clearly about how their publishing strategy served the museum beyond ticket sales.

> It is important for brand awareness, and it's really good for our kind of aims as an educational charity. It doesn't necessarily matter to us if 300,000 people watch a video. Those 300,000 people don't have to necessarily then go and buy a ticket, but those 300,000 people might know a little bit more about the [region], a little bit more about what we stand for, about our story, about our messaging, and that's just as important really. (P5)

They noted just how useful it was to have a colleague who was an avid user of the platform – someone who could report back on trends and what audiences may want to see.

> [My colleague] knew loads about the platform, [they] knew what was trending – classic 2020 style – had spent hours and hours and hours and hours a day on this app because there was nothing else to do, so [they'd] really got [their] finger on what was successful and what people wanted to see. (P5)

This approach had been successful; however, it is somewhat dependent on individual staff members. This posed a difficulty when staff members leave.

> We had two paid for attendants . . . one of them it was very keen on social media, so he got a lot of the YouTube type things going, Instagram, and so on. Now he's now moved to [a larger institution] as a media officer for them, which has left us at the museum with no one to actually do a lot of this social media posting. (P10)

This is important in the light of the number of interns, volunteers and staff on short-term contracts who run museum social media accounts and presents an ongoing problem for museums' digital adoption. If staff with short-term contracts are developing digital skills and leaving these institutions, much of the digital infrastructure they have created, as well as hard-won knowledge about successful online publishing strategies, is lost. In more than one interview, it transpired that the passwords for social media accounts had been misplaced during handover periods, in one case, leading to a platform being abandoned entirely.

Few museums in the UK have a dedicated digital team, and those that exist often sit uneasily between departments. Of the many responsibilities that our participants held, social media was rarely a primary focus. P7 typifies our discussions with smaller organizations. As one of only two paid staff members at the museum, their responsibilities included opening the site, applying for grants, managing volunteers and while they did look at insight figures for their website and social media, 'the board have never asked for that data, so [they were] not worried about it'. Of the ten participants we interviewed, only one's main responsibility was social media, and as they noted, it is rarely prioritized.

> Social media is often considered to be a bit like, you don't really need to know what to do on social media. Like, 'blah blah blah, we'll just shove it on an intern'. (P5)

Over half of the organizations we interviewed had relied on unpaid team members – including interns and work experience students – to manage social media accounts.

> We did have a work experience student last year who did two Instagram reels . . . I certainly think they were very good quality for what was, you know, something for a work experience student to do. (P8)

Many museums have unrealistic expectations of such setups, likely encouraged by the sector's few success stories. However, a 'calibrated amateurism' is widely used by social media influencers to establish a relatable presence; this facade obscures the long hours, business acumen, and equipment that are essential to growing an online audience (Abidin 2017; Marwick 2013). This contributes to the prevailing belief that anyone – no matter how under-resourced – can achieve social media success (Ashton and Patel 2018).

With barely enough resources to maintain a presence on social media, it is unsurprising that many museums are not able to invest in producing anything beyond event advertisements and basic updates. Speaking in 2009, Shelley Bernstein highlighted that her work at the Brooklyn Museum was 'not about using social media as just another marketing and visitor experience tool-set', and that social media was 'not an intern role' (Reynolds 2009). Yet, this requires significant time and buy-in from the museum's management, and the kind of sustained investment required to build a social media following is not feasible for most museums. As Nesta highlighted in 2017, in the wider arts and cultural sector, it is 'heritage organisations (the majority of which are Museums) [that] are the least active on social media' (2017a, 17).

To make matters worse, multiple studies have highlighted that the visual content and rich media are preferred, especially by younger audiences (Perez 2022; Barry and Graça 2018). A study by Moran, Muzellec and Johnson found that on Facebook 'all rich media formats encourage more clicks than static plain-text content, but video-based content has the greatest impact on encouraging clicking behaviours; thus, videos are the best source of encouraging content discovery' (2019, 541). This suggests that if museums want more people – including younger audiences – to share or interact with their posts, they should upload videos. Yet, in comparison with text, video content is far more time-consuming to make and requires a greater degree of specialist knowledge and equipment.

Q3. What are the barriers to publishing, and has this influenced the frequency or location of publication? What would be the ideal place for publication be otherwise?

Platforms that are based on video content are therefore less attractive to most museums, and comparing the use of YouTube and Facebook illustrates museums' preference for the latter. 94 per cent of UK adults online and 77 per cent of museums have a Facebook account, whereas while 92 per cent of adults watch YouTube, it is estimated that only 46 per cent of accredited museums have an account (Larkin, Ballatore and Mityurova 2023, 634; Charlesworth, Beresford, et al. 2023, 10; Ofcom 2022, 32). By eschewing video-based platforms, museums are likely skewing their online audiences towards older demographics.

Ofcom found that YouTube, Snapchat, and TikTok – which are all based on sharing videos – were more often used by younger age groups. In 2022, just over half of both TikTok's (52 per cent) and Snapchat's (51 per cent) UK adult visitors were between 15 and 34, in contrast to the two-thirds of Facebook's users over the age of thirty-five (Ofcom 2022, 32, 2021, 59–60). Museums are almost entirely absent from Snapchat and TikTok – on which only 7 per cent of accredited museums have an account (Charlesworth, Beresford, et al. 2023, 10). Our interviews have reaffirmed that difficulty creating videos may have contributed to a reluctance to use these platforms.

We have dabbled with TikTok. And we do have a video officer who's trying to do a few more things on that, but we found it very, very time consuming to do properly. I think the individual communications officers are a bit more wary about starting something like that off without the means to be able to continue it. (P2)

How platforms shape texts

There was an awareness amongst our participants that different audiences were to be found on different platforms, and to reach them required tailoring the text of what they publish to each site. Of course, the large uptake of social media amongst many different types of museums means there is a range of publishing strategies used amongst our participants. One interviewee summarized theirs:

I just put the same thing on three times across the [three different] platforms. (P8)

Which contrasts with another participant, who described how they changed the focus of each text depending on where it would be published.

From Facebook to Twitter, we have to completely overhaul [our posts] because of the text and the character length. Instagram tends to get more engagement because of the visual, so even when we've tried to change the text within it, we've found that it hasn't made the biggest difference. However, what we do find is that we have to make sure we've got stronger imagery . . . as opposed to a gallery of images that we might utilise more on Facebook. (P6)

There was no prevailing method amongst our participants regarding how they changed their publishing practices in response to texts' reception. It depended on the organizational aims of the museums; for some, qualitative feedback from on-site visitors was prioritized, while academically oriented institutions cared more about research outcomes.

Of course, the 'feedbacks' present on social media do not accurately capture the type of in-depth engagement museums are trying to foster. Likes, reach, page views and shares are all metrics that are predominantly designed to serve the customers of social media sites – that is advertisers (Gillespie 2010). To clarify what these terms mean, Facebook produced a disambiguation, which declares:

Page views are the number of times that a Page's profile has been viewed by people, including people who are logged into Facebook and those who aren't.

Reach is the number of people who saw any content from your Page or about your Page. This metric is estimated.

Impressions are the number of times any content from your Page or about your Page entered a person's screen. (Facebook 2024a)

The substitution of 'was loaded into a browser' with 'saw' is misleading, especially when 'entered a person's screen' is also used. Short of implementing eye-tracking technologies on every device, it is impossible to tell whether a user was looking somewhere else, either on their screen or off.[3] Here, Hall's breakdown of the stages of mass communication are useful. He notes that 'production', 'circulation', 'distribution/consumption' and 'reproduction' are each distinct stages (1980, 163). As is implied by the slash, 'distribution' and 'consumption' were often synonymous in mass media and print advertising. Yet on social media, this boundary blurs further to become 'circulation/distribution/consumption'. How many people 'see' a post is decided by the social media site itself.

This is because across all major social media platforms, the main way users discover new content is not via search but through the platforms' personalized recommendation systems (Zhou et al. 2016). This is true of younger audiences, who Hassoun et al. found to have a 'preference for algorithmically-tailored information sources' (2023, 6). In 2022, a Senior Vice President at Google, Prabhakar Raghavan, mentioned that 'in [Google's] studies, something like almost 40% of young people, when they're looking for a place for lunch, they don't go to Google Maps or Search.... They go to TikTok or Instagram' (Moreno 2022; Raghavan 2022). The dataset underlying this statistic has not been published, but it points to the increasing prominence of 'social search'. This new trend sees people rely on their social media networks to find trusted information rather than turning to Google. Hassoun et al. also found that when looking for information, 'many [young users] felt that they would *encounter* important or personally relevant information, rather than needing to search for it' (2023, 6). This reliance on algorithmically curated content means it is therefore necessary to be cautious before ascribing the seeming popularity of a post to the communities and demographic groups that inhabit each platform.

Q4. What do the metrics you are using represent? Are they an accurate proxy for what you are trying to measure?

It is likely younger audiences will first and foremost search social media for cultural venues and heritage sites, presenting a difficulty for museums, the majority of whom are not on younger-leaning platforms. Simply being on Snapchat or TikTok is not enough to reach young audiences. Because users discover new content through the platform's recommendation system, museums are beholden to the types of content they prioritize. For example, TikTok's recommendation system is more likely to share your videos with users if you upload regularly, something that was lamented by our participants.

> TikTok is super hard work because the algorithm rewards people that post five times a week, every day. (P5)

---

[3] This also ignores more complex behaviours such as ironic engagement or sharing to deride, which are outside of the scope of this chapter, but are well worth an investigation if studying an online community (Yus, Colston, and Gibbs Jr 2023).

> I think you need such a big team to do these things successfully. And you really, you need to be doing it every day, twice a day, to get it done properly. So yeah, we can't do that at all. (P2)

This not only presents an issue in terms of resources but also what the recommendation systems prioritize is liable to change with no notice. One of the interviewees who had cultivated the largest online followings noted the fragility of their success.

> I think it's hard to be successful on the platform consistently. . . . You have to recognise that just because you understand it one week, doesn't mean that you can apply the same knowledge the next. You just have to be aware that everything's constantly evolving, and you've just got to try and stay on top of that. (P5)

Still others were baffled by the apparent changes to the platform – likely a result of changes to the recommendation system – but were unable to pinpoint what (Meese and Hurcombe 2021, 3). Three participants highlighted that their Facebook engagement had changed dramatically over the past five years, although none of them were unable to pinpoint exactly what had changed or why.

> I think Facebook is changing drastically, and what people are seeing from our own accounts is vastly different to what they *were* seeing. (P2)

Part of the difficulty this presents is that many museums may conflate adapting their content for their audience – which is considered good practice – with adapting their texts in such a way that the platform, not the audience, shares their content. For example, if audiences stop engaging with certain types of posts, staff may assume this is because they are no longer interested and not realize that their content is not being shown to users because the platform is 'pushing' a different type of post. Such misunderstandings are likely exacerbated by a lack of platform expertise in the majority of museums. As Michela Arnaboldi and Melisa Diaz Lema concluded in their study of Italian Archaeological museums, 'the platform itself also determines the rules of dissemination, and the percentage of followers who are shown the material may vary continuously' (2021, 12). The opaque recommendation system highlights the intermediary role that platforms play between museums and their audiences.

> Q5. Which mechanisms – aside from the content of the text – may be affecting its reception?

This is important because the companies that own platforms – and thus the recommendation systems they create – have very different priorities from those of museums. David Berman's prescient paper in 1995 highlighted the danger that 'we [museums] will be squeezed out of the Global Information Infrastructure (GII) by a commercial content that embodies very different values from our own' (1995,

'Conclusions'). For the most part, the priority of these companies is increasing the amount of time users spend on the site. In 2023, Meta saw their largest profit in years, which they attributed to an increase in the amount of time users were spending on Facebook (7 per cent increase) and Instagram (6 per cent increase) (Meta 2023). Mark Zuckerberg attributed this increase to 'recommendation improvements', which consequently have improved the company's advertising revenue (Paul 2023).

In this context, certain types of content do well. On Facebook, emotive posts are more likely to be shared, an effect that is increased for those that inspire negative emotions (Ji et al. 2019). This is seen in the dataset of Facebook posts and Tweets put together by the Mapping Museum team (Ballatore and Candlin 2023). In this data set, the most shared posts were dominated by war, conflict, and animals in distress.[4] Our previous research explored this trend in depth, using a case study of a emotive picture to showcase how this effect can be seen on museums' posts (Charlesworth, Warwick, et al. 2023). This raises the important question of how this may change audiences' relationships to museums and their content. Museums have been criticized for adopting an unemotive 'pedagogical register' (Crang and Tolia-Kelly 2010, 2315). But could social media become a driving force for a change in approach? It seems unlikely that social media would facilitate empathetic discussion about complicated and nuanced histories at scale. In the UK, museums have maintained a degree of public trust (Martin 2020; BritainThinks 2013). How might this be impacted if they started creating content tailored to the recommendation algorithm – either geared towards entertainment or in this darker vein?

Two further examples came up in interviews. One participant's most popular post regarded a distressing theft at the museum, and they recounted the way local groups on Facebook rallied to the museum's aid. While this was initially much appreciated, they also expressed discomfort at the way the story had been spread and co-opted by local organizers – in some cases it was used as justification to abuse a marginalized community living near the site. A more benign example of how much more engaging negative posts can be arose in a second interview.

> For example, if something difficult has happened ... it might be litter or something. There's a real reaction, 'oh no, we must do more' and 'we must do better' – an attempt to push that message forward. It's not against the site in any way, but simply just in a kind of 'come on people, let's do it', that kind of camaraderie, I guess. (P6)

Therefore, it is worth considering how the platforms that museums choose to publish on may affect the texts they publish. These content recommendation systems are 'black box' algorithms – the underlying mechanisms of which are not interpretable – no one, not even by their creators, can be certain why these algorithms recommend one video

---

[4] This also ignores more complex behaviours such as ironic engagement or sharing to deride, which are outside of the scope of this chapter, but are well worth an investigation if studying an online community (Yus, Colston, and Gibbs Jr 2023).

over another. While it is possible to identify key elements of a video, for example, the regularity of an account's posts, corporate entities do not share details of these ever-changing algorithms, which remain opaque to researchers and users alike (Bishop 2018; Cunningham, Craig and Silver 2016). If museums continue to pursue larger online audiences, they must strike a balance between creating texts that meet their organizational aims and those that meet the unspecified criteria of social media platforms.

It is not the case that museums have imported old approaches to publishing to new platforms, but there is a deeper similarity in publishing practices on social media and mass media, and that is in the power of selection. Bruce Williams and Michael Delli Carpini posited in 2000 that new media would circumvent the traditional gatekeeping mechanisms of print and television – 'if there are no gates, there can be no gatekeepers' (Williams and Delli Carpini 2000, 61). Yet, as Ralph Schroeder highlights, 'the way that content is tailored to audiences via search engines means that there are new gatekeeping mechanisms' (2018, 324). Recommendation algorithms pose a similar issue, and although the internet circumvents the upfront costs of print production, human selection is increasingly replaced by algorithmic curation (Vos 2015).

This is evermore relevant to researchers, as not only do these companies control the circulation and distribution of posts on the platform, but also access to the platform data. Researchers are required to use an application programming interface (API) to access the data; however, Daniel Thiele discovered that when using Meta's API, 'the data returned sometimes exhibits gaps or skewness for unclear reasons' (2022, 193). Furthermore, following the Cambridge Analytica scandal and increasing concerns about user privacy, there has been a move to reduce API services, most recently seeing the closure of Meta's Crowdtangle platform (Facebook 2024b; Venturini and Rogers 2019; Freelon 2018). Increasingly, it may be necessary for researchers to adopt web scraping techniques to collect or verify the data they require.

> Q6. What are the limitations on the data you have access to? Is the data you receive accurate?

Conclusion

The data and interviews paint a worrying picture of online publishing practices in museums. While the vast majority of the population is on social media, most museums have so far been unable to reach younger and more diverse audiences online (Ofcom 2022).

The issue is compound; many museums have transposed older modes of publishing onto social media, adopting an 'unassailable voice' that alienates twenty-first-century audiences (Walsh 1997). Yet, the majority of museums do not have the resources to experiment with video and upload schedules that are compatible with the established format of younger-leaning social media platforms such as TikTok. The social media landscape has shifted over the last decade, and high-quality video is now essential to growing online audiences, presenting a high barrier of entry to many organizations. Financial limitations prevent museums from investing in sufficient training, equipment and staff to build and maintain a sizeable audience. However, the attitude of management teams within an organization also shapes digital strategy and the level of investment available. The museums we spoke to had very limited digital resources, and social media was often relegated to the preserve of junior staff or volunteers. While some staff excelled in this role, it is highly contingent on the individual and their personal familiarity with the trends and communication norms of a platform.

However, looking more broadly at publishing practices, it is not merely a case of lack of resources. Audiences will not just 'discover' museum content by themselves. In order to reach new audiences, museums are required to deftly navigate the ever-changing demands of platforms' recommendation systems. The large companies that build these systems have different – and occasionally conflicting – priorities to museums, making the balancing of creative control and pragmatism immensely difficult. In this context, it is reasonable that some museums avoid social media due to ethical concerns or have apprehensions of how these platforms impact the way their audiences perceive them. For some collections and topics, social media is simply not conducive to open and educational discussions.

This raises the question of how we, as researchers, should engage with these platforms. Studying social media presents several intertwined obstacles: appropriate data collection and sampling, inaccurate measures of audience reception and an increasingly hostile relationship between social media owning conglomerates and academia. To help navigate this difficult field, we have posed the following questions to guide researchers new to social media data.

1. What are the limitations of your data? Who/What is missing?
2. How do the texts you are working with conform – or not, as the case may be – to conventions of the medium? What does this reflect about the priorities of the author?
3. What are the barriers to publishing, and has this influenced the frequency or location of publication? What would be the ideal place for publication be otherwise?
4. What do the metrics you are using represent? Are they an accurate proxy for what you are trying to measure?
5. Which mechanisms – aside from the content of the text – may be affecting its reception?
6. What are the limitations on the data you have access to? Is the data you receive accurate?

Bibliography

Abidin, Crystal. '#familygoals: Family Influencers, Calibrated Amateurism, and Justifying Young Digital Labor'. *Social Media + Society* 3, no. 2 (2017): 2056305117707191. https://doi.org/10.1177/2056305117707191.

Andersen, Kurt. 'The Age of Unreason'. *The New Yorker*, 26 January 1997.

Arnaboldi, Michela and Melisa L. Diaz Lema. 'The Participatory Turn in Museums: The Online Facet'. *Poetics* 89 (2021): 101536. https://doi.org/10.1016/j.poetic.2021.101536.

Ashton, Daniel and Karen Patel. 'Vlogging Careers: Everyday Expertise, Collaboration and Authenticity'. In *The New Normal of Working Lives*, 147–69. Edited by Stephanie Taylor and Susan Luckman. Cham: Springer International Publishing, 2018. https://doi.org/10.1007/978-3-319-66038-7_8.

Ballatore, Andrea and Fiona Candlin. 'A Geography of UK Museums'. *Transactions of the Institute of British Geographers* 48, no. 1 (2023): 213–29. https://doi.org/10.1111/tran.12578.

Barry, James M. and Sandra S. Graça. 'Humour Effectiveness in Social Video Engagement'. *Journal of Marketing Theory and Practice* 26, no. 1–2 (2018): 158–80. https://doi.org/10.1080/10696679.2017.1389247.

Bearman, David. 'Museum Strategies for Success on the Internet'. In Science Museum: Museums and the Web, 1995. http://web.archive.org/web/20010211004518/http://www.nmsi.ac.uk/infosh/bearman.htm.

Belfiore, Eleonora. '"Impact", "Value", and "Bad Economics": Making Sense of the Problem of Value in the Arts and Humanities'. *Arts and Humanities in Higher Education* 14, no. (2015): 95–110. https://doi.org/10.1177/1474022214531503.

Bishop, Sophie. 'Anxiety, Panic and Self-Optimization: Inequalities and the YouTube Algorithm'. *Convergence: The International Journal of Research into New Media Technologies* 24, no. 1 (2018): 69–84. https://doi.org/10.1177/1354856517736978.

Bode, Katherine. *A World of Fiction: Digital Collections and the Future of Literary History*. Edited by Julie Thompson Klein, Tara McPherson, and Paul Conway. Ann Arbor: University of Michigan Press, 2018. https://doi.org/10.1353/book.59018.

Bødker, Henrik. 'Stuart Hall's Encoding/Decoding Model and the Circulation of Journalism in the Digital Landscape'. *Critical Studies in Media Communication* 33, no. 5 (2016): 409–23. https://doi.org/10.1080/15295036.2016.1227862.

Bowen, Jonathan P. 'A Brief History of Early Museums Online'. *The Rutherford Journal* 3 (2010). https://web.archive.org/web/20231031205301/https://www.rutherfordjournal.org/article030103.html.

BritainThinks. 'Public Perceptions of – and Attitudes to – the Purposes of Museums in Society'. Museums Association, 2013. https://archive-media.museumsassociation.org/05042013-britain-thinks-3.pdf.

Candlin, Fiona and Jamie Larkin. 'What Is a Museum? A New Approach'. *Museum and Society* 18, no. 2 (2020): 115–31. https://doi.org/10.29311/mas.v18i2.3147.

Candlin, Fiona, Jamie Larkin, Andrea Ballatore and Alexandra Poulovassilis. 'The Missing Museums: Accreditation, Surveys, and an Alternative Account of the UK Museum Sector'. *Cultural Trends* 29, no. 1 (2019): 50–67. https://doi.org/10.1080/09548963.2019.1690392.

Chadwick, Andrew. *The Hybrid Media System: Politics and Power*, 2nd ed. New York: Oxford University Press, 2017.

Charlesworth, Ellen, Andrew M. Beresford, Claire Warwick and Leonardo Impett. 2023. 'Understanding Levels of Online Participation in the UK Museum Sector'. *Museum Management and Curatorship* 40, no. 2 (2023): 1–24. https://doi.org/10.1080/09647775.2023.2188478.

Charlesworth, Ellen, Claire Warwick, Leonardo Impett and Andrew M. Beresford. 'Designing for Audience Engagement Exploring the Use of Online Metrics in the GLAM Sector: Exploring the Use of Online Metrics in the GLAM Sector'. *Magazén*, no. 1 (2023), JournalArticle_13185. https://doi.org/10.30687/mag/2724-3923/2023/07/005.

Crang, Mike and Divya P Tolia-Kelly. 'Nation, Race, and Affect: Senses and Sensibilities at National Heritage Sites'. *Environment and Planning A: Economy and Space* 42, no. 10 (2010): 2315–31. https://doi.org/10.1068/a4346.

Cunningham, Stuart, David Craig and Jon Silver. 'YouTube, Multichannel Networks and the Accelerated Evolution of the New Screen Ecology'. *Convergence: The International Journal of Research into New Media Technologies* 22, no. 4 (2016): 376–91. https://doi.org/10.1177/1354856516641620.

Da, Nan Z. 'The Computational Case against Computational Literary Studies'. *Critical Inquiry* 45, no. 3 (2019): 601–39. https://doi.org/10.1086/702594.

Deakin, Tim. 'In Conversation with Adam Koszary, Head of Digital, The Audience Agency'. *MuseumNext, Marketing* (blog). 6 November 2021. https://web.archive.org/web/20231107110044/https://www.museumnext.com/article/people-behind-the-museums-adam-koszary-head-of-digital-the-audience-agency/.

Deodato, Joseph. 'The Patron as Producer: Libraries, Web 2.0, and Participatory Culture'. *Journal of Documentation* 70, no. 5 (2014): 734–58. https://doi.org/10.1108/JD-10-2012-0127.

Douglas, Ollie and Adam Koszary. 'The History Behind an Absolute Unit'. 10 April 2018. https://web.archive.org/web/20231107105416/https://merl.reading.ac.uk/blog/2018/04/history-behind-absolute-unit/.

Elliott, Philip and David Chaney. 'A Sociological Framework for the Study of Television Production'. *The Sociological Review* 17, no. 3 (1969): 355–75. https://doi.org/10.1111/j.1467-954X.1969.tb01191.x.

Facebook. 'Differences Between Page Views, Reach and Impressions'. 9 October 2024a. https://www.facebook.com/help/274400362581037.

Facebook. 'Research Tools and Datasets: CrowdTangle'. 16 August 2024b. https://web.archive.org/web/20240909204220/https://transparency.meta.com/en-gb/researchtools/other-datasets/crowdtangle/.

Falk, John and Lynn Dierking. *Learning from Museums: Visitor Experiences and the Making of Meaning*. New York: AltaMira Press, 2000.

Fletcher, Adrienne and Moon J. Lee. 'Current Social Media Uses and Evaluations in American Museums'. *Museum Management and Curatorship* 27, no. 5 (2012): 505–21. https://doi.org/10.1080/09647775.2012.738136.

Fransen-Taylor, Pamela and Bhuva Narayan. 'Challenging Prevailing Narratives with Twitter: An #AustraliaDay Case Study of Participation, Representation and Elimination of Voice in an Archive'. *Journal of Librarianship and Information Science* 50, no. 3 (2018): 310–21. https://doi.org/10.1177/0961000618769981.

Freelon, Deen. 'Computational Research in the Post-API Age'. *Political Communication* 35, no. 4 (2018): 665–8. https://doi.org/10.1080/10584609.2018.1477506.

Giannini, Tula and Jonathan P. Bowen. 'Museums and Digitalism'. In *Museums and Digital Culture: New Perspectives and Research*, 3–26. Edited by Tula Giannini and Jonathan P. Bowen. Springer Series on Cultural Computing. Cham: Springer, 2019.

Gillespie, Tarleton. 2010. 'The Politics of "Platforms"'. *New Media & Society* 12 (3): 347–64. https://doi.org/10.1177/1461444809342738.

Gooding, Paul, Melissa Terras and Claire Warwick. 'The Myth of the New: Mass Digitization, Distant Reading, and the Future of the Book'. *Literary and Linguistic Computing* 28, no. 4 (2013): 629–39. https://doi.org/10.1093/llc/fqt051.

Hall, Stuart. 'Encoding/Decoding'. In *Media and Cultural Studies: Keyworks*, rev. ed., 163–73. Edited by Meenakshi Gigi Durham and Douglas Kellner. Blackwell, 1980.

Hassoun, Amelia, Ian Beacock, Sunny Consolvo, Beth Goldberg, Patrick Gage Kelley, and Daniel M. Russell. 'Practicing Information Sensibility: How Gen Z Engages with Online Information'. In *Proceedings of the 2023 CHI Conference on Human Factors in Computing Systems*, 1–17. ACM, 2023. https://doi.org/10.1145/3544548.3581328.

Hogan, Bernie. 'The Presentation of Self in the Age of Social Media: Distinguishing Performances and Exhibitions Online'. *Bulletin of Science, Technology & Society* 30, no. 6 (2010): 377–86. https://doi.org/10.1177/0270467610385893.

Hooper-Greenhill, Eilean. *Museums and the Shaping of Knowledge*. Heritage. Abingdon: Routledge, 1992.

Hooper-Greenhill, Eilean. 'Museum Education: Past, Present and Future'. In *Towards the Museum of the Future*. Abingdon: Routledge, 1994.

Ignatow, Gabe and Laura Robinson. 'Pierre Bourdieu: Theorizing the Digital'. *Information, Communication & Society* 20, no. 7 (2017): 950–66. https://doi.org/10.1080/1369118X.2017.1301519.

Jenkins, Henry. *Confronting the Challenges of Participatory Culture: Media Education for the 21st Century*. The John D. and Catherine T. MacArthur Foundation Reports on Digital Media and Learning. Cambridge, MA: MIT Press, 2009.

Ji, Yi Grace, Zifei Fay Chen, Weiting Tao and Zongchao Cathy Li. 2019. 'Functional and Emotional Traits of Corporate Social Media Message Strategies: Behavioral Insights from S&P 500 Facebook Data'. *Public Relations Review* 45, no. 1 (2019): 88–103. https://doi.org/10.1016/j.pubrev.2018.12.001.

Kaplan, Andreas M. and Michael Haenlein. 'Users of the World, Unite! The Challenges and Opportunities of Social Media'. *Business Horizons* 53, no. 1 (2010): 59–68. https://doi.org/10.1016/j.bushor.2009.09.003.

Larkin, Jamie, Andrea Ballatore and Ekaterina Mityurova. 'Museums, COVID-19 and the Pivot to Social Media'. *Curator: The Museum Journal* 66, no. 4 (2023): 629–46. https://doi.org/10.1111/cura.12558.

Lievrouw, Leah A. 'Social Media and the Production of Knowledge: A Return to Little Science?' *Social Epistemology* 24, no. 3 (2010): 219–37. https://doi.org/10.1080/02691728.2010.499177.

MacDonald, George F. and Stephen Alsford. 'Conclusion: Toward the Meta-Museum'. In *The Wired Museum: Emerging Technology and Changing Paradigms*. American Association of Museums, 1997.

Martin, Emma. 'Trusting Museums'. *Journal of Museum Ethnography*, no. 33 (2020): 1–6.

Marwick, Alice E. *Status Update: Celebrity, Publicity, and Branding in the Social Media Age*. New Haven: Yale University Press, 2013.

Meese, James and Edward Hurcombe. 'Facebook, News Media and Platform Dependency: The Institutional Impacts of News Distribution on Social Platforms'. *New Media & Society* 23, no. 8 (2021): 2367–84. https://doi.org/10.1177/1461444820926472.

Meta. 'Meta Reports Third Quarter 2023 Results'. Financial Quarter Results 3rd Quarter 2023. Meta. https://web.archive.org/web/20231115131727/https://s21.q4cdn.com/399680738/files/doc_news/Meta-Reports-Third-Quarter-2023-Results-2023.pdf.

Moran, Gillian, Laurent Muzellec and Devon Johnson. 'Message Content Features and Social Media Engagement: Evidence from the Media Industry'. *Journal of Product & Brand Management* 29, no. 5 (2019): 533–45. https://doi.org/10.1108/JPBM-09-2018-2014.

Moreno, Johan. 'Google Is Evolving Search As Zoomers Use TikTok, Instagram To Find Things Online'. *Forbes*, 19 July 2022. https://web.archive.org/web/20231103133802/https://www.forbes.com/sites/johanmoreno/2022/07/19/google-is-evolving-search-as-zoomers-are-using-tiktok-instagram-to-find-things-online/.

NEMO. 'Survey On the Impact of the COVID-19 Situation on Museums in Europe: Final Report'. 2020. https://www.ne-mo.org/fileadmin/Dateien/public/NEMO_documents/NEMO_COVID19_Report_12.05.2020.pdf.
Nesta. 'Digital Culture 2017'. Digital Culture'. *Nesta*, 2017a. https://web.archive.org/web/20230626181420/https://media.nesta.org.uk/documents/digital_culture_2017.pdf.
Nesta. 'Digital Culture 2017: Museums'. Digital Culture. *Nesta*, 2017b. https://web.archive.org/web/20231114105411/https://media.nesta.org.uk/documents/dc2017_museums_factsheet.pdf.
Ngai, Eric W. T., Spencer S. C. Tao and Karen K. L. Moon. 2015. 'Social Media Research: Theories, Constructs, and Conceptual Frameworks'. *International Journal of Information Management* 35, no. 1 (2015): 33–44. https://doi.org/10.1016/j.ijinfomgt.2014.09.004.
Noehrer, Lukas, Abigail Gilmore, Caroline Jay and Yo Yehudi. 'The Impact of COVID-19 on Digital Data Practices in Museums and Art Galleries in the UK and the US'. *Humanities and Social Sciences Communications* 8, no. 1 (2021): 236. https://doi.org/10.1057/s41599-021-00921-8.
Ofcom. 'Online Nation, 2021 Report'. *Ofcom*, 2021. https://www.ofcom.org.uk/__data/assets/pdf_file/0013/220414/online-nation-2021-report.pdf.
Ofcom. 'Online Nation, 2022 Report'. Ofcom, 2022. https://www.ofcom.org.uk/__data/assets/pdf_file/0023/238361/online-nation-2022-report.pdf.
Parry, Ross, ed. *Museums in a Digital Age*. Leicester Readers in Museum Studies. London: Routledge, 2010.
Paul, Kari. 'Meta Earnings Report Reveals Most Profitable Quarter in Years'. *The Guardian*, 25 October 2023, sec. Tech. https://web.archive.org/web/20231115132015/https://www.theguardian.com/technology/2023/oct/25/meta-earnings-report-profitable-quarter-facebook.
Perez, Sarah. 'Google Exec Suggests Instagram and TikTok Are Eating Into Google's Core Products, Search and Maps'. *TechCrunch*, 12 July 2022. https://web.archive.org/web/20231103135316/https://techcrunch.com/2022/07/12/google-exec-suggests-instagram-and-tiktok-are-eating-into-googles-core-products-search-and-maps/.
Rabinovitch, Victor and Stephen Alsford. 'Museums and the Internet. Reflections on Eight Years of Canadian Experience.' In , 1–7. Canadian Museum of History. https://web.archive.org/save/https://www.historymuseum.ca/learn/research/resources-for-scholars/essays/museums-and-the-internet-eight-years-of-canadian-experience/.
Raghavan, Prabhakar. 'Organizing the World's Information'. 2022. https://web.archive.org/web/20231103133809/https://fortune.com/conferences/fortune-brainstorm-tech-2022/agenda.
Reynolds, Paul. 'Shelley Bernstein Talks about the Brooklyn Museum at the NLNZ'. *Peoplepoints* (blog), 11 March 2009. https://web.archive.org/web/20230202124606/http://www.peoplepoints.co.nz/2009/03/shellyey-bernstein-talks-about-brooklyn.html.
Rosen, Jay. 'The People Formerly Known as the Audience'. In *The Social Media Reader*, 13–16. Edited by Michael Mandiberg. New York: New York University Press, 2012. https://doi.org/10.18574/nyu/9780814763025.003.0005.
Schroeder, Ralph. 'Towards a Theory of Digital Media'. *Information, Communication & Society* 21, no. 3 (2018): 323–39. https://doi.org/10.1080/1369118X.2017.1289231.
Shirky, Clay. *Here Comes Everybody: The Power of Organizing Without Organizations*. New York: Penguin Press, 2008.
Speight, Catherine. 'Museums and Higher Education: A New Specialist Service?' In *Museums and Design Education: Looking to Learn, Learning to See*, 11–28. Edited by Beth Cook, Rebecca Reynolds, and Catherine Speight, eBook. Routledge, 2016.
The Audience Agency. 'Digital Audience Survey: Findings'. The Audience Agency. June 2021. https://www.theaudienceagency.org/evidence/digital-audience-survey-findings.

Thiele, Daniel. 'Pandemic Populism? How Covid-19 Triggered Populist Facebook User Comments in Germany and Austria'. *Politics and Governance* 10, no. 1 (2022): 185–96.

Trant, Jennifer. When All You've Got Is "The Real Thing": Museums and Authenticity in the Networked World'. *Archives and Museum Informatics* 12, no. 2 (1999): 107–25. https://doi.org/10.1023/A:1009041909517.

Underwood, Ted. 'Distant Reading and Recent Intellectual History'. In *Debates in the Digital Humanities 2016*, 530–3. Edited by Matthew K. Gold and Lauren F. Klein. Minneapolis: University of Minnesota Press, 2016.

Venturini, Tommaso and Richard Rogers. '"API-Based Research" or How Can Digital Sociology and Journalism Studies Learn from the Facebook and Cambridge Analytica Data Breach'. *Digital Journalism* 7, no. 4 (2019): 532–40. https://doi.org/10.1080/21670811.2019.1591927.

Vos, Tim P. 'Revisiting Gatekeeping Theory During a Time of Transition'. In *Gatekeeping in Transition*. Edited by Tim P. Vos and François Heinderyckx. New York: Routledge, Taylor & Francis Group, 2015.

Walker, Dominic. 'Towards the Collaborative Museum? Social Media, Participation, Disciplinary Experts and the Public in the Contemporary Museum'. University of Cambridge. Apollo - University of Cambridge Repository, 2016. https://doi.org/10.17863/CAM.7082.

Walmsley, Ben, Abigail Gilmore, Dave O'Brien and Anne Torreggiani. 'Culture in Crisis: Impacts of Covid-19 on the UK Cultural Sector and Where We Go from Here'. Culture in Crisis. The Centre for Cultural Value, 2022. https://www.culturehive.co.uk/CVIresources/culture-in-crisis-impacts-of-covid-19/.

Walsh, Peter. 'The Web and the Unassailable Voice'. *Archives and Museum Informatics* 11, no. 2 (1997): 77–85. https://doi.org/10.1023/A:1009086030363.

Warwick, Claire. 'The Jar of Moles: Twitter Celebrities and Visitors' Favourite'. In *Conversation Pieces: Inspirational Objects in UCL's Historic Collections*, 34–5. Edited by Mark Carnall. London: Shire Publications, 2013.

Williams, Bruce A. and Michael X. Delli Carpini. 2000. 'Unchained Reaction: The Collapse of Media Gatekeeping and the Clinton–Lewinsky Scandal'. *Journalism* 1, no. 1 (2000): 61–85. https://doi.org/10.1177/146488490000100113.

Wong, Amelia S. 'Ethical Issues of Social Media in Museums: A Case Study'. *Museum Management and Curatorship* 26, no. 2 (2011): 97–112. https://doi.org/10.1080/09647775.2011.566710.

Yus, Francisco, Herbert L. Colston and Raymond W. Gibbs Jr. 'Inferring Irony Online'. In *The Cambridge Handbook of Irony and Thought*, 160–80. Cambridge University Press, 2023. https://www.cambridge.org/core/books/abs/cambridge-handbook-of-irony-and-thought/inferring-irony-online/889E0C973CDED795A47046B893E325D9.

Zhou, Renjie, Samamon Khemmarat, Lixin Gao, Jian Wan and Jilin Zhang. 'How YouTube Videos Are Discovered and Its Impact on Video Views'. *Multimedia Tools and Applications* 75, no. 10 (2016): 6035–58. https://doi.org/10.1007/s11042-015-3206-0.

CHAPTER 13
DESCRIBING NEW MEDIA
STRATEGIES AND RECOMMENDATIONS FOR TEACHING STRUCTURED DATA IN MULTIDISCIPLINARY HUMANITIES CONTEXTS

Kristen Schuster

Knowledge organization is a rather broad field of work and theory, and my perspectives and claims are rooted in my background as a library and information science professional. I am a librarian who works in academia – which is a roundabout way of saying I teach knowledge organization more often than I do any practical cataloguing or collections management. However, teaching knowledge organization has given me a particular perspective on why standards, guidelines and good practices might hinder rather than facilitate interdisciplinary practices. Particularly interdisciplinary practices that use media. This is not to say we should do away with standards, but it is my way of saying I will not be describing or prioritizing a specific standard in this chapter. Instead, I reflect on the ways teaching has helped me approach knowledge organization as a flexible and iterative practice supported with discussion, debate, and troubleshooting.

The idea of flexible models for organizing information is by no means a new concept or a even new practice. Ontologies, as philosophical areas of work and technical practices within information science, are broadly speaking methods and practices that allow us to map, model and structure knowledge organization systems (Nurmikko Fuller et al. 2015; Jett et al. 2016; Thompson et al. 2020). I don't want to dwell on the semantic meaning of ontologies, but I would like to flag the fact that they are a fruitful area of interdisciplinary work on knowledge organization (Ribes and Bowker 2005; Bowker 2010; Edwards et al. 2011). There are quite a few ontologies to choose from, and my goal in this chapter is to highlight an ontology that has facilitated interdisciplinary work between librarians and book historians: Functional Requirements for Bibliographic Records (FRBRoo). My attention to FRBRoo is strategic because it is a model that has generated diverse practices within book history and is an opportunity to explore methods for integrating new media into digital humanities practice and research.

After discussing knowledge organization and FRBRoo, I will consider how media pose challenges and opportunities for integrating digital methods into book history projects. Interdisciplinary work is a negotiation of lexical meanings, which requires semantic disambiguation. The process of disambiguating meaning through knowledge organization does not, as one might assume, demand the adoption of hard and fast definitions and classification schema. Instead, there are opportunities for pluralities and nuance in meaning because of data models adopted in digital methods for book history. Understanding that disciplinary knowledge shapes understandings of how research generates data is an essential first step towards acknowledging the possibilities for data to be diverse.

Function before form: Knowledge organization, semantics and syntax

The histories of classification and categorization is one way to bridge digital and analogue approaches to book history and media studies (Bowker and Star 1999; Svenonius 2000; Adler 2016). The practical considerations of cataloguing and classification present opportunities to consider the ways we generate or reproduce meaning through acts of cataloguing (Turner 2016; Adler 2017). What, for example, do we mean by author? Is an author the individual who conceptualized a story? At first glance, yes. This definition would fit nicely with popular conceptualizations novelists, poets, essayists and so on. But what happens when we try to apply this definition to forms of new(er) media like fanfiction? The notion of originality throws a semantic spanner in the works, and it is the possibility of semantic ambiguity that makes knowledge organization a challenge. I would like to explore the possibilities for book history to act as an intellectual space that brings together different disciplinary perspectives on knowledge organization and, thus, facilitate more creative forms of cataloguing and classification. Book historians have quite a bit to say about authorship, and my example, while very simplistic, highlights the possibilities of using methods for studying print culture and readers to better understand media – particularly new forms of new media that use digital methods and tools to adapt, modify, manipulate and transform content.

Histories of printing and the book can help us understand why semantic ambiguities pose exciting challenges and offer important insights into new media and modes of communication (Hayles 2002, 2008; Bode 2017; Tonra 2021). This is because histories of the book invest in understanding the ways writing, editing, and publishing resist standardization because of the creative and innovative practices of authors and publishers. The framing of authorship and publishing as disruptive processes may seem at odds with the material reality of books. However, when we investigate the nuances of editions, translations and adaptations, we gain opportunities for forming networks and associations between styles, genres, and formats of print media (Radway 2009; Bode 2017; Johns 2019). In many ways, then, working with databases and metadata is a contemporary iteration of long-standing interests in the evolution of authorship and printing technologies.

There are quite a few interdisciplinary approaches to defining and theorizing knowledge organization. In information science Christine Borgman and Elaine Svenonious have put forward theories about the importance of semantic clarity and syntactic flexibility (Svenonius 1986; Borgman 2003; Svenonius 2004). Their work highlights the ways we use technology to reproduce culturally mediated forms of categorization and classification. Much of their work focuses on database technologies and offers critical insights into knowledge organization as a field of research and practice that contextualizes human-computer interactions as socially and culturally situated practices. Their work considers the ways semantics – the meaning of words – and disciplinary knowledge confound notions that technology might produce neutral or universal knowledge. Along these lines, Susan Star's work considers knowledge organization in even broader contexts (Star 1990; Bowker and Star 1999; Star 1999; Lampland and Star 2009). Her work takes principles of knowledge organization and applies them to everyday practices. Highlighting the often-mundane process of classifying in many ways demystifies the idea that technology somehow solves or enhances knowledge organization. The human factor involved in the production and circulation of information calls for interdisciplinary approaches to thinking about information needs. Let's look at two examples of semantic ambiguity – homonyms and synonyms – that showcase the ways book history and new media can help contextualize the importance (and complexity) of knowledge organization.

Homonyms occur when two words spelled the same way (and usually pronounced the same way) have different meanings (Svenonius 1986, 2004). What is a nook? This is a rather esoteric question, but in asking it, we can begin to think about the ways book history and theories of new media help us use descriptive language consistently – even when there are complex nuances in meaning. Is a nook a small convex space, or is it a proprietary digital e-reading device? The answer to each of these questions, broadly speaking, is yes. Each instance depends on a person's ability to infer meaning based on semantics and syntax, which in many ways depends upon statements being syntactically appropriate. For example, it is not too difficult to parse the semantics of nook in this sentence: They were reading *Pride and Prejudice* on their Nook in their favourite nook under the stairs. Capitalization of proper nouns and prepositions provides context to logically infer that nook and Nook are homonyms, whereas a sentence like this, I am reading a nook in a nook, provides little to no semantic context for us to infer meaning and seems rather bizarre.

Now let's consider an example of synonyms (when different words mean the same thing) (Svenonius 1986, 2004), and let's use author and creator as an example. Hans Christian Andersen wrote *The Little Mermaid*. Surely this means he is the author – he wrote the story and is credited with the creation of the characters and plot. If we search in a library database, or even generally with a web browser, metadata will indicate that he is the author of the story. However, on platforms like Disney+, Amazon and Netflix (where we are likely to find film adaptations of *The Little Mermaid*), there is no explicit search field for author. Director, producer, actors, yes, but not author. However, if you were to search on one of these streaming platforms for Hans Christian Andersen, you would likely retrieve various Little Mermaid and possibly even Snow Queen-inspired results. So, what is Hans Christian Andersen in relation to a film adaptation of his work? He is the creator of characters, the creator of a story, the inspiration for a film and so on. Creator and inspiration, then, become potential synonyms for author but who formulates the semantic equivalencies between synonyms?

My examples highlight a key point we should keep in mind while considering methods for creating, interpreting, and reusing information. Namely, we should remember that categorizing information can happen in several ways, for several reasons, which means there is no 'one system' to rule them all. Nor should there be – plurality in meaning is essential; semantics along with syntax helps us disambiguate meaning and challenge assumptions about accuracy and precision. Categories pose their own problems in terms of boundaries and limits to meaning, and interdisciplinary collaborations between information science and book history can help us theorize and operationalize effective systems for creating, manipulating and managing media.

Much of the library and information science curriculum for cataloguing and metadata will touch upon issues of semantic precision. Given the constraints of training sessions and academic semesters, it is rather difficult to really delve into the details of semantics. However, it is important to frame semantic ambiguity in terms that provoke reflective and inclusive work, and in the case of new media and book history, there are a few possible approaches:

> **Avoid using technical jargon** – semantics are daunting, particularly in the context of technical work like cataloguing. Providing definitions and examples that are straightforward and basic are more likely to encourage discussion and requests for more complex examples.
>
> **Provide examples that encourage discussions about practitioner and disciplinary trends, debates, and emerging practices.** There are quite a few exciting developments in database technologies and cataloguing standards. Connecting theoretical concepts to emerging areas of work and research is likely to encourage discussion and will help contextualize the value of more theory-oriented research.

So far, I have reviewed ideas used in library and information science to broadly contextualize knowledge organization. The examples I have used reflect my interest in building bridges between areas of scholarship that examine the ways technology produces knowledge *and* simultaneously create new modes of transmitting and transforming knowledge. Now, I would like to use the ideas and concepts outlined in the previous section to discuss classification and categorization in more detail. Looking into the ways production and reproduction of content of printed materials from a historical perspective offers insight into the social and cultural practices that shape demands for certain types of media (Radway 2009; Johns 2019). This, in turn, can help us consider the need for organizational systems and standards . . . which is to say, the importance of metadata. There are many types of metadata, and in this chapter, I will focus on descriptive metadata. Broadly speaking, descriptive metadata enables the consistent and coherent application of terms, phrases, and concepts to describe an information resource (Gilliland 2008). Often, information professionals will use controlled vocabularies to generate descriptive metadata. In general, controlled vocabularies are lists of terms, concepts, events, names, and places developed and maintained by professional bodies – they are a bit like dictionaries and thesauri because they provide preferred spellings, uses and applications of descriptive terminology (Gilliland 2008; Adler 2017).

While controlled vocabularies are far from perfect, comprehensive, or neutral, they are a resource that allows for practitioners from many different disciplines to review, select and implement descriptive terminology while creating metadata (Turner 2016; Adler 2017). When I am teaching introductory courses on metadata, I use the colour 'blue' as an example to illustrate how controlled vocabularies – particularly thesauri – can help us balance semantic accuracy with accessible terminology. If you search the Getty Art and Architecture Thesaurus using 'blue' a rather daunting list of terms comes back. However, if you click on one term and scroll down the entry a bit, you will see a hierarchical list that organizes different iterations of 'blue' into materials, concepts, pigments and so on.

Looking at the list in Figure 13.1, it is possible to identify appropriate terms and see how they relate to similar semantic instances. Testing out the appropriateness of different semantic instances in a museum or archive database is an opportunity to evaluate how precise your use of a term needs to be (or can be). I use the term blue as an example to encourage students to think about semantics in relation to their everyday practice. It is also a bit of an homage to the reference services joke that goes something like 'a patron walks up to the reference desk and asks for a book . . . the only thing they remember about it is that it is blue'.

Understanding the value of descriptive metadata and the role of controlled vocabularies is, in my opinion, essential in the organization, management and reuse of any media. Additionally, understanding the complexities of descriptive metadata is an excellent entrée to the technical aspects of information retrieval, which is essential in any conversation about AI, big data, and the semantic web. Earlier I discussed synonyms and homonyms and used creator, author, and nook as examples. Now, let's build on this example using principles of knowledge organization to structure this information in a logically consistent and coherent fashion so that it is retrievable.

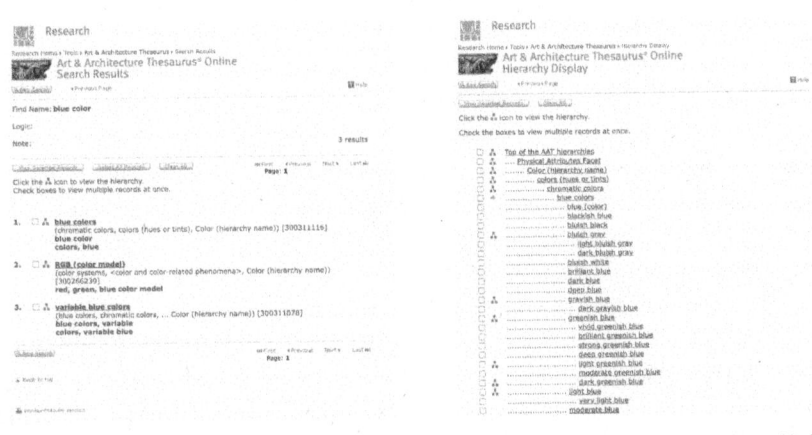

Getty Art and Architecture Thesaurus concise results for 'blue color'

Getty Art and Architecture Thesaurus hierarchical display for 'blue colors'

Figure 13.1 Getty Art and Architecture thesaurus results for 'Blue'.

We can use the example of author/creator and structure information about works inspired by Hans Christian Andersen in a way that enables basic information organization in local digital contexts (e.g. a database):

\<creator\> Walt Disney Company \</creator\>
\<contributor\> Andersen, Hans Christian (Danish writer and artist, 1805-1875) \</contributor\>
\<title\> Little mermaid (Motion picture: 1989) \</title\>
\<type\> motion pictures (visual works) \</type\>

We can refine this example by unambiguously indicating the source of our terminology used to describe our information object (a film):

\<creator xsitype= "dcterms:ULAN"\> Walt Disney Company \</creator\>
\<contributor xsitype= "dcterms:ULAN"\>
Andersen, Hans Christian (Danish writer and artist, 1805-1875) \</contributor\>
\<title xsitype= "dcterms:LCNAF"\> Little mermaid (Motion picture: 1989) \</title\>
\<type xsitype= "dcterms:AAT"\> motion pictures (visual works) \</type\>

Here I have used a combination of controlled vocabularies – the Getty Union List of Artist Names, the Getty Art and Architecture Thesaurus and the Library of Congress Name Authority Files. Using standardized forms of names is a core practice in knowledge organization because it ensures that the spelling, meaning and order of information making up a term are consistent. Consistency in turn ensures that information can be entered into database forms and parsed into machine-readable content. However, the selection of terms is by no means a simple process. Disciplinary knowledge and familiarity with user needs will influence which controlled vocabularies we consult, which database technologies we install, and what we expect users to know about information resources in a collection. Even in the humanities. Let's use the term 'print' as an example. Art historians may understand 'print' as a process that produces visual resources, while a book historian may understand 'print' as a process that produces textual resources. Here we have a homonym that context could disambiguate, and the role of controlled vocabularies is to provide catalogues with the means to make at least small inroads into minimizing ambiguity caused by homonyms.

What might this look like in practice? Let's return to our example of *The Little Mermaid*: We can further refine our metadata by indicating the source of the terms to identify what we are describing (e.g. our search fields in a database): use the example of author/creator and structure information about works inspired by Hans Christian Andersen in a way that enables basic information organization: in local digital contexts (e.g. a database):

```
<dc:creator source= "ULAN"> Walt Disney Company </dc:creator>
<dc:contributor source="ULAN">
Andersen, Hans Christian (Danish writer and artist, 1805-1875)
</dc:contributor>
<dc:title source="LCNAF"> Little mermaid (Motion picture : 1989) </dc:title>
<dcterm:type source="AAT"> motion pictures (visual works) </dcterm:type>
```

Here I have indicated that the Dublin Core Metadata Data Initiative (DCMI) is the source of terms for creator, contributor, title and format. As a resource for structuring information so that it is machine readable, Dublin Core attempts to provide a functional set of terms and guidelines for using terms to structure data. While it is by no means flawless, Dublin Core does provide accessible definitions for terms like 'creator' and 'title' and 'type'. The affordances of accessible definitions provide semantic clarity for what a term means so that it is easier to implement and use. Likewise, there are technical specifications that allow for syntax to be both human and machine readable. This can go a long way to ameliorating (or at least not adding to) semantic ambiguity for Web-accessible resources. For example, we can take the example of *The Little Mermaid* and make it retrievable in more complex digital environments like a search engine.

```
<dc:creator xsitype="dcterms:URI">
http://vocab.getty.edu/page/ulan/500115074
</dc:creator>
<dc:contributor xsitype="dcterms:URI">
http://vocab.getty.edu/page/ulan/500130208
</dc:contributor>
<dc:title xsitype="dcterms:URI">
http://id.loc.gov/authorities/names/n90699307
</dc:title>
<dcterm:type xsitype="dcterms:URI">
http://vocab.getty.edu/page/aat/300136900
</dcterm:type>
```

Here we have associated forms of meaning with an information object, and we have thus classified and categorized the media so that, in theory, we can find, identify, select and obtain a particular instance of Disney's *The Little Mermaid* inspired by the story authored by Hans Christian Andersen. The three iterations of *The Little Mermaid* are examples of how strategic approaches to knowledge organization. Focusing on the ways classification requires the use of semantics and syntax requires we begin thinking about standardization, and the ways standards can limit the flexibility of any system of knowledge production. However, the possibilities for innovation and creativity are not necessarily diminished. In fact, the possibility for technology, particularly technologies used to produce media can lead to interesting challenges for locating, using, reusing and even re-representing information and necessity living with plurality or instability in the semantic values of categories. This means we need to think of systems for information management, exchange and use that are flexible and scalable.

The technical possibilities of knowledge organization shouldn't be separated from the social practices of media and knowledge production (Bowker and Star 1999; Turner 2016; Adler 2017). Histories of print and book history are areas of research that can provide unique insights into the technologies and practices that facilitate (and require) classification and categorization (Hayles 2008; Johns 2019; Guldi 2023). Of particular interest for our discussion of knowledge organization and new media are the intersections between technologies that (re)produce content and technologies that facilitate information retrieval. Book history in particular offers insights into the value of studying editing practices for the sake of understanding the interpretive acts and creative decisions (Gitelman 2008; Ballatore and Natales 2016; Tonra 2021). Likewise, histories of print shed light onto the intersections between creative, political, and economic systems influencing understandings of authorship (Adler 2017; Johns 2019; Guldi 2023). In each instance, scholarship critically engages with concepts like creativity, originality, and authenticity. All of which are essential concepts to the organization, classification, and management of information and media. Scholarship about the histories of technologies by no means disregards the importance of metadata; however, it often relies on intensely technical details and specifications of computers and computer programmes. While these details are essential to the functional systems and infrastructures that enable information retrieval in increasingly complex ways, there is an equal need to think through how we are discussing technology in relation to the content we expect machines to sort, sift, process and increasingly interpret for us. The growing potential for technical infrastructures to facilitate sort, sift, process and interpret data has caused quite a bit of anxiety, and many of these anxieties seem to dance around perceptions of information being too complex to understand or users not being able to perceive and cope with nuances in meaning (Ng et al. 2021; James and Filgo 2023; Lo 2023). Counter to these notions, while teaching metadata I have learned that good practices aimed at introducing and contextualizing technical concepts have the ability to help interdisciplinary scholars with varying technical skills to contribute to the creation of sustainable, versionable, and user-friendly descriptive metadata. To this end, while writing guidelines for metadata creation and management, it is important to:

- **Balance technical precision with commonly used terms** – new media and printing techniques may be debated and semantically diverse within academic disciplines, or widely understood within digital preservation communities . . . but this does not mean users and new the field academics or practitioners will be familiar with the nuances and particularities of file formats, media genres and historical terminologies for printing.
- **Don't assume that a term in a controlled vocabulary will be familiar to experts.** Working with database design and user interface experts can help you understand ways to catalogue resources using technical terminology, while also developing accessible interfaces and mechanisms for information retrieval.

- **Explore information organization strategies outside of your everyday practices and expertise.** While your disciplinary and professional knowledge can contribute to the development or implementation of knowledge organization practices, it is important to remember other people have expertise that might be of use. Either because it adds technical, social, or cultural nuance to your understanding of media, or because it presents new information about how people perceive and engage with the media you are managing.
- **Write down workflows, standards, good practices, and resources you regularly reference and implement.** Map these practices onto the strategies, mandates and guidelines promoted or mandated by your employer.

While my recommendations seem like common sense, it is important to remember that the knowledge, expertise and resources you are familiar with may not be obvious to someone new to a role or to someone with different technical, professional and disciplinary training. So, sharing common sense, negotiating meaning(s) and documenting strategies for organizing and managing semantic and syntactic information that describes different types of media.

I have spent quite a bit of time discussing how semantic ambiguity (homonyms and synonyms) can cause confusion. The possibility for misunderstanding then requires us to think about meaning and sense making from many different points of view. To this end, I would like to add another layer of nuance to our discussion of knowledge organization: FRBRoo. The Functional Requirements for Bibliographic Records (FRBRoo) is a set of conceptual models developed by the International Federation of Library Associations (IFLA) Cataloguing Section Working Group (Tillet 2005). The FRBRoo conceptual models outline an approach to logically articulating relationships between items, creators, and owners of creative works. FRBRoo emerged at a time of rapid and dynamic change in information communication technologies. The advent of linked data, excitement about semantic web technologies and the explosion of media call for more dynamic methods for classifying and cataloguing (Evans et al. 2020; Gartner 2021). Knowledge organization and information retrieval, while always complex, became increasingly dependent on interdisciplinary practices capable of blending computer science and library science methods and practices to develop infrastructures capable of supporting complex and increasingly unstructured information-seeking practices. The ability for databases to facilitate finding, selecting, and obtaining information increasingly required flexible and iterative and polysemous expressions of key terms like author, creator, contributor, and editor. Ontologies like FRBRoo have become essential to developing information architectures for complex information processing systems (CIDOC CRM 2024). So, what does the FRBRoo Group 1 entity model look like?

The diagram represented in Figure 13.2 is not terribly intuitive – between terminology, arrows and descriptions, there are quite a few different features we need to consider. As we work through this diagram, I will use *Alice in Wonderland* as an example.

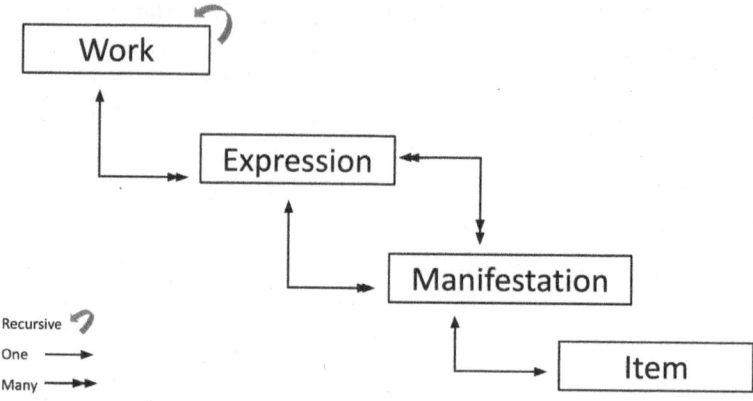

Figure 13.2 FRBRoo Group 1 entities.

Work

A work is intangible. The printed editions of *Alice in Wonderland* did not just appear one day. Lewis Carroll's creative process of imaging characters and a plot constitutes a Work. The potentially immaterial qualities of a work give us a context for thinking about the importance of identifying and describing the ideas, artistic movements, genres, and social connections that enabled Lewis Carroll to imagine and conceptualize *Alice in Wonderland*. How then might we describe a Work? We can start by saying that a Work has a creator, and in this instance Lewis Carroll is the creator of *Alice in Wonderland*. You'll notice that I used a particular syntax in this example – A Work has a creator, and a Work has a genre are examples of triples where we have a subject, predicate and object. In this instance, Lewis Carroll is our subject, *is* functions as a predicate and the Creator is our object. This semantic structure establishes the basic syntax for mapping out relationships we might express in a Linked Open Data (LoD).

Expression

Expressions are instances of a work. Expressions can take the form of notes, drafts, ephemera and so on that represent the concepts and ideas developed in a work. *Alice in Wonderland* evolved through many drafts and revisions – these drafts constitute Expressions. An expression will not actually be the edition of a book we pick up and read or even a complete or coherent draft sent to an editor or publisher, which is rather frustrating because it means we still don't have what we could easily identify as *Alice in Wonderland*. However, the use of semantic triples can help us map out relationships between different types of media to conceptualize how an idea takes shape and evolves. For example, sketches of characters, letters to friends and notes on plot are all semantic triples that can help us organize and manage relationships between ephemera that contribute to the development of the story we know as *Alice in Wonderland*. The flexibility of what might constitute an Expression allows us to bring in theories of new media to evaluate what edited volumes and editorial projects negotiate and include in different editions of Lewis Carroll's classic story.

Manifestation

A Manifestation is an instance of an Expression. While an Expression is the beginnings of a creative process coming into physical form, a Manifestation is the outcome of drafts, revisions and so on. The important thing to keep in mind is that a Manifestation is not a single object, copy or item. It is more of a placeholder to represent editions, series or runs, which means it is a way to acknowledge that multiple versions of an Expression might come into being either through a Creator's actions or later acts of interpretation and editing. So, what might this look like as a triple? *Manifestations have editions*. Editions, it is important to note, do not have to be traditional forms of print or even print based. An edition can be an opera score, the plans for an installation or multimedia interpretation of a text. This is where digital methods developed in book history contexts, and the multidisciplinary approaches adopted in the digital humanities can help us conceptualize the value and complexity of media (be it analogue or digital).

Item

An Item is an instance of a Manifestation, or in more direct terms: An Item is the copy of an edition we find on a library or bookshop shelf, or a specific musical performance, or a specific copy of a recording of a film. If Manifestations *have Editions*, and an *Item is an instance of a Manifestation*, in the case of *Alice in Wonderland*, we could say that *Alice in Wonderland* illustrated by Chris Riddell is a manifestation of Lewis Carroll's creation, and the copy on my bookshelf in West London (where I happen to be working while writing this chapter) is an Item. (See Figure 13.3)

The FRBRoo Group 1 Entities exist alongside similar models that map out relationships between people and descriptive terms and subjects. It is beyond the scope of this chapter to outline these additional models, but in general it is valuable to acknowledge that practices designed for bibliographic description have encouraged librarians, book historians and digital humanities practitioners to collaboratively engage in discussion about how we can represent complex relationships between ideas, editions, to hand copies alongside relationships between authors, editors and publishers. This gives us a good framework for thinking about what we want metadata to do, and the infrastructures we need to operationalize our expectations. I have a few recommendations that will be of use to colleagues who are both new to digital methods and established in their practices and managing teams with varying disciplinary backgrounds.

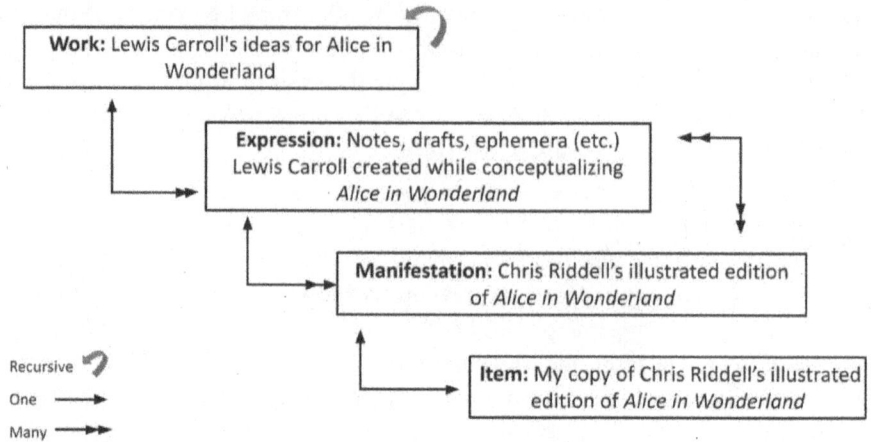

Figure 13.3 FFRBR Group 1 entities as *Alice in Wonderland*.

- **Start small** – identifying relationships between works, expressions, manifestations, and items takes time and practice. Starting with media you are familiar with (possibly even an expert on) will help you identify the most appropriate terminology to use to create descriptions and to express relationships. As you gain confidence in the practices you are developing, you can develop more complex connections and relationships.

- **Develop documentation** – Consistency is essential to any knowledge organization process because it increases the likelihood of replicating procedures for selecting and entering descriptive and technical information about media. Consistency is not at all easy to implement, but writing down basic guidelines that reference or point to more detailed instructions can be immensely helpful.

- **Test information retrieval** – FRBRoo works with a very particular form of logic that is not always easy to follow. While you might gain proficiency describing, cataloguing, and organizing media following these logics, that doesn't mean they will work for everyone (or every database or search engine). Check to see how information you have organized is retrieved and represented in the digital tools, platforms, or environments you are working in.

- **Share your experiences** – There is no one perfect way to organize information, work with media or develop digital methods. Talking about your practices, opinions and experiences is important. Not only because you can receive feedback on your decisions, but you might also learn a few new things along the way.

Postscript: The limits of categories and classification

Much of the discussion and review in the chapter has a positive (or academically neutral) tone. I won't lie, I love categories and I love classification systems. However, as I have learned about different cataloguing standards and managed different database systems, I have become aware of the limits of information organization practices. So, I would like to take a moment to reflect on some of the challenges and limitations of cataloguing, classification, and knowledge organization. This is by no means a rejection of the theories, work, and practices that I love ... but it is an acknowledgement of a need for research and social justice informed practices that embrace new forms of media and challenge hierarchies that affect the adoption and dissemination of technology-enhanced information processing.

My interest in semantics and syntax has provided a starting point for interrogating and examining the potential for interdisciplinary collaborations between library and information scientists and book historians to conceptualize more creative descriptions of media. Identifying approaches to understanding the production of knowledge through the examination of media and understanding the historical contexts for newness provide robust frameworks and methodologies for destabilizing assumptions about meaning, function and value. While semantics and syntax offer systems for recognizing the meaning and function of words, networked and digital contexts require information management and media theories recognize the possibilities for complex and plural meanings. It also requires critically examining the possibility of reproducing problematic or harmful assumptions about meaning, value and purpose. Interdisciplinary work and critical perspectives from book historians and information scientists can shed light on the assumptions and biases that reproduce problematic and/or uncontested meanings.

Bibliography

Adler, Melissa. 'The Case for Taxonomic Reparations'. *KO Knowledge Organization* 43, no. 8 (2016): 630–40.

Adler, Melissa. *Cruising the Library: Perversities in the Organization of Knowledge.* Fordham University Press, 2017.

Ballatore, Andrea, and Simone Natale. 'E-readers and the Death of the Book: Or, New Media and the Myth of the Disappearing Medium'. *New Media & Society* 18, no. 10 (2016): 2379–94.

Bode, Katherine. 'The Equivalence of "Close" and "Distant" Reading; or, Toward a New Object for Data-rich Literary History'. *Modern Language Quarterly* 78, no. 1 (2017): 77–106.

Bode, Katherine. 'Looking (Im) properly: Women Objectifying Men's Bodies in Contemporary Australian Women's Fiction'. In *Women Constructing Men: Female Novelists and Their Male Characters*, 185–206. Edited by Katharina Rennhak and Sarah S. G. Frantz. Lexington Books, 2000.

Borgman, Christine L. *From Gutenberg to the Global Information Infrastructure: Access to Information in the Networked World.* MIT Press, 2003.

Bowker, Geoffrey. 'A Plea for Pleats'. In *Deleuzian Intersections: Science, Technology, Anthropology*, 123–38. Edited by Casper Bruun Jensen and Kjetil Rödje. Berghahn Books, 2010.

Bowker, Geoffrey and Susan Leigh Star. *Sorting Things Out: Classification and Its Consequences.* MIT Press, 1999.

CIDOC Conceptual Reference Model retrieved from https://www.cidoc-crm.org/.

Edwards, Paul N., Matthew S. Mayernik, Archer L. Batcheller, Geoffrey C. Bowker and Christine L. Borgman. 'Science Friction: Data, Metadata, and Collaboration'. *Social Studies of Science* 41, no. 5 (2011): 667–90.

Evans, Rachel S., Robin Fay and Linh Uong. 'Linked Data for the Real World: Leveraging Metadata for Cataloging'. Presentations, 2020. https://digitalcommons.law.uga.edu/speeches/207.

Gartner, Richard. *Metadata in the Digital Library: Building an Integrated Strategy with XML*. London: Facet Publishing, 2021.

Gilliland, Anne J. 'Setting the Stage'. *Introduction to Metadata* 2, no. 1–19 (2008): 7.

Gitelman, Lisa. *Always Already New: Media, History, and the Data of Culture*. MIT Press, 2008.

Guldi, Jo. *The Dangerous Art of Text Mining: A Methodology for Digital History*. Cambridge University Press, 2023.

Hayles, N. Katherine. *Electronic Literature: New Horizons for the Literary*. University of Notre Dame Press, 2008.

Hayles, N. Katherine. *Writing Machines*. MIT Press, 2002.

James, Amy B. and Ellen Hampton Filgo. 'Where Does ChatGPT Fit Into the Framework for Information Literacy? The Possibilities and Problems of AI in Library Instruction'. *College & Research Libraries News* 84, no. 9 (2023): 334.

Jett, Jacob, Terhi Nurmikko-Fuller, Timothy W. Cole, Kevin R. Page and J. Stephen Downie. 'Enhancing Scholarly Use of Digital Libraries: A Comparative Survey and Review of Bibliographic Metadata Ontologies'. In *Proceedings of the 16th ACM/IEEE-CS on Joint Conference on Digital Libraries*, 35–44. IEEE, 2016.

Johns, Adrian. *Piracy: The Intellectual Property wars from Gutenberg to Gates*. University of Chicago Press, 2019.

Lampland, Martha and Susan Leigh Star, eds. *Standards and Their Stories: How Quantifying, Classifying, and Formalizing Practices Shape Everyday Life*. Cornell University Press, 2009.

Lo, Leo S. 'The CLEAR Path: A Framework for Enhancing Information Literacy Through Prompt Engineering'. *The Journal of Academic Librarianship* 49, no. 4 (2023): 102720.

Nurmikko-Fuller, Terhi, Kevin R. Page, Pip Willcox, Jacob Jett, Chris Maden, Timothy Cole, Colleen Fallaw, Megan Senseney and J. Stephen Downie. 'Building Complex Research Collections in Digital Libraries: A Survey of Ontology Implications'. In *Proceedings of the 15th ACM/IEEE-CS Joint Conference on Digital Libraries*, 169–72. Association for Computing Machinery, 2015.

Ng, Davy Tsz Kit, Jac Ka Lok Leung, Kai Wah Samuel Chu and Maggie Shen Qiao. 'AI Literacy: Definition, Teaching, Evaluation and Ethical Issues'. *Proceedings of the Association for Information Science and Technology* 58, no. 1 (2021): 504–9.

Radway, Janice A. *Reading the Romance: Women, Patriarchy, and Popular Literature*. University of North Carolina Press, 2009.

Ribes, David and Geoffrey C. Bowker. 'A Learning Trajectory for Ontology Building'. In *Annual Knowledge and Organizations Conference*. 2005.

Star, Susan Leigh. 'The Ethnography of Infrastructure'. *American Behavioral Scientist* 43, no. 3 (1999): 377–91.

Star, Susan Leigh. 'Power, Technology and the Phenomenology of Conventions: On Being Allergic to Onions'. *The Sociological Review* 38, no. 1_suppl (1990): 26–56.

Svenonius, Elaine. 'The Epistemological Foundations of Knowledge Representations'. *Library Trends* 52, no. 3 (2004).

Svenonius, Elaine. *The Intellectual Foundation of Information Organization*. MIT Press, 2000.

Svenonius, Elaine. 'Unanswered Questions in the Design of Controlled Vocabularies'. *Journal of the American Society for Information Science* 37, no. 5 (1986): 331–40.

Thompson, Luke, Bin Hu, Ruth Timme, Elisha M. Wood-Charlson et al. *Introduction to Metadata and Ontologies: Everything You Always Wanted to Know About Metadata and Ontologies (but Were Afraid to Ask)*. Lawrence Berkeley National Laboratory (LBNL), Berkeley, CA (United States). National Microbiome Data Collaborative (NMDC), 2020.

Tillett, Barbara. 'What is FRBR? A Conceptual Model for the Bibliographic Universe'. *The Australian Library Journal* 54, no. 1 (2005): 24–30.

Tonra, Justin, ed. 'Book History and Digital Humanities in the Long Eighteenth Century'. Special issue of *Eighteenth Century Studies* 54 no. 4 (2021): 765–83.

Tonra, Justin. *Write My Name: Authorship in the Poetry of Thomas Moore*. Routledge, 2020.

Turner, Hannah. 'Critical Histories of Museum Catalogues'. *Museum Anthropology* 39, no. 2 (2016): 102–10.

CHAPTER 14
HONEY, AI SHRUNK THE ARCHIVE
ARTIFICIAL INTELLIGENCE AS COMPRESSION ALGORITHM
Jon Ippolito

The digital age reshaped the foundations of knowledge; generative AI promises to overturn them completely. The advent of academic repositories like ARTstor and Europeana alongside the quotidian world wide web challenged the primacy of scholarly narrative in the tradition of authors like Erwin Panofsky and Jacques Derrida. Yet while these database-driven methods offered new ways to discover knowledge buried in primary sources, large language models threaten to replace sources with a compacted surrogate that generates rather than discovers knowledge. Understanding the statistical engine behind these lossy substitutes for the archive can help us choose the best strategies for combating the homogenizing tendencies of transformer models.

How AI bends the archival arc

Scholarship has always had a presumed trajectory that starts with a collection of data. Exactly what the researcher discovers in her purview depends on the discipline: an astronomer might find evidence of a black hole in a star's spectrographic signature, while a historian might find evidence of fierce anticlericalism in something William Blake scribbled in a manuscript margin. Domain specifics notwithstanding, the researcher is likely then to hunt for additional evidence in the same range, or contrast the discovery with discoveries from other ranges, or wrap the discovery in an explanatory framework. Regardless of which 'archive' a scholarly process starts with, its endpoint has traditionally been some sort of publication, whether gracing the pages of the *Antioch Review* or the *Open Journal of Astrophysics*.

From Galileo's telescope to Anne Kelly Knowles's viewshed analyses, emerging technologies and techniques have forged spurs alongside this well-worn path and expanded the scope of valid evidence. In 1999, media scholar Lev Manovich pointed to the displacement of a traditional narrative approach to humanities scholarship by the increasing influence of databases, which culminated a decade later in an academic obsession with 'big data' (Manovich 1999). From ArcGIS to the blockchain, data structures became both a new ground for archival research as well as a potential archive in which to publish it.

Creators have traditionally fed the opposite stream of this cultural trajectory. Photos were shot with a camera and then digitized, or born digital when snapped with someone's phone; images selected by the photographer then circulated through the Internet via Instagram or Flickr; those deemed sufficiently notable to preserve for the future made their way into an archive or museum. At that final destination, conservators ingested them into databases or preservation software, and thus presumably into the historical record. Rather than starting with a collection and producing original research as researchers do, artists start by producing original research, publishing what they deem worthy of public view in a gallery or online, and then (with sufficient talent and luck) selling or donating their work to a public or private collection (Blais and Ippolito 2006).

As artist Eryk Salvaggio points out, the advent of generative AI could more than any other recent technology bend the archival trajectory for both scholars and creators back upon itself.[1] This bend is not a distortion due to bias in the archival collection – a valid concern in itself – but a flip of the arrow of contingency. Whether trained on a highly curated photo collection or the billion web pages of the Common Crawl, large language models start by atomizing content in the archive and then compressing it into an engine that can produce new artefacts derived from that original content. Salvaggio has described generative AI as 'an archive in reverse', in that culture produced by AI actually starts with curation (an archive of source material) and ends with creation (an artefact generated from this archive). The implications of a twist in the archival trajectory could be dramatic for both scholars and creators alike, calling into question deeply held beliefs about ground truth and creativity.[2]

The shifting repositories of information

The word 'scholarship' has its roots in the concept of an illuminating conversation,[3] so it's natural that the original paradigm for conveying knowledge would be discursive. Memory palaces and other artifices provided information architectures – almost literally – to help bards recall the scenes of a story or parts of an argument. Over time, as these narratives evolved into written forms, their genres multiplied and became codified, but

---

[1] Technically, Salvaggio only described the reversal of the archival trajectory for creators: 'Generative AI is digital humanities in reverse. Any description of an archive becomes a formula for the production of similar content. This reversal makes digital humanities an essential lens for understanding the cultural questions surrounding AI. To do that, we have to start imagining archives in reverse.' Threads, 3 September 2024. https://www.threads.net/@cyberneticforests/post/C eCLsUIR6S, accessed 16 November 2024.

[2] This fact complicates both sides of the copyright debate, adding a new wrinkle to disputes over the nature of authenticity and attribution. At the time of writing, US law provides no recourse or control over the creation and distribution of these automated offspring.

[3] The Greek word σχολή (skholḗ), which originally meant spare time, later became 'conversations and the knowledge gained through them during free time; the places where these conversations took place'. 'Scholar,' Wikipedia, https://en.wiktionary.org/wiki/scholar, accessed 16 November 2024.

the overt goal was generally to convey complex ideas in an accessible manner (even if the covert goal might have been to dominate a debate or rise in an intellectual hierarchy).

Manovich's 'Database as Symbolic Form' argues that the rise of software shifted the paradigm of knowledge stockpiles from narrative to database. He posits that the emergence of databases decentered the academic narrative in favour of a more modular, data-driven approach to scholarship. Manovich states, 'If after the death of God (Nietzsche), the end of grand Narratives of Enlightenment (Lyotard) and the arrival of the Web (Tim Berners-Lee) the world appears to us as an endless and unstructured collection of images, texts, and other data records, it is only appropriate that we will be moved to model it as a database'. In Manovich's view, the database becomes a matrix for grounding scholarship, for which coding an interface to a database on Salman Rushdie might be more significant than writing an essay about his literary relevance.[4]

In the mid-2000s, cryptocurrency enthusiasts popularized distributed ledgers, decentralized kinds of databases that evolved into programmable blockchains like Ethereum. These platforms enabled artists and scholars to create smart contracts that modify, fork, or merge records upon access, transforming transactions into dynamic components of the creative process. For the most experimental crypto-artists, these transactions are not mere exchanges but integral to their medium. While some archives experimented with blockchains, many faced challenges due to their computationally intensive nature and inherent risks.[5]

The latest evolution in accumulated knowledge is generative AI, epitomized by large language models like ChatGPT. These models consolidate vast amounts of online knowledge into standalone chatbots, offering a new paradigm of interaction. However, this shift raises concerns about Euro-ethnic bias and the limitations of accessing the deep web (see Bergman 2000). Large language models predict the likelihood of a word following a given sequence of words, using complex neural networks to analyse and generate human-like text. More cogent to a discussion about the evolution of cultural repositories, however, is the fact that ChatGPT's one-field interface presents it as an all-knowing oracle,[6] threatening to replace academic scholars and creative professionals with a superior intelligence that digests and synthesizes the sum of human knowledge.

---

[4]Many digital scholarly editions provide comprehensive access to authorial works and related materials. Beyond database interfaces, computational humanities projects like the Mining the Dispatch project use data analysis to extract insights from cultural records, presenting findings through charts and visualizations that reveal patterns and trends that otherwise might be hidden in traditional narratives. See also Miller Prosser's essay in this volume (Chapter 5) for more on the database paradigm in textual editing.

[5]Notable examples include the Zentrum für Kunst und Medien (ZKM), which accidentally burned two valuable NFTs by sending them to an inaccessible wallet; and ARCHANGEL, an initiative of the University of Surrey with the UK National Archives that explored blockchain's potential as a 'trusted archive of digital public records' before recognizing its limitations.

[6]For more on how chatbot interfaces obscure the vagaries of generative AI models, see Ippolito (2024b).

Yet this personification conceals mechanistic frailties of actual large language models, from data poisoning to reinforcing stereotypes to numerous other downsides.[7]

Beyond the animate AI metaphor

To reconcile the interdependence of generative AI and the archive, we need to challenge some prevailing assumptions about the lifelike qualities of large language models. When DALL-E 2 and ChatGPT exploded on the scene in April and November 2022, respectively, these tools seemed unlike anything that came before – not just because they vaulted ahead of prior attempts to generate images and text with artificial intelligence, but also because the astronomical scale of these systems – trained on billions of documents found on the web – was all but incomprehensible to users accustomed to managing a few thousand documents on their hard drives. The marketing rhetoric of OpenAI and its successors in the AI industry fed the impression that these tools had no precedent, often falling back on anthropomorphic metaphors to reinforce the impression that never-before-seen beings were emerging from torrents of matrix multiplication. In Silicon Valley's view, AI was 'growing up fast' and 'would understand exactly what you wanted, and it would give you the right thing' (Marr 2017).

At the same time, several critics have warned that envisioning algorithms as children or superorganisms can foster misunderstandings about their capabilities and limitations (Bender et al. 2021; Bali et al. 2024). When we describe AI systems as 'thinking' or 'understanding', we risk attributing emotions, intentions, and consciousness to systems that are no less mechanistic than a roulette wheel. It's a short hop from presuming AI has consciousness to presuming it has a conscience. That could result in misplaced trust in AI agents to make moral or ethical decisions without human oversight, whether betting on the stock market or reading an x-ray.

Anthropomorphism also obscures accountability. For years, vehicle companies neglected to mention the remote assistance provided to their so-called 'autonomous' vehicles by humans behind the scenes.[8] The very term 'self-driving cars' insinuates that these machines have a self, and presumably therefore free will and possibly even an ethical compass. On the flip side, humanizing AI also risks exacerbating fears about it surpassing human intelligence, fueling dystopian narratives about killer robots that can hinder productive discourse about the integration of AI into society.

As complex as a trillion-parameter large language model might be, we are only obscuring its mechanism by comparing it to an organism or superbeing. Organic life is complex on a vast array of levels, from the electron-transport chain in the mitochondria of a cell to insulin's effect on the bloodstream to the unique body language of Italian

---

[7]For a compact list of potential AI downsides, see the IMPACT RISK framework created by the author at https://AI-Impact-Risk.com, accessed 15 November 2024.
[8]Compare to Metz (2024).

gestures. Chatbots are complex on pretty much one level: the billions of matrix parameters involved in training and generating outputs. To some observers, LLMs exhibit emergent linguistic or even conceptual structures. But these structures are not the product of a heterogeneous architecture. They are the product of a homogenous mechanism that has more in common with the messiness of a bowl of spaghetti than the intricacy of a living cell. And since these models are ultimately assemblages of wire and silicon, comparing their behaviour to actual machines might be more appropriate than reaching for animistic comparisons. And their mechanistic counterparts have the virtue of being a lot simpler than organic ones.

AI as a cup of coffee

Emily Bender's provocative disparagement of large language models as 'stochastic parrots' (Bender et al. 2021) has the benefit of countering the narrative of large language models as superhuman sentients. Unfortunately, this metaphor's association with another life form – even if one associated more with meaningless chatter than intelligent conversation – distracts from the mechanistic qualities of generative AI. The 'stochastic' half of her moniker, on the other hand, reflects a core tenet of how generative AI works. Stochastic systems are composed of so many random bits that their microstates can't be predicted but its overall statistics can. So let's consider something less animate and more stochastic for our metaphor: a cup of coffee.[9]

This metaphor goes deeper than caricaturing AI models as 'full of hot air' or capable of 'burning their users'. Imprecise metaphors aside, a cup of coffee, bowl of soup, or even a balloon shares mathematical properties with a large language model that help reveal what's going on inside generative AI's 'magic box'. Mugs of coffee and large language models are both thermodynamic systems that have achieved a state of equilibrium thanks to trillions of probabilistic interactions. For coffee, these interactions are molecules of caffeine and milk that move in seemingly random directions in a physical cup. For an LLM, they are numerical weights that move in seemingly random directions in a mathematical space.

While such desultory beginnings would seem to yield nothing more than useless randomness, applying a constraint to such 'stochastic' systems can rein in these haphazard processes and, surprisingly, deliver the entire state to a stable equilibrium. For a drink, this constraint is nature's commandment that drives all systems to get cooler and more disordered; it's why your morning brew gets cold and the 'latte art' poured by your barista eventually dissipates.

---

[9]Educator Lance Cumming also draws an analogy between AI and coffee, though he describes temperature as variation in bean selection rather than a thermodynamic property. https://www.linkedin.com/posts/lance-cummings-phd_with-the-help-of-ai-and-my-love-for-coffee-activity-7273346174491754496-DJ7, January 2025, accessed 4 March 2025.

Although a large language model is a human construct rather than a natural system, AI engineers can still 'train' the system into equilibrium by adding an artificial constraint. To do this, they test to see how well the model identifies some input – say, photographs of cats – while at the same time randomly tweaking the weights. A 'cost' function measures the incremental gain or loss in accuracy after each tweak; beneficial tweaks are retained and detrimental ones discarded. Automating these tweaks across the ten-thousand CUDA cores on each of ten-thousand GPUs enables the model to explore a huge space of possible weights, just as the septillion (10^{24}) molecules in a cup of coffee are free to explore a vast space of possible positions.

A coffee or chatbot may seem a single entity to macroscopic creatures like us, but both contain the possibility of a myriad of different microstates, whether the specific jumble of molecules in a latte or the specific word sequences produced by a chatbot. (Here the 'micro' in microstate here doesn't refer to a system that is small in scale, but refers to the entire drink or model at the deterministic level of individual molecules or numbers in matrices.)[10] The microstate a coffee gravitates to when we stir it, or a chatbot when we query it, depends on a few properties common to all stochastic systems.

Energy is one such property. For a liquid, it's a measure of internal movement, that is, how much its molecules are deviating from a condition of complete rest. Energy for an LLM can be thought of as how far the model deviates from real-world data. In nature, the arrangement of molecules will naturally tend toward the lowest possible energy, which is why your coffee cools off. For a large language model to be accurate, however, it requires that engineers train it into a state with as low an energy as possible. While training large language models has a more structured series of steps than pouring espresso into a cup, in the end an LLM also reaches a point where the energy is at a minimum as measured by how close its output fits the training data.

The disorder within a thermodynamic system, meanwhile, is represented by its entropy. The mathematical definition of entropy for a liquid counts how many possible microstates look like the current microstate. A latte with all the milk molecules bunched together in one-half and all the coffee molecules bunched together in the other would be unlikely indeed – not because there aren't multiple microstates that could look like this, but because the number pales in comparison to the myriad of possible configurations of molecules in which the milk and coffee molecules are intermixed. (That's why 'latte art' doesn't spontaneously form in your macchiato.) Entropy for a large language model, meanwhile, corresponds to the uncertainty and variability of its possible outputs, which influences the diversity of generated content.

While energy and entropy are properties of the entire system, they can be observed indirectly by sampling. Measuring the momentum of the septillion molecules in a coffee cup is beyond the reach of contemporary scientific instruments, but a few drops sprinkled on your tongue can tell you if the entire cup is too hot to drink. Likewise, if a

---

[10] It is possible for a deterministic system to exhibit stochastic behaviour (Carleson 1989).

chatbot gives a different answer every time you ask it for the best tennis player of all time, that would be a condition of high energy, while a chatbot with zero energy might always respond 'Serena Williams'.

Natural systems aim for a balance of minimizing energy and maximizing entropy.[11] In practice, AI engineers also have to strike a balance between outputs that are creative yet trustworthy. It's great to have a chatbot that responds 'Paris' every time it's asked for the capital of France; but if 'princess' is the only response you get from prompting a chatbot to complete the sentence, 'Once upon a time there was a,' the energy is too low to qualify as 'generative' AI.

Bringing a drink or a model to equilibrium requires an interplay between energy and entropy. If all the milk is at the top of your drink and you don't have a spoon, heating up your coffee will increase the kinetic energy of its molecules, causing them to scatter more evenly, eventually mixing the ingredients thoroughly and maximizing your drink's entropy. Likewise, when a model always returns the same results, it has been 'overfitted' to its training data and needs more entropy. During training, engineers can respond by injecting more energy into the model with techniques like dropout and weight decay that add randomness to the system. This increases the number of available microstates and thus diversifies the possible answers to a prompt. Add a smidgen of energy and your chatbot might offer 'Once upon a time there was a queen'; add a lot and you might get 'Once upon a time there was a donut'.

Even after a model has been trained, it's possible for users to coerce it into more diverse responses by adjusting the model's 'temperature' setting. For a coffee, temperature is the average kinetic energy of its molecules. For a model, it can be thought of as the 'creativity' or randomness in LLM outputs. Far from a vague analogy, the concept of temperature has an exact parallel in the mathematics of liquids and chatbots. Near equilibrium, the energies of molecules in a liquid or gas are distributed according to an equation first formulated by physicist Ludwig Boltzmann:

$$P(E_i) = \frac{e^{\frac{-E_i}{kT}}}{\sum_j e^{\frac{-E_j}{kT}}}$$

The exponential function in the equation, symbolized by Euler's number e, is a mathematician's way of exaggerating the difference in a spread of numbers. e to the power of 0 is 1; e to the power of 2 is 2.7; e to the power of 3 is 20; e to the power of 4 is 55. The numbers zero through four may only be four units apart, but when cast as exponents, the 3 and 4 get much further apart than the 1 and 2. Because the exponent in the formula is negative, that imposes a dramatically lower probability for high-energy states than low-energy ones. For coffee, this bias means a cup left alone is likely to cool off.

---

[11] This law can be generalized as the concept of Gibbs Free Energy. 'Gibbs Free Energy,' Wikipedia, https://en.wikipedia.org/wiki/Gibbs free energy, accessed 16 November 2024.

For large language models, this bias favours only the word predictions with the highest correlations, and can even prevent a chatbot from ever returning anything but the best fit. That can be desirable when you're asking for a factual answer like the capital of France, but this 'degenerate' condition can never produce creative or unexpected results.

That's where temperature comes in, symbolized by the T in the denominator of the exponent. The higher this value is for a liquid, the more the distribution of molecular energies will spread out. At absolute zero degrees, all the molecules would literally be frozen in place, corresponding to an extremely tall and narrow curve near zero. At high temperatures, the curve widens, allowing molecules to explore higher energies far from the zero state. In that case, some of the molecules might still be slow, but others will be moving fast enough to burn your tongue.

Not by coincidence, temperature is the parameter that controls the sharpness of a function called at the end of an AI inference that steers the likely outputs to an AI prompt. As in the formula for the distribution of molecular energies, this AI 'Softmax' function includes a temperature parameter in the denominator of the exponent to adjust the distribution's spread:[12]

$$P(z_i) = \frac{e^{\frac{z_i}{T}}}{\sum_j e^{\frac{z_j}{T}}}$$

AI tools with knobs you can turn to control the temperature – common in image generators and open-weight models – allow users to constrain outputs to only the most likely outcomes or to expand the possibilities by 'rolling the dice' for more fanciful results.[13] This is in marked contrast to the oracular interface of ChatGPT and the like, which as noted above make it seem like AI utterances come from some omnipotent oracle.

The importance of AI's thermodynamic pedigree

To see how AI companies have buried generative AI's thermodynamic pedigree, look no further than the 2024 Nobel Prize. Angry physicists booed when the 'Godfather of AI' Geoffrey Hinton shared the Nobel prize in Physics, while Silicon Valley cheered confirmation that AI has become the driver of all innovation. Both sides got the lesson exactly wrong.

---

[12] For more on how the temperature changes chatbot output, see ML Tech Lead, 'What is this Temperature for a Large Language Model?', YouTube, 17 May 2024, https://www.youtube.com/watch?v=FMPzS2gQrNI, accessed 16 November 2024.

[13] The parallels between the Boltzmann distribution and softmax function don't stop with temperature. Both equations are 'normalized' so that the sum of all microstates will be 100 per cent – whether those are possible energies of a molecule or words in the response – ensuring that every probability is correctly accounted for.

Observers who didn't bother to read the official Nobel award citation probably assume Hinton, a computer scientist, was honoured because his AI contributions made possible so many wonderful achievements in physics. Computing has certainly opened entirely new directions of physics research, but that was true long before generative AI. Contrary to the narrative pushed by AI boosters, the fact that the 2024 Physics Nobel was shared by a computer scientist and a physicist is less proof of computing's influence on physics than of physics' influence on computing.

The Nobel committee reported that the breakthroughs of Hinton and his fellow awardee, physicist John Hopfield, 'stand on the foundations of physical science' (Taylor, Metz and Milller 2024). In fact, Hopfield's insights from thermodynamics were one of the jolts that propelled the field of artificial intelligence out of the so-called 'AI winter'.[14] In 1982 Hopfield drew inspiration from emergent properties of the randomized states of particles in 'spin glasses' to show that artificial neural networks with analogous states could store information in a kind of memory. Building upon these concepts, Hinton and his collaborators developed pattern-recognizing networks called Boltzmann machines. These statistical models are named after the same Boltzmann who founded thermodynamics, laying the groundwork for the probability distribution common to coffee cups and large language models described above. Hinton name-checked Boltzmann because finding a pattern in the noise turned out to be equivalent to finding the lowest-energy state of a system. As Salvaggio reminds us, image generators like Midjourney render the pope wearing Prada or a capybara on Mars by looking for those images in noise (Salvaggio 2023). Hinton nabbed the Nobel because a technique he added, backpropagation, dramatically improved the pattern recognition of these networks.

Why should we care about whether generative AI came from physics or computer science? Because seeing large language models as statistical engines rather than artificial brains reminds us of their fallibility. And thermodynamic concepts like energy and temperature can help explain why they seem at turns big-brained or pea-brained depending on the context.

One paradox that concepts like temperature can help explain is that models scoring highest on hard problems requiring mental creativity and lateral thinking may ironically score the lowest on easy problems requiring short, fact-seeking answers. As a case in point, GPT-4, a model OpenAI touted for its superior reasoning ability, scored less than 40 per cent on OpenAI's own SimpleQA benchmark (OpenAI 2024; Tangermann 2024). We can explain this using the homomorphism between large language models and thermodynamic systems. The higher you raise the temperature, the more solution

---

[14]"The revival of the field had to await two events which occurred in the next decade. In 1982, physicist John Hopfield published a paper in which he showed how networks of simple neurons could acquire the ability to calculate, and explained this behavior with a mathematical theory similar to thermodynamics' (Crevier 1993, 215).

states a model will sample, but that also means the more likely it is to settle in one that is incorrect. To put it crudely, the 'smarter' they are, the more they can be wrong.

The thermodynamic view of chatbots reminds us that they are stochastic systems whose effects vary dramatically based on hidden properties of the system like entropy and temperature. The manifest commonalities between chatbots and mechanistic systems break the often implicit parallel between electronic neural networks and biological brains. And the thermodynamic revelation that microscopic states may obey universal laws even if they cannot be directly apprehended debunks the common perception of large language models as inscrutable black boxes that cannot be explained or tuned.

AI as a compression algorithm

There are of course ways in which a large language model is not at all like a cup of coffee. Training an LLM involves numerous intertwined processes that can't be captured simply by the activity of molecules bouncing around a mug. Additionally, a cup of hot liquid achieves equilibrium on its own thanks to deterministic physical laws, while a large language model must be trained by engineers on data created by free-spirited humans; the first embodies natural laws, the second emulates them. This makes generative AI's outcomes less predictable and more varied than those in thermodynamic systems near equilibrium.

As useful as concepts like energy and temperature are for understanding AI models, it's unclear at first how they would help assess AI's threat of supplanting the archive. As stochastic engines, large language models can accommodate all possible microstates, but archives don't have the shelf or server space for that. Jorge Luis Borges's famous combinatorial library aside, archivists have to curate their selections of dusty books or retro MP3s because they can't accommodate everything. Even the World Wide Web, for all its strange nooks devoted to Flat Earth theories and Rent-a-Chicken enterprises, is but a tiny subset of every possible web page.

Since large language models can essentially accommodate every linguistic utterance, real or imagined, researchers looking to expand their range of scholarly inquiry may choose to consult AI instead of a librarian (or Google). Science fiction tells us where this line of thought is going, in examples like the synthetic Librarian of Neal Stephenson's novel *Snow Crash* (1992). But again we don't need to resort to an animate metaphor to imagine a mechanism capable of digesting a library full of documents into a concise summary. Another precedent for AI models captures its relationship to a human-made archive in a way that is simple yet rigorous. And that precedent is as ubiquitous in our digital workplaces as hot beverages are on our desks.

Today's digital workflows would slow to a crawl without algorithms like JPEG and AAC to share images and stream songs, or the ZIP file format we use to speed attachments to and fro. The Internet's architects have entrusted one particular utility, gzip, with the responsibility for compressing web traffic, data archives, software downloads, container images, database backups, and file transfers. So it may come as a surprise that generative

AI models can be viewed as an advanced equivalent of the humdrum compression algorithms that we use every day.

For the lay user, PNG and JPEG may be the most familiar compression formats. A raw digital photo is essentially a two-dimensional array of numbers, each corresponding to the colour of a pixel. The resolution of your smartphone camera is on the order of 100 megapixels, so reducing redundancy is essential to making room for all those holiday and pet snapshots on your phone. You can think of PNG compression as counting the number of contiguous pixels with the same colour. To represent a row of five white pixels in a logo background, a raw photo might include the block 'white white white white white'; PNG replaces that thirty-character string with the eight-character string 'white 5x'. JPEG, on the other hand, is meant more for photos than graphics, so it aims to replace transitions from one colour to another rather than uniform colour blocks. In a sunset snapshot, JPEG might represent the gradual fade from a blue sky to an orange horizon with a uniform gradient between those two colours.

Regardless of the compression format, what's important is that such interpolations deliberately discard any deviation from uniformity. When you load a JPEG onto your phone, the photo uncompresses back into an array of pixels. But this new, streamlined version may omit some tiny blips in the original gradient that were in fact birds in the far distance. This interpolation can be counterproductive when image compression blurs over subtle fractures in medical images or licence plates in crime scene photographs. But it is a known cost of compressing raw data into a digested deliverable.

Science fiction author Ted Chiang describes the parallel in his essay 'ChatGPT Is a Blurry JPEG of the Web':

> Imagine that you're about to lose your access to the Internet forever. In preparation, you plan to create a compressed copy of all the text on the Web, so that you can store it on a private server. Unfortunately, your private server has only one per cent of the space needed; you can't use a lossless compression algorithm if you want everything to fit. Instead, you write a lossy algorithm that identifies statistical regularities in the text and stores them in a specialized file format. Because you have virtually unlimited computational power to throw at this task, your algorithm can identify extraordinarily nuanced statistical regularities, and this allows you to achieve the desired compression ratio of a hundred to one.
>
> Now, losing your Internet access isn't quite so terrible; you've got all the information on the Web stored on your server. The only catch is that, because the text has been so highly compressed, you can't look for information by searching for an exact quote; you'll never get an exact match, because the words aren't what's being stored. To solve this problem, you create an interface that accepts queries in the form of questions and responds with answers that convey the gist of what you have on your server.
>
> What I've described sounds a lot like ChatGPT, or most any other large language model. (Chiang 2023)

AI in education enthusiast and Wharton professor Ethan Mollick puts it more simply:

> We now have the world's most advanced compression system for knowledge. Anyone can download, for free, a 235 GB file that can answer questions in many languages based on a vast swath of all human writing (even if it makes some errors, unsurprising as compression isn't perfect). (Mollick 2024)

These comparisons may sound like figures of speech, but taking the compression analogy literally can help us shed some of the hype around AI models to see them with greater clarity. Take GPT-3, an early version of ChatGPT for which OpenAI has disclosed more details than with subsequent models. Training the GPT-3 model distilled word correlations in 300 billion tokens of source data down to 500 matrices with a total of 150 million parameters. In principle, GPT-3 is able to reproduce information digested from the original data on demand. This compression is lossy, which explains why retrieved content can feel boring for some queries yet farcical for others (Ippolito 2024a). Despite their occasional misfires, generative AI models are a remarkably compact and efficient representation of the original material. Their formidable 2000-to-1 compression ratio demonstrates the ability of large language models to distil and generalize vast textual information into a manageable utility. Recent research supports a correlation between LLM compression efficiency and success on intelligence benchmarks.[15] Indeed, the Hutter Prize rewards improvements in compressing a subset of Wikipedia with the expressed intention of spurring advances in AI.[16]

As in the case of the coffee metaphor, an examination of the underlying mathematics shows deep parallels between compression algorithms and generative AI. Although they were not originally intended to generate novel results, modern compression algorithms identify implicit features in source text, code or media, and then map them into a vector space and compute the similarities among them.[17] To reduce storage requirements while preserving core information, a common compression technique involves replacing groups of data points with their midpoints.[18] This has a striking parallel in the weighted vector sums by which inferences derive outputs from large language models, which in a crude sense are regressions to the mean.[19]

---

[15] 'We find that LLMs' intelligence – reflected by average benchmark scores – almost linearly correlates with their ability to compress external text corpora. These results provide concrete evidence supporting the belief that superior compression indicates greater intelligence' (Huang et al. 2024).
[16] Wikipedia contributors. 'Hutter Prize.' Wikipedia, https://en.wikipedia.org/wiki/Hutter_Prize, accessed 4 March 2025.
[17] 'Compression algorithms implicitly map strings into implicit feature space vectors, and compression-based similarity measures compute similarity within these feature spaces' (Sculley and Brodley 2006).
[18] See the discussion of k-means clustering in Cohen-Addad and Epasto (2023).
[19] In another parallel, large language models privilege information repeated frequently in their training data; likewise, gzip encodes data with variable-length codes, assigning shorter codes to more frequent elements.

The most convincing validation of this view of generative AI models is the fact that some compression algorithms can be pressed into service as language models, even when they were originally developed purely to reduce a file's footprint when saved on a hard drive or streamed over the Internet. Indeed, a text classifier that combined gzip with the neighbourhood averaging technique described above actually outperformed a 2018 language model developed by researchers at Google (Jiang et al. 2023). The surprising success of gzip as a word predictor further underscores the value of viewing generative AI as a sophisticated compression tool. Perhaps it is no wonder that before OS 10.5 Leopard, the Apple command for compressing a folder was 'Create Archive'.[20]

Conclusions from mechanistic AI analogues

Seeing a large language model as a compression algorithm is useful when considering the model's ability to summarize and condense vast amounts of information. Indeed, since the 1990s, some researchers have argued that compression is equivalent to intelligence (Huang 2024). However, the analogy between large language models and compression algorithms falls short in capturing the LLM's capability to generate novel content. This limitation can be explained, however, by combining our understanding of LLMs as compression algorithms with our understanding of them as thermodynamic systems.

We can view compression algorithms as extreme cases of a more general class to which large language models belong. Because their goal is to reproduce as closely as possible the original Word document or Quicktime movie, gzip aims to match the entropy of the original file. In this sense, gzip is a large language model with the temperature set to zero. Nevertheless, the fact that entropy is a key parameter in this process allows us to see how large language models deviate from this restriction by enabling the user to adjust a model's temperature. While you wouldn't want to do this for most compression contexts, large language models can be viewed as a generalization of compression that permits deviations from exact reproduction of the original data.

What makes these analogues more useful than the stochastic parrot metaphor is that thermodynamic and compression operations do not merely replicate what is in their training data, but they transform it through a process of normalization. A dollop of milk poured into espresso produces a homogenized new hybrid with a different flavour and texture than black coffee or milk alone. That said, while they are more expressive than hot liquids or compression algorithms, AI models may limit the amount of deviation due to the way they produce results by 'averaging' derivations from their training data (Ippolito 2024c).

Apart from disarming the temptation to ascribe lifelike qualities to chatbots, the mechanistic analogues we've reviewed each help in their own way to reveal two diametrical

---

[20] "List of Built-in MacOS Apps: Archive Utility," Wikipedia, https://en.wikipedia.org/wiki/List of built-in macOS apps#Archive Utility, accessed 16 November 2024.

flaws in large language models that make them ill-suited as replacements for an archive. As argued above, thermodynamic systems aim towards equilibrium, which minimizes anomalous microstates. Stir your coffee (or just wait long enough) and you'll end up with a liquid homogeneous in makeup and temperature; left to its own devices, your cappuccino isn't going to spontaneously divide into espresso on one side and milk on the other, much less create a stunning work of latte art. Likewise, compression algorithms like gzip privilege the presentation of items that occur frequently in the training data;' this makes gzip a stochastic system, which tends to repress outliers in favour of the most common features in the source material.

On the other side of the coin, large language models can invent bogus records not present in the original archive. JPEG is typically enlisted to compress and then reconstruct a photo for which it has been fed a complete array of pixels. But users can easily prompt generative AI to return information for which there is no training data, like 'Explain the Treaty of Versailles as a Choose-Your-Own-Adventure story' or 'Show the pope wearing a puffer coat'. This is like feeding JPEG a photo with large patches of pixels missing, and like any good compression algorithm ChatGPT and DALL-E will do their best to reconstruct the data void. While these examples are fun, no researcher wants her librarian to make up books that don't exist, which makes generative AI a poor substitute for an archive.

The reverse archive

If generative AI tends to smooth over outliers while fabricating interpolated points, what future could that imply for scholars and creators? As mentioned in the introduction, AI tools may twist the archival arc into an unfamiliar trajectory. Comparisons to mechanistic analogues like thermodynamic and compression processes suggest that large language models are neither superintelligences nor Xerox machines, but technologies that replace diverse content with normalized hybrids. By comparison, an archive has less entropy and more energy than a large language model; most of us go to archives to discover ground truth, however messy. Compressing an archive removes the unique factuality that makes it useful to us.

But what if the ease and ubiquity of chatbots inspires the public to consult them rather than direct sources? The danger is that a large language model is not meant to retrieve knowledge from an archive but to replace it with a homogenized surrogate, with the long-term risk of reconstruction turning into replacement. If a lay user needs a photo of the Colosseum for her website, it's going to be faster and cheaper to prompt Stable Diffusion to create one than to pay for a stock photo or a professional photographer.

Human creators and cultural heritage professionals may react to this forecast with panic, though it's reminiscent of a panic that those of us who lived through the dot-com era have felt before. Back then we worried that digitizing and uploading Guernica or the Grateful Dead would mean people spent less time at the real canvas or concert, and this has basically come to pass. It's conceivable that the same fate could befall the same digital media that usurped analogue media; perhaps people in the future will interact less with actual photos and songs, and more with surrogates conjured up via impromptu conversations with chatbots. The original web chopped up the seamless pages of printed books and magazines into separate items like text, styles, and images. Generative AI goes a step further by atomizing the web itself into individual words that are recombined probabilistically when the reader asks for new content. While these models clearly wouldn't exist without archives, they also shatter the authority of the archive's status as the standard bearer for truth.

A preview of this disturbing vision that you can explore right now is Websim,[21] a site that is effectively a version of the Internet created on the fly by user prompts. The site presents you with a fake web browser; type a web domain you want to visit, like malaysia.travel or pumpkin.recipes, in its location bar and behind the scenes a large language model generates the HTML and images for a website that seems to be a probable match for that web address. Clever prompters have even managed to get Websim to produce playable 2- and 3-D games without ever touching the code or making an actual website. The result is a sort of mirror of the web, created not by HTML coders and web designers but by the spur-of-the-moment desires of its viewers.

While Salvaggio describes generative AI as an 'archive in reverse', AI may engender an even more contorted twist in the trajectory of cultural production. While there's broad consensus that scaling up the amount of data fed into these models has produced remarkable results from fairly simple mathematical constructs, companies like open AI and Google are running out of data to scrape. To feed future expansion of these ravenous models, some engineers have proposed using the models themselves to generate 'synthetic data' to train future releases. Even if AI companies are wary of depending on this lab-grown data, they may not be able to avoid training on AI-generated content. After all, the current landing place for AI-generated PNGs of unicorns with rollerblades and AI rehashes of popular news stories is social media and websites. At that point, the products of previous models posted to the Internet will in turn become fodder for training the next models.

In this dystopian curatorial ouroboros, archives will no longer be just the starting or end point of a cultural artefact, but both origin and destination. In the extreme case, this paradigm shift could make coming into contact with actual human-made artefacts even less likely for the average person. For archival sources that we depend on for ground truth, from Wikipedia to Reddit to the Internet Archive, the danger is becoming overrun with AI-generated slop. For the AI models themselves, the danger is overfitting or even model collapse. A 'synthetic archive' would offer a perpetual source of training data, but it also threatens to create evermore inbred generations of output. This vicious circle could

---

[21] Websim, https://websim.ai, accessed 16 November 2024.

amplify the numerous ways models can misrepresent the truth, whether by reproducing bias in their training data or by reducing the diversity of archival records to averages.[22]

Conclusion

As a general rule, collecting institutions haven't stayed abreast of the implications of generative AI as much as fields like education, software development, or even the arts. Some intrepid experimentation has demonstrated how useful AI tools can be for the digital humanities and data science; researchers have demonstrated the value of generic chatbots to automate dreary tasks like adding metadata to photographs (Brumfield and Brumfield 2023) or cleaning up bioinformatic data in a spreadsheet (Stapleton 2023).

While these experiments are essential, we must not let them distract us from the looming threat that generative AI poses to the content and relevance of formal and informal archives. Keeping alert to the potential risks and benefits of generative AI means being clear-eyed about the fundamental mechanisms by which it works – and steering clear of animistic metaphors that obscure those mechanisms.[23]

Acknowledgement of AI use

The author used GPT-4.0 extensively for research, but not for sources, conclusions or editing prose.

---

[22] When Salvaggio prompted an image generator for an obsolete photograph format (stereoview), he saw another example of how AI can surface stereotypical content in an archive: 'when I went into the training data for these image models and explored open repositories for where these images may have been sourced from, I discovered that there was a vast collection of stereoview images from the Library of Congress that referred to stereoview images – and specifically, as a tool for circulating images of the US occupation of the Philippines. The United States circulated these images deliberately to tell a story glorifying that project. As expected for a cultural institution, the Library of Congress shared these images online, contextualizing them in an exhibition that showed how this storytelling was crafted and the goals it served. Nonetheless, when encountered simply as data, these images became strongly associated with the imagery of stereoview images, even to the extent that the very hallmark of the media format – two photos, side by side – would sometimes go away. At the same time, pictures of colonization would remain, as if the word stereoview was more strongly correlated to colonization than to a media format' (Salvaggio 2024).

[23] It is important to be both open-minded about potential solutions as well as recognize their limitations. In particular, solutions that favour voluntary interventions by humans may prevail over attempts to legislate blanket compliance that leave too many loopholes. For example, mandating watermarks for AI-generated content is unenforceable, while adding digital signatures to genuine archival material is a tried-and-true way to ensure evidence is trustworthy or creations are human-made. Likewise, outlawing deep fakes will be less effective than supporting local journalism that can debunk fake news. Standing up for diversity amidst the homogenizing tendencies of generative AI will be a priority going forward.

Bibliography

Bali, Maha, Anuj Gupta, Yasser Atef and Anna Mills. 2024. 'Assistant, Parrot, or Colonizing Loudspeaker? ChatGPT Metaphors for Developing Critical AI Literacies'. arXiv:2401.08711, 15 January. https://arxiv.org/abs/2401.08711.

Bender, Emily M., Timnit Gebru, Angelina McMillan-Major and Shmargaret Shmitchell. 2021. 'On the Dangers of Stochastic Parrots: Can Language Models Be Too Big?' *FAccT '21: Proceedings of the 2021 ACM Conference on Fairness, Accountability, and Transparency* (March): 610–23. https://doi.org/10.1145/3442188.3445922.

Bergman, Michael K. 'The Deep Web: Surfacing Hidden Value'. *BrightPlanet*, July 2000. https://resources.mpi-inf.mpg.de/d5/teaching/ws01_02/proseminarliteratur/deepwebwhitepaper.pdf (accessed 16 November 2024).

Blais, Joline and Jon Ippolito. *At the Edge of Art*. Thames & Hudson, 2006.

Brumfield, Sara and Ben Brumfield. 2023. '10 Ways AI Will Change Archives'. *YouTube*, 27 October 2023. https://www.youtube.com/watch?v=Fmgbk1x6RSY (accessed 16 November 2024).

Carleson, Lennart. 1989. 'Stochastic Behaviour of Deterministic Systems'. IUI Working Paper, No. 233, The Research Institute of Industrial Economics (IUI), Stockholm. https://www.econstor.eu/bitstream/10419/95223/1/wp233.pdf. (accessed 16 November 2024).

Chiang, Ted. 'ChatGPT Is a Blurry JPEG of the Web'. *The New Yorker*, 9 February 2023. https://www.newyorker.com/tech/annals-of-technology/chatgpt-is-a-blurry-jpeg-of-the-web.

Cohen-Addad, Vincent and Alessandro Epasto. 'Differentially Private Clustering for Large-scale Datasets'. *Google Research*, 25 May, 2023. https://research.google/blog/differentially-private-clustering-for-large-scale-datasets.

Crevier, Daniel. *AI: The Tumultuous Search for Artificial Intelligence*. BasicBooks, 1993. https://archive.org/details/aitumultuoushist00crev/page/214/mode/2up?q=hopfield.

Huang, Yuzhen, Jinghan Zhang, Zifei Shan and Junxian He. 'Compression Represents Intelligence Linearly'. arXiv:2404.09937v1, 15 April, 2024. https://arxiv.org/html/2404.09937v1.

Ippolito, Jon. 'AI Made Me Basic'. *Still Water Blog*, 2024a. https://blog.still-water.net/ai-made-me-basic (accessed 16 November 2024).

Ippolito, Jon. 'Why You Should Generate AI Images in Your Classroom'. *Still Water blog*, 2024b. https://blog.still-water.net/why-you-should-generate-ai-images-in-your-classroom. Accessed 16 November 2024.

Ippolito, Jon. 'Why Your AI Outputs Feel Average'. *Still Water Blog*, 2024c. https://blog.still-water.net/why-your-ai-outputs-feel-average, accessed 16 November 2024.

Jiang, Zhiying, Matthew Yang, Mikhail Tsirlin, Raphael Tang, Yiqin Dai and Jimmy Lin. '"Low-Resource" Text Classification: A Parameter-Free Classification Method with Compressors'. In *Findings of the Association for Computational Linguistics: ACL* (2023), 6810–28. Association for Computational Linguistics, 2023. https://aclanthology.org/2023.findings-acl.426 (accessed 16 November 2024).

Manovich, Lev. 'Database as Symbolic Form'. *Millennium Film Journal* No. 34 (1999). http://www.mfj-online.org/journalPages/MFJ34/Manovich_Database_FrameSet.html (accessed 12 November 2024).

Marr, Bernard. '28 Best Quotes About Artificial Intelligence,' *Forbes*, 2017. https://www.forbes.com/sites/bernardmarr/2017/07/25/28-best-quotes-about-artificial-intelligence (accessed 15 November 2024).

Metz, Cade, Jason Henry, Ben Laffin, Rebecca Lieberman and Yiwen Lu. 'How Self-Driving Cars Get Help From Humans Hundreds of Miles Away'. *New York Times*, 3 September 2024.

Mollick, Ethan. 'An Underutilized Perspective...'. *LinkedIn*, October 2024. https://www.linkedin.com/posts/emollick-an-underutilized-perspective-on-ai-for-non-technical-activity-7243309260212699136-lzXx. (accessed 16 November 2024).

OpenAI. 'Introducing SimpleQA.' 2024. https://openai.com/index/introducing-simpleqa (accessed 15 November 2024).

Salvaggio, Eryk. 'Flowers Blooming Backwards into Noise'. *YouTube*, 1 June 2023. https://www.youtube.com/watch?v=zNA7sPm-zlQ. (accessed 16 November 2024).

Salvaggio, Eryk. 'Infrastructures of Memory,' *Cybernetic Forests*, Oct 19, 2024. https://cyberneticforests.substack.com/p/infrastructures-of-memory (accessed 16 November 2024).

Sculley, D. and C. E. Brodley. 'Compression and Machine Learning: A New Perspective on Feature Space Vectors.' *IEEE Explore*, 10 April 2006. https://ieeexplore.ieee.org/document/1607268 (accessed 16 November 2024).

Stapleton, Andy. 'A Literal AI Game Changer for Research & Academia'. *YouTube*, 12 July 2023. https://www.youtube.com/watch?v=yklFHtlK4sQ (accessed 16 November 2024).

Tangermann, Victor. 'OpenAI Research Finds That Even Its Best Models Give Wrong Answers a Wild Proportion of the Time'. *Futurism*, 2 November 2024. https://futurism.com/the-byte/openai-research-best-models-wrong-answers (accessed 15 November 2024).

Taylor, D. B., C. Metz and K. Milller. 'Nobel Physics Prize Awarded for Pioneering A.I. Research by 2 Scientists'. *New York Times*, October 8, 2024. https://web.archive.org/web/20241008123756/https://www.nytimes.com/2024/10/08/science/nobel-prize-physics.html (accessed 5 March 2025).

CHAPTER 15
BOOK HISTORY FOR THE FUTURE
CONNECTING COMMUNICATIONS MEDIA
Leah Henrickson

There are, admittedly, few clear career paths for those with degrees in book history. I remember one of my eventual employers looking at that line on my CV shortly before my graduation and bluntly asking, 'what's that piece of paper going to get you?' It took great restraint not to reply with something along the lines of 'if I roll it up, something to whack you with'. Having spent years studying the history of books and authorship and reading, I knew why a book history degree was valuable. I could enthusiastically dive into convoluted conversations about communications media, drawing upon thousands of years of examples of how ideas transcend space and time. After hours spent in Special Collections, I could comfortably identify the fine details of books and then document those details for others through bibliographic notation. I could read between the lines, figuratively and literally, to investigate how books are more than just containers for words. It was clear to me how books are social artefacts, reflecting and influencing social contexts in ways both subtle and overt. Yet when my employer questioned why my degree mattered, I couldn't articulate a compelling response.

It wasn't until years later, while writing a PhD thesis about computer-generated texts, that I was finally able to explain book history's relevance. Book history is not just about documenting and analysing the past, although book historians do these things well. Book history is also about laying foundations for critically considering current media and imagining media futures. To be trained as a book historian is to be familiarized with frameworks of production, dissemination and reception that can add structure to otherwise overwhelming interrogations of communications media. A book historian understands the importance of systematic investigation of material objects because every material object (even an electronic one) has its own story to tell, even if it might look similar to another. Awareness of each object's unique story also means that a book historian is comfortable rambling in grey areas, following breadcrumb trails that lead towards unexpected people and places. Book history is a necessarily interdisciplinary area of study that trains students for inquiry into the uncertain. Big-picture thinking and attention to detail converge in the objects being studied.

Those objects have tended to be physical, but increasingly we are seeing book historians move into digital spaces, reflecting on the materiality and infrastructures of digital media objects, the transposition of physical objects into digital forms, and the use of digital tools to support research (Henrickson 2020; Kirschenbaum 2012). We are also seeing book historians confidently integrate themselves into broader discussions of emerging media: discussions that are often driven by others' discomfort with those grey areas where book historians feel most at home.

This chapter argues for the particular value that book history brings to considerations of emerging media. I begin by acknowledging that books and bookishness are frequently used as baselines for such considerations. However, whether or not this baseline is used, there are numerous other entry points into ongoing conversations about emerging media that book historians may exploit. These entry points will be illustrated using the case study of Inflection AI, a new (at the time of writing) company based around AI-driven personal assistant chatbots. I conclude with a call to action, under the guise of guiding questions, for book historians to celebrate the worth of their insights for questioning, developing and evaluating modern communications media.

Some readers may roll their eyes at how obvious some of this chapter's points are. Ideally, one day, that will be every one of this chapter's readers. For now, I write for those who feel why book history matters but can't yet articulate to others the intricacies of that feeling. I write too for my past self, standing in front of my employer, scrambling to explain why book history matters. Because it *does* matter. Book history is bigger than people might think. It's for the past, of course, but also for the future: the future that the world would be privileged to have trained book historians help build.

The book as baseline

While digital media now abound – and somehow *still* spur regular declarations of the book's decline or even death – the book continues to serve as a measure for emerging media (Striphas 2011). Let's start with the following passage attributed to author Ray Bradbury (1984):

> A computer is a book. No, a computer is an encyclopedia. No, a computer is a whole damned library.
>
> And yet we constantly hear the cry: Aren't you afraid of computers?
>
> To which my response is, I don't shiver or quake when I walk past a library, I don't shake with fear when I enter a reading room, so why should I be afraid of computers when they perform the same functions as a library, an encyclopedia or a book?
>
> The thing is, of course, that computers don't *look* like books, which makes some people uncomfortable. They have been raised with the idea that machines are enemies and since a computer is a machine it *must* be hostile to mankind. The notion is an old one, going back to the Luddites who kicked and beat devices because, in varieties of ways, they feared them.
>
> Well, I for one will not listen to our neo-Luddites. With a book tucked in one hand, and a computer shoved under my elbow, I will march, not sidle, shudder or quake, into the twenty-first century.

To so staunchly liken a computer to a book or library – while perhaps comforting to those 'raised with the idea that machines are enemies' – is to discount computers' unique affordances. Yes, computers can store texts, link between those texts and perform many of 'the same functions as a library, an encyclopedia or a book', but those functions are completed within markedly different circumstances. The computer may be a library, but it is a library that facilitates certain kinds of social interactions in spaces that are fundamentally distinct from physical libraries. Nevertheless, Bradbury's comparison is useful for this discussion because it shows how connections have been, and continue to be, made between books and digital media: connections that are sometimes made explicitly, but also through assumptions related to shared understandings of bookishness.

Jessica Pressman (2020, 150) has expanded on the idea of bookishness to consider 'the complex bundle of emotions that come with recognizing that a relationship to books has changed – this relationship, for many readers and writers, is both personal and cultural'. In her book about the concept, Pressman reflects on how books are framed as sites of refuge and shelter from, and even weapons against, emerging media. Indeed, books are commonly evoked in such ways for critique of these media. An article about virtual reality in the popular magazine *GQ*, for instance, calls the book 'the ultimate piece of mobile and social technology. [. . .] In a frenzy of seemingly endless digital possibility, books are the ultimate experience machine – a window on other worlds that remind us we are still embedded in this real, imperfect one' (Davies 2016). And the range of potential experiences books can offer is vast. As technology critic Jaron Lanier has been quoted, 'Wikipedia is run by super-nice people who are my friends. But the thing is it's like *one* encyclopedia. Some of us might remember when on paper there was both an Encyclopedia Britannica and Encyclopedia Americana and they provided different perspectives. The notion of having the perfect encyclopedia is just weird' (Hattenstone 2023). While a reader's experience of Wikipedia differs greatly from that of a physical encyclopaedia, the direct comparison between Wikipedia and bookish counterparts is indicative of users' book-informed expectations of digital options. Despite Lanier's point being made nearly forty years after Bradbury's, both men default to bookishness.

Although bookish expectations often direct our experiences of emerging media, the 'book' has become so familiar that individuals often forget that it is indeed a medium. Book history calls attention to the mechanical and experiential codicological elements that many take for granted until they are faced with newer, more novel media formats (Price 2019, 26–50). Book history also calls attention to the historical continuities of textual media, serving as much-needed reality checks for unmitigated claims of novelty about those media. In this way, book historians contribute valuably to cultural studies conversations (Brown 2004). Books are so deeply embedded in cultural consciousness that, even with digital innovation, we continue to live in an Order of the Book (van der Weel 2011). In other words, books are our baseline for considering emerging media, and bookishness is our baseline for culture.

New Directions in Digital Textual Studies

A reflection on Inflection

If books are our baseline, I *could* spend the remainder of this chapter simply comparing recent digital innovations to bookish counterparts. As Bradbury and Lanier's quotations suggest, such comparisons can shed light on trajectories of media evolution that are sometimes neglected in hyped-up sales pitches. Comparisons can help us take stock of where we are, where we've been and where we'd like to go. By comparing media, we may also discover fresh ways of combining media forms, creating original experiences that merge the unique affordances of different media. There are, in short, good reasons for comparing digital and written or printed textual media.

But this is not that kind of chapter. I am here to spark inquiry, not satisfy it. The case study below is arbitrary, representing my own research interests (Henrickson 2021), and is used to demonstrate the expansive relevance of book history. In the spirit of expansiveness, the discussion below is more stream-of-consciousness than argument, representing the start – rather than the end – of a potential book history-informed analysis.

The case study is a new company called Inflection AI. Inflection AI describes itself as 'an AI studio creating a personal AI for everyone'. Its current core product is Pi, short for 'personal intelligence', which is advertised as using large language models (LLMs) to offer a 'supportive and empathetic' conversational experience (Inflection AI 2023). A version of Pi is available for public use on Web browsers or text messaging applications like WhatsApp. A conversation with Pi is similar to one with other LLM-driven chatbots like OpenAI's ChatGPT or Google's Gemini, but the tone is lighter due to Pi's more liberal use of informal language and peppering of exclamation marks and emoji. In addition to maintaining Pi, Inflection AI is now working to make its technology more accessible to commercial customers hoping to create bespoke chatbots.

Inflection AI was founded by three entrepreneurs with existing connections to a wide range of industrial and educational organizations, stemming from their impressive track records of commercial technological success (see Hu and Varghese 2024). Combining these track records evidently filled investors with confidence in the company. Within months of its inception, Inflection AI secured $225 million in funding from industry leaders like Microsoft; within about a year, this amount had reached $1.525 billion. This funding is ostensibly more for public, rather than private, good, with Inflection AI being registered as a public benefit corporation. A public benefit corporation

> is intended to produce a public benefit or public benefits and to operate in a responsible and sustainable manner. To that end, a public benefit corporation shall be managed in a manner that balances the stockholders' pecuniary interests, the best interests of those materially affected by the corporation's conduct, and the public benefit or public benefits identified in its certificate of incorporation. (Delaware Code Revisers n.d.)

The narrative framing of Inflection AI's registration as a public benefit corporation is noteworthy. This is a technology company with substantial financial resources and potential profit margins, but it is also one that is marketed as working towards public benefit. Precisely what 'public benefit' means in this context, however, is unclear in both corporate and legislative documentation.

Book historians are acutely aware of how conceptions of 'public benefit' – or, inversely, public risk – have been used to maintain social and financial orders. Socrates (as depicted in Plato's *Phaedrus*) declared that the written word 'will create forgetfulness in the learners' souls, because they will not use their memories; they will trust to the external written characters and not remember of themselves' (Plato 2008). This passage shows us just how powerful our means of communication have always been perceived to be – changes to media can prompt anxiety about the disruption of established social systems, despite the recognized benefits of those media. Once writing had become an established cultural technique, the content of that writing itself was put under scrutiny, again under perceptions of public risk. For example, in 1557, London's Stationers' Company received a royal charter for blocking the production and distribution of 'seditious and heretical books' critical of the monarchy and state religion to prevent civil disobedience and blasphemy (Deazley n.d.). Sure, this charter could be considered an effort to maintain public order and uphold the integrity of London's book trade, but it also effectively cemented the Stationers' Company's monopoly over print. Under this monopoly, the Stationers' Company issued copyrights in perpetuity, meaning that publishers could price their books however they liked, without fear of competition. High prices eventually led to the 1710 'Bill for Encouragement of Learning, and for Securing the Property of Copies of Books to the Rightful Owners thereof', more commonly known as the Statute of Anne. By assigning authors time-limited copyrights in their own works, the Statute of Anne undermined the Stationers' Company's monopoly, lowering book prices and allowing for a much greater variety of titles to be produced – all in the name of public education (never mind the economic benefits of reviving London's book trade). Not everyone believed in the variety afforded by the extended trade, though. One 1780 item in *Lady's Magazine*, for example, lambasts the 'Modern Novel' as 'the literary opium, that lulls every ſenſe into delicious rapture'. Ruing the apparent desolation of respectable representations of love, the author declares that '[i]t is a misfortune incident to human nature, that its fineſt qualities may be perverted to the moſt deſtructive ends' (Author Unknown 1780). These are just a few of the countless examples of how the 'public benefit' (or risk), whatever its contemporary interpretation, has informed discussions and regulations related to books.

These examples show how interpretations of 'public benefit' work to solidify power. For Socrates, this power is social, with aural communication and memory being privileged as forms of intelligence and social capital. The 1557 royal charter makes no effort to hide the King and Queen's feeling threatened by the contents of published works. Some have called the Statute of Anne a 'trade regulation statute intended to destroy the booksellers' monopoly of the book trade' (Patterson 2001, 437); although the Statute facilitated sharing of more diverse political and religious ideas, it still enforced regulatory oversight. Readers could evidently not be trusted to decide for themselves what ideas were worth reading; as the item in *Lady's Magazine* indicates, women have been especially vulnerable to reading's 'moſt deſtructive ends'. All of these examples were driven by efforts to assert power under the guise of protecting the public.

Similar efforts have been made in recent discussions about LLMs driving technologies like Inflection AI. Numerous organizations representing authors have published open letters and survey results raising concerns about the use of human-written textual corpora to train LLMs that could potentially produce literary works (Weber 2023). These are the same organizations that have repeatedly criticized the digitization of books by private companies like Google/Alphabet – projects also advertised as being for the public good (Marcum and Schonfeld 2021). The open letters published by these organizations primarily advocate for financial remuneration for authors, but they also refer to broader cultural implications of computational consolidation of text. For instance, the press release accompanying the Authors Guild's (2023) open letter attempts to evoke conceptions of public benefit: 'When writers have to give up their profession, it is a grave problem for all of us, not just the writers, because far fewer great books get written and published; and a free, democratic culture depends on a healthy, diverse ecosystem in which all views and voices are heard and ideas exchanged.' This is ostensibly more than a financial matter – democracy itself is on the line. Philosopher Daniel Dennett (2023) makes a similar appeal to democratic values in his argument against computer-generated texts. 'Democracy depends on the informed (not misinformed) consent of the governed,' he writes:

> By allowing the most economically and politically powerful people, corporations, and governments to control our attention, these systems will control us. Counterfeit people [text generators], by distracting and confusing us and by exploiting our most irresistible fears and anxieties, will lead us into temptation and, from there, into acquiescing to our own subjugation. The counterfeit people will talk us into adopting policies and convictions that will make us vulnerable to still more manipulation. Or we will simply turn off our attention and become passive and ignorant pawns.

In Dennett's view, LLMs may contribute to an alternative manifestation of reading's 'moſt deſtructive ends', except women are not the only ones at risk – *everyone* is. Some texts uphold public benefit, while others oppose it. In 1780, the 'Modern Novel' was considered by some to be dangerous. Now, it seems that we would welcome opportunities to read those same books in defiance of computer-generated texts.

The FAQ section on Inflection AI's website indicates the company's awareness of public skepticism towards AI technologies and commercial interests. Inflection AI's website also includes a safety commitment wherein surveillance (e.g. collection of personal data and monitoring of conversations with Pi) is justified under 'review and improvement' that verifies compliance with company policies. The company's privacy policy does offer some transparency regarding the use of such surveillance but, given Pi's proprietary nature, detailed information about the software's technological architecture is not publicly available. To its credit, Inflection AI has acknowledged that software like Pi is never neutral, and that the company accepts the curatorial responsibilities that inform Pi's user experience. Yet in the words of one of Inflection AI's co-founders (Suleyman 2023), 'we have to figure out as a society which bodies we trust to make decisions. [. . .] And that means that democratic structures need to sort themselves out pretty sharpish, and actually have some functioning bodies that can provide real oversight without everybody fainting over the accusations that this is censorship.' Easier said than done, perhaps, when private commercial interests like those of Inflection AI often mean guarding the information that is necessary for public oversight. Another publishing monopoly – a kind of technopoly, to adapt Neil Postman's (1992) term – arises: one that is determined by the exorbitant costs of LLM infrastructures, deep and inaccessible-to-many technological know-how, and ardent protection of intellectual property. We are again subject to claims of 'public benefit' that in actuality reinforce social and financial hierarchies that may only benefit a minority.

By looking to book history, we can see that modern technopolies are hardly without precedent. Text and power are inextricably linked, albeit often in complex and covert ways (Ezell 2008; Lamal, Cumby and Helmers 2021), and computer-generated texts like those produced by Inflection AI's Pi represent just the latest ways for that power to be made manifest. Book historians know that we cannot study texts without also studying the relationships between those producing, distributing and consuming those texts. This is, in essence, what conceptual models like Darnton's (1982) and Adams and Barker's (1993) communications circuits facilitate, as is evident by other circuits that they have inspired (e.g. Murray and Squires 2013; Thompson 2021, 451–62; van der Weel 2001). These models help us map social connections around textual artefacts. Even for AI systems, like Pi, that appear to run autonomously, human intervention is prevalent at every stage of development and use (Broussard 2018; Crawford 2023). A conceptual model like a communications circuit can help us look deeper than the seamless graphical user interface that may mask those humans.

Still when we consider Inflection AI's Pi, we must do so with attention to Pi's 'chat' interface. This is somewhat complicated because there are various ways to chat with Pi: through a Web browser; through private messaging sections of platforms like Instagram, WhatsApp and Facebook; through SMS; or through the Inflection AI app. While the quality and content of Pi's responses may not be platform-dependent, user experiences of Pi will differ, even if only slightly, across the different platforms. In the oft-cited article 'Print Is Flat, Code Is Deep', N. Katherine Hayles argues for media-specific analyses that pay special attention to the materiality of texts and 'the interplay between a text's physical characteristics and its signifying strategies'. In Hayles's own review of the material implications of electronic hypertexts, she uses book history as her starting point, framing computer code as existing within a lineage of textual media (Hayles 2004). Computing is, in a sense, writing; '[a]ll programs are texts that read texts and write other texts' (Bolter 1991, 9). Just like every book prompts its own experience, however, so too does every program. Fear not – I will not delve into reviewing Pi's various interfaces in this chapter. It is sufficient to simply acknowledge that a full analysis of Pi must include the experiences of both the text that Pi gives us (textual output) and the texts that Pi uses to run (software and platforms).

Analysing experiences of Pi's textual output is fairly straightforward. Simply pick which platform you would like to chat with Pi on and type a message as you would to any other conversational partner. In what contexts do you receive Pi's texts, and through what media? How do you interact with these texts, and why? Different media afford different kinds of interactions. Moving from the scroll to the codex, for instance, afforded opportunities for indexical and discontinuous reading (Stallybrass 2012). Pi's most prominent affordance is related to personalization. Readers do not just make Pi's texts their own by, for example, annotation (Dahlström 2011). These texts are, like many Books of Hours (Reinburg 2012), bespoke for users who take on patron-like status through typed prompts. How does knowing that a text has been produced just for you inform your response?

And, as book historians are aware, reader response cannot be divorced from material experience. The digital materiality and fluidity of Pi's texts speak to Johanna Drucker's reconceptualization of book history wherein a book is not considered to be an autonomous object that passes between people (as implied by many communications circuits), but an event space within ever-changing conditions. 'However fluid the text,' Drucker (2014, 24) writes, 'the documents have their own kinds of persistence and permanence, however palimpsestic and complex their relations to the streams of production in which they participate may be.' By likening Pi's chat interface to a palimpsest, both literal and figurative, a fresh set of questions emerges for our critical consideration (Carruthers, Chai-Elsholz and Silec 2011). Is the 'blank screen' of a new chat really blank? If not, what are we adding our text to? What are we erasing or covering with our additions? How many layers of text does this screen hold, and what does each layer mean for individual and societal experiences of Pi?

The underlying layers are the codes and datasets responsible for Pi's functionality – its software and platforms. The LLMs upon which Pi depends all involve processes of encoding and decoding textual information, much like in bibliography. Bibliography encodes textual and material elements to judge relationships between variants, assess textual authority and record the evolution of texts (Gaskell 1995). Digital bibliographic efforts include the use of similar encoding and knowledge organization such as Optical Character Recognition (OCR) (Cordell 2017) and Extensible Markup Language (XML) (Cummings and Willcox 2013), as well as database systems for similar purposes. A bibliographic approach to reading Pi's code and datasets, if they were to be made available for public perusal, could allow for documentation that identifies Pi's learning trajectories and contributes to more explainable AI. As Simone Murray (2021, 976) has noted in her book history-informed analysis of Goodreads, such '[p]roprietary data are [. . .] unlikely ever to be regarded as sufficiently historical to be discarded or gifted to public institutions. It follows that book history cannot simply transpose its human-centred schemas and public-interest assumptions to a digital environment premised on a data-hoarding commercial paradigm'. Nevertheless, bibliographical practice is a form of systematic datafication that is comparable to that which drives computational systems like Pi, and the act of reading code is comparable to the act of reading a natural language text (Vee 2017). Even without the precise data required to conduct a digital bibliographical analysis of the software, those trained in bibliography may approach Pi with eyes trained to examine minute details. Bibliographers, and book historians more generally, already work in code.

Through the booking glass

What constitutes 'book history' is not always clear, especially given the diversity of the field's activities. Some book historians track the production, circulation and sales of material artefacts; others maintain more literary emphasis, tending towards textual analysis (Howsam 2008). There are also scholars who combine these two approaches to produce archives and editions (McKenzie 1999; Van Hulle 2022). Book historians are active in digitization efforts, creating digital research resources and using digital tools to approach old materials in new ways (Rippl and Lenker 2021; Tonra 2021). In her consideration of book history as an 'interdiscipline', Leslie Howsam goes so far as to assert that book history is not an academic discipline in itself, but a conceptual meeting space for scholars of varying disciplines to reflect upon media of communication. 'What is shared is not method, and not subject matter, but rather that way of thinking, that sense of the creation, mediation and consumption of the objects of communication being crucial to the way that culture and society work,' Howsam writes. 'And all the more when those objects are multiplied. Not only medium and message, but also infrastructure' (2016, 14). Book history is therefore about more than just books. It is also about how and why books are made and shared, by whom they are made and used, and the cultural circumstances within which they exist. It is also a space for play and mischief, for revelling in what Beth Driscoll and Claire Squires deem the 'slipperiness' of books (2020), or in what Stephen Ramsay has called the 'hermeneutics of screwing around' (2010). Each book historian is left to self-determine what the field means to them, with books not just containing language and culture, but also serving as cultural metaphors and touchpoints.

But just as book historians make their own borders, they also build their own bridges. The Inflection AI case study shows one potential bridge between book history and an emerging media space. This single example revealed various avenues for bookish exploration, from cultural studies to bibliographic encoding. Perhaps you identified even more avenues as you read. If I've succeeded in my aim for this chapter, you're beginning to see how book history training can support the development and analysis of new forms of media, as well as how book historians can add layers of nuance that deepen our understanding of how these media work and why.

By the time you read this chapter, circumstances will have changed. Inflection AI may have grown, releasing products that expand its remit. The company may have folded. New AI and/or media companies have undoubtedly cropped up, and one of the products touted by these companies is probably the subject of overhyped news articles, some of whose predictions likely verge on the apocalyptic. All of these changes create opportunities for a book historian's intervention.

Start by focusing on one case study centred on an emerging medium at one point in time, as I did with Inflection AI and Pi. Consider the following questions, each of which is accompanied by a suggested task and selection of readings to guide your thinking.

- Who is involved in the production, distribution and consumption of your chosen case? What do each of these people or organizations do to contribute to your case?
    - Map these parties' relationships to one another. Your map may not be as visually tidy as the communications circuits that book historians have published. You may even find that a 'circuit' format does not suit your case. That's fine. You are exploring uncharted terrain, and you can continue to adjust this map as you undertake the next few tasks.
    - Book history inspiration: Adams and Barker 1993; Darnton 1982; Murray and Squires 2013; Thompson 2021; van der Weel 2001
- Now that you have identified who is involved in your case and what they do, consider the nature of everyone's relationships. Who holds power over others, and when, how and why? Who has a financial stake in your case? What other factors might contribute to interpersonal power dynamics contributing to and informing your case?
    - For each party you have included on your map, note what you think their motivations for, and interests in, engaging with your case might be. Perhaps they are seeking financial gain, social or political dominance, or something else. Then, specify how each party is actually contributing to your case. Do they have expert knowledge, money or other resources to share? How are they compensated for their contributions?
    - Book history inspiration: St Clair 2004; Walsh 2009
- What is your case's materiality? How do you interact with it? As a user of your case, what are you expected to do with it? How are 'typical' users engaging with your case?
    - Use your case. Observe what your body is doing as you engage with the case and how what you do with your body influences the way it works and/or produces output. What hardware and software does your case rely on, if any? Does your case require specialist knowledge or training for use? Once you have used your case, try to identify who your case is intended for and why. Explain how you have reached your conclusion.
    - Book history inspiration: Drucker 2013; Gruber Garvey 2012; Mak 2011
- After identifying your case's materiality, consider how you could systematically document that materiality so that future scholars may track the lifecycle of your case. Which elements of your case are important to record, and why?

- List each element that you feel is important to record. Define each element in one or two sentences. Then, for each element, note how one might go about documenting it. What language or notation should be used? Will your documentation be qualitative, quantitative or a mix of both? Once you have created your own guidelines for documentation (and if you are feeling up to it), try actually documenting your case according to those guidelines.
- Book history inspiration: Carter, Barker and Thadani 2024; Gaskell 1995

• How is your case framed in popular and scholarly discourse? If it is advertised, what language and tone are used to describe its functionality and purpose? If it is the subject of news or scholarly articles, what language and tone are used to describe, praise and/or critique its functionality and purpose? Does the rhetoric you observe correspond with actual usage?
- Collect examples of your case being discussed. Note which words and phrases evoke affective responses. Reflect on how your examples make you feel about your case. Observe whether or not these feelings align with what you know about your case from the previous tasks.
- Book history inspiration: McKenzie 1999; Price 2019

• How might one use your case for unintended and/or subversive purposes, such as creative expression and advocacy?
- Embrace your inner science fiction author and imagine the world in five years. Ten years. Fifteen years. Where does your case fit within those contexts? As social, political and economic circumstances change, how does your case change with them, if at all?[1]
- Book history inspiration: Coker 2017; Driscoll and Squires 2020

If you find it challenging to answer these questions, good. That means you are in a grey area – and book historians love grey areas. The beauty of book history training is that there is rarely a 'right' answer, and if there *is* a right answer, it might not stay right for long. Approaching your case study with the openness that book history requires means that you will be able to see things that may be invisible to others. Read what is around you; let yourself be guided through the story of your case.

Conclusion

Book historians know the power of communications media. They have millennia of examples of the innovative and impactful applications of these media – examples that

---

[1] This exercise is adapted from the University of Queensland's WhatIF Lab (e.g. Wilkins, Bennett and Marshall 2023).

comprise a wide range of ways to share knowledge, facilitate self-reflection and build connections. Books, bookishness and book history are not just suitable baselines for conceptualizing new media; they comprise some of the very foundations of these media.

As a book historian, you are well-equipped to (*quelle surprise!*) study books. However, you are also well-equipped to study emerging media. You may apply your deep knowledge of the past to interrogations of the present and imaginations of the future. You may turn your bibliographic attention to detail to other systematic forms of encoding. You may adapt your bigger-picture models to new and fluid circumstances, guiding and recording your thinking about media and the human relationships that drive them. Your insight into the past will help us better understand how our relationships with media – through which we create, consume and share knowledge – are changing, and the skills you have developed through your training will help us navigate those changing media landscapes.

So, what is book history? The future.

Acknowledgements

Thanks are due to the attendees of the 2022 *On the Margins: Hypertext, Electronic Literature, Digital Humanities* conference (London, UK), who provided invaluable feedback on the early thoughts that inspired this paper. Special thanks to Mark Bernstein for his critical questioning and reading recommendations.

Bibliography

Adams, Thomas R. and Nicolas Barker. 'A New Model for the Study of the Book'. In *A Potencie of Life: Books in Society*, 5–43. Edited by Nicolas Barker. London: The British Library, 1993.

Alvis, Alexandra. 'Books of Ours: What Libraries Can Learn about Social Media from Books of Hours'. In *Intermediate Horizons: Book History and Digital Humanities*, 109–19. Edited by Mark Vareschi and Heather Wacha. Madison: University of Wisconsin Press, 2022.

Author's Guild. 2023. 'More than 10,000 Authors Sign Authors Guild Letter Calling on AI Industry Leaders to Protect Writers'. *The Author's Guild*, 18 July 2023. https://authorsguild.org/news/thousands-sign-authors-guild-letter-calling-on-ai-industry-leaders-to-protect-writers (accessed 31 July 2023).

Author Unknown. 'Cursory Thoughts on the Modern Novel'. *The Lady's Magazine; or Entertaining Companion for the Fair Sex, Appropriates folely to their Use and Amusement (Supplement for 1780)* 11 (1780): 693.

Bolter, Jay D. *Writing Space*. Hillsdale, NJ: Erlbaum, 1991.

Bradbury, Ray. 'Another Computer Definition'. In *Digital Deli: The Comprehensive User-Lovable Menu of Computer Lore, Culture, Lifestyles and Fancy*, 201. Edited by S. Ditlea. New York: Workman Publishing, 1984.

Broussard, Meredith. *Artificial Unintelligence: How Computers Misunderstand the World*. Cambridge, MA: MIT Press, 2018.

Brown, Matthew P. 'Book History, Sexy Knowledge, and the Challenge of the New Boredom'. *American Literary History* 16, no. 4 (2004): 688–706.

Silec, Tatjana, Raeleen Chai-Elsholz and Leo Carruthers. *Palimpsests and the Literary Imagination of Medieval England: Collected Essays*. New York: Palgrave Macmillan, 2011.
Carter, John, Nicholas Barker and Simran Thadani. *ABC for Book Collectors, Ninth Edition*. New Castle, DE: Oak Knoll, 2024.
Coker, Catherine. 'The Margins of Print? Fan Fiction as Book History'. *Transformative Works and Cultures* 25 (2017).
Cordell, Ryan. '"Q i-jtb the Raven": Taking Dirty OCR Seriously'. *Book History* 20, no. 1 (2017): 188–225.
Crawford, Kate. 'Data from the Atlas of AI31'. *Missing Links in AI Governance* (2023): 111.
Cummings, James and Pip Willcox. 'Stationers' Register Online: A Case Study of a Byte-Reduced TEI Schema for Digitization (tei_corset)'. *Journal of the Text Encoding Initiative* 6 (2013).
Dahlström, Mats. 'A Book of One's Own: Examples of Library Book Marginalia'. In *The History of Reading, Volume 3: Methods, Strategies, Tactics*, 115–31. London: Palgrave Macmillan, 2011.
Darnton, Robert. 'What is the History of Books?' *Daedalus* (1982): 65–83.
Davies, Sally. 'Why Books Are the Best Form of Virtual Reality'. *GQ*, 23 February 2016. https://www.gq-magazine.co.uk/article/why-books-will-always-beat-virtual-reality (accessed 4 August 2023).
Deazley, Ronan (Ed). 'Stationers' Charter, London (1557)'. *Primary Sources on Copyright (1450–1900)*, n.d. https://www.copyrighthistory.org/cam/tools/request/showRecord.php?id=record_uk_1557 (accessed 31 July 2023).
Delaware Code Revisers. 'TITLE 8: Corporations'. *Delaware Code Online*. https://delcode.delaware.gov/title8/c001/sc15 (accessed 27 July 2023).
Dennett, Daniel C. 'The Problem with Counterfeit People'. *The Atlantic* 16 (2023). https://www.theatlantic.com/technology/archive/2023/05/problem-counterfeit-people/674075 (accessed 31 July 2023).
Driscoll, Beth and Claire Squires. 'The Epistemology of Ullapoolism: Making Mischief from within Contemporary Book Cultures'. *Angelaki* 25, no. 5 (2020): 137–55.
Drucker, Johanna. 'Diagrammatic Writing'. *New Formations* 78, no. 78 (2013): 83–101. https://ubu.com/media/text/vp/drucker_diagrammatic_writing_2013.pdf.
Drucker, Johanna. 'Distributed and Conditional Documents: Conceptualizing Bibliographical Alterities.' *MATLIT: Materialidades da Literatura* 2, no. 1 (2014): 11–29.
Ezell, Margaret J. M. 'The Laughing Tortoise: Speculations on Manuscript Sources and Women's Book History'. *English Literary Renaissance* 38, no. 2 (2008): 331–55.
Gaskell, Philip. *A New Introduction to Bibliography*. New Castle, DE: Oak Knoll, 1995.
Garvey, Ellen Gruber. *Writing with Scissors: American Scrapbooks from the Civil War to the Harlem Renaissance*. Oxford: Oxford University Press, 2012.
Hattenstone, Simon. 'Tech Guru Jaron Lanier: "The Danger Isn't that AI Destroys Us. It's That it Drives Us Insane"'. *The Guardian*, 23 March 2023. https://www.theguardian.com/technology/2023/mar/23/tech-guru-jaron-lanier-the-danger-isnt-that-ai-destroys-us-its-that-it-drives-us-insane (accessed 7 August 2023).
Hayles, N. Katherine. 'Print Is Flat, Code is Deep: The Importance of Media-specific Analysis.' *Poetics Today* 25, no. 1 (2004): 67–90.
Henrickson, Leah. 'The Book in the Digital Age: An Introduction'. *Publishing History* 83 (2020): 7–16.
Henrickson, Leah. *Reading Computer-Generated Texts*. Cambridge: Cambridge University Press, 2021.
Howsam, Leslie. 'Thinking through the History of the Book'. *Mémoires du livre* 7, no. 2 (2016).
Howsam, Leslie. 'What is the Historiography of Books? Recent Studies in Authorship, Publishing, and Reading in Modern Britain and North America'. *The Historical Journal* 51, no. 4 (2008): 1089–101. https://doi.org/10.1017/S0018246X08007206.

Hu, Krystal and Harshita Mary Varghese. 'Microsoft Pays Inflection $650 mln in Licensing Deal While Poaching Top Talents, Source Says'. *Reuters*, 22 March 2024. https://www.reuters.com/technology/microsoft-agreed-pay-inflection-650-mln-while-hiring-its-staff-information-2024-03-21 (accessed 20 August 2024).

Inflection AI. 'About'. *Inflection AI*, 2023. https://inflection.ai/about (accessed 31 July 2023).

Kirschenbaum, Matthew G. *Mechanisms: New Media and the Forensic Imagination*. Cambridge, MA: MIT Press, 2012.

Koutras, Nikos. 'Copyright as Property Right: Its Historical Evolution'. In *Intellectual Property Forum: journal of the Intellectual and Industrial Property Society of Australia and New Zealand*, no. 104 (2016): 21–31. https://www.copyrighthistory.org/cam/tools/request/showRecord.php?id=record_uk_1557 (accessed 31 July 2023).

Lamal, Nina, Jamie Cumby and Helmer J. Helmers. *Print and Power in Early Modern Europe (1500–1800)*. Leiden: Brill, 2021.

Mak, Bonnie. *How the Page Matters*. Toronto: University of Toronto Press, 2011.

Marcum, Deanna and Roger C. Schonfeld. *Along came Google: A History of Library Digitization*. Princeton: Princeton University Press, 2021.

McKenzie, D. F. *Bibliography and the Sociology of Texts*. Cambridge: Cambridge University Press, 1999.

Murray, Padmini Ray and Claire Squires. 'The Digital Publishing Communications Circuit'. *Book 2.0* 3, no. 1 (2013): 3–23. https://doi.org/10.1386/btwo.3.1.3_1.

Murray, Simone. 'Secret Agents: Algorithmic Culture, Goodreads and Datafication of the Contemporary Book World'. *European Journal of Cultural Studies* 24, no. 4 (2021): 970–989.

Patterson, L. Ray. 'Nimmer's Copyright in the Dead Sea Scrolls: A Comment.' *Houston Law Review* 38 (2001): 431.

Plato. 'Phaedrus'. Translated by B. Jowett, *Project Gutenberg*, 2008. https://www.gutenberg.org/files/1636/1636-h/1636-h.htm (accessed 31 July 2023).

Postman, Neil. *Technopoly: The Surrender of Culture to Technology*. New York: Vintage, 1992.

Pressman, Jessica. *Bookishness: Loving Books in a Digital Age*. New York: Columbia University Press, 2020.

Price, Leah. *What We Talk About When We Talk about Books: The History and Future of Reading*. New York: Basic Books, 2019.

Ramsay, Stephen. 'The Hermeneutics of Screwing Around; or What You Do with a Million Books.' *Pastplay: Teaching and Learning History with Technology* (2010): 111–20.

Reinburg, Virginia. *French Books of Hours: Making an Archive of Prayer, c. 1400–1600*. Cambridge: Cambridge University Press, 2012.

Rippl, Gabriele and Ursula Lenker. 'Book Histories in the Digital Age: Challenges, Promises, Achievements'. *Anglia* 139, no. 1 (2021): 1–5. https://doi.org/10.1515/ang-2021-0001.

Stallybrass, Peter. 'Books and Scrolls: Navigating the Bible'. In *Books and Readers in Early Modern England*, 42–79. Edited by S. Orgal, E. Sauer and J. Andersen. Philadelphia: University of Pennsylvania Press, 2012.

St Clair, William. *The Reading Nation in the Romantic Period*. Cambridge: Cambridge University Press, 2004.

Striphas, Ted. *The Late Age of Print: Everyday Book Culture from Consumerism to Control*. New York: Columbia University Press, 2011.

Suleyman, Mustafa. 'Will Everyone Have a Personal AI? With Mustafa Suleyman, Founder of DeepMind and Inflection'. Interviewed by E. Gil and S. Guo. 11 May 2023. *No Priors*. https://open.spotify.com/episode/4U2e4xgSyPPPcKruJJ80ij?si=328b9788875d44d6 (accessed 31 July 2023).

Thompson, John B. *Book Wars: The Digital Revolution in Publishing*. Oxford: John Wiley & Sons, 2021.

Tonra, Justin. 'Book History and Digital Humanities in the Long Eighteenth Century'. *Eighteenth-Century Studies* 54, no. 4 (2021): 765–83. https://doi.org/10.1353/ecs.2021.0091.

Van der Weel, Adriaan. *Changing our Textual Minds: Towards a Digital Order of Knowledge*. Manchester: Manchester University Press, 2011.

Van der Weel, Adriaan. 'The Communications Circuit Revisited'. *Jaarboek voor Nederlandse boekgeschiedenis* 8 (2001): 13–25.

Van Hulle, Dirk. *Genetic Criticism: Tracing Creativity in Literature*. Oxford: Oxford University Press, 2022.

Vee, Annette. *Coding Literacy: How Computer Programming Is Changing Writing*. Cambridge, MA: MIT Press, 2017.

Walsh, John. 'Literary Patronage in Medieval England, 1350–1550'. *Library Review* 58, no. 6 (2009): 451–60. https://doi.org/10.1108/00242530910969802.

Weber, Millicent. 'Authors Are Resisting A with Petitions and Lawsuits. But They Have an Advantage: We Read to Form Relationships with Writers'. *The Conversation*, 2023. https://theconversation.com/authors-are-resisting-ai-with-petitions-and-lawsuits-but-they-have-an-advantage-we-read-to-form-relationships-with-writers-208046 (accessed 31 July 2023).

Wilkins, Kim, Lisa Bennett and Helen Marshall. 'Calibrating Possibility'. *Possibility Studies & Society* 1, no. 1–2 (2023): 230–5. https://doi.org/10.1177/27538699231166486.

AFTERWORD
ON TEXTUAL EDITING AND DIGITAL SCHOLARLY CURATION
Dirk Van Hulle

As this volume shows, we have a lot to gain from combining textual editing, book history, and digital curation. One of the major developments in textual editing in the course of the twentieth and twenty-first centuries is the steady increase of transparency and accountability in the sense that editors have quite consistently deployed new tools and techniques to enable readers to check the editors' work. In the print paradigm, the authority of the editor was to some extent assumed because readers had to rely on this authority as a guarantor of textual integrity. The opportunities to check the editor's decisions were limited, unless one had access to the original documents, often dispersed in various archives around the globe. The digital paradigm not only enables and facilitates accessibility, searchability, usability and computability: it also comes with increased levels of accountability. This implies a certain textual awareness, a sense that the text one is reading is one among many versions and the product of several agents of textual change.

Textual awareness

Just imagine walking around in a bookshop, and on a display table with the advertisement 'Buy one, get one free' you see, lying next to each other, two editions of the same book by Mary Shelley, one saying *Frankenstein* and the other saying *Frankenstein: 1818 text*, both presented by the same publisher. Instead of combining *Frankenstein* with, say, *Dracula* – 'Buy one, get one free' –you let yourself be lured into purchasing two versions of *Frankenstein* for the price of one.

This may seem a banal commercial anecdote, based on a true story, but it is much more than that. It is the result of a long, gradual process in scholarly editing: the growing awareness that texts exist in many versions. The past four decades have been crucial to enhancing this awareness of multiple versions, not only in editorial theory (McGann 1991; Stillinger 1994; Shillingsburg 1996; McKenzie 1999; Bryant 2002; Van Hulle 2004, Eggert 2009; 2019; Ohge 2021; Van Mierlo 2025) but also in practice. Thus, for instance, Hans Walter Gabler's edition of *Ulysses* was followed by Jeri Johnson's edition, which followed a different rationale and reproduced the 1922 text (a copy of the first edition held at the Bodleian Library). Next to M. K. Joseph's 1969 edition of Mary Shelley's *Frankenstein* based on the *ultima manus* edition of 1831 (representing Shelley's final authorial intentions), the same publishing house, Oxford University Press, made available another edition, by Marilyn Butler. Instead of letting one edition 'supersede' a newer one, making the former 'obsolete' in the process, both editions were allowed to exist side by side; they both remain on offer in the very affordable Oxford World's Classics series (as in the anecdote above).

The digital medium has contributed significantly to this development. For a very long time, the tradition of scholarly editing was conditioned by the print medium, which often seemed to be patronizing readers as creatures who could not make up their own minds about textual variation. This attitude had an impact on the role of the editor. Since publishers assumed that 'the reader' did not want to be bothered by textual variants and was not interested in knowing about the text's revision history, the editor was supposed to be or act as the absolute authority who had to (and may have felt entitled to) make textual decisions for their readers. When one speaks of a critical edition, it is often implied that it will include (and usually be centred around) a critical reading text. An illustration of this development is that the various 'orientations to text' proposed by Peter Shillingsburg in *Scholarly Editing in the Computer Age* (3rd ed., 1996) were revisited two decades later (Van Hulle and Shillingsburg 2015), to add an orientation that was not necessarily geared towards the production of an edited text: the genetic orientation involves an editorial strategy that displays creativity in motion rather than settling on a final version as the main object of editing. Developments like these often make use of the digital medium's affordances to make readers aware of and offer them access to the material traces of creative writing processes.

Material awareness

Textual scholars make editions of material that is housed in, and very often also digitized by, holding libraries. This digitization is, and should be recognized as, a scholarly enterprise in and of itself. It is a critically informed process. As Merisa Martinez has shown, the critical decisions made by archivists during the production of digital artefacts significantly condition their use and reuse in digital scholarly editions (Martinez 2024). This situation calls for a rapprochement between library digitization and digital textual scholarship. As Martinez argues, this scholarly collaboration is necessary, especially at the start, or in the preparatory phase, of new digital scholarly editions (DSE).

The same mutual respect and curatorial-editorial collaboration would be beneficial at the end of digital editorial projects. More than ever, a rapprochement between digital curation and textual scholarship is necessary to guarantee the longevity of digital scholarly editions. Libraries and scholarly editions in print used to be natural allies. Even the most voluminous complete-works editions usually found a shelf in any self-respecting research library. And compared to the digital medium, paper has proven to be a stable material to future-proof scholarly editions. The first few decades of digital scholarly editing have shown to what extent this close connection had been taken for granted. Editors used to be able to rely on a distributed publication and preservation mechanism that took over the task of distributing the edition. While the editor's role was to produce the edition, the publisher took care of its publication, but this distribution of labour is often less clear in the digital age, as in the case of many digital scholarly editions the editor often de facto remains responsible for keeping their edition accessible – and is often left alone with this responsibility. As a result, instead of the distributed preservation model for print editions, digital scholarly editions often run from a single server hosted by a generous Humanities Faculty and financed with a project budget that is limited, also in time. This is a precarious situation against the background of the centuries-old preservation model of printed books, based on the distribution of many copies.

A rapprochement between digital curation and textual scholarship implies a bidirectional effort: from an editorial perspective, this effort entails the full appreciation of the scholarly dimension of library digitization; from a curatorial perspective, it implies the attentive concern and sense of responsibility to help take care (from Latin 'cura') of the products of digital edition projects in order to future-proof their continued accessibility. For understandable reasons, not all libraries are eager to take on – or even share – this responsibility if it involves the constant maintenance and updating of software.

There are several views when it comes to this question of digital maintenance of digital scholarly editions. One approach is to agree on a particular set of tools and build a community around it (such as e-editiones.org around TEI Publisher) to sustain the set.

Another view is to use emulation or encapsulation software such as Docker, which works well for born-digital material (Granger 2000; Van der Hoeven, Lohman and Verdegem 2007), but as Vincent Neyt notes, it may be less useful for digital scholarly editions because it attempts to solve an issue of software obsolescence by means of more software (Neyt and Van Hulle 2024). The result could be a matryoshka-doll effect of infinite regress, the digital equivalent of the homunculus problem in philosophy and Daniel Dennett's 'Cartesian theatre': if one tries to explain the workings of the mind by imagining a homunculus sitting in the brain observing and processing the sensory data that come in, one implicitly assumes that inside this homunculus's brain there is an even smaller homunculus etcetera, *ad infinitum*.

Instead of solving the software problem by means of more software, a third approach does the opposite by trying to turn the digital scholarly edition into a static website to preserve it. This approach, advocated by the Endings project at the University of Victoria (endings.uvic.ca), is well received by some of the most prominent pioneers of digital scholarly editing (Robinson 2023).

Yet another view is that it makes no sense to try and keep the digital scholarly edition as is. The argument is that, since the interface or the 'initial presentation' of the encoded texts is 'only a single perspective on the data' (Turska, Cummings and Rahtz 2016), it would therefore be better to regard the interface as just a temporary, disposable shell, and to focus only on preserving the source files (the image files and XML documents) in repositories (Rosselli Del Turco 2016; Turska, Cummings and Rahtz 2016). The extreme version of this view is to reduce the act of scholarly editing to creating a set of data, and then speculating that, with those data, AI will soon be able to make a DSE-on-demand. The question is to what extent it is wise to see digital scholarly editions as a form of datafication and to whom it is beneficial to reduce the role of the editor to that of a datafier, as it were. In this context, Joanna Tucker asks a few pertinent questions from a humanities perspective: 'Do we as researchers prefer to start with a fresh slate (if that is ever possible), rather than inheriting the nuances or "biases" from previous research projects? And are these nuances in the data not in fact what make our research valuable (and fundable) in the first place?' (Tucker 2022, 100)

Curatorial awareness

The principles for digital longevity by the Endings project at the University of Victoria (endings.uvic.ca; see above) are an excellent starting point for new edition projects. But in the meantime, there is a whole generation of pioneering digital scholarly editions that have been built according to different and divergent principles. In the case of long-standing projects, with a significant code base, complying to the Endings principles presents a challenge, but it is a challenge many editors will take up if it helps them future-proof their edition.

From the perspective of digital humanities, the idea of a decrease in technological sophistication (as in the third approach sketched above, turning a dynamic edition into a static website as a form of digital curation) does not fit in comfortably with the rhetoric of ceaseless innovation, disruptive trailblazing, uprooting, groundbreaking, perpetual pioneering, and pushing of boundaries.

But let us also take a moment to look at it from an editorial point of view. In bibliography and scholarly editing, the notions of versions and editions have played a crucial role for many decades. They are inherent to the discipline and define numerous other concepts, such as textual variants, collation, critical apparatus, and so on. The discipline of bibliography is built on notions such as 'edition', 'impression', 'issue' and 'state'. Before the digital age, and still today, outside the realm of the digital, an 'edition' in bibliographical terms refers to a book set in type, and all subsequent impressions based on that setting, whether printed from the original type or reproduced photographically. If this is the first appearance of a book it is the 'first edition'. When the same text is reset it becomes the 'second edition' and so on.

Textual scholars and bibliographers have always paid careful attention to textual variants between editions (and even *within* editions: collation in the early modern period is often employed to determine stop-press corrections). But when it comes to digital editing, we tend to accept that its result – whether it is called a digital 'archive' or 'edition' or 'arsenal' (Price 2009) – is treated as just a website which, thanks to the flexibility and affordances of the medium, can be emended at any time. But, this emendability takes for granted that there is, and assumes there will always be, someone who not only makes the emendation, but also keeps the edition alive.

The software editors use to create digital scholarly editions – which enables collaborative work, facilitates the addition of new data, makes collations and provides visualizations of our TEI-XML transcriptions – is essential for the development process.

However, once the development process is over and the edition is complete, its users will notice little difference whether the pages they browse are dynamically generated by server software or provided as static web pages. Instead of presenting a static website as an admission of failure in the dominant rhetoric of dynamics, editors and curators can also frame their sustainability plan differently and positively, as the rediscovery of a crucial concept in textual scholarship: the edition (in the bibliographical sense of a work's first, second, third edition). Making a static version of a digital scholarly edition would be the digital equivalent of publishing a first edition, which can then be followed by a revised second, third, . . . edition whenever the editorial-curatorial team would deem it appropriate.

A major task of a scholarly editor is that of 'a maker of connections' (Van Hulle 2024, 40) – connections in terms of the chronological succession of versions; connections between versions in the form of textual variants; connections between texts and external source texts. If we see this act of connecting as a crucial task of scholarly editing, it is worth making a case for the curation of static versions or first, second, . . . editions as an alternative to regarding every form of sustainability in terms of datafication. Archiving an edition is not necessarily a form of data management. Under the label of 'sustainability', digital scholarly editions are sometimes reduced to a set of data, dividing the edition into a container with images on the one hand and a container with text or transcription files on the other. The connections are conveniently forgotten because – according to the logic of data management – that is something that future scholars, software engineers or AI will be able to reconstruct themselves, as long as they have the data. Some editors might respectfully disagree. Making these connections according to a stated rationale is the scholarly editor's job; and preserving and curating these connections is the very purpose of an edition. That is also the reason why every scholarly edition of a particular text tends to be different.

Let's return to the example of James Joyce's *Ulysses*, mentioned above. Now that the text is in the public domain, the centenary of the novel's first publication in 1922 was celebrated by numerous new editions. The long list of editions of *Ulysses* may suggest 'the idea that each one of these editions is somehow not quite right and thus warrants superseding', as Georgina Nugent and Sam Slote note (2024, 1), but the fact that several editions have come out in the past forty years does not make, say, the 1984 Gabler edition obsolete. On the contrary, forty years after its publication, an entire volume of retrospective essays was dedicated to this critical and synoptic edition (Nugent and Slote 2024). In a similar way to 'the pertinence of being provisional' (1) in print editions, the interface of a digital scholarly edition is inherently interim. This realization 'does not render interfaces obsolete', as Rasmussen et al. argue: 'it just means they should not be considered permanent' (Rasmussen et al. 2024). If the interface is indeed 'an integral part of the argument that an edition makes about a text', surely it is worth preserving (Andrews and van Zundert 2018, 8). A digital edition's interface may be '*only* a single perspective on the data' (Turska, Cummings and Rahtz 2016; emphasis added), but the question is whether that makes it disposable. One could argue that, on the contrary, *because* it is a single perspective on the data, it is a unique critical-editorial argument about the connections between the textual material and therefore deserves to be cherished and curated.

Bibliography

Andrews, Tara L. and Joris J. van Zundert. 'What Are You Trying to Say? The Interface as an Integral Element of Argument'. In *Digital Scholarly Editions as Interfaces*, 3–33. Edited by Roman Bleier, Martina Bürgermeister, Helmut W. Klug, Frederike Neuber, and Gerlinde Schneider. Schriften des Instituts für Dokumentologie und Editorik 12. Norderstedt: Books on Demand, 2018.

Bryant, John. *The Fluid Text: A Theory of Revision and Editing for Book and Screen*. Ann Arbor: University of Michigan Press, 2002.

Cummings, James. 'Academics Retire and Servers Die: Adventures in the Hosting and Storage of Digital Humanities Projects'. *Digital Humanities Quarterly* 17, no. 1 (2023).

Driscoll, Matthew J. and Elena Pierazzo, eds. *Digital Scholarly Editing: Theories and Practices*. Cambridge: Open Book Publishers, 2016.

Eggert, Paul. *Securing the Past: Conservation in Art, Architecture and Literature*. Cambridge: Cambridge University Press, 2009.

Eggert, Paul. *The Work and the Reader in Literary Studies, Scholarly Editing and Book History*. Cambridge: Cambridge University Press, 2019.

Eve, Martin Paul. 'Digital Scholarly Journals Are Poorly Preserved: A Study of 7 Million Articles'. *Journal of Librarianship and Scholarly Communication* 12, no. 1 (2024).

Fenlon, Katrina Simone. 'Sustaining Digital Humanities Collections: Challenges and Community-Centred Strategies'. *International Journal of Digital Curation* 15, no. 1 (2020).

Granger, Stewart. 'Emulation as a Digital Preservation Strategy'. *D-Lib Magazine* 6, no. 10 (2000).

Holmes, Martin, Janelle Jenstad and J. Matthew Huculak. 'Introduction to Special Issue: Project Resiliency in the Digital Humanities'. *Digital Humanities Quarterly* 17, no. 1 (2023a).

Holmes, Martin and Joey Takeda. 'From Tamagotchis to Pet Rocks: On Learning to Love Simplicity through the Endings Principles'. *Digital Humanities Quarterly* 17, no. 1 (2023b).

Kirschenbaum, Matthew. *Mechanisms: New Media and the Forensic Imagination*. Cambridge, MA: MIT Press, 2008.

Martinez, Merisa Ariel. *Material Awareness: Exploring the Entanglement of Library Digitization and Digital Textual Scholarship*. The Swedish School of Library and Information Science, 2024.

McGann, Jerome J. *The Textual Condition*. Princeton: Princeton University Press, 1991.

McKenzie, D. F. *Bibliography and the Sociology of Texts*. Cambridge: Cambridge University Press, 1999.

Neyt, Vincent and Dirk Van Hulle. 'Sustaining Digital Editions: The Case of the Beckett Digital Manuscript Project'. Paper presented at the conference of the European Society for Textual Scholarship., Budapest, 2024. elte-dh.hu/ests-2024-program

Nugent, Georgina and Sam Slote, eds. *Ulysses Forty Years: A Critical Retrospective of Hans Walter Gabler's Critical and Synoptic Edition of Ulysses*, 1–14. Liverpool: Liverpool University Press, 2024.

Ohge, Christopher. *Publishing Scholarly Editions: Archives, Computing, and Experience*. Cambridge: Cambridge University Press, 2021.

Price, Kenneth M. 'Edition, Project, Database, Archive, Thematic Research Collection: What's in a Name?' *Digital Humanities Quarterly* 3, no. 3 (2009).

Rasmussen, Krista Stinne Greve, Katrine Frøkjær Baunvig, Jon Tafdrup, Kirsten Vad, Kim Steen Ravn. 'One Edition – Multiple Interfaces: Dissemination and Preservation of Sustainable Digital Scholarly Editions'. In *Open Up Digital Editions*. Edited by Elena Spadini and Yann Stricker. Zürich and Basel: Center Digital Editions & Edition Analytics / Research and Infrastructure Support RISE, 2024. https://doi.org/10.5281/zenodo.10400571

Robinson, Peter. 'The Endings Project and the Canterbury Tales Project (and also, Boccaccio and Dante)'. *Scholarly Digital Editions blog*, 2023. scholarlydigitaleditions.blogspot.com/2023/07/the-endings-project-and-canterbury.html

Rosselli Del Turco, Roberto. 'The Battle We Forgot to Fight: Should We Make a Case for Digital Editions?' *Digital Scholarly Editing: Theories and Practices*, 219–38. Edited by Matthew J. Driscoll and Elena Pierazzo. Cambridge: Open Book Publishers, 2016.

Sahle, Patrick. 'What is a Scholarly Digital Edition?' *Digital Scholarly Editing: Theories and Practices*, 19–40. Edited by Matthew J. Driscoll and Elena Pierazzo. Cambridge: Open Book Publishers, 2016.

Shillingsburg, Peter. *From Gutenberg to Google: Electronic Representations of Literary Texts*. Cambridge: Cambridge University Press, 2006.

Shillingsburg, Peter. *Scholarly Editing in the Computer Age*, 3rd edition. Ann Arbor: University of Michigan Press, 1996.

Shillingsburg, Peter. *Textuality and Knowledge*. University Park, PA: Penn State University Press, 2017.

Stillinger, Jack. 'A Practical Theory of Versions'. In *Coleridge and Textual Instability: The Multiple Versions of the Major Poems*, 118–40. Oxford: Oxford University Press, 1994.

Tucker, Joanna. 'Facing the Ecologies of the Far Right: Fanning the Flameschallenge of Digital Sustainability as Humanities Researchers'. *Journal of the British Academy* 10 (2022): 93–120.

Turska, Magdalena, James Cummings and S. Rahtz. 'Challenging the Myth of Presentation in Digital Editions'. *Journal of the Text Encoding Initiative* 9 (2016). https://doi.org/10.4000/jtei.1453

Van der Hoeven, Jeffrey, Bram Lohman and Remco Verdegem. 'Emulation for Digital Preservation in Practice: The Results'. *International Journal of Digital Curation* 2, no. 2 (2007). https://doi.org/10.2218/ijdc.v2i2.35

Van Hulle, Dirk and Peter Shillingsburg. 'Orientations to Text, Revisited'. *Studies in Bibliography* 59 (2015): 27–44.

Van Hulle, Dirk. 'Creative Ecologies: The Complete-Works Edition in a Digital Paradigm'. In *Futures of Digital Scholarly Editing*, 33–49. Edited by Matt Cohen, Kenneth M. Price, and Caterina Bernardini. Minneapolis: University of Minnesota Press, 2024.

Van Hulle, Dirk. 'Digital Library History: The Virtual Bookcases of James Joyce and Samuel Beckett'. *Quaerendo* 46, no. 2–3 (2016): 192–204.

Van Hulle, Dirk. *Textual Awareness: A Genetic Study of Late Manuscripts by Joyce, Proust, and Mann*. Ann Arbor: University of Michigan Press, 2004.

Van Mierlo, Wim. *Scholarly Editing in Perspective*. Cambridge: Cambridge University Press, 2025.

INDEX

Note: Page numbers followed by 'n' denotes note numbers, while in *italics* represents figures.

abolitionist movement in the US   120
Act for the Encouragement of Learning   285
Adler, Melissa   30
Airoldi, Edoardo   28
ALGOFOLK digital project   201
algorithmic folklore   201
Alice in Wonderland (Carroll)
   creative process, work   256
   expressions, work instances   256–7
   FFRBR Group 1 entities as   *258*
   FRBRoo Group 1 entities model   *256*
   manifestation, and item   *257*
Alsford, Stephen   228
American Contact (2024)   6
American Folklife Center at the Library of Congress (LC)   200
American folklore archives   195–6
Ancient Mysteries Described (Hone)   55–7, 62
Andersen, Hans Christian   249, 252
Andersen, Kurt   227
Annif   28–9. *See also* digital catalogues
annotation   8, 85, 86, 87, 88, 90, 92, 113, 122, 124, 127, 133–4, 137–41, 144–50, 152, 192, 288
AntConc software programme   145–7
Antioch Review   263
anti-slavery hymn book (Garrison)   119
anti-slavery literature anthologies   117–18
Archaeology of Reading project   4
archives
   'authors'   3, 82
   digital   79, 81, 174, 176, 201
   documents, archival   178
   and 'editions'   4, 6, 79
   and folklore, digitization   8, 191–4, 196–8
   and libraries   87, 89, 91
   online, digitization in   149–50
   personal   83, 87, 92
   publishers'   70
   Whistlestop Project   210–12
Archives of Northwest Folklore   191, 199
Archives Toolkit (AT)   195
archivists, defined   195
Arnaboldi, Michela   238

artefact analyses, *oby Dick*   142–4, *143–4*
   'digital' approaches   143–4
   objects selection   143
artificial intelligence (AI)   2, 3, 9, 73, 85, 266, 271
   'AI winter' Hopfield's insights   271 n.14
   analogy, as coffee cup   267–70, 267 n.9
   archival research   263–4
   assisted, digital teaching   6
   Boltzmann distribution and   270 n.13
   ChatGPT, and Chatbots   265, 267, 273
   compression algorithm, modern   272–5, 274 n.17
   diverse responses   269
   GPT-3/4 model   271, 274
   humanizing, risks   266
   implications, archival trajectory   263–4, 264 nn.1–2
   mechanistic analogues   275–6
   pattern-recognizing networks   271
   PNG compression   273
   reverse archive as   264, 276–8
   'Softmax' function   270
   'synthetic data' to train, risks   277–8, 278 n.22
   thermodynamic concepts and   271–2
artificial languages   26
ARTstor   263
audience-driven museums   228
audiovisual technology   182–3
augmented reality (AR)   176
Austen, Jane   135
automatic subject classification tools   30

ballads and chapbooks, collections   61–2
Balliol College, Oxford   180
Batchelar, Thomas   59–60, 62–3, 73–4
   Hone's visit to   55, 61–2
   printer of songbooks   55–6
Batten, Mollie   164
Beckett Digital Library   80–1, 94
Bedford, Leslie   138, 141
Bender, Emily   267
Berman, David   238
Bewick, Thomas   59–60, 71
bibliography   1, 3–5, 6, 50, 60, 63, 68, 70, 110, 113, 288–9, 300

Index

'bibliomania' 60
Bibliothèque nationale de France 43, 46
Bird, Eleanor 122
Bischof, Jonathan M. 28
Bitstreams (Kirschenbaum) 3
Black Bibliography Project 6
black-and-white photography 48
Blake, William 179, 263
blockchains, programmable 265 n.5
Bødker, Henrik 227
Bodleian Library catalogue 19
Boltzmann, Ludwig 269, 271
Boltzmann machines 271
Book Historian's Digital Toolkit (London Rare Books School) 129
book historians, significance 281–3, 292
book history 5, 7, 289
    authorship and publishing 248
    bibliography and 6, 288
    bookishness 283, 292
    computers *vs.* book or library 282–3
    degrees in 281
    digital approaches to 2, 5–6, 72, 286, 289
    electronic hypertexts 287
    emerging media evolution 5, 282–4, 287, 289
    Inflection AI, case study 284–5, 289
    interdisciplinary area 281, 289
    Intermediate Horizons (2022) 6
    LLMs driving technologies 284–7
    print histories and 248, 252, 254
    project management in 221
    projects, digital methods into 247–8
    relevance 281–2
    semantic ambiguities, challenges 248
    textual materialism and 70
    training, new media analysis 289–91
'bookishness' (Pressman) 283
Borwick, Jim 207–8, 211, 213, 222 n.1
Boswell, James 61–2
Bourdieu, Pierre 46, 227
The Bow in the Cloud (1834), anthology 8, 117
    and abolitionist movements 118–21
    authors' names, consistency 123–5
    Buxton's letter extract 128, *129*
    collaborations 123–4, 128
    compiled/edited by, Rawson 117
    creative-critical approaches 127–8
    data analyses 124–6
    digital edition, purpose 117, 119–20, 129–30
    layout/pages 118
    overview 117–19
    preface versions 123–5
    Prince and Equiano's narrative *vs.* 126
    published version 120–1, 124
    religious affiliations, contributors 125, *126*

    revision narratives 127–8
    sentiment scores 126, *127*
    TEI-XML transcriptions 119, 126
    unpublished material 120–1, 125
    vocabulary density 124 n.6
Boyle, Robert 16–17
Bradbury, Ray 282–4
British abolitionist movement 121
British Library (BL) 175, 179, 180
broadside ballads 59–61
Bryant, John 86
    'fluid text' theory 122
    revision narrative 127–8
Bulgarian Academy of Sciences (BAS), Folklore Institute 197–8
Bush, Vannevar 104–5
Buzzetti, Dino 103, 110

Cambridge Analytica scandal 240
Canterbury Tales 175
Capmas, Charles 40
CARE principles 129
Carpini, Michael X. Delli 240
Catalogue of the Large and Curious English Library of Mr. John Hutton 22
catalogues 7
    archives, hierarchical system 194
    associative approach 28
    auction 80
    Bayesian approach 27
    biases into, knowledge organization 25–6, 32
    bibliographical ways, term use 17
    classifications granularity, issues 30
    critical cataloguing 30–1
    de Chauliac remarks 16
    decision-making process 25–6
    digital tools 26–9
    Enlightenment influences on 15–16, 18, 22, 24
    essential tools 15
    extant and virtual libraries 83
    guide, library owners 22
    Hierarchical Poisson Convolution 28
    key categories 16
    lexical approach 28
    library 16, 32
    literary figures, works 17
    medicines 16, 16 n.1, 17
    Medieval 15, 19
    Milton's works 17
    multiple categories 25–7, 29–30
    online, of books 4
    problematic subject classifications 30–1
    scholarly enquiries 18–19
    subject-based classifications 22, 25–6, 30–1
    tables classification 25

Index

technical methods use 23–4
term, refers to 16–17, 18 n.3
CAVE projection screens 182
Cecil, Richard 124–5
Critical Editions for Digital Analysis and Research (CEDAR) project 111–12
Center for Technology Innovations in Education (CTIE) 208
chatbots 275–7
   complex nature 267
   stochastic systems 272
   temperature concept 269
ChatGPT 265–7, 273, 276
Chiang, Ted 273
Chicago Online Research and Publication Services (CORPUS) 113–15
Childhood in Dickensian London 181
Christen, Kim. 194
Codd, E. F. 104–5
Colored Conventions Project 6
Common Crawl 264
community-built digital archives 194
compression formats 272–3
computational editing platform 99
Computer Lib/Dream Machine (Nelson) 102
Conder, Eliza 125
Conder, Josiah 121, 125
Connell, Sarah 119, 127
Conrart, Valentin 38
content management system (CMS) 114, 180, 194, 196
Contextualising the Archives (Kolovos) 195
controlled vocabularies 250–1
copper-plate engraving 46
Cordell, Ryan 50
Coulet, Henri 42, 43 n.5
critical cataloguing 30–1
critical edition 4, 101, 105, 298
Cruikshank, George 57, *58*
cryptocurrency 265
Cults3D 149
curatorial practices 8, 153, 175, 177, 180, 182
Cutter, Charles Ammi 24
Cutter's Expansive Classification system 23–4

d'Alembert, Jean le Rond 20, 22–3
DALL-E 276
data normalization principle 104–5
database paradigm 107
databases 2, 4, 7, 10, 52, 80, 193, 195, 197–8, 248, 255, 263–5
   digital, establishment 80
   graph 8, 105–8, *106*
   OCHRE, research platform 109
   relational 105

data-driven approach, to scholarship 9, 265
Davis, Tom 63, 65
de Chauliac, Guy 16
de Maupertuis, Pierre Louis Moreau 42–3, *44*, 49
Dead Sea Scroll dating 102
Deanesly, Margaret 164
'Dear Dirty Dublin' 3D model 187
decimal classification system 23–4
Deciphering Dickens project 180–1
Derrida, Jacques 263
Derrida's Margins 80
descriptive metadata 217, 250–1, 254
Dever, Maryanne 178
Dewey Decimal System (DDC) 23–4, 29
Dewey, John 134, 138, 141
Dewey, Melvil 23
Dicey, Cluer 61
Diderot, Denis 20, *21*, 22, 24
Dietz, Laura 3
DigiBoard 200
digital catalogues 31
   associative approach 28
   critical cataloguing 30–1
   Finto AI 28
   granularity in classifications, issues 30
   LCC terminologies 30
   metadata, increased quantities of 30
   multiple subjects classification 29–30
   real-time changes to 31
   solutions, for cataloguers 27
   TEXTA Toolkit 29
   topic modelling 27–9
   user-generated tags, benefits 29–30
digital collections 2, 7
digital concepts 7
digital curatorship 176, 184
digital display cabinet
   advantages, and drawbacks 179
   for displaying, rare books 179–80
   Turning the Pages 179–80
digital editions 4, 50, 117, 123–4, 129, 180–1
   challenges, established concepts 86–7
   digital archives, distinction 79
   image-enhanced 47
   modelling challenges for 88
   production of 84–6
   study of reading traces 87–8
   Vetusta Monumenta 4
digital facsimile 1, 4, 72
   and block printing 55
   connecting with narrative 130
   facsimile editions 49
   manuscripts 180
   'transformed text' 5

Index

Turning the Pages   179
writers' libraries   80–1
digital forms of engagement   151
digital humanities (DH)   1–2, 4–7, 70, 72, 79, 81, 91, 119, 135–6, 147, 197, 219–21, 247, 257, 264 n.1, 278, 300
   book history   6
   changing media conceptions   5
   genealogy of, hypertext   219–20
   integrating new media   247–50, 264 n.1
   librarians/archivists, relevance   6
   matching and sequencing impressions   64, 65, 68–9
   project management   217–18, 221
   projects, and digital archives   4
   records management   221
   research   136, 147
   texts, multitudes   100
   tools and datasets use   220
   visualization tools   135, 197
digital imaging   55, 66, 69, 72
digital management software   29
digital museum guide systems   183
digital photography   69
digital pluralism theory (Shillingsburg)   122
digital publications   49, 113–15, 127
digital recordkeeping   197
digital scholarly editions (DSE)   88, 180, 183, 265 n.4, 298–301
   datafication   300–1
   development process   300–1
   digital maintenance, views   299
   editor's role   298–9
   interface, single perspective on data   299, 301
   source files preservation, in repositories   299
   static website, turning into   299–1
   'sustainability' plan   301
   TEI-XML transcriptions   300
   textual variants, editions   297–8, 300
digital storytelling   184–5
   and hypertext   220
   Museum of Literature Ireland (MoLI) case   186–7
   Wordsworth Grasmere case study   185–6
digital technologies, for galleries/museums
   Adobe Flash Player   182
   'audience-driven museum'   228
   audio-visual technology   182–3
   cost issue   180
   digital museum guide systems   183
   exhibition space, virtual tour   181–2
   gap between materiality and immateriality   176, 184
   GPS technology   183
   interactive, gamification tools   183
   materiality and immateriality, gap between   176, 184
   online exhibitions   181–2
   participatory approach   228
   personal digital assistants (PDA)   183
   QR codes   182
   rare books, display   178–9
   RFID reader   183
   scepticism about usage   176, 229
   social media practices   180, 227–9
digital textual editing, methodologies
   approaches to   100–2, 121–4
   case of an *editio princeps*   102
   computation and text analysis   103–4, 124–7
   data normalization, Codd's   104–5
   discrete granular items, texts as   104–5
   document paradigm   107–8
   graph database model   8, 105, *106*, 107–8
   Hebrew Bible complexity   102
   linearity of digital text, issues   103–4
   McGann's theories   101
   Nelson's intertwingularity concept   101, 104
   OCHRE graph data model use   108–10
   TEI, for data publication or sharing format   103–4, 106, 119, 123–4
   text schema   104
digital writing   51
'Digitales Osmantinum' system   183
digitization   5, 298
   3D modelling   150
   advantages   91
   affordances, and object   72
   large-scale, projects   69, 72 n.12
   photography for   47–8
   of printing surfaces   70
   textual materialism, cognizant of   70
   writer's library   84–6
digitized archives
   'born digital' folklore collections   200
   case studies   196–200
   community-built, using Mukurtu   194
   Dublin Core metadata schema   199
   opportunities and challenges   197
   purposes and benefits   194
   struggles, issues of training   195–6
   successes and problems   199–200
   wider availability and access   200
diplomatic transcription   41, 43, 46–7, 49
discourse units   109
Dondi, Cristina   4
Dorothy Howard collection, Australia   197–8
Douglass, Frederick   121
Dove Cottage   185–6
Drescher, Tim   136
Driscoll, Beth   289

Index

du Châtelet, Marquise
    ambiguities in letter 45
    diplomatic transcription 49
    letter juxtaposed with, Besterman's transcription 43-4, *45*, 49
    letter to Maupertuis 42-3, *45*
    punctuation use, Sgard views 42-3
Dublin Core (DC) 113
Dublin Core Metadata Initiative (DCMI) 212, 253
Duchêne, Roger 40-1, 49

Early Caribbean Digital Archive 6
Early English Books Online (EEBO) 4, 48
East India Company 118
e-books 6, 29
Eclectic Review magazine 121
edited collections
    contributors to, theology and divinity field 158 (*see also* theological publishing)
    data availability, issue 161-2
    defined 158
    as a format 157-8
    profile of contributors, shift in 159, 166, 168
    scholarly journal issue *vs.* 158
    specialist audiences for 161
    volumes increase 158, 168
editing, writer's library
    biases 91-2
    corpus, selection criteria 88-9
    marginalia 81, 83, 85, 87-8
    material and spatial nature 89-90
    prioritizing material 91
    reading traces encoding, challenges 90-1, 90 n.15
Eighteenth Century Collections Online (ECCO) 4
electronic cataloguing system 27
Electronic Enlightenment database 43
Empson, William 134
encapsulation software 299
Encoding/Decoding model (Hall) 227-8
encyclopaedia, purpose 20
encyclopaedic narrative 133-5
    readers' engagement 133-4
Encyclopedia Americana 283
Encyclopedia Britannica 283
'encyclopedic' texts 133
Encyclopédie, (Diderot and d'Alembert) 20, 24
    article on woodcut in 58, *59*
    hierarchical and relational methodologies 22-3
    relief depictions of blocks 71
    system devised for 20, 22
    'Système figuré des connoissances humaines' 20, *21*

Endings project, University of Victoria 299-300
Enlightenment period, catalogues problems 15-16. *See also* catalogues
enumerative cataloguing 23-4
epigraphic units 109
epistolary editing 40
epistolary punctuation 42-3
Equiano, Olaudah 126
Estonian Folklore Archives (EFA) 191
Ethereum 265
Europeana 263
Europeana Data Model (EDM) 113
Eve, Martin Paul 3
Evelyn, John 22
Everyday Book (Hone) 60, 62
exhibit environment, engagement 138-9
    3D printing use 139, 144-5
    aesthetic experience 141, 152
    keywords, object based 140-1
    material annotation impact 141, 144-5
    with novel (*see Moby-Dick* (Melville))
    tactile 134
Extensible Markup Language (XML) 6, 27, 50, 85, 90-1, 93, 102, 106, 108, 112, 119, 123-4, 126, 183, 212, 288, 299-300
extraction *vs.* extractivism 133-4

Fertel, Martin Dominique 42, 44
findable, accessible, interoperable, and reusable (FAIR) 129
    data formats 123, 130
Finto AI 28
Flickr 180
folklore archives 191-2
    cataloguing, hierarchical system 194
    digitization, case studies 19 n.3, 196-201
    Dublin Core metadata schema 199
    history and evolution of 192-3
    management, 'hybrid practice' 195
    online systems for 194
    opportunities and challenges 8
    in Oregon 199-200
    Romanian Academy's 198-9
    University of Oregon (OU) Folklore Programme 199
folklorists, and archivists 195-6
Frankenstein (Shelley), multiple textual versions 297-8
Freedom Burning (Huzzey) 121
Functional Requirements for Bibliographic Records (FRBRoo) 247, 254-5, *256*, *257*, *258*

Gabler, Hans Walter 49-50
Gallimard Pléiade edition 40
Gallinari, Laura 152

Index

gamification tools   183
Garrison, William Lloyd   119, 121
Gaskell, Elizabeth   177
Gaskell, Philip   15
generative AI   6, 129, 264 n.1, 265, 270, 276, 278 n.23. *See also* large language models
   archive in reverse   264, 276-7
   compression algorithms   272, 274-5
   limitations   278 n.23
   mechanistic qualities   267
   thermodynamic metaphor   270-2
Georgitis, Nathan   193, 195
Getty Art and Architecture Thesaurus   *251*, 252
Getty Union List of Artist Names   252
Gilmore, J. C.   195-6
Global Information Infrastructure (GII)   238
Goethe Bibliothek Online   80, 83
Goffman, Erving   227
Google's Gemini   284
graph database model   105, *106*, 107 n.5
grapheme   99 n.1, 102, 105, 108-10, 112
Greenblatt, Stephen   175, 177-8
Greetham, David C.   100
Griffith, Jim   191-2
Groom, Nick   61

Hackman, Larry   211-12
Hall, Stuart   227-8, 237
handwritten text. *See also* letters editions
   association, with individuality   39, 52
   Duchêne's assessment   40-1
   editing, for readability   7, 38-9
   diplomatic approach   45-6
   Voiture's works   38
Harry S. Truman Presidential Museum and Library   205-9, 211-16, 218, 220-1
Hassoun, Amelia   237
Hayles, N. Katherine   2, 287
Hebrew Bible   102
Henrickson, Leah   9
Heritix web crawler tool   200
Hinton, Geoffrey   270-1
The History Men (Kenyon)   157
The History of Mary Prince   119
Hjørland, Birger   30
Hodgson, Thomas   62
holographic screens   182
Hone, William
   Ancient Mysteries Described   55-6, *57*, 62
   ballads/chapbooks collection, 1843 catalogue   62 n.6
   Cruikshank, collaboration with   57-8
   Everyday Book   60, 62
   illustrations of episodes, life of Christ   56, *57*

   political satires by   62
   visual language, adoption   57-8
Hooke, Robert   16
Hopfield, John   271
Hopkins, Gerard Manley   186
Howard's End (Forster)   133
Hubble, Gwenyth   164
Hutter Prize   274
Hyde, Thomas   19
hyperspectral and CT imaging   69
hypertext   3, 219-20

IIIF-based storytelling tool (Exhibit)   129
IIIF image viewer (Mirador)   119
imaging technologies
   classification task   65-6
   hyperspectral and CT imaging   69
   Reflectance Transformation Imaging (RTI)   71
   resolution, improvements   48-9
Indiana State University Folklore Archives   194
Inflection AI   282
   funding, and success   284
   Pi core product   284, 286-7
   private commercial interests   287
   public benefit corporation, registered as   284-5
   safety commitment   286
information repositories   264-6
Insko, Jeffrey   133-4
Institute of Museum and Library Services   211
Intermediate Horizons (2022)   6
International Image Interoperability Framework (IIIF)   4, 47, 93, 119, 129, 181
'intertwingularity' concept (Nelson)   8, 101
Intner, Sheila   26
Irving, Washington   121
Italian Archaeological museums   238

Jauss, Hans Robert   134
John Rylands Library   119, 175
Johnson, Samuel   134
Johnston, John   73
journal-as-network   157
Joyce, James   81, 186-7, 301
   Finnegans Wake   186
   A Portrait of the Artist as a Young Man   186

Keats, John   175
Kirschenbaum, Matthew   2
   Bitstreams   3, 50
   text and image   50
Kittler, Friedrich A.   73, 73 n.13
knowledge organization   19, 26, 248-55
   Alice in Wonderland, example   256-8, *258*
   biases   19-20, 25-6
   categories and classification, limits   258-9

consistency in   258
controlled vocabularies   250–2
descriptive metadata, importance   250–3
everyday practices   249
as evolution of authorship and publishing   248
forms of categorization and classification   248–50, 254
Getty Art and Architecture Thesaurus   *251*
in histories of print and book history   248, 252, 254
information retrieval and   255, 258
The Little Mermaid example   249, 252–3
metadata creation and management, guidelines   254–5
new media and   250, 254
semantic ambiguities in   248, 250
Knowles, Anne Kelly   263
Kochtanek, Thomas.   207
Koszary, Adam   231
Kovacs, Beatrice   26–7
Kratt tool   28–9

Lady's Magazine (1780)   285–6
Lanier, Jaron   283–4
large language models (LLMs)   130, 284, 286–8
  artificial constraint   268
  Bender's disparagement   267
  ChatGPT   266–7
  claims of 'public benefit'   287
  compression algorithm   274–5
  cup of coffee, analogy   267–70
  Dennett's view   286
  energy/entropy concepts for   268–9, 272
  gzip   272, 275–6
  intelligence   274 n.15
  letters and survey, raising concerns   286
  thermodynamic systems   267–8
  training   272, 274 n.19
Larkin, Jamie   229
Latent Dirichlet Allocation (LDA)   28
Latour, Bruno   227
Leibniz, Gottfried Wilhelm   25
Leiva, Isidoro Gil   30
Lema, Melisa Diaz   238
letters editions
  'accurate' representations   48
  'authenticity' of documents   37–8, 46 n.8
  diplomatic transcription   41, 43, 46–7
  editorial polishing for publication   37–8
  epistolary qualities   38
  Gallimard Pléiade edition   40
  original punctuation in   43
  Persian Letters   37
  personal punctuation   43 n.5
  photographic transcriptions   47–8

prefaces role   37, 39
punctuations usage in   42–3
seventeenth-and eighteenth-century   7, 38
Sévigné's correspondence   38–9
transcribing for print edition   45
Voiture's works   38
letterpress printing   55
Leviathan Book Club   152
Liberty Bell (edited by Chapman)   119 n.2
library catalogues   16, 80
  Annif, use   28
  during the eighteenth century   23
  growth in popularity of   18
  hierarchical and relational methodology   22–3
  Mabinogion case   25–6
  mediating function   32
  subject classifications   22, 25–6
Library of Congress Classification System (LCC)   23, 29
Library of Congress Name Authority Files   252
LibraryThing   30
Linked Open Data (LoD)   256
literary heritage   176
  artefacts, and emotion elicited   176, 178
  'aura' of documents   178
  defined   177
  digital media use, neglect in   176
  digital opportunities, and media   180–4
  emotional attachment to records and memory   176, 178
  memory and legacy, preservation   177
  sense of critical curiosity   177
  in terms of 'resonance' and 'wonder'   177–8
  theory of affect   176–8
  Yeats exhibition for the web   179, 181
lithography   46
The Little Mermaid (Andersen)   249
Locke, John   17, 19
London's Stationers' Company (1557)   285
Ludwig Tiecks Bibliothek   80, 83 n.11
Lumsden, James   60
Lydgate, John   19
Lyell Lectures in Bibliography, 2014   5

Mabinogion   25, 29
McCreery, John   56
McCullough, David   221
MacDonald, George   228
McGann, Jerome   8, 99, 114
  digital editorial practice, methodologies   48–49, 101
  facsimile and critical editing   110
  image of text, and text relationship   48–9
  linear text markup issue   103
  n-dimensional, textual fields   100, 101

Index

McKenzie, Donald F. 6, 50, 70
machine-assisted AI methods 6
machine learning 63–4, 73
Madden, Frederic 61–2
Magnino, Bennett 207, 210, 212–13
Manchester Digital Collections 119
manuscript *vs.* printed text. *See also* textual scholarship
    Besterman's transcribing for print edition 43–5
    diplomatic transcription 41, 43, 46–7, 52
    document's 'authenticity' 37–8, 41, 46 n.8
    Duchêne's assessment 40
    editors' role/accountability 297–8
    epistolary punctuation, adherence to 42–3, 52
    'exact transcription' of original 46
    facsimiles 46 n.7, 50
    Gabler's conception, transmissibility of text 49, 51
    handwritten text, imitation for print 45–6
    image resolution, changes 48 n.9
    incommensurability, in relationship 39–40
    letter, documentary singularity 42
    as literary artefact 175
    mediated 'translation' 39, 41
    non-print documents, problem 52
    photos transform texts 47–8
    progress towards exactitude 47
    resolution, improvements in 48–9
    spelling or non-systematic syntax 42–3, 52
    substantives and accidentals, distinction 42
    TEI Guidelines, modelling text 49–50, 112, 119, 126, 129
    typographic punctuation 42
Mapping Museums Project 230, 239
Marr, Tim 141–2
Mascall, E. L. 166
Mascall, Eric 167
Mason, George 19
material annotation idea 8, 139, 145, 149–50
    concordance features 145, *146*
Material Evidence in Incunabula (Dondi) 4
material text, term 2–3, 5, 70 n.10
matryoshka-doll effect 299
Medieval catalogues 15, 19
Medieval Hebrew Leningrad Codex 112
Melville, Herman 4, 8
Melville Electronic Library (MEL) 153
Melville's Marginalia Online (MMO) 4, 81, 88
memex (Bush) 104
Mendelson, Edward 133
Midjourney images 271
Milton, John 17
Moby-Dick (Melville) 8, 134
    chapter titles, 'glossing' 139–40
    gaming experience 152

immensity, understanding 135, 145, 151
keywords, object-based 139–41, 139 n.3, *140*, 152
lexicographical richness 135
material annotation, approach to 134, 138–41
multiple discourses, of whaling 135–6, 135 n.2, 138, 141–2
multiple levels, engagement 134–9
mural and novel, relationship between 136
nautical vocabularies 149
'The Quadrant' contextual glossing 139–40, *140*
'word cloud' strategy, text *135*
World of Whaling in the Digital Age 141–4
Moby-Dick in Pictures: One Drawing for Every Day (Kish) 151
Mollick, Ethan 274
Moorcroft, Heather 30–1
'The Mother' poem, (Gilbert) 119, *120*
movable type printing 45–6
Mukurtu 194
Museum of Literature Ireland (MoLI) 186–7
museum theory 138
    artefact analysis 142–4, *143–4*
    connection, tangible experiences of 138–9
    Conn's account 138
    'digital assets' 145
    exhibitions 141–2
    'interpretive exhibitions' 138
    items selection, for 3D-printing 139, 144–5
    outreach, step to re-imagining 9
    sense of artworks, Dewey's 138
museums' social media practices
    APIs, Meta and Google 229
    brand awareness 233
    case study of UK museums' 228
    circulation/distribution/ consumption 237
    content recommendation systems 237–40
    during COVID pandemic, changes 230, 232
    data-led research with interviews 229–30, 231
    digital expertise shortage 234–5
    distant reading of texts 229–30
    emotive posts 239
    Facebook engagement 238–40
    growth of 229
    lack of platform expertise 238
    monologues and sales pitches 232–3
    Nesta survey 229, 235
    questions to guide researchers 241
    resources issue 233–6
    sampling bias issue 232
    size of online audiences 231, 240
    TikTok engagement 235, 237–8

Index

Unassailable Voice use   229, 233
   using Twitter   230–2, 236
   video-based content   235
MyMiniFactory (formerly MyMiniVerse)   149

National Archives and Records Administration (NARA)   218
National Art Library (NAL)   180–1
National Library of Finland (NLF)   28
National Library of Ireland (NLI)   179–80
National Library of Scotland (NLS)   180–1
Naudé, Gabriel   22
Nelson, Ted   8, 99, 101, 112, 114
Network of European Museum Organisations (NEMO)   230
New Bedford Whaling Museum   142
New Essays Concerning Human Understanding (Leibniz)   25
new media
   appeal and challenges   229
   in digital humanities   247–50, 264 n.1
   knowledge organization and (*see* knowledge organization)
   online museums (*see* museums' social media practices)
   studies   1–2, 9
Newman, John Henry   186
Neyt, Vincent   299
Nobel prize   270–1
Noel, Will   5
nook, semantics   249

Oeuvres complètes de Voltaire (OCV)   43
Ohge, Christopher   8, 102, 107, 113
Oldenburg, Henry   16–17
Olsen, Hope A.   27
Olsen-Smith, Steven   4, 27, 85
Online Cultural and Historical Research Environment (OCHRE)
   CHOIR text category in   108–9
   digital publications, production   113–14
   digital text editing through   108–9
   graph database platform   108
   hierarchies, epigraphic and discourse   109
   hypergraph approach   112
   as literary machine   112–13
   supports multiple text editions   111, *112*
   used for facsimile editing   110, *111*
   Xanadu *vs.*   112–13
online exhibitions   181–2
Online Public Access Catalogues (OPACs)   80
ontologies   247
Open Journal of Astrophysics   263
OpenAI, ChatGPT   271, 274, 284

Optical Character Recognition (OCR) tools   50, 288
Or, the Whale (Sances)   136–7. *See also Moby-Dick* (Melville)
   Catalogue Key to, Drescher   136–7
   'Or, the Eye', StoryMap   137
oral histories   206
ordered hierarchy of content objects (OHCO)   103
Oregon Heritage Commission (OHC)   199–200
Orley, Emily   129
Ozment, Kate   30

Pale Fire (Nabokov)   3
Panofsky, Erwin   263
'Pardoner's Tale' (Chaucer)   6
Partington, Gill   3
part-of-speech (POS) tagging   147
Percy, Thomas   18, 61–2
Perrin, Denis-Marius   38–41, 47
The Persian Letters   37 n.1
personal digital assistants (PDA)   183
personal intelligence (Pi), AI chatbot   284
   bibliographic approach   288–9
   'chat' interface   287–8
   personalization feature   288
   user experience   284, 286–7
Peterson, Jeff   137
photo-etching method   70
Physics Nobel (2024)   270–1
Pinchesne, Martin   38
Plantin-Moretus Museum, Antwerp   55
Plateau Peoples' Web Portal   194
PNG compression   273
Polyani, Michael   134
Porter, Roy   165
Postman, Neil   287
Presidential Libraries Act (PLA 1955)   205
Pressman, Jessica   283
Priestley, Joseph   20, 22
Primo software   29
Prince, Mary   126
Print & Probability project   4, 78
print technology   7
   alternative methods   46
   Cliché reproduction   62
   image processing   69–70
   image resolution, changes   48 n.9
   Ivins's claim   63
   stereotype plates   62–3
   technical developments   59–60
printing surfaces
   article on woodcut, *Encyclopédie*   58, *59*
   ballads and chapbooks, blocks for   60, *61*
   block impressions, using VGG VISE   64, 65
   Cliché reproduction   62

313

Index

digital registration method 66, 68
digitization of 63–5, 70, 72
history of blocks 55–6
media production, quantitative shift in 59
object detection, illustrations 64
technical developments 57–9
woodblocks studies, with computers 63–4, 64, 65
Pritchard, J. W. H. (Reverend) 124, 128
private libraries 79
project management, importance 217–18, 221
Project StoryMachine 201
Proust, Jacques 42–3
Prown, Jules David 177
Prusa Printables (3D printing) 149
'public benefit' (or risk)
    Dennett's view, democratic values 286
    interpretation, examples 285
    Socrates' views 285

Rader, Dean 100
Raghavan, Prabhakar 237
Ramsay, Stephen 289
Ramsey, Michael 166
Rawson, Mary Anne 8, 117–27
recommendation systems/algorithms 237–40
recordkeeping courses 221
Reflectance Transformation Imaging (RTI) 71
relational database approach 105, *106*
relief woodcuts 55
religious studies and theology, in U.K. 157–9
Reliques of English Poetry (Percy) 61
Research Assessment Exercise 162
Research Excellence Framework (REF) exercise 158
'reverse archive' 276–8. *See also* artificial intelligence (AI)
Riddell, Chris 257
Robinson, J. W. 57
Robinson, Peter 46, 49
Romanian Academy's folklore archive 198–9
Root, Howard 165
Rosen, Jay 227
Royden, Maude 164
Rules for a Printed Dictionary and Catalogue (Cutter) 24

sales catalogues 18, 22
Salvaggio, Eryk 264, 271, 277, 278 n.22
Samuel Beckett Digital Manuscripts Project 4, 80–1, 93, 180
Sayers, Dorothy L. 164
Schloen, J. David 99, 103–4, 107
Schloen, Sandra R. 99, 103–4, 107
scholarship, and conversation, concept 264 n.3

School of Library and Informational Science (SLIS) 207
Schroeder, Ralph 227, 240
Science pratique de l'imprimerie (Fertel) 42
Serrell, Beverly 138
Sévigné's letters 38. *See also* letter editions
    Duchêne views 40
    edited and published, Perrin in 1734–7 38–9, 41
    'new expanded edition' in 1754 38
    originals, Capmas's edition 40 n.4
    polishing for publication 39–41, 40 n.3
    preface 39
Sgard, Jean 42, 43 n.6
Shakespeare, William 102, 135
Sheffield Ladies Anti-Slavery Society 121
Shillingsburg, Peter 102, 113, 122
    Scholarly Editing in the Computer Age 298
Show Me Learning 212–13
Sigourney, Lydia Huntley 123
Silverman, Jonathan 100
Slave Trade Act, 1807 123
Slavery Abolition Act, 1833 120, 123
Smithsonian 3D Digitization programme 144–5
Smyth, Adam 3, 6
Sobkiw-Williams, Elizabeth 146
social media 1, 9, 176, 180, 227. *See also* museums' social media practices
'social search' prominence 237
Socrates 285
souvenir sets 150
Squires, Claire 289
Stable Diffusion 276
Star, Susan Leigh 249
Statute of Anne 1710 285
stochastic systems 267
Swain, Ellen D. 206
Sweeney, Fionnghuala 118

tangible and intangible heritage 176–7
Tanselle, G. Thomas 16
Taylor, Wilson 144
Technology Innovation Challenge Grant (TICG) 206
technopoly, term 287
Temple of Glass (Lydgate) 19
Text Encoding Initiative (TEI) 27, 49, 50, 90–1, 93, 103–4, 106, 108, 112, 119, 126, 129, 183, 300
    guidelines, representing text 49–50, 103
    scholarly editions using 4
TEXTA Toolkit 29
text-secure watermarks 198 n.4
textual analysis 99–100, 124–7, 289
textual materialism framework 70, 73
textual scholarship 1, 3, 6

Index

'Beyond Gutenberg' approach to digital text   104, 107, 122
  comparison to quantum particles   46
  and complex media forms   3, 9, 101
  conceptions, changes   50
  creative-critical approaches   8, 119, 122, 127
  data analysis tools   124–6
  database approach to   99, 107–8
  definition, in computing world   51
  digital approaches to   2–4, 102–3, 127
  digital curation   299
  dimensional complexity   99, 101
  as discrete granular tokens   104
  editors' role   297–8
  Gabler's conception, transmissibility   49, 51
  graph database approach   8, 105, *106*, 107–8
  'intertwingularity'   101
  McGann's framework   48–9
  multi-author digital edition project (*see The Bow in the Cloud* (1834), anthology)
  Schloen and Schloen's work on   99, 103–4, 107
  technologies   2–3
  various 'orientations to text'   297–8
  written text, complexity   99–100
textual variants, editions   297–8, 300
theological publishing   158–60
  authorship, by professional status   166, *167*
  Christology, soteriology scholarship stuff   161 n.1
  constraints   159, 163
  country-wise, geographic   167–8, *168*, 168 nn.2–3
  data   162–3
  denominations represented   159
  exclusion criteria, volumes   161
  gender, and authorship   163–5, *164*
  institutions of learning in   165–7
  at international levels   159
  method of data collection   160–1
  periodisation (1919 to 1999)   162–3
  principles of inclusion   160–2
  professional scholars   159–60, 166–7
  volumes essays written by experts   161
  women, opportunities for   159, 163
Theories of the Text (Greetham)   100
theory of affect   176–8
Theses on the Metaphors of Digital-Textual History (Eve)   3
Thiele, Daniel   240
Thingiverse   149
Thomas Mann Nachlassbibliothek Online   80
Thomas Mann's library   80, 86
Thrall (Bangor), Margaret   164
Tonra, Justin   6
topic modelling   28–9

Townley, James   125
Trans Metadata Collective (TMDC)   31
Transcribe Bentham project   183
Transkribus   6
Trant, Jennifer   229
Truman, Harry S.   205–6, 208, 215–16, 221
Truman Presidential Library & Museum website   *219*
Trumanlibrary.org (2001-2019)   205, 209, 214–15
  accessibility of materials   216–17
  archival records, digitization   215
  Collections with Online Content section   214, 216
  formats, and metadata   216–17
  Online Documents section   214–15
  Other Online Collections section   214, 216
  project's funding, and focus   214
  relevance/value based, digitization   215, 217
  Research Files section; tabs   215
  series-level digitization   214, 217
  social media use   214
Turning the Pages' (Armadillo Systems)   179–80
typographic punctuation   42

UChicago Node   114 n.8, 115
Ulysses (Joyce)   301
  editions, multiple   297, 301
  Gabler's edition   297, 301
  Johnson's edition   297
Underhill, Evelyn   164
Unicode Transformation Format-8   51
Universal Short Title Catalogue (USTC)   4
University of Oregon (OU) Folklore Program   199

Van Hulle, Dirk   89
  creative ecologies   7, 122
Vareschi, Mark   6
Vercruysse, Jeroom   42
VGG Visual Search Engine (VISE) tool   64, 65
video-based content   235
Vinci, Leonardo da   179
virtual reality (VR)   176
virtual tour, exhibition space   181–2, 182 n.1
Voiture, Vincent   38
Voyant tools   135 n.2, 145, 147–8, 153

Wacha, Heather   6
Wallace, Robert   151
Walpole, Horace   18, 60
Walsh, Peter   228–9, 233
Warton, Thomas   18–19
Web Cultures Web Archive (WCWA)   200
Webcomics Web Archive (WWA)   200
Websim   277

Index

The West Indies and Other Poems (Montgomery)   123
Whistlestop Project   206. *See also* Trumanlibrary.org (2001-2019)
   aim/initial funding   207, 211
   archivist role, in project management   217–18, 221
   Borwick's job, remembrances   207–8
   context, and origins   206
   'Daily Presidential Appointments Calendar'   213
   digital standards for   212
   digitizing documents   208–9, 211
   hardware obsolescence, concern   212
   hypertext systems as   219–20
   Kochtanek, key role in   207–9, 211, 213–14
   lesson plans   212–13
   Magnino' contributions   207, 210–13
   migrating database to the Truman site   209, 214, 218–19
   NARA relaunched   218, *219*
   progressions (1996 to 2019)   210–14
   project-based learning   205–6
   publicity   213
   source materials, and backups   208, 212–13, 220
   'The Spy's Dilemma'   213
   staff, and scientists' role   207–8, 222 n.1
   teachers training, and contribution   209
   Truman Library's digital collections, impact on   221
   Truman presidency, 'official documents'   206
Whistlestop.org   205, 209, *210*
Whitney, Katherine   138
Wieland, Christoph Martin   183
Wieland Museum   183
Wiffen, Jeremiah Holmes   124
Wikipedia   283
Williams, Bruce   240
women in academic publishing   163–5, *164*. *See also* theological publishing
woodblock studies
   with computers   63–4, *64*, *65*
   damages   66, 68, *69*
   dating, external/publication   66
   depth capture   70
   overlay visualization   66, *68*
   RTI capture, Newcastle ballad-printer's   *71*
wood-engraving   59–60
Woolf, Virginia   175

Wordsworth Grasmere
   archives' 'aura'   185
   Dove Cottage   185–6
   From Goslar to Grasmere   180–1, 185–6
   The Prelude and *Home at Grasmere*   180, 186
Wordsworth, William   118, 121, 185–6
work expressions   256–7
work of art, conception   138
The World is a Text   100
World of Whaling in the Digital Age, and Moby Dick
   artefact analysis   142–3
   hybrid experience, NEH Institute   141–2
   'material annotation' activity   145
   'quadrant' case, 'concordance'   145–6, *146*
   reading and conversation   142
   site-specific experiences   142
World Cat   27
Woudhuysen, H. R.   5, 17
writers' libraries   8
   'adaptive revision'   86
   archives   4, 8
   authorship notions   82, 87
   bibliographic classifications, dynamic   86
   challenges for modelling, digital edition   88
   defined   81
   digital editions, production   79, 81, 84–7, 93
   digitization, as scientific method   84–5
   editing, problems   80–1, 88–92
   'extant' and 'virtual' libraries   82–4
   fluid (hyper-)text   86
   future editions   93
   marginalia   81, 83, 87–8
   object of study   83
   OCR and HTR programmes   93
   online platforms dedicated to   80
   oral texts   84
   physical collection access   90
   positivist approach to material   87–9
   problems with, editorial process   88–92
   textual and non-textual elements   83–4
written texts, complexity   99–101

Xanadu project (Nelson)   99, 101, 112–13

Yeats exhibition, for Web   179, 181

Zimmer, Erica   8, 137
ZIP file format   272
Zipf's Law   147, *148*
Zuckerberg, Mark   239